P9-ELG-920

Drug Use in Assisted Suicide and Euthanasia

ALL PHARMACEUTICAL PRODUCTS PRESS BOOKS
AND JOURNALS ARE PRINTED
ON CERTIFIED ACID-FREE PAPER

Published by

Pharmaceutical Products Press, 10 Alice Street, Binghamton, NY 13904-1580 USA

Pharmaceutical Products Press is an imprint of The Haworth Press, Inc., 10 Alice Street, Binghamton, NY 13904-1580 USA.

Drug Use in Assisted Suicide and Euthanasia has also been published as *Journal of Pharmaceutical Care in Pain & Symptom Control*, Volume 3, Numbers 3/4 1995 and Volume 4, Numbers 1/2 1996.

© 1996 by The Haworth Press, Inc. All rights reserved. No part of this work may be reproduced or utilized in any form or by any means, electronic or mechanical, including photocopying, microfilm and recording, or by any information storage and retrieval system, without permission in writing from the publisher. Printed in the United States of America.

The development, preparation, and publication of this work has been undertaken with great care. However, the publisher, employees, editors, and agents of The Haworth Press and all imprints of The Haworth Press, Inc., including The Haworth Medical Press and Pharmaceutical Products Press, are not responsible for any errors contained herein or for consequences that may ensue from use of materials or information contained in this work. Opinions expressed by the author(s) are not necessarily those of The Haworth Press, Inc.

This is a scholarly work. The diverse views of many professionals are expressed in an attempt to illustrate in a balanced way issues that are highly controversial. Sections dealing with legal matters are current as of the publication date. However, as laws are subject to change and judicial interpretation, nothing in this work should be used as legal advice. Legal advice should be obtained from professional consultation with an attorney. The Haworth Press, Inc. assumes no responsibility for the subject matter contained herein.

Library of Congress Cataloging-in-Publication Data

Drug use in assisted suicide and euthanasia / Margaret P. Battin, Arthur G. Lipman, editors.
    p. cm.
    Includes bibliographical references and index.
    ISBN 1-56024-814-9
    1. Assisted suicide–Moral and ethical aspects. 2. Assisted suicide–Law and legislation. 3. Euthanasia–Moral and ethical aspects. 4. Euthanasia–Law and legislation. 5. Drugs–Prescribing–Moral and ethical aspects. 6. Pharmacists–Professional ethics. I. Battin, M. Pabst. II. Lipman, Arthur G.
R726.D78 1996   95-49632
179'.7–dc20   CIP

Drug Use
in Assisted Suicide
and Euthanasia

Margaret P. Battin, PhD
Arthur G. Lipman, PharmD
Editors

Pharmaceutical Products Press
An Imprint of
The Haworth Press, Inc.
New York • London

INDEXING & ABSTRACTING

Contributions to this publication are selectively indexed or abstracted in print, electronic, online, or CD-ROM version(s) of the reference tools and information services listed below. This list is current as of the copyright date of this publication. See the end of this section for additional notes.

- *Abstracts in Social Gerontology: Current Literature on Aging,* National Council on the Aging, Library, 409 Third Street SW, 2nd Floor, Washington, DC 20024

- *AnalgesiaFile,* Dannemiller Memorial Educational Foundation, 12500 Network Boulevard, Suite 101, San Antonio, TX 78249-3302

- *CINAHL (Cumulative Index to Nursing & Allied Health Literature),* in print, also on CD-ROM from CD PLUS, EBSCO, and SilverPlatter, and online from CDP Online (formerly BRS), Data-Star, and PaperChase. (Support materials include Subject Heading List, Database Search Guide, and instructional video). CINAHL Information Systems, P.O. Box 871/1509 Wilson Terrace, Glendale, CA 91209-0871

- *CNPIEC Reference Guide: Chinese National Directory of Foreign Periodicals,* P.O. Box 88, Beijing, People's Republic of China

- *Excerpta Medica/Secondary Publishing Division,* Elsevier Science Inc., Secondary Publishing Division, 655 Avenue of the Americas, New York, NY 10010

(continued)

WITHDRAWN

AUG - 1997

- *InPharma Weekly DIGEST & NEWS on: Pharmaceutical Literature, Drug Reactions & LMS,* Adis International Ltd., 41 Centorian Drive, Mairangi Bay, Auckland 10, New Zealand

- *International Pharmaceutical Abstracts,* ASHP, 7272 Wisconsin Avenue, Bethesda, MD 20814

- *INTERNET ACCESS (& additional networks) Bulletin Board for Libraries ("BUBL"), coverage of information resources on INTERNET, JANET, and other networks.*
  - JANET X.29: UK.AC.BATH.BUBL or 00006012101300
  - TELNET: BUBL.BATH.AC.UK or 138.38.32.45 login 'bubl'
  - Gopher: BUBL.BATH.AC.UK (138.32.32.45). Port 7070
  - World Wide Web: http://www.bubl.bath.ac.uk./BUBL/ home.html
  - NISSWAIS: telnetniss.ac.uk (for the NISS gateway)
  The Andersonian Library, Curran Building, 101 St. James Road, Glasgow G4 ONS, Scotland

- *Leeds Medical Information,* University of Leeds, Leeds LS2 9JT, United Kingdom

- *Medication Use STudies (MUST) DATABASE,* The University of Mississippi, School of Pharmacy, University, MS 38677

- *Referativnyi Zhurnal (Abstracts Journal of the Institute of Scientific Information of the Republic of Russia),* The Institute of Scientific Information, Baltijskaja ul., 14, Moscow A-219, Republic of Russia

(continued)

SPECIAL BIBLIOGRAPHIC NOTES

related to special journal issues (separates)
and indexing/abstracting

☐ indexing/abstracting services in this list will also cover material in any "separate" that is co-published simultaneously with Haworth's special thematic journal issue or DocuSerial. Indexing/abstracting usually covers material at the article/chapter level.

☐ monographic co-editions are intended for either non-subscribers or libraries which intend to purchase a second copy for their circulating collections.

☐ monographic co-editions are reported to all jobbers/wholesalers/approval plans. The source journal is listed as the "series" to assist the prevention of duplicate purchasing in the same manner utilized for books-in-series.

☐ to facilitate user/access services all indexing/abstracting services are encouraged to utilize the co-indexing entry note indicated at the bottom of the first page of each article/chapter/contribution.

☐ this is intended to assist a library user of any reference tool (whether print, electronic, online, or CD-ROM) to locate the monographic version if the library has purchased this version but not a subscription to the source journal.

☐ individual articles/chapters in any Haworth publication are also available through the Haworth Document Delivery Services (HDDS).

Drug Use in Assisted Suicide and Euthanasia

CONTENTS

LEGAL AND REGULATORY ISSUES IN ASSISTED SUICIDE AND EUTHANASIA

DRUG USE IN ASSISTED SUICIDE AND EUTHANASIA

COMMENTARIES

ABOUT THE EDITORS

Margaret P. Battin, PhD, is Professor of Philosophy in the College of Humanities at the University of Utah. She also serves as Adjunct Professor of Internal Medicine in the Division of Medical Ethics at the University of Utah School of Medicine. Dr. Battin has authored several books, including *Ethical Issues in Suicide* and *The Least Worst Death: Essays in Bioethics on the End of Life.* She has also served as Co-Editor of several books, including *Changing to National Health Care: Ethical & Policy Issues,* which she co-edited with Robert P. Heufner, and *Suicide & Ethics: A Special Issue on Suicide and Life-Threatening Issues,* which she co-edited with Ronald Maris.

Arthur G. Lipman, PharmD, is Professor of Clinical Pharmacy in the College of Pharmacy at the University of Utah. He also practices at the Pain Management Center of the University Hospitals and Clinics at the University of Utah. Dr. Lipman has been a consultant on pain management to the Federal Interagency Committee on Pain and Analgesia, the American Cancer Society, and the National Cancer Institute. Dr. Lipman has served on a number of national and international pain management bodies. He is one of the first hospice practitioners in the United States, and in 1973 was a co-investigator on the National Cancer Institute demonstration project on hospice care. His hospice experience includes work in England, Connecticut, and Salt Lake City.

About the Contributors

Robert T. Angarola, JD
Hyman, Phelps & McNamara, P.C.
Washington, DC

Margaret P. Battin, PhD
Professor of Philosophy
and Adjunct Professor
of Internal Medicine
Division of Medical Ethics
University of Utah
Salt Lake City, Utah

William S. Breitbart, MD
Associate Attending Psychiatrist
Memorial Sloan-Kettering Cancer
Center and
Associate Professor
of Psychiatry
Cornell University
Medical College
New York, New York

C. Richard Chapman, PhD
Professor of Anesthesiology,
Psychology, and Psychiatry
and Behavioral Sciences
University of Washington School
of Medicine and
Director, Pain and Toxicity
Research Center
Fred Hutchinson
Cancer Research Center
Seattle, Washington

Charles Corr, PhD
Professor, Department
of Philosophical Studies
Southern Illinois University
at Edwardsville
Edwardsville, Illinois

Karen M. Corr, PharmD
Clinical Pharmacy Coordinator
F.D.R. Veterans Hospital
Montrose, New York

Barbara Insley Crouch, PharmD
MSPH
Director, Utah Poison Control
Center and
Assistant Professor
of Pharmacy Practice
College of Pharmacy
University of Utah
Salt Lake City, Utah

Betty R. Ferrell, PhD, FAAN
Associate Research Scientist
City of Hope Medical Center
Duarte, California

Jonathan Gavrin, MD
Assistant Professor
of Anesthesiology
University of Washington School
of Medicine and Associate
in Clinical Research, Pain
and Toxicity Research Center
Fred Hutchinson Cancer
Research Center
Seattle, Washington

Derek Humphry
Euthanasia Research
& Guidance Organization (ERGO!)
Junction City, Oregon

Stephen Jamison, PhD
Director
Life and Death Consultations
Mill Valley, California

Peter J. Katsufrakis, MD
Associate Dean
for Student Affairs
Clinical Assistant Professor
of Family Medicine and
Director of Clinical Training
Pacific AIDS Education
and Training Center
University of Southern California
School of Medicine
Los Angeles, California

Gerrit K. Kimsma, MD, MPH
Department of Family
and Nursing Home Medicine
Free University
Amsterdam, The Netherlands

Arthur G. Lipman, PharmD
Professor of Clinical Pharmacy
College of Pharmacy and
Pain Management Center
University Hospitals and Clinics
University of Utah
Salt Lake City, Utah

Richard MacDonald, MD
Medical Director
The Hemlock Society
Megalia, California

Kristine Carlson Marcus, RPh
Portland, Oregon

Fred S. Marcus, MD
Medical Oncologist,
Redwood Medical Group
Attending Physician
Sequoia Hospital,
Redwood City and
Stanford University Hospital
Stanford, California

William L. Marcus, JD
Deputy Attorney General
California Department of Justice
Los Angeles, California

Margaret V. McDonald, CSW
Research Associate
Memorial Sloan-Kettering Cancer
Center
New York, New York

Barbara Jean McGuire, RN,
MN, PhC
The Fielding Institute
Santa Barbara, California

Ralph Mero, MDiv, DD
Executive Director
Compassion in Dying
Seattle, Washington

Gail Middlekauf, JD
Hyman, Phelps & McNamara, P.C.
Washington, DC

Ronald Baker Miller, MD
Clinical Professor
of Medicine and
Director of the Program
in Medical Ethics
University of California at Irvine
Orange, California

Jerome A. Motto, MD
Department of Psychiatry
Langley Porter Psychiatric
Institute
University of California–
San Francisco
San Francisco, California

Steven D. Passik, PhD
Assistant Attending Psychologist
Memorial Sloan-Kettering Cancer
Center and Assistant Professor
of Psychology in Psychiatry
Cornell University Medical
College, New York, New York

Thomas A. Preston MD
Professor of Medicine
University of Washington
and Chief of Cardiology
Pacific Medical Center
Seattle, Washington

Lynne M. Rivera, RN, MSN
Research Specialist
City of Hope Medical Center
Duarte, California

Barry D. Rosenfeld, PhD
Research Associate
Memorial Sloan-Kettering
Cancer Center
New York, New York

John Samuel Rozel, BA
Medical Student
Brown University School
of Medicine and
Consultant on the ethical
and clinical management
of suicidal and violent behavior
Providence, Rhode Island

Michael T. Rupp, PhD
Associate Professor
of Pharmacy Administration
School of Pharmacy
and Pharmacal Sciences
Purdue University
West Lafayette, Indiana

Judith M. Saunders, RN,
DNSc, FAAN
Assistant Research Scientist
City of Hope National
Medical Center
Duarte, California
and Assistant Professor
Department of Nursing
University of Southern California
Los Angeles, California

Cheryl K. Smith, JD
Eugene, Oregon

Bryan Tanney, BSc, MD,
FRCPC
Professor of Psychiatry
Calgary General Hospital
Calgary, Alberta, Canada

Kathryn L. Tucker, JD
Perkins Coie
Seattle, Washington

Sharon M. Valente, RN, PhD,
FAAN
Assistant Professor
Department of Nursing
Center for Health Professions
University of Southern California
Los Angeles, California

James L. Werth, Jr., BS
Psychology Intern
Counseling and Consultation
Arizona State University
Tempe, Arizona

Bruce D. White, DO, JD
Clinical Director
Clinical Ethics Center
Saint Thomas Hospital
Nashville, Tennessee

Introduction:
The Need to Objectively Examine Issues
in Assisted Suicide and Euthanasia

Margaret P. Battin

Arthur G. Lipman

SUMMARY. Many issues relating to drug use in assisted suicide and euthanasia are explored. The papers which follow in this volume discuss ethical and institutional background policy issues, the patient's situation, legal and regulatory issues in assisted suicide and euthanasia, and drug use in assisted suicide and euthanasia. Several papers contain accounts of current practice, both legal and extra-legal, of drug use in assisted suicide and euthanasia. Commentaries include position papers on assisted suicide and euthanasia, and a set of discussion cases addressed by an interdisciplinary panel. *[Article copies available from The Haworth Document Delivery Service: 1-800-342-9678.]*

KEYWORDS. Euthanasia, assisted suicide, drugs, law, lethal drugs, policy, physician-assisted suicide, ethics, cases, commentaries

---

Margaret P. Battin, PhD, is Professor of Philosophy in the College of Humanities and Adjunct Professor of Internal Medicine (Division of Medical Ethics) in the School of Medicine, University of Utah. Arthur G. Lipman, PharmD, is Professor of Clinical Pharmacy in the College of Pharmacy and the Pain Management Center, University Hospitals and Clinics, University of Utah.

Address correspondence to: Dr. Arthur G. Lipman, College of Pharmacy, University of Utah, Salt Lake City, UT 84112.

[Haworth co-indexing entry note]: "Introduction: The Need to Objectively Examine Issues in Assisted Suicide and Euthanasia." Battin, Margaret P., and Arthur G. Lipman. Co-published simultaneously in *Journal of Pharmaceutical Care in Pain & Symptom Control* (Pharmaceutical Products Press, an imprint of The Haworth Press, Inc.) Vol. 3, No. 3/4, 1995, pp. 1-10; and: *Drug Use in Assisted Suicide and Euthanasia* (ed: Margaret P. Battin, and Arthur G. Lipman) Pharmaceutical Products Press, an imprint of The Haworth Press, Inc., 1996, pp. 1-10. Single or multiple copies of this article are available from The Haworth Document Delivery Service [1-800-342-9678, 9:00 a.m. - 5:00 p.m. (EST)].

© 1996 by The Haworth Press, Inc. All rights reserved.

1

In the vigorous and increasingly politicized discussion of assisted sui-cide, physician-assisted suicide, and euthanasia in terminal illness, drugs are an often unrecognized centerpiece. Virtually all comment, both for and against the moral acceptability of assisted suicide and for and against the legalization of these practices, assumes that death is to be caused by lethal doses of drugs–not guns, or trauma, or other violent means. Indeed, it is drugs which are assumed to be capable of providing what a terminally ill person may be seeking: a gentle, painless way of dying that will be peace-ful and dignified both for the patient and for any family members or others who may be present.

Since drugs are at the center of this controversy, we seek in this publica-tion to directly address issues about the use of drugs in actively bringing about death. There are many sorts of issues–empirical issues, ethical issues, legal issues, issues of prudent public policy, among others. What drugs are used? How are they used? What are the potential problems and advantages of some drugs over others in bringing life to a close? What are the risks? Does providing information about drugs, or assisting in the use of drugs, or administering drugs violate ethical, legal, or professional obligations of physicians, pharmacists, nurses, family members, and others who might be involved? Is providing a lethal drug the same as killing? Or is access to drugs a basic right–some would argue a constitutional right–of the person who is terminally ill and faces death in any case?

Most health professionals and many other persons have adopted posi-tions in opposition to or in support of terminally ill patients having the prerogative to actively end their own lives and of health professionals participating in the ending of these patients' lives. We often base our positions on personal values, religious beliefs or emulation of persuasive mentors. Positions on the issues of assisted suicide and euthanasia more often than not are intense and highly personal. When individuals' posi-tions on these important societal issues are challenged by thoughtful, even scholarly, arguments that oppose those individuals' beliefs, many people become more entrenched in their positions and do not allow themselves to objectively examine the issues.

Whether one favors or opposes permitting patients with advanced, irre-versible disease who wish to actively end their lives having access to assisted suicide and euthanasia, we believe that a careful examination of the issues relating to these acts is in order. Health professionals may expect to receive increasing inquiries about life-ending acts. Both the lay press and the professional literature are focusing on these issues. Physicians are asked to prescribe life-ending drugs, nurses are asked to participate in the procurement and use of these agents, and pharmacists are asked to provide information on the use of these drugs and often, to provide the drugs themselves with or without a prescription. The authors of the papers in this work hold widely ranging views on these issues. Even the editors of this volume disagree on fundamental aspects of health practitioner participation in active ending of life. But we all agree that careful examination of the issues should be a prerequisite to an individual's taking a position on hastened and assisted death.

Some of the authors presented here believe that assisted suicide, physician-assisted suicide, and euthanasia arc wrong, both on ethical and prudential grounds, and that legalizing these practices would be dangerous and immoral. Others take these practices to be a fundamental right of the dying patient, and favor full legalization. Still others hold a variety of positions in between. This volume itself does not seek to take a stance on these larger issues, but it does insist on one thing, that we cannot pretend that these practices are not now happening, whether we take this to be good or bad. Hence this volume focuses not just on theoretical issues, but on actual practice, and on how drugs can be and are used in bringing about death.

The purpose of this volume therefore is not to support or denounce, but to elucidate. Some readers may find that the papers which follow provide support for positions that they currently hold on assisted suicide and euthanasia. Others may find themselves troubled by arguments that effectively oppose their previously held positions. Still others may wish to redefine their own beliefs based upon objective re-examination of the issues. No one, we think, can agree with all the positions advocated in the papers presented here. However, we also believe that most thoughtful readers will find something of importance in all of them.

What do we mean by "suicide," "euthanasia" and "assisted suicide," the practices addressed in this volume? At a minimum, "suicide" means "self-killing," "euthanasia" means killing by another person in a medical context, and "assisted suicide" means self-killing in which another person supplies aid in doing so. But these terms are heavily laden with connotations, connotations which are exploited in negative ways by some speakers, positive ways by others. "Euthanasia," for example, has strongly positive connotations in the Netherlands, where it means "voluntary death in the interest of the person whose death it is," or "good death." But in Germany, the same term has very strong associations with Nazism, and it means something closer to "politically motivated murder using medical situations as a pretext." The term "suicide" tends to have negative connotations in English. But the connotations of the same term in the expression "physician-assisted suicide" are much less negative. Because of these variations in terminology, it is not possible to provide rigorous, objective, neutral definitions of any of them; and it is critical to be alert to the shifting senses in which they are used by various authors. It is important to note that some of the position statements presented in the last section of this volume use different definitions–for example, the Compassion in Dying and the National Hospice Organization position papers use definitions that imply the acceptability or lack of acceptability of euthanasia, respectively. Similarly, the authors of the various papers also employ a wide range of working definitions. Readers should not expect to find uniformity among them.

Some of the papers in this volume are formal analyses of the issues; others are quite informal, comparatively personal accounts of individual experience. But all are important in seeing the context and complexity of the broad social questions now facing us about how we die.

The volume opens with physician-ethicist Ronald Miller's broad survey of the arguments for and against assisted suicide, physician-assisted suicide, and euthanasia. The article modestly claims that it presents "some" arguments. But in fact it is close to exhaustive, a very broad look at the arguments as they have been pursued in public, academic, and professional spheres. Any one of its entries can be–and many have been–expanded into a sustained debate, and much of the argumentation displayed here plays a role in the papers that follow.

Next in the volume, Michael Rupp explores these issues as they confront pharmacists and provides data on pharmacists' attitudes about assisted suicide and euthanasia. Pharmacists' cooperation, knowing or unknowing, is expected when a physician provides a terminal patient with a prescription for drugs specifically intended to bring about the end of life. Oregon's Measure 16, approved at the polls in November 1994 (though under current legal challenge), casts pharmacists in precisely this role. Measure 16 permits physicians to prescribe lethal doses of drugs for terminally ill patients who request them, subject to a variety of safeguards. But Measure 16 is silent about the role of pharmacists. It simply assumes that pharmacists will fill the prescriptions as a matter of course. Must the pharmacist fill such a prescription, whether as a matter of moral, legal, or professional duty? Much has been made of physicians' rights to refuse to provide aid-in-dying to their patients, even in jurisdictions where it is legal to do so. Rupp and colleagues outline a conscience clause that would permit pharmacists to opt out, without violating standards of practice in disobeying physicians' orders even if Measure 16 or a similar measure were law. This paper does not presuppose that all pharmacists will wish to opt out, but insists that the rights of those who wish to do so must be respected.

In discussing the issues that the practice of assisted suicide and euthanasia pose for nurses, Betty Ferrell and Lynne Rivera review nurses' attitudes about them, as assessed in a variety of studies. These authors describe why assisted suicide and euthanasia can pose dilemmas for nurses. Nurses are subject to conflicting obligations: the obligation to protect life, the obligation to provide care by relieving suffering and pain, and the obligation to respect patients and their autonomous choices. To some nurses, this seems to speak for participation in aid-in-dying; to others, it does not. Published studies reflect a substantial diversity of opinion about whether nurses may participate in assisted suicide. And these differences are not likely to be reduced. Ferrell and Rivera emphasize the way in which conflicts for nurses will become even more acute as the health-care system changes and terminal care is more frequently provided in the home. In this private setting, nurses often become even more intimately involved with dying patients and their families than in the traditional institutional environment. As nurses increasingly assume the primary role in home care for the dying, the dilemmas nurses face increase in frequency and intensity. Often, nurses are the persons whom patients ask for assistance in dying.

The focus of this volume then turns to patient decision-making concerning suicide and euthanasia. This section addresses patient motivation: what leads patients to make such choices. An important framework for patient decisions is laid out by C. Richard Chapman and Jonathan Gavrin in their discussion of suffering as experienced by terminally ill patients. Not uncommonly, patients seek to end their lives due to the assumption that this is the only way they can escape the suffering associated with their disease. Pain and most other physical symptoms can be well managed today in many–even most–patients with advanced, irreversible disease. Nevertheless, many patients suffer unnecessary pain and other terribly distressing symptoms because their caregivers are not aware of medications and other treatment modalities that are available and effective. The rapid growth of the hospice movement in the United States from one demonstration project in 1974 to about 2,000 active programs today speaks for improved symptom control in terminally ill patients, but complete relief of all pain and suffering in the terminally ill has hardly been achieved. Chapman and Gavrin also describe the emotional suffering that accompanies advanced disease for many patients. Their paper recognizes that not all suffering is due to physical symptoms and not all suffering is amenable to drug therapy or counseling. They explore how suffering influences patient decisions about their lives.

Steven Passik, Margaret McDonald, Barry Rosenfeld and William

Breitbart then examine clinical and research considerations concerning patients in the terminal stages of AIDS. This work focuses particularly on the key psychiatric, medical and social factors that require assessment, when such patients express the desire for a hastened death, for physician-assisted suicide, or for euthanasia. They look carefully at issues about depression, pain, psychological distress, anxiety, organic mental disorders, and a variety of demographic and social variables. One surprising finding of their research is an inverse relationship between pain and positive attitudes towards physician-assisted suicide. Although they acknowledge that this finding requires further study, it is surprising, since intractable pain is often cited by the lay public and by medical experts as the motivation for patients' requests for assistance in suicide. This thus challenges the widespread assumption that good palliative care will obviate the desire for hastened death in most patients, though they believe it to be generally true in both AIDS and cancer. However, the patient population studied by these authors–a New York City HIV(+) population, including a majority of persons other than gay white males–favorably endorsed statements supporting physician-assisted suicide at a considerably lower rate (65%) than other groups studied, including gay white HIV(+) males (whose rate of approval was over 90%). Perhaps this is due to a historical lack of access to medical services and the absence of close ties to doctors among members of minority groups.

Legal and regulatory issues in assisted suicide and euthanasia are addressed in the third section of the volume. Robert Angarola and Gail Middlekauff discuss advanced directives in the context of withdrawing and withholding treatment. They explore some of the law now on the books in five jurisdictions. They do not discuss changes currently proposed; theirs is a picture of the law as it has been assumed to stand.

Following this, attorney Kathryn Tucker presents the case that she made in Federal District Court in the State of Washington, namely that the right to assist persons in actively ending their lives is constitutionally protected as a privacy issue in which the government has no role. Although her argument did prevail initially, it was reversed in the Ninth Circuit Court of Appeals in May 1994. Whether such an argument will in the future be entertained in the U.S. Supreme Court is difficult to tell at this time, but virtually all observers agree that some such case will eventually be heard there.

Cheryl Smith, an attorney who has been actively involved in right-to-die cases describes the state of the current law pertaining to assisted suicide and euthanasia. She discusses what the law is, how it is enforced, and recent challenges and changes to the law. This paper describes a number of cases in which assisted suicide was carried out and the legal outcomes. Her portrait of changes underway in the law reveals considerable ferment in the legal arena.

Measure 16, the Oregon Death with Dignity Act that passed as a ballot initiative in November 1994 (but at the time of this writing is under legal challenge which has delayed implementation) permits physicians to prescribe life ending drugs. However, this act does not address the role of pharmacists. Kristine Marcus, in the following paper, articulates some of the concerns that many Oregon pharmacists have about Measure 16. She also describes formal actions taken by Oregon pharmacy organizations in response to Measure 16. Her account is sensitive to many of the conflicting expectations patients, other pharmacists and society at large have concerning pharmacists' roles.

Turning to issues of public policy, William Marcus addresses issues of legal and professional regulation of health care professionals who are state licensees. If assisted suicide and euthanasia are illegal, he argues, the issues are comparatively simple in providing a basis for action against a licensee. But if they are not, the matter is far more complicated. Marcus explores in some detail the gray areas a regulatory agency would need to explore in attempting to ensure that such practices were conducted in an acceptable manner, and to decide whether licensees should be disciplined for killing patients or assisting patients in killing themselves when that is the patient's expressed wish. If either assisted suicide or euthanasia is legalized, he writes, the performance of the act will involve the licensee's professional judgment. Such judgment is the province of the licensing board, which is obligated to monitor the competence and prudence of its licensees. Marcus argues that probably the safest, most productive involvement for regulators is to ensure informed consent on the part of the patient and to require that baseline medical procedures, including safety, sanitation, and careful patient evaluation and treatment are provided in causing or aiding death.

It is noteworthy that several states have recently passed laws and enacted regulations to ease prescribing restrictions for analgesics to be used by patients with terminal disease. Oregon, which passed Measure 16, is one of the states which has recently recognized the need for fewer restrictions on medications to be used for symptom control. For example, in May, 1995, the Oregon Senate unanimously passed SB671, which paves the way for physicians to prescribe larger doses of opioid analgesics for patients who suffer from intractable pain. The sentiment of that legislative body was articulated by Senator Bill Kennemer, who responded to an allegation that this bill would allow people to become more addicted to drugs by saying:

This is not about making illicit drugs available. This is about competent medicine, and about fairness and quality patient care. This bill creates a much-needed solution in our society.

The fourth section of this volume examines the actual practice of drug use in assisted suicide, physician-assisted suicide, and euthanasia. Derek Humphry, the British journalist, former president of the Hemlock Society, and author of the guide on ending one's life entitled *Final Exit,* which sold over half a million copies and reached the top of the *New York Times'* how-to bestseller list, describes how patients actually obtain and stockpile the drugs they use to end their lives. Physician Thomas Preston and minister Ralph Mero, who are respectively on the medical advisory board and executive director of Compassion in Dying, an organization located in the state of Washington that provides support to terminally ill patients who choose suicide, provide an account of Compassion's experience. They describe in detail the characteristics of these patients whose suicides were performed with drugs obtained from the patients' own physicians. They describe these patients' choices and their experiences. They note that many patients wish to avoid a death that would involve continuous sedation, loss of dignity or an unacceptable quality of life.

Until recently, the Netherlands was the only country which had permitted physicians to actively end patients' lives when they so request. (In May, 1995, the Northern Territory of Australia enacted legislation which permits both physician-assisted suicide and, in some cases, active voluntary euthanasia, though this law has not yet been implemented.) Writing from the Netherlands, physician Gerrit Kimsma describes in detail the types of euthanizing drugs employed, together with a brief history of how information about appropriate and inappropriate drugs has been disseminated to physicians in his country. Kimsma describes the professional expectations and norms surrounding the practice of euthanasia, recounting the development of these expectations and norms in a series of reports from 1977, 1980, 1987, and 1994. The most recent report provides extensive information about drugs used and experience with them, providing specific information about time lapse between administration and death and side effects experienced. Of particular interest to U.S. audiences is the advice to avoid morphine and the benzodiazepines, drugs most commonly assumed in the United States to be appropriate for ending life. Kimsma notes that morphine can result in the patient waking up and that benzodiazepines can result in an extended dying process of "torturing duration," a situation reflected in Stephen Jamison's account in the final paper of this section. Kimsma also discusses dilemmas that remain for Dutch physicians, despite the fact that in the Netherlands most issues surrounding euthanasia and assisted suicide are dealt with in an open fashion. He describes the lessons he has learned in the cases in which he himself has performed euthanasia.

Continuing this section's attention to concrete issues of drug use in assisted suicide and euthanasia, clinical toxicologist Barbara Insley Crouch critiques the types of "euthanasia recipes" that appear in Derek Humphry's *Final Exit* and other such publications in this country and elsewhere. Both pharmacokinetic and toxicological assumptions that are made by proponents of euthanizing drugs are often flawed. Crouch points out that there are few objective data about the lethal doses of various drugs or toxins in humans, and discusses the nature of some of the animal data available. She discusses differences among the kinds of drugs covered in *Final Exit,* describing their various forms of pharmacologic activity, and discusses why some would be far less satisfactory choices than others. Crouch also discusses factors that affect the absorption, distribution, metabolism, and elimination of a drug and so enhance or reduce its toxicity. In sum, she says, there are no good scientific data available to identify the fatal dose of a drug in humans. While the doses listed may produce fatal outcomes for some individuals, it is not clear that death could be reliably produced in a gentle, pain-free way in all cases. This conclusion, based on the current toxicological literature and experience of American poison control centers, is more cautious than that of Preston and Mero's or Kimsma's accounts, both of which provide observations concerning drug combinations reported to reliably produce easy death.

In an informal narrative, Stephen Jamison portrays what happens when drugs go wrong. Jamison tells the stories of patients whose efforts at suicide, with and without the assistance of friends or physicians, went awry, and what impact this had on family members or others involved. Particularly poignant in the stories Jamison tells is the frequent way in which drug failures compel family members or other assisters to assume far more active roles in causing death than they had anticipated, roles far more active than they were prepared for, either practically or emotionally. Drug failures occur with doctors as well as assisters who are not medical professionals, and in some particularly difficult cases, nothing seems to work. Not infrequently, physicians who lack sophisticated pharmacological and toxicological expertise advise–even provide–drugs which do not produce a rapid and comfortable death. These troubling stories underscore the insistence of this volume that we not pretend that drugs are not now being used in assisted suicide and euthanasia; they are, but with sometimes difficult results. The stories Jamison presents force us to take seriously issues about drug use in assisted suicide and euthanasia among terminally ill patients, and not to assume that discussion of the ethical, institutional, and policy issues, including issues about patients' rights, attitudes, and preferences, is sufficient to address these issues without also looking at the facts of what is actually the case.

The final section of this volume contains commentaries on these issues. Position papers of various organizations on the issues are reprinted with permission. Some of these are endorsements of active participation in assisted suicide and euthanasia; some are condemnations. Each represents a legitimate position of thoughtful individuals and organizations. The position paper of the Society for Health and Human Values is of particular interest because it does not attempt to resolve the issue. Rather, it asks important questions and examines them in a balanced and scholarly manner. These position papers are followed by a series of brief clinical vignettes and commentaries edited by Sharon Valente and Judith Saunders that are presented for sustained reflection. Commenting on these cases are a number of distinguished authors, including practitioners, ethicists and investigators in the various fields covered by the pieces in this volume. The attitudes they display are extremely diverse, but in discussing and disagreeing over these cases, they exhibit why the issues here are so volatile, so complex, and so important in contemporary times.

These are complex issues. Many people hold strong opinions either opposing or supporting individuals' rights to actively end their own lives and to seek assistance from others in the act. The collection of papers in this volume provides the basis for thoughtful readers to analyze their personal positions on active life-ending acts and to draw conclusions based on effective articulation of arguments both favoring and opposing assisted suicide and euthanasia.

AUTHOR NOTE

Dr. Margaret Battin has published extensively in end of life issues. She has authored or edited nine books, including *Ethical Issues in Suicide, Ethics in the Sanctuary,* and *The Least Worst Death: Essays on Bioethics at the End of Life.* Dr. Battin has conducted research on physician-assisted suicide and euthanasia in the Netherlands and Germany.

Dr. Arthur Lipman was an investigator in the original National Cancer Institute-funded Demonstration Project of Hospice Care in the 1970s and has been an investigator and practitioner in palliative care for over 25 years. He has published and consulted extensively on symptom control in terminal disease. He has also served on numerous federal and professional society panels relating to these issues, including the panels that wrote the federal Agency for Health Care Policy and Research Clinical Practice Guidelines on Management of Acute Pain in 1992 and Cancer Pain in 1994.

ETHICAL AND INSTITUTIONAL BACKGROUND POLICY ISSUES

Assisted Suicide and Euthanasia: Arguments For and Against Practice, Legalization and Participation

Ronald Baker Miller

SUMMARY. Conceptual and pragmatic arguments are presented supporting and opposing the following topics: the practice of suicide, assisted suicide, and voluntary active euthanasia; the legalization of assisted suicide or euthanasia; and the participation of physicians in these acts (whether or not they are legalized). Safeguards for

Ronald Baker Miller, MD, is Clinical Professor of Medicine and Director of the Program in Medical Ethics, University of California at Irvine, and Clinical Consultant and Chairman, Scientific Advisory Board, Spectra Laboratories (a national End-Stage Renal Disease laboratory) in Fremont, CA.

Address correspondence to: Dr. Ronald Baker Miller, Program in Medical Ethics, University of California, Irvine Medical Center, 101 The City Drive–Mail Route 81, Orange, CA 92668.

[Haworth co-indexing entry note]: "Assisted Suicide and Euthanasia: Arguments For and Against Practice, Legalization and Participation." Miller, Ronald Baker. Co-published simultaneously in *Journal of Pharmaceutical Care in Pain & Symptom Control* (Pharmaceutical Products Press, an imprint of The Haworth Press, Inc.) Vol. 3, No. 3/4, 1995, pp. 11-41; and: *Drug Use in Assisted Suicide and Euthanasia* (ed: Margaret P. Battin, and Arthur G. Lipman) Pharmaceutical Products Press, an imprint of The Haworth Press, Inc., 1996, pp. 11-41. Single or multiple copies of this article are available from The Haworth Document Delivery Service [1-800-342-9678, 9:00 a.m. - 5:00 p.m. (EST)].

© 1996 by The Haworth Press, Inc. All rights reserved. *11*

physician-assisted suicide and euthanasia are proposed. The morally problematic role of the pharmacist in physician-assisted suicide and euthanasia is discussed as are appropriate responses of healthcare professionals to the public's demand for assistance in suicide and euthanasia. *[Article copies available from The Haworth Document Delivery Service: 1-800-342-9678.]*

KEYWORDS. Suicide, assisted suicide, physician-assisted suicide, assisted death, physician-assisted death, euthanasia, voluntary active euthanasia, pharmacists

This paper surveys some of the conceptual and pragmatic arguments favoring and opposing assisted suicide and voluntary active euthanasia, their legalization and safeguards, and the participation of healthcare professionals. It begins with consideration of suicide itself (i.e., unassisted suicide), then turns to considerations related to all three practices (suicide, assisted suicide, and euthanasia). Thereafter this paper reviews some positive and negative assertions regarding each. Following a consideration of the legalization or quasi-legalization of physician-assisted suicide and euthanasia, safeguards that might be appropriate and the roles of physicians and pharmacists are discussed. Finally, actions which healthcare professionals might make, individually or collectively, in response to the public demand for assistance in suicide or assistance in death (i.e., euthanasia) are described.

This survey is not intended to champion a point of view or to provide dogmatic answers. Rather, it is intended to present a sufficient number of the arguments that have been asserted on both sides of the issues that the reader may formulate his or her own opinion on these matters.

SUICIDE

Suicide may be defined as an elective, self-determined death, or as voluntary, intentional, deliberate self-killing. More broadly the term may refer to any activity that increases the chance of death and is undertaken knowingly. One writer stated "Although suicide is often popularly understood in a narrower sense of active, pathological, self-killing, traditionally abhorred, the underlying issue most broadly conceived concerns the role the individual may play in bringing about his or her own death."[1] Do we then include in the meaning of "suicide" the refusal of treatment of a terminal illness, high-risk behavior, self-destructive behavior, or martyr-dom?[1] Do we include suicidal gestures or attempts that represent a cry for help? To avoid denial of life insurance benefits, advance directive legislation commonly states death due to refusal of treatment is not suicide, but what would we think if the treatment were penicillin for pneumonia or insulin for diabetes in a patient who was not terminally ill?

There are innumerable reasons patients commit suicide. Some are that patients may be depressed, lonely (desolate), have physical or mental illness and suffering, be fearful of illness or its consequences, or that they wish to leave an inheritance or life-insurance proceeds to their family. Suicide may be other-regarding (altruistic) or self-regarding.[2] Hill categorizes the latter as impulsive suicide, apathetic suicide (stemming from a loss of interest in life), self-abasing suicide (due to a "sense of worthlessness or unworthiness"), and hedonistic calculated suicide (which is "decided upon as the result of a . . . cost/benefit calculation").[3]

A fundamental question is whether suicide is a right. Many assert it is a right justified by the principle of autonomy. Doerflinger, however, notes the religious view that the fundamental "first right of the human person is his life." On this view, he states "suicide is not the ultimate exercise of freedom but its ultimate self-contradiction."[4] Although suicide is largely prohibited in Christianity, Judaism, and Islam, the question remains whether suicide is ever morally acceptable. A related question is whether suicide can be rational. Battin lists five criteria for rational suicide: the ability to reason logically, a realistic view of the world, adequacy of accurate information about one's circumstances and options, avoidance of harm (harm to oneself, "unless of course some greater good is thereby to be attained") and accordance with the individual's fundamental interests.[5]

Although, suicide is not invariably due to or even always associated with mental illness, depression is often present. Suicide may nevertheless be rational if either the depression is situational (and the situation warrants suicide) or if the depression is untreatable (and sufficiently severe that it is a rational basis for suicide).

Next we may ask if assistance in rational suicide is legitimate or culpable. Assistance in suicide is a crime in the majority of states and a felony in many.[6,7] On the other hand, a Federal District Judge ruled a Washington state law against assisted suicide unconstitutional.[6] The Ninth Circuit Court of Appeals overruled this decision, in keeping with the legal opinion of several experts.[6-9]

In judging whether assistance in suicide is legitimate or culpable, is it morally relevant to ask how much assistance is given? Is it acceptable for a physician to prescribe medication even knowing the patient may be stockpiling it and even to warn the patient of the consequence if an excessive dose is taken, so long as the physician is not present at the time the dose is taken? And what are the consequences (of assistance) for others: other patients, non-patients, and for physicians or other healthcare professionals if they learn of the assistance? Conversely what are the consequences of *not* providing assistance to individuals intent upon ending their lives?

If assistance in suicide is permissible, which–if any–healthcare professionals (physicians, pharmacists, others) should provide what assistance? Does assistance corrupt the profession or the professional? Are pharmacists especially positioned to be helpful on the one hand and vulnerable on the other? And if a pharmacist suspects a patient is stockpiling medication in potentially lethal amounts, does he or she have an obligation to report this concern to the prescribing physician, to the Medical (Licensing) Board, or to some other authority?

As previously noted I will separately consider arguments supporting and opposing suicide, assisted suicide, and euthanasia. I will begin with arguments relevant to all three methods of termination of life.

ARGUMENTS SUPPORTING THE INTENTIONAL TERMINATION OF LIFE BY SUICIDE, ASSISTED-SUICIDE, OR VOLUNTARY ACTIVE EUTHANASIA UNDER CERTAIN CIRCUMSTANCES

There are a number of arguments which favor the termination of life under the specific circumstances of unrelievable suffering and a patient's determination that death is the lesser of evils, particularly if the patient is terminally ill.

The most compelling argument is that of mercy or compassion. Illness may be debilitating, disabling, demoralizing, and degrading with loss of independence, competence, memory, continence, ability to care for oneself, or even the ability to express oneself. Public health measures and advances in medical science have resulted in prolonged life expectancy, but morbidity from degenerative disease in many cases makes survival less than desirable. Suffering may be unrelievable and unbearable as well as prolonged. Death itself may be delayed and dying prolonged, lingering, painful, and degrading. Suicide, assisted-suicide, and voluntary euthanasia are possible solutions to these unfortunate problems. They allow termination of life whose burdens outweigh the benefits as when there is uncontrollable physical pain, severe psychological suffering, advanced dementia, a bilateral stroke with loss of mobility, continence and dignity; permanent unconsciousness (in which case, though the patient may not suffer, the patient's family and caretakers often do), or illness with such loss of quality of life as judged by the patient that the burdens of illness greatly outweigh the benefits of living. In these circumstances, one wishes to be sure there is no relievable underlying depression or remediable situational stress.

Pain cannot always be managed effectively (without obtunding the patient), even with modern medications and patient-controlled devices for their parenteral administration.[11] And under these circumstances, especial-ly when death is inevitable and imminent, one asks, Why must life be prolonged? Indeed, once death is accepted, it may be merciful to end life quickly. Many patients fear having their life prolonged by "machines" in hospitals with little benefit and at great cost. Others simply fear not being in control. Nursing homes are "deeply depressing because hopelessness in most facilities is overwhelming."[12] All argue that physician-assisted sui-cide or death (voluntary euthanasia) would allow "death with dignity" and allow control over the time and manner of one's own death.

Anxiety is often associated with these fears of terminal pain and suffer-ing, of death-delaying, life-sustaining technology, of not being in control and of being vulnerable, of loss of dignity or respect, and of having one's wishes overridden perhaps by a physician-stranger. Such anxiety is often alleviated if the patient is assured his or her physician will provide relief. And most such individuals never request assistance in dying.

The second major argument favoring termination of life under such circumstances is the right of individuals to self-determination and to con-trol the time, place, and nature of their death. Sometimes this is called "the right to die," but this is an inherently flawed concept. We are all obligated to die, and what is usually meant by "the right to die" is the right to control one's dying. Many believe we should have the right to a dignified, humane, painless, and quick death. Do we also have the right to a "con-trolled, comfortable, convenient death?"[13] Many believe that free choice (autonomy) justifies assisted suicide and euthanasia, but Callahan argues "The self-determination in that case [euthanasia] can only be effected by the moral and physical assistance of another. Euthanasia is thus no longer a matter of only self-determination, but of a mutual, social decision be-tween two people: the one to be killed, and the other to do the killing."[14] Davies argues poignantly that "kill" is the wrong word for an act of active voluntary euthanasia.[15]

A very thoughtful proposal would permit physician-assisted death (in-deed would legalize it) in the "extraordinary circumstance when it is requested voluntarily by a patient whose suffering has become intolerable and who has no other satisfactory options," though the authors believe patients do not "have a right to physician-assisted death as they do to standard medical care."[16]

Some contend the distinction between forgoing life-sustaining treatment and suicide (intentional self-killing) is artificial[17] and may in fact be cruel.[18,19] Similarly, the distinction between physician-assisted suicide and active voluntary euthanasia is said by some to be morally irrelevant.[17,20-23] Relevant considerations before forgoing life-sustaining treatment or considering physician-assisted suicide or euthanasia were outlined by the Task Force on Physician-assisted Suicide of the SHHV.[10] One must consider the extent of the patient's suffering, both physical and emotional, as well as the certainty of the diagnosis and prognosis. One must consider alternative treatments including hospice. One should consider the probable duration of life both with and without the assisted suicide or death and whether the means to be used are conventional or appropriate. One wishes to know whether the patient's preferences are free of coercion, depression, and mental illness, are coherent and understandable (even if not reasonable), and whether they are expressed consistently in an enduring fashion. One should evaluate the motivation of each of the parties and consider the effect of the action upon other patients and professionals.

ARGUMENTS OPPOSING THE INTENTIONAL TERMINATION OF LIFE BY SUICIDE, ASSISTED SUICIDE OR VOLUNTARY EUTHANASIA UNDER ANY CIRCUMSTANCE

A sacrosanct, deontologic argument is that killing is always wrong. This is frequently a religious argument such as the "Jewish and Christian belief that humans are stewards and not the absolute masters of the gift of life."[24] The faithful believe only God has dominion over life and death.[17] Life is sacred, and furthermore Christians believe that suffering is ennobling. Similar moral beliefs need not have a religious basis.[25] There are many in our society who believe that killing–even though out of mercy and compassion–is intrinsically wrong, and that assisted suicide and euthanasia devalue life and are disrespectful of persons.[14,24,26-31]

Of great importance is the fact that a seeming autonomous request for assisted suicide or euthanasia is often a cry for help. Such requests, no matter how subtle, should not go unanswered. Depression (whether endogenous or situational) frequently underlies a desire to end life. And unfortunately, depression is seriously under-diagnosed, particularly in the elderly.

Traditional state interests are the four "Ps": the preservation of life, the prevention of suicide, the protection of innocent third parties, and the preservation of the ethical integrity of the medical profession. Of these, the protection of innocent third parties probably carries the most weight today. Nevertheless, solidarity and communitarian concerns favor preservation of life so long as it is not exceedingly burdensome.

A pragmatic argument relates to the messages sent by a society which condones physician-assisted suicide or euthanasia. The messages include the devaluation of human life (disrespect for persons), an emphasis on individual rights rather than responsibility to community, and a threat to the doctor-patient relationship.[31] Indeed, laws change attitudes,[31] and "the right to die" could become "the duty to die," a quip often attributed to Richard Lamm, former governor of Colorado.

Some believe assisted suicide and euthanasia are unnecessary because most deaths are not painful.[22,23] Furthermore, pain and depression are nearly always treatable: statistically very few patients have unrelievable pain and depression. Of greater concern is that ready availability of assisted suicide and death would take the pressure off our profession to do a better job in treating pain and suffering. They would divert attention from hospice and pain management.

Most individuals who oppose assisted suicide and euthanasia are concerned with the dangers of erroneous diagnosis and prognosis, and with the dangers of abuse and the slippery slope. It is commonly feared that assisted suicide and euthanasia would be extended from terminally ill, competent, assertive patients, to the non-terminally ill, the incompetent, and the vulnerable (the elderly, the young, and the poor). Callahan argues "There is . . . no reasonable or logical stopping point: if we really believe in self-determination, then any competent person should have the right to be killed by a doctor for any reason that suits him. If we believe in the relief of suffering, then it seems cruel and capricious to deny it to the incompetent."[29] And Kass asks, "Will we not sweep up, in the process, some who are not really tired of life, but think others are tired of them; some who do not really want to die, but who feel that they should not live on, because to do so when there looms the legal alternative of euthanasia is to do a selfish or cowardly act? Will not some feel an obligation to have themselves "eliminated" in order that funds allocated for their terminal care might be better used by their families or, financial worries aside, in order to relieve their families of the emotional strain involved?"[30] Indeed, the risk of abuse of assisted suicide or death is increased by the pressures of cost containment in our health care system.[16]

The Task Force on Physician-assisted Suicide of the SHHV noted that a number of American attitudes are in keeping with the notion that slippery slope fears are real.[10] Too many of us are prejudiced against the elderly, the chronically ill, and people with disabilities. The lack of access for the poor and minorities to health care raises "the specter that someday assisted death could be seen as a form of medical cost control." Our "emphasis on curative care . . . and the lack of support for hospice, mental health services, and primary care . . ." are further threats. Our "death phobia" and our "tendency to seek mechanical or technical answers to what is at bottom a problem of meaning and spirituality" pose yet additional threats. Furthermore, we have "relied . . . upon . . . death as a way to resolve certain [of our] social problems." Our lack of adequate long-term care and of respite care produces fatigue of caretakers "so that the ill person may receive a variety of subtle and not so subtle messages that he would be more valued . . . if he elected a quicker end . . . . "[10]

There are, of course, counter-counter arguments. Slippery slope arguments tend to reflect an unreasonable demand for certainty, and stem from a refusal to discern significant differences. They may represent an abuse of data and reason, and may demonstrate a distrust of safeguards. Commonly there is a failure to identify the force causing the slide down the slope, a failure to recognize means of arresting the slide, a failure to clearly identify the feared outcome (the bottom of the slide), or a failure to demonstrate the badness of the outcome (i.e., that the outcome is worse than the general state).[32]

Yet another counter-counter argument: Rachels noted that if suicide is sometimes rational, and if suicide assistance is sometimes morally acceptable, and if the distinction between assisted suicide and voluntary euthanasia is morally insignificant, then we are on a slippery slope, but "if we went to the bottom of this particular slope, our attitudes towards suicide and euthanasia would have become not worse, but better."[19]

ARGUMENTS JUSTIFYING SUICIDE
UNDER CERTAIN CIRCUMSTANCES

There are many reasons for suicide. Perhaps the most common are pain, suffering and depression. Pain and suffering may be chronic, terminal, or due to mental illness. Depression is very common, and may be situational (as following the death of a spouse) or endogenous (idiopathic). Guilt, shame, humiliation, and dejection are additional reasons for suicide. One cause of guilt is the fear of burdening others: suicide then is self-sacrifice. Physical disability and dependence are common reasons for the fear of burdening others (and for suicide), whereas martyrdom for a religious or other heroic cause is nowadays rare even though belief in an afterlife (for one's soul) is common.

Suicide is said by some to represent the ultimate right of self-determination. However, the belief that it harms only the individual is rarely true as we are all "connected." Though not true in the past, presently it is widely believed "if a competent patient expresses a clear desire to die, the state's interest in protecting the individual's life ceases to exist."[33] And, interestingly, the argument that suicide is prohibited when it harms others, might logically be turned about to *require* suicide if it would help others.[5]

The treatment of suicidal ideation, suicide attempts, and suicide includes recognition of causes and premonitory symptoms, and prevention by preemptive treatment of psychological conditions and relief of situational circumstances. Intervention is indicated for suicide that is imminent or already underway. Postvention is therapy of an individual who attempted suicide or of the family of one who accomplished suicide (for surviving loved ones have an increased risk of suicide themselves).[32]

ARGUMENTS OPPOSING SUICIDE
UNDER ANY CIRCUMSTANCE

Epistomologically, suicide can never be rational (at least not fully informed) since one cannot know what, if anything, follows death–i.e., know what the full consequences of death are to be.[1] To be sure, suicide always represents a tragedy for the individual unless the burdens of his or her life so outweigh the benefits. Clearly suicide causes suffering for those who remain (family, friends, and especially dependent children or parents). That is, suicide is a selfish act. It is thought to be an "incoherent end [to one's] biographical narrative."[10] There is social stigma attached to suicide which adversely affects how the individual is remembered, and may extend to the family and friends of the departed as well.

"Although U.S. law does not prohibit suicide, it is not usually interpreted to recognize suicide as a right."[1] In the past, suicide was taken to be a wrong against the state, and perhaps this was true when the strength of a state could be measured by the number of its citizens. But it is no longer true: conceivably suicide may even help society (at least one that is over populated). Also in the past suicide was considered a wrong against God (because we are each a steward of our own body) and this was a powerful argument for many.

ARGUMENTS SUPPORTING ASSISTED SUICIDE
UNDER CERTAIN CIRCUMSTANCES

Battin defines physician-assisted suicide as a practice whose purpose is "to help a patient in need avoid what he or she perceives as a far worse death, or avoid continued existence in a state he or she perceives [to be] worse than death."[5] Physician-assisted suicide has become a matter of considerable public interest and concern. Reasons for this include: increased life expectancy, an increase in degenerative diseases, the ascendance of autonomy and the "right to die," rethinking of religious and cultural assumptions, and the psychosocial and economic costs of chronic illness.[5]

Battin asks, "If the patient is entitled to refuse life-prolonging treatment while he or she is still competent, and so die, or to direct in advance that treatment be withheld after he or she is no longer competent, and so die, why isn't the patient entitled to choose to die by more direct and immediate means?"[5] Indeed, in May of 1994, Barbara J. Rothstein, Chief U.S. District Judge, found the Washington State statute against assistance in suicide unconstitutional on the grounds of undue burden to exercise a constitutionally protected right and on the grounds of denying plaintiffs equal protection (i.e., those with life-threatening illness can refuse therapy and so die, but . . .).[6] This decision was appealed to the Ninth Circuit Court of Appeals which ruled the state law is constitutional. Although there could yet be a ruling en banc by the full panel of 12 circuit judges, several scholars state there is no fundamental or constitutional right to suicide or assisted suicide.[6-9]

A *Harvard Law Review* article notes "Many states expressly prohibit suicide assistance . . . These laws imply that patients do not have the right to authorize suicide assistance. However, current right-to-die case law strongly suggests the opposite–that patients do have a right to determine how and when they die. Thus, the laws against suicide assistance must be reconciled with the principle of self-determination found in current right-to-die doctrine." Furthermore, the article states there are "no inherent distinctions between letting a patient die and assisting a patient's suicide . . . To say that the patient's illness, rather than the withdrawal of life-sustaining treatment "causes" the patient's death simply means that a court will not hold the physician liable for the death."[33]

The laws against suicide itself were dropped in order to encourage psychiatric treatment of those who attempt suicide and fail, and also to lessen the impact on the family.[8] Perhaps legislators also thought, as the saying goes, "It is wrong to kick someone when he is down": that is, to punish someone who is so distraught that he (or more commonly she) attempted suicide and failed at it. More properly we might say depression and mental illness deserve treatment, not punishment (and furthermore, a law against suicide is unlikely to dissuade someone intent upon it).[7] And it goes without saying that accomplished suicide is unpunishable.[7]

The SHHV Task Force noted, "If one views suicide itself as morally unproblematic, and morally defensible in a particular case, then assisting in that case would probably be viewed as morally praiseworthy."[10] In other words, if a suicide is appropriate (or rational), then *assistance* is also morally appropriate (or rational):

a. if the patient is uninformed regarding how to commit suicide,
b. if the patient might otherwise botch it or fears botching it,
c. if the patient prefers medication to other means at his or her disposal, and
d. if the patient wants not to be alone at the time of suicide.

A further argument in favor of physician-assisted suicide is that if it is not allowed, there will be increased social pressure to allow physician-performed euthanasia. Compared with euthanasia there is less chance of involuntary or non-voluntary death with physician-assisted suicide. Furthermore, it can be done at home (with family and friends in attendance) if medications are stockpiled or provided. And finally, with physician-assisted suicide there is a greater sense of control by the patient and perhaps therefore, less chance of the patient actually committing suicide.

Additional arguments favoring physician-assisted suicide are that individuals have the right to determine the time, cause, and nature of their death; that no one should have to endure unrelievable suffering; that a goal of medicine is to relieve suffering when cure is not possible; that it would be unjust if individuals dependent upon life sustaining treatment were allowed to die with physician attendance but those with equally intolerable, but treatment-independent conditions were not; that protections against abuse can be devised and enforced; and that—when death is voluntary—it may contribute to justice by relieving families and society of social and economic burdens. [5]

ARGUMENTS OPPOSING ASSISTED SUICIDE
UNDER ANY CIRCUMSTANCE

Although a particular suicide might be appropriate (from the point of view of the patient, or even from the point of view of others), some would say it is never appropriate for the patient to ask anyone else to participate, least of all, a healthcare professional. This is because there are adverse consequences for persons who assist, and these may be legal (assistance in suicide is illegal in most states), social (stigma), or psychological (guilt, remorse, callous indifference or insensitivity) effects. The principal arguments opposing physician-assisted suicide are that life is sacred, that slippery-slope abuses will occur, and that the practice will corrupt physicians.[5]

The life is sacred argument may be extended to suggest that suffering is redemptive, that suicide is never rational, and that killing (assisted suicide) is intrinsically wrong. Patients should not request physicians to do what is wrong.

Slippery slope concerns are that the practice of physician-assisted suicide would be abused and extended from the few intolerably-suffering, terminally-ill patients who might request it to the many vulnerable, non-terminally ill, non-voluntary, depressed individuals who might be coerced to request (or unable to refuse) assistance in death.

Assisted suicide as compared with suicide increases the risk of abuse (of pressuring persons to allow assisted suicide). This may justify the illegality of assisted suicide.

The corruption concern is that physicians will become callous if not unscrupulous. Furthermore, they will be relieved of the responsibilities of better care for patients, and of more research to improve the treatment of pain and suffering. Patients will then lose trust in, and respect for, physicians.

ARGUMENTS SUPPORTING EUTHANASIA UNDER CERTAIN CIRCUMSTANCES

Physician-assisted suicide may be defined as the "prescription of medication or the counseling of an ill patient so he or she may use an overdose to end his or her life." [34] Physician-assisted death (voluntary, active euthanasia) may similarly be defined as the "deliberate administration of an overdose of medication to an ill patient at his or her request with the primary intent to end his or her life."[34] Alternatively, euthanasia has been defined as "the art of painlessly [and, I would add, compassionately] putting to death persons suffering from incurable conditions or diseases,"[35] or as "the deliberate termination of a patient's life in order to prevent further suffering."[36]

Is there a significant moral difference between physician-assisted suicide and voluntary active euthanasia (physician-performed death)? Brock argues there is not: "The only difference that need exist between the two is the person who actually administers the lethal dose. In each, the physician plays an active and necessary causal role." Brock further argues that the same values that support the patient's right to refuse life sustaining treatment "support the ethical permissibility of euthanasia: individual self-determination or autonomy and individual well being."[21] Battin further argues as previously noted, "If the patient is entitled to refuse life-prolonging treatment while he or she is still competent, and so die, or to direct in advance that treatment be withheld after he or she is no longer competent, and so die, why isn't the patient entitled to choose to die by more direct and immediate means?"[5] The advantage of physician-performed euthanasia compared with physician-assisted suicide (or compared with unassisted suicide) is that there is less chance of botching the death, more social acceptance, and the methods are preferable to some.

There are several categories of arguments in favor of physician-performed euthanasia.[22,23,29] First is the right of self-determination for patients who may or may not be terminally ill and whose suffering may be unrelievable, unbearable, and prolonged. Second, some believe euthanasia is compatible with the practice of medicine, that is with the duty of the physician to relieve suffering, and even that it is immoral to withhold it if it is requested for unbearable suffering. Although Callahan would not agree [29] some feel the difference between killing and allowing to die is irrelevant.[20] Of particular interest in this regard is the fact that "the Dutch apparently regard Americans' willingness to cease an incompetent patient's life-sustaining treatment as more morally problematic than their own policy of active euthanasia for competent patients."[37]

Last, but not least, is the lack of evidence that legalization will result in harm. The only truly extensive experience in this regard is that of the Netherlands, where euthanasia is not actually legal, but where it is not prosecuted if certain conditions are met. These include: the suffering is intolerable and unrelievable; a voluntary, repeated, and consistent request for euthanasia by an informed, competent adult; concurrence of a consulting physician; and report by the physician to the medical examiner who, in turn, reports to the prosecutor.[32,38]

The Dutch themselves wished to assess their practice of voluntary, active euthanasia. Incidentally, they believe the term "euthanasia" sufficient, and the term "voluntary, active euthanasia," as we use it, redundant. Their survey of the practice of 400 physicians and review of the cause of death of 8500 patients was the basis of the Remmelink Report. This review covered four categories of cases: withholding or withdrawing life-sustaining treatment, the alleviation of pain and suffering by use of large doses of opioids or other drugs even though death might ensue, euthanasia and physician-assisted suicide, and life-ending actions without specific request. The all-encompassing term for the Dutch is "MDEL" (Medical Decisions at the End of Life). "Euthanasia" for the Dutch does not include cases where lethal doses of medication were given to hasten or cause death of patients in pain, and does not include the purposeful death of patients incapable of giving consent, but data in these regards as well as concerning "euthanasia" were presented in several publications.[39-48] In 1990 there were 128,786 deaths of which 22,500 (17.5%) were due to a refusal of treatment (passive euthanasia). Another 22,500 deaths (another 17.5%) were "APS," (that is, deaths while Alleviating Pain and Symptoms) which may have shortened life (i.e., what we would call "double effect"). In 1990 it is estimated that 25,000 patients initiated discussions about euthanasia, and there were 9,000 explicit requests for euthanasia. Two thousand three hundred patients (26% of requests) underwent voluntary active euthanasia which accounts for 1.8% of all deaths. In addition, there were 1,000 cases of "LAWER" (Life-terminating Acts Without Explicit Request). These amounted to 0.8% of all deaths. In these cases there was intentional ending of life for unbearable suffering without the explicit and persistent request of the patient. However, many patients (59%) had engaged in prior discussion with their physician; many (41%) were unconscious; and in most cases (86%) life was shortened less than one week. Finally, there were 400 cases of assisted suicide, amounting to 0.3% of deaths.

To summarize, then, 17.5% of deaths were what we would call "passive euthanasia" or refusal of life-sustaining treatment; 17.5% deaths caused by alleviating pain (double effect); 1.8% voluntary active euthanasia; 0.8% non-voluntary active euthanasia (life termination without explicit and persistent request at the time); and 0.3% were physician-assisted suicide. To further summarize, 35% of deaths in the Netherlands were due to refusal of life-sustaining treatment or due to pain medication, (not remarkably different from what I suspect is the experience in the United States), and 3% of deaths were either voluntary active euthanasia, non-voluntary active euthanasia, or assisted suicide (although perhaps a low percentage for what we assume to be the case in the Netherlands, a greater percentage than we admit to be the case in the United States). In contrast to the conclusion of some observers,[41,48] I interpret the Dutch experience to refute the notion of failure to avoid the slippery slope.

ARGUMENTS OPPOSING EUTHANASIA UNDER ANY CIRCUMSTANCE

As previously noted and discussed, the primary arguments against euthanasia are the messages it conveys, the danger of the slippery slope and abuse, and diversion of the physician's attention from comprehensive care of the dying. Perhaps most fundamental is an appreciation that just as in the case of abortion, "pro-choice" does not mean "pro-abortion." So too, in this context, "pro-choice" does not mean "pro-euthanasia." The reasons underlying the need for such a choice are always tragic.

Regarding the slippery slope, Singer and Siegler list four ways in which voluntary euthanasia could lead to involuntary euthanasia: Crypthanasia (secret euthanasia), encouraged euthanasia (pressure on chronically ill or dying patients to accept euthanasia), surrogate euthanasia (euthanasia upon a proxy's decision for an incompetent), and discriminatory euthanasia (euthanasia of vulnerable groups).[27] In contrast to the Dutch, German physicians did slide down the slippery slope in the 1930s and 1940s. Alexander wrote, "Whatever proportion the [Nazi] crimes finally assumed, it became evident to all who investigated that the crimes had started from small beginnings. The beginnings at first were merely a subtle shift in emphasis in the basic attitude of physicians. It started with the acceptance of the attitude, basic in the euthanasia movement, that there is such a thing as a life not worthy to be lived."[49]

ARGUMENTS FAVORING LEGALIZATION OF PHYSICIAN-ASSISTED SUICIDE OR EUTHANASIA

The history of accepted or legalized euthanasia begins in ancient times. There was widespread acceptance of euthanasia in ancient Greece and Rome, but this was challenged by the minority of physicians who were part of the Hippocratic school.[22,23] Assisting suicide is not a crime in Germany so long as the individual is not depressed or coerced. Although physicians could administer a lethal drug, apparently they rarely do so, and they are rarely present when a patient takes an overdose. Curiously "once the patient has taken the drug and becomes unconscious, the physician incurs a duty to resuscitate him or her."[52]

Although many have mistakenly thought euthanasia is legal in the Netherlands, it remains technically prohibited by statute although under a variety of legal and policy decisions. Physicians will not be prosecuted if explicit safeguards and reporting requirements are met. Nevertheless, the quasi-legal agreement not to prosecute if safeguards are met by physicians has allowed for a substantial experience there.

In November of 1994 the voters of Oregon by the slim margin of 51 to 49% approved Measure 16, permitting physician-assisted suicide for terminally ill patients (expected to live less than six months) who make two informed oral requests more than 14 days apart and a written request (with two witnesses) more than 48 hours before the physician writes the prescription for the lethal dose of medication which the patient then takes him or herself.[50]

Most recently, in May 1995, by a vote of 15 to 10 (initially 13 to 12) the Northern Territory of Australia passed a statute permitting both physician-assisted suicide and physician-performed euthanasia for terminally-ill patients (expected to live less than 12 months) who are competent adults without depression and who have "severe suffering, pain, or distress" for which no medical treatment is "reasonably available or acceptable."[51] Following the request the patient must wait seven days, then sign a formal request and wait an additional two days. Thereafter medication can be administered by the patient or the physician, and the death must be reported to the coroner.

For most of the world, physician-assisted suicide and euthanasia remain illegal. Gostin and Weir state "Life-and-Death choices across the country could sink to the low level where people must deliberately marshal their legal evidence in the fear that their government will fail to respect their wishes and privacy. Alternatively, states can enact creative ways to encourage meaningful dialogue with family and physicians on final care, assist people in making clear and simple statements of their preferences and adopt legal presumptions about the closeness of family life that best reflect the value system and behavior of most Americans."[53] Indeed, a *Harvard Law Review* article states "because this type of physician-assisted suicide (withdrawal of life sustaining treatment) has been legalized, there is no objective reason why courts cannot create exceptions in similar cases that involve lethal injections and prescription drugs."[33] Margaret Battin points out that active euthanasia is "much more overt and conspicuous" than withdrawing and especially withholding treatment (passive euthanasia), and thus potentially less susceptible to abuse.[54]

Many believe that autonomy should include the right to determine the nature, place, and time of one's death. Battin states, "To restrict the right to die to the mere right to refuse unwanted medical treatment and so be "allowed" to die . . . is an indefensible truncation of the more basic right to choose one's death in accordance with one's own values. Thus, advance directives, . . . do-not-resuscitate orders, and other mechanisms for withholding and withdrawing treatment are inadequate to protect fundamental rights." [1]

Brock believes the good consequences of permitting euthanasia include: (1) demonstration of respect for the self-determination of competent patients who want it, (2) a reassurance to people if they ever want it they can get it, (3) relief of pain and suffering, and (4)"once death has been accepted, it is often more humane to end life quickly and peacefully, when that is what the patient wants."[21] Legislation then would: (1) respect the rights of those who request it *and* (2) protect those who provide it, (3) reduce the fear of an unpleasant death and of loss of control when dying– i.e., reassure people that a humane end of life will be available to them, and (4) "provide a more humane and peaceful death than some patients would otherwise have."[17]

In simple terms one might argue that if voluntary active euthanasia is sometimes appropriate, it should be legal. Indeed, if an act is justified, why not a practice? CeloCruz notes that another argument for the legalization of assisted suicide or euthanasia (though she does not find it compelling) is the fact that juries are reluctant to indict or convict doctors for assisted suicide or euthanasia.[7] Laws should be reasonable, realistic, and should meet the needs of society. Patients should not have to die alone, but they should not put loved ones who assist them in dying in jeopardy by having them present at the time of assisted death.

It is unfair to ask physicians to break the law to relieve the suffering of even those few patients for whom euthanasia is a reasonable solution, and who request it. Patients should not have to ask physicians to break the law to assist them in dying. If euthanasia is practiced, even occasionally, it would be better to have it done openly with public scrutiny rather than clandestinely, hidden from the public. If done openly, we can learn its extent, the problems, the abuses. If done openly, we can regulate it; that is, we can require safeguards. Thus legalization should actually protect against the slippery slope and the discriminatory dispatching of patients.

Brock submits, "The case against . . . the likely policy consequences of permitting voluntary active euthanasia . . . is sufficiently weak to warrant a limited and controlled experiment with it, such as would follow one or a few states permitting it."[20] Indeed, it seems appropriate to legalize physician-assisted suicide and/or euthanasia in some jurisdiction as an experiment, perhaps simply allowing the Oregon statute to stand. Thereby we can learn empirically whether the practice should be extended to other jurisdictions or should be illegal in all jurisdictions (or possibly legal in some, illegal in others). Weir recommends "A preferable alternative to the current patchwork of state laws on assisted suicide would be for the National Conference of Commissioners on Uniform State Laws, working with appropriate medical groups, to develop model legislation on physician-assisted suicide that might be adopted throughout the country. . . ."[55] Weir also believes "legal restrictions on assisted suicide should be lifted only for physicians."

ARGUMENTS OPPOSING LEGALIZATION OF BOTH PHYSICIAN-ASSISTED SUICIDE AND EUTHANASIA

Again, history is of interest. In 1906 an Ohio bill to legalize euthanasia failed. It had been inspired by a prominent Harvard professor, Charles Elliot Norton, who advocated euthanasia. And in 1936 a bill to legalize euthanasia was defeated in Britain.[22,23] In more recent times, initiatives to legalize assisted suicide and euthanasia were defeated 54% to 46% in the state of Washington (Initiative 119)[56] in 1991, and by the same margin in California (Proposition 161) in 1992.[50] Canada's Supreme Court ruled there was no constitutional right to assisted suicide in 1993 by a 5 to 4 decision, and the Michigan Supreme Court ruled in the same direction in 1994.[57]

Even though euthanasia might be morally permissible, perhaps even obligatory, under certain circumstances, many believe it would be bad public policy to legalize it. They argue there are insufficient numbers of cases to warrant legislation, and passive euthanasia should suffice. Abuses and the slippery slope are serious risks of legalization: the frail and the vulnerable might well be coerced. Furthermore, the message such laws would send (regarding the kind of society we have and devaluing the importance of individuals in our society) is inappropriate.[31]

It is stated that most suicides and requests for euthanasia are due either to treatable pain or to treatable depression (or the fear of such pain and suffering). Thus, laws should discourage not encourage suicide or physician-assisted death (euthanasia).

Legislation will lead to the slippery slope and involuntary killing.[58] It is much easier for physicians to allow a patient to die than to keep trying to treat recalcitrant pain and suffering. Furthermore, the cost of health care may pressure many patients, especially the elderly, into acquiescence even though the cost savings may not be substantial.[59] Should we legalize the right to death on command when we have not even legislated the right to health care? How can we legalize the right to die when we have not provided entitlement to healthcare (except to the elderly, to patients with end-stage renal disease, and to prisoners), and when those who cannot afford healthcare may be pressured or feel obligated to accept euthanasia?

Bayley[31] and CeloCruz[7] assert that laws do influence public opinion and societal attitudes and values. Bayley believes that even if we do not become callous, we are likely to lose our sense of righteous indignation when patients' lives are terminated. Condoning the autonomous request for euthanasia is an affront to communitarian values and even to respect for the lives of persons requesting it. We cannot be so naive as to believe that patients who are sick and dying make free and voluntary decisions, untainted by economic concerns, feelings of being a burden to others, or confusion about what is possible and desirable for them. To legalize euthanasia will vastly increase its practice and its abuse.[14,29,30,58] Thus it would be better to keep it illegal, and to have the burden of justifying it on those who practice it.[60] For similar and other reasons the New York State Task Force on Life and the Law unanimously recommended that laws not be changed to permit assisted suicide or euthanasia. They "concluded that legalizing assisted suicide would be unwise and dangerous public policy."[9] Our society is too pluralistic, relativistic, diverse and intolerant to avoid abuses were euthanasia to be legalized. If euthanasia were legalized, it could become expected: vulnerable patients might feel obligated to accept it in order to reduce the burden on their families, their caretakers, their healthcare professionals, and even on society. Children of elders and other caretakers, even healthcare professionals, might expect reasonable patients to accept it. If euthanasia were legalized, it would be easier to pressure those who cannot afford medical care to be eliminated.

If euthanasia were to become a legal right for competent, suffering, terminally ill patients who are a burden to themselves, it would likely be extended to the incompetent (or never competent) and to those with treatable suffering or even those without demonstrable suffering, those with treatable terminal illness or non-terminal illness, and those who are simply a burden on others.

If legalized with tight restrictions (such as requiring competence, terminal illness, suffering, exclusion of depression, explanation of options, counseling) the restrictions might well be lifted in the future allowing a slip down the slope. And if euthanasia were legalized, it would be more difficult to detect and to avoid abuses. Indeed, if we allow death for the good of the patient, may we not also accept it for the good of the patient's loved ones, family, or beneficiaries?

And most importantly (I fear) legalization of euthanasia may lessen the need for the medical profession to improve pain control, and to integrate hospice care into general medical practice. Furthermore, it lessens the need for research in pain control, hospice, and care of the dying. It reduces the pressure on physicians to better meet the spiritual (as well as emotional and physical) needs of mentally or terminally ill or dying or suicidal patients. It allows too easy a way out for healthcare professionals caring for difficult patients.

pros

SAFEGUARDS FOR PHYSICIAN-ASSISTED SUICIDE AND EUTHANASIA

With moral indignation[28] over the brief, inflammatory essay, "It's over Debbie"[61] and widespread controversy over the behavior of Dr. Jack

Kevorkian,[2,62] no one would dispute the necessity of safeguards for practices as potentially susceptible to abuse as assisted suicide or death. Despite generally laudatory responses to the compassionate admissions of Dr. Timothy Quill,[63,64] most individuals seem to favor writing safeguards into law[65] rather than having guidelines adopted by professional medical societies[66] or standards of practice defined by the behavior of "reasonable" physicians. A very thoughtful proposal suggests both state legislation and professional regulation by palliative care consultants and regional palliative-care committees.[16] It is widely believed that the ballot initiatives in the state of Washington and in California failed because of insufficient safeguards.[16,67] This was corrected, at least in part, for Oregon's Measure 16, which was passed by the voters but is presently restrained by the Court. Oregon's physician-assisted suicide measure requires the physician to inform the patient of alternative treatments as well as of his diagnosis, prognosis, and of the risks and benefits of taking the prescribed medication. A consulting physician must confirm that the illness is terminal, that the patient is competent, and that decision making is voluntary and informed. The physician must ask the patient to notify next of kin, and if either the physician or consultant is concerned, the patient must be referred for psychological counseling. There is to be a 15 day interval between the request and prescription of medication, and the physician must offer the patient an opportunity to rescind the request.[50]

Quill, Cassel, and Maier proposed seven criteria justifying and regulating physician-assisted suicide which, incidentally, they believe has less risk of coercion than voluntary active euthanasia.[68] The criteria are: incurable disease, severe untreatable pain, competence of the patient, a meaningful doctor-patient relationship and consultation, the request must be initiated by the patient and repeated, and documentation of all of the above. Similarly, Battin has categorized protections against abuse of physician-assisted suicide or voluntary active euthanasia as (1) confirmation of diagnosis, prognosis, treatment options, and competence, (2) mandatory, non-directive, non-paternalistic counseling, (3) education of physicians, (4) education of the public, and (5) regulation to prevent abuse.[1,5,32]

Additional comments on these protections address the above points: (1) Confirmation of diagnosis, prognosis, treatment options, and competence includes confirmation that the illness is not readily reversible, that suffering is not relievable, that the patient does not have treatable depression or mental illness, that the request is stable, authentic, and informed, and that the patient has been offered all available care. (2) The mandatory, non-directive, non-paternalistic counseling is intended to explore the patient's understanding of his or her illness and the therapeutic options, and to understand the patient's decision in light of his or her personal, cultural, and spiritual values, to uncover any coercion, manipulation, or misunderstanding, and to review the impact of the patient's decision upon others. (3) Education of physicians is to enable communication about serious illness (without raising false hopes or overly pessimistic fears), effective counseling of patients, knowledge of pharmacologic and other techniques of suicide and euthanasia, and understanding by the physician of his or her own moral values, and minimizing adverse emotional consequences for the physician and for other healthcare professionals. (4) Education of the public is also essential. (5) Regulations to prevent abuse should include all of the above and also a waiting period between the request and the act; witnessing of the request, of the informed consent, and of the act; and mandatory documentation, reporting, and auditing.[1,5,32]

There are a number of other suggestions that might be considered as safeguards. Surely a request for assisted suicide or death must be revocable at any time, but should it be revocable if the patient has become incompetent (whereas he or she was competent when the request was previously made)? Coercion should be a punishable crime. The request should not only be rational, but should be authentic (i.e., consistent with the patient's values). Does the patient need to be terminally ill or simply to have a serious, poorly treatable illness? Should all patients have consultations to exclude depression (by psychiatrists, psychologists, or psychiatric social workers)? Should all patients have a hospice evaluation? Can economic factors be primary in the patient's wish to terminate his or her life? Should there be review by an institutional ethics committee or by a panel like an IRB?[16] Must the patient's primary physician be involved (at least in counseling of the patient), and how long need the primary physician have known the patient? Should payment for euthanasia be precluded? Should the death itself be witnessed and/or video-taped? Model legislation or regulations with safeguards are under consideration in a number of jurisdictions including Los Angeles and Boston.[69,70]

ARGUMENTS FAVORING PHYSICIAN PARTICIPATION IN ASSISTED SUICIDE OR DEATH

Physicians are the logical professionals in our society to assist patients in death desired because of illness. They are trained in, or have experience with, many of the necessary skills such as assessment of competence; detection of depression; balancing benefits to health and burdens of illness in medical decision making; matters of severe disabling, debilitating, incapacitating illness; matters of life and death; evaluating and treating illness;

pain control; and hospice. Brock quipped to make a serious point, "Killing patients is not, to put it flippantly, understood to be part of physicians' job description . . . but some killings are ethically justified, including many instances of stopping life support."[21] Indeed, he stated "morally justified killing of patients is a proper part of medical practice."[20] Griffiths reports that the Dutch public generally believe that physician-assisted suicide and euthanasia must be performed by a physician to be "legitimate."[42] A survey published in the JAMA indicated 64% of Americans thought physicians should be allowed by law to respond to a request for aid in dying by a competent, terminally ill patient in pain.[71] Two surveys of physicians showed far fewer thought physicians should participate than thought euthanasia should be legalized.[34,72]

Physicians ideally have a long-standing relationship with patients, and know them as persons. They know the patient's condition and prognosis, and they are generally highly ethical, highly responsible, and most are committed to quality of life as well as to the longevity and welfare of their patients. Physicians should manage death with compassion, care, respect, and skill just as they do the treatment of illness. They are able to effect a humane, dignified, swift, painless, gentle, and certain death. The alleviation of pain and suffering is as fundamental to the practice of medicine as the prolongation of life.

The SHHV Task Force made a number of cogent observations. "Once patients understand that the physician would assist them in the end, they will more openly discuss their true fears and needs, thereby leading in most cases to better alternatives for relief of suffering."[10] The physician's usual role in prolonging life at nearly all costs may make physicians appropriate protectors of their patients and defenders against the abuse of dispatching them. Which should take precedence: the physician's duty to attempt to prolong life, or the duty to relieve suffering?[10] "Which will better cement the patient's trust in the physician: the knowledge that the physician will never directly act to end the patient's life? Or the knowledge that the physician will accede to the patient's voluntary request for assistance in certain specified circumstances?"[10] An article in the *Harvard Law Review* observed, "Courts routinely mention safeguarding the integrity of the medical profession as a valid state interest, but just as routinely find that this interest does not conflict with the patient's right to die."[33] That physicians are paid for continuing the care of patients may be viewed as a safeguard rather than as a conflict of interest.

Allowing physician assistance of suicide or death could strengthen the doctor-patient relationship: when the patient knows that his or her physician cares enough about him or her to be willing to do what is at best unpleasant, and at worst immoral or illegal, he or she is doubtless appreciative. Miller and Fletcher go so far as to state, "If legalized euthanasia is confined to killing at the request of competent patients, then it should not undermine trust."[65]

If physicians assist in suicide or death the pressure on relatives, friends, and loved ones to do so for unfortunate patients is markedly reduced. Some believe that the *only* healthcare professional who should participate in assisted suicide or death is the physician. Brock states physicians need to be involved in developing safeguards, and in limiting the people allowed to perform these functions in order to hold them accountable.[21]

Physicians vary considerably in their opinions of participation in physician-assisted suicide and euthanasia. Some would be willing to assist under some circumstances even though illegal. Others (substantially more) would be willing to assist if physician-assisted suicide or death were legalized. Some believe patients have a right to physician assistance, but virtually all believe that no individual physician should be obligated to provide it. Some believe that physician assistance should be permitted (as a treatment of last resort), but that it is not a right of patients to receive assistance as standard medical care.[16] Other positions of physicians are more negative, and will be noted in the next section.

ARGUMENTS OPPOSING PHYSICIAN PARTICIPATION IN ASSISTED SUICIDE OR DEATH

Kass is convinced physician-assisted suicide and euthanasia are antithetical to the goals of medicine.[30] Callahan stated, "It is not Medicine's place to determine when lives are not worth living or when the burden of life is too great to be borne. Doctors have no conceivable way of evaluating such claims . . . Medicine should try to relieve human suffering, but only that suffering which is brought on by illness and dying . . . not that suffering which comes from anguish or despair at the human condition."[29] Indeed, some believe even if it were appropriate public policy to legalize assisted suicide and death, it would be inappropriate for physicians to be the agents of death. It would jeopardize patient trust in physicians, the cornerstone of the doctor-patient relationship. Killing brutalizes the killer, even if the patient voluntarily requests it. At best it is emotionally traumatic for the euthanizer, and at worst, it is corrupting. Some believe that pain control, psychological intervention, and hospice care are sufficient to avoid the need for physician-assisted suicide and death.[26] Certainly participation would reduce the sensitivity of physicians to death and would risk a callous attitude. Even if most physicians were unaffected, a few irresponsible physicians could abuse enormous numbers of patients and seriously damage the reputation of the profession. Patients would come to fear their own physicians. The potential for abuse by well-intended but misguided physicians is enormous, yet unlikely to be evident to the public or even to legal authorities. On the other hand if we cannot trust physicians to do it, whom could we trust?

One might preserve the trust of patients in their physician if primary-care physicians were precluded by law from practicing euthanasia, and if the practice were restricted to a small group of specialists ("obitiatrists" in Jack Kevorkian's parlance).[36] The SHHV Task Force asks, "If physicians cannot in good conscience as professionals assist a patient in suicide, but if the moral defense of suicide assistance in the face of serious illness and suffering is otherwise compelling, should a separate body of non-physicians be created for the purpose of offering this assistance? Would other health professionals such as nurses or pharmacists volunteer?" [10]

If physicians are to participate, they must be willing. Many state they would not participate on religious, moral or psychological grounds; others because it is illegal. Some feel assisted suicide or death are appropriate for a few desperate patients but that assistance is beyond the scope of appropriate physician responsibilities. These attitudes are thought by some to be hypocritical since such a high percentage of physicians (and of other healthcare professionals as well) state they can conceive of circumstances in which they would commit suicide or request another physician to assist them. Some even state they have such a covenant with another physician. If it's good for the goose (the physician) shouldn't it be for the gander (the public)?

Some might say it is unethical for a patient to ask a physician to participate in his or her death. On the other hand this argument would apply to anyone legally entitled to practice euthanasia. The role of healthcare professionals other than physicians, such as pharmacists, nurses, social workers, and chaplains, vis-à-vis physician-assisted suicide and death is similarly problematic. The code of ethics of the American Medical Association states "the physician should not intentionally cause death."[73] Similarly, the American Nurse's Association Code of Ethics prohibits assisted suicide and euthanasia.[74] I will not specifically consider the role of all healthcare professionals, but will explore the role of pharmacists.

THE PHARMACIST
AND PHYSICIAN-ASSISTED SUICIDE AND DEATH

Because of the pharmacists' knowledge and responsibilities, they are situated in a morally problematic position relative to both the patient and the physician with regard to the issues of assisted suicide. Pharmacists may have knowledge exceeding that of the average physician with regard to lethal substances and how best to administer them. Thus, the physician might ask the pharmacist for advice to assist a patient to die. What should the pharmacist do if presented with a single prescription for a lethal dose of medication? Presently pharmacists are required by law to educate the patient with respect to medications they dispense, but also to review that the medication and its dosage are appropriate. What if this requirement were extended to a prescription of a lethal medication or of a usually non-lethal medication in lethal dosage? Might pharmacists find themselves in an untenable or at least an undesirable or an uncomfortable position professionally or personally? Even if the pharmacist did not feel morally responsible (i.e., guilty), he or she might still be emotionally stressed especially since the pharmacist may not know of the discussion that presumably occurred between the patient and the physician regarding their plans for assisted suicide.[74]

What should a pharmacist do if he or she suspects a patient is stockpiling drugs to be able to achieve a potentially lethal dose? This question might be looked at from a medical or informational perspective, a legal perspective, and an ethical perspective. From the medical perspective, if the prescribing physician were unaware that the patient was stockpiling, he or she might appreciate the pharmacist's informing him or her of the stockpiling. On the other hand, from a legal perspective if the physician failed to respond after the pharmacist told him of the patient's stockpiling, there could be legal implications. So might there be if suicide were illegal in the state. And from an ethical perspective, if the pharmacist believed that suicide was wrong, there would be a problem even if assisted suicide were legal in the state. If the pharmacist believed suicide were inappropriate for the patient, but the physician wished to assist the patient, there could be major professional conflict.

If physician-assisted suicide or death were legal and a pharmacist was aware of the patient's intention to end his or her life with medication, the pharmacist would be put in the potentially uncomfortable position that nurses are now put in relative to passive euthanasia (i.e., relative to patients who are allowed to die). A pharmacist who is asked or ordered to fill a lethal prescription might feel even more responsible for the patient's death (i.e., that he or she were the executioner, or at the very least that he or she were an accomplice). This might be the case even though the pharmacist believed the primary moral agent was the prescribing physician and even though the pharmacist was personally opposed to the action (though not to the extent of countermanding the physician's order), and perhaps even if the pharmacist had personally tried to talk the physician and/or patient out of proceeding with the suicide or euthanasia (or asked to be excused from having to fill the prescription).

Thus, the pharmacist is in a morally sensitive position in a case in which medication is the agent selected to assist the patient in suicide or death. This is true even though the pharmacist's role is secondary to that of the physician. The moral ante would be raised substantially were the pharmacist asked by the physician to prescribe or dispense lethal medication or non-lethal medication in a lethal dose. The American Pharmaceutical Association Code of Ethics for Pharmacists (1994) does not include a prohibition against assisted suicide or euthanasia as does the American Nurses' Association Code of Ethics.[74] For some this might increase (for others decrease) the moral stress of being even an unwilling accomplice.

RESPONSE OF HEALTHCARE PROFESSIONALS TO THE PUBLIC'S DEMAND FOR ASSISTANCE IN SUICIDE OR DEATH WHEN THE BURDENS OF LIFE EXCEED THE BENEFITS

Whether physician-assisted suicide or voluntary euthanasia is legalized or not, healthcare professionals have moral obligations to patients who request help in these matters. First and foremost we should stop regarding death as a failure in all cases. Second, we should communicate effectively with patients and their families about treatment options (including supportive care only) as well as about death and dying and about the natural fear thereof. We need to provide better care for seriously or terminally ill patients from the standpoint of pain control, hospice, social service, and pastoral care. Professionally and politically we need to advocate universal access to care (including nursing home care, hospice, and home care). Brody expresses these thoughts eloquently:[75] "Those on both sides of the debate over assisted death can agree that all patients should be confident that physicians will aid them with the latest palliative care to relieve terminal suffering and will respect their right to refuse life-prolonging treatment and to execute advance directives. One hopes that this view . . . would considerably reduce the number of patients who will request a physician's aid in dying. One also hopes that clearly labeling a good death a medical success will spur a better understanding of the remaining barriers that keep physicians from the appropriate use of palliative measures . . . and tendencies to deny that the patient is approaching death."[75] As the New York State Task Force on Life and the Law noted "a serious gap exists between what medicine can achieve and the palliative care routinely provided to most patients."[9]

There are many alternatives to euthanasia. These include better palliative care, better hospice service, emotional and spiritual support, and respite care for the spouse or other caretaker of seriously ill patients, allowing to die, suicide, and assisted suicide. To reduce the incentive for euthanasia, healthcare professionals should improve their management of pain and care for the dying, allay patients' fear of pain and fear of dying, allow patients to forgo treatment, accept that death is not always a failure, and utilize hospice and pain specialists. "Hospice and palliative care can relieve suffering in the vast majority of cases of terminal illness," and good hospice care reduces requests for euthanasia.[76] We need to do a better job in management of pain and suffering, in recognition of depression, but also in treating the fear of pain and suffering, the fear of dying, the fear of over-treatment, the financial burden of terminal illness, and the sense of loss of control in severe and terminal illness.[77] There is need for greater education of medical students in care of the dying,[78] and the same is true of physicians generally.[11,79] And clearly we need more research not only of palliative, hospice, and respite care but also of responses we might make to bereavement. We also need further research into the personal, spiritual, and cultural meaning of death and of various ways of dying.

If assisted suicide and death become legalized, we must learn the law and all its provisions regarding assisted suicide, active euthanasia, death certificate reporting, and the like. We will also need to ascertain whether our institution has policies regarding assisted suicide and death, and if not we need to work with the ethics committee to develop necessary policies. We will need to decide whether our personal moral values will allow us to provide assistance in suicide or euthanasia upon request. We need to decide what to do if the patient wishes euthanasia but refuses counseling or refuses psychiatric evaluation to exclude depression. We also need to decide what we will do if the patient refuses to inform family members of his or her desire for euthanasia, and what to do if the patient wishes the death certificate not to state suicide as it normally would (unless precluded by statute, which would be unfortunate from a public health perspective). Finally we will need evaluative research to assess the law, both its procedural aspects and the substantive consequences of it. And, as suggested in a very thoughtful article, we need "research into the personal and cultural meaning of physician-assisted death."[16]

In conclusion, the issues of suicide, assisted suicide and assisted death pose challenges for patients, physicians, pharmacists, and other healthcare professionals, as well as for society at large. It is hoped that the questions and perspectives raised in this paper may help us to respond appropriately to our individual, professional, and communal challenges.

REFERENCES

1. Battin MP. Suicide. In Reich WT, editor, Encyclopedia of Bioethics, revised edition, New York, Simon and Schuster Macmillan, 1995; p. 2444-2449.

2. White RF. Physician-assisted suicide and the suicide machine. In Misbin RI, editor, Euthanasia: The Good of the Patient, The Good of Society. Frederick MD, University Publishing Group, 1992.

3. Hill, TE Jr. Self-regarding suicide: A modified Kantian view, in Autonomy and Self-respect, Cambridge, Cambridge University Press.

4. Doerflinger R. Assisted suicide: pro-choice or anti-life? In Howell JH and Sale WF, editors, Life Choices: A Hastings Center Introduction to Bioethics, Washington, DC, Georgetown University Press, 1995.

5. Battin MP. Ethical Issues in Suicide. Englewood Cliffs, NJ, Prentice Hall, 1995.

6. Capron AM. At law: Easing the passing. Hastings Center Report 1994; 24(4):25-26.

7. CeloCruz MT. Aid-in-dying: Should we decriminalize physician-assisted suicide and physician-committed euthanasia? Amer J Law and Med 1992; 28: 369-394.

8. Kamisar Y. Are laws against assisted suicide unconstitutional? Hastings Center Report 1993; 23:32-41.

9. New York State Task Force on Life and the Law. When Death is Sought: Assisted Suicide and Euthanasia in the Medical Context. Albany, NY, New York State Task Force on Life and the Law, May, 1994.

10. Task Force on Physician-assisted Suicide of the Society for Health and Human Values. Physician-assisted suicide: Toward a comprehensive understanding. Report of the Task force on Physician Assisted Suicide of the Society for Health and Human Values. Acad Med 1995; 70:583-590.

11. Quill TE, Brody RV. "You promised me I wouldn't die like this!": A bad death as a medical emergency. Arch Intern Med 1995; 155:1250-1254.

12. Cassell EJ. Dying in a technological society. In Steinfels P and Veatch RM, editors, Death Inside Out. New York, Harper and Row, 1974, p. 47.

13. Fitzgerald F. Physician aid in dying–Finding the middle ground. West J Med 1992; 157:193-19.

14. Callahan D. When self-determination runs amok. Hastings Center Report 1992; 22(2):52-55.

15. Davies J. Raping and making love are different concepts: so are killing and voluntary euthanasia. J Med Ethics 1988; 14:148-14.

16. Miller FG, Quill TE, Brody H, Fletcher JC, Gostin L, Meier DE. Regulating physician-assisted death. N Eng J Med 1994; 331:119-123.

17. Brock DW. Death and dying: euthanasia and sustaining life. In Reich WT, editor, Encyclopedia of Bioethics, revised edition, New York, Simon and Schuster Macmillan, 1995; p. 554-587.

18. Rachels J. Active and passive euthanasia. N Eng J Med 1975; 292:78-80.

19. Rachels J. The End of Life: Euthanasia and Mortality. New York, Oxford, 1986.

20. Brock DW. Life and Death: Philosophical Essays in Biomedical Ethics, New York, Cambridge University Press, 1993.

21. Brock DW. Voluntary active euthanasia. Hastings Center Report 1992; 22(2):10-23.

22. Emanuel EJ. Euthanasia: Historical, ethical and empiric perspectives. Arch Intern Med 1994; 154:1890-1901.

23. Emanuel EJ. The history of euthanasia debates in the United States and Britain. Ann Intern Med 1994; 121:793-802.

24. Pellegrino ED. Doctors must not kill. J. Clinical Ethics 1992; 3(2):95-102.

25. Kant I. Suicide. In Luper-Foy S and Brown C, editors, The Moral Life. Orlando, Harper Brace, 1992.

26. Beltran JE. Legalizing physician-assisted suicide and death is flawed public policy: The slippery slope is subtle. Personal communication, 1995.

27. Singer PA, Siegler M. Euthanasia: A critique. N Eng J Med 1990; 322: 1881-1883.

28. Gaylen W, Kass LR, Pellegrino ED, Siegler M. Doctors must not kill. JAMA 1988; 259:2139-2140.

29. Callahan, D. Aid-in-Dying: The social dimensions. Commonweal, Sept 1992, Supplement:12-16.

30. Kass LR. Why Doctors Must Not Kill. Commonweal, Sept 1992; Supplement:8-12.

31. Bayley CM. Proposition 161: California Death with Dignity Initiative. A debate for the Schneiderman Memorial Lecture, University of California, Irvine, Oct 29, 1992.

32. Battin MP. The Least Worst Death: Essays in Bioethics on the End of Life. New York, Oxford University Press, 1994.

33. Anonymous. Physician-assisted suicide and the right to die with assistance. Harvard Law Review 1992; 105:2021-2040.

34. Cohen JS, Fihn SD, Boyko EJ, Jonsen AR, Wood RW. Attitudes toward assisted suicide and euthanasia among physicians in Washington State. N Eng J Med 1994; 331:89-94.

35. Gillon R. Acts and Omissions, Killing and Letting Die. Brit Medl J 1986; 292:126-127.

36. Benrubi GI. Euthanasia: the need for procedural safeguards. N Eng J Med 1992; 326:197-198.

37. Capron AM. Euthanasia in the Netherlands: American observations. Hastings Center Report 1992; 22(2):30-33.

38. Battin MP. Voluntary euthanasia and the risks of abuse: Can we learn anything from the Netherlands? Law Med Health Care 1992; 20:133-143.

39. deWachter MAM. Euthanasia in the Netherlands. Hastings Center Report 1992; 22(2):23-30.

40. ten Have HAMJ, Welie JVM. Euthanasia: Normal medical practice. Hastings Center Report 1992; 22(2)34-39.

41. Keown J. On regulating death. Hastings Center Report 1992; 22(2):39-43.

42. Griffiths J. Medical behavior that shortens life. Current developments in the Netherlands. Clinical Ethics Report (Bioethics Consultation Group, Berkeley, Calif.) 1994; 8 (2 and 3):1-24.

43. Kimsma GK, van Leeuwen E. Dutch euthanasia: background, practice and present justifications. Cambridge Quarterly of Healthcare Ethics 1993; 2:19-35.

44. van Delden JJM, Pijnenborg L, van der Maas PJ. The Remmelink Study: Two years later. Hastings Center Report 1993; 23(6)24-27.

45. van der Maas PJ, van Delden JJM, Pijnenborg L, Looman CWN. Euthanasia and other medical decisions concerning the end of life. Lancet 1991; 338: 669-674.

46. Pijnenborg L, van der Maas PJ, van Delden JJM, Looman CWN. Life-terminating acts without explicit request of patient. Lancet 1993; 341:1196-1199.

47. van Delden JJM, Pijnenborg L, van der Maas PJ. Reports from the Netherlands: Dances with data. Bioethics 1993; 7(4):323-329.

48. Gomez CF. Regulating Death: Euthanasia and the Case of the Netherlands. New York. The Free Press (Macmillan), 1991.

49. Alexander, L. Medical science under dictatorship. N Eng J Med 1949; 241:39-47.

50. Capron AM. At law: Sledding in Oregon. Hastings Center Report 1995; 25(1) 34-35.

51. Anonymous. Euthanasia bill approved by legislature: World history is made. Last Rights World News, Internet, May 24, 1995.

52. Battin MP. Assisted suicide: Can we learn from Germany? Hastings Center Report 1992; 22:44-51.

53. Gostin L, Weir RF. Life and death choices after Cruzan: Case law and standards of professional conduct. Milbank Quarterly 1991; 69:143-173.

54. Battin MP. Euthanasia: The way we do it, the way they do it. J Pain Sympt Manage 1991; 6:298-305.

55. Weir RF. The morality of physician-assisted suicide. Law Med Health Care 1992; 20:116-126.

56. Carson R. Washington's 119. Hastings Center Report 1992; 22(2):7-9.

57. American Medical Association News. January 2, 1995, page 2.

58. Grant ER, Forsythe CD. From natural death to aid in dying: Reflections on the American judicial experience. In Misbin RI, editor, Euthanasia: The Good of the Patient, the Good of Society. Frederick, MD, University Publishing Group, 1992.

59. Emanuel EJ, Emanuel LL. The economics of dying: The illusion of cost savings at the end of life. N Eng J Med 1994; 330:540-544.

60. Lo B. Assisted Suicide and Active Euthanasia in Resolving Ethical Dilemmas: A guide for Clinicians. Baltimore, Williams and Wilkins 1994, pp. 168-177.

61. Anonymous. It's over Debbie. JAMA 1988; 259:272.

62. Cassel CK, Meier DE. Morals and moralism in the debate over euthanasia and assisted suicide. N Engl J Med 1990; 323:750-752.

63. Quill TE. Death and dignity: A case of individualized decision-making. New Eng J Med 1991; 324:692-694.

64. Quill TE. Death and Dignity: Making Choices and Taking Charge. New York, WW Norton and Company, 1993.

65. Miller FG, Fletcher JC. The case for legalized euthanasia. Perspectives in Biol and Med, 1993; 31:159-176.

66. White MH. Proposition 161: California Death with Dignity Initiative. A debate for the Schneiderman Memorial Lecture, University of California, Irvine, Oct 29, 1992.

67. Grochowski E, Cassel CK. Care of the dying patient: Is physician-assisted suicide an acceptable practice? Amer J Ethics Med, (Fall)1993: 3-8.

68. Quill TE, Cassel CK, Meier DE. Care of the hopelessly ill: Proposed clinical criteria for physician-assisted suicide. N Eng J Med 1992; 327:1380-1384.

69. Landis KW. Proposed guidelines for physician-assisted suicide. Draft for Los Angeles California Bar Association Bioethics Committee, 1994.

70. Boston Working Group. An act authorizing and regulating medically assisted suicide: The model law. In draft, 1994.

71. Blendon RJ, Szalay US, Knox RA. Should physicians aid their patients in dying? The public perspective. JAMA 1992; 267:2658-2662.

72. Heilig S. The SFMS Euthanasia survey: Results and analyses. San Francisco Medicine. May 1988; 24-26 and 34.

73. Gorlin RA. Codes of Professional Responsibility, 2nd ed, Washington DC, Bureau of National Affairs, 1990.

74. Haddad AM. Physician-assisted suicide: The impact on nursing and pharmacy. Of Value (Society for Health and Human Values) 1994; 24(4) 1 and 6.

75. Brody H. Assisted death–a compassionate response to a medical failure. N Eng J Med 1992; 327:1384-1388.

76. Miller RJ. Hospice care as an alternative to euthanasia. Law, Med, and Health Care, 1992; 20(1-2):127-132.

77. Wanzer SH, Federman DD, Adelstein SJ, Cassel CK, Cassem EH, Cranford RE, Hook EW, Lo B, Moertel CG, Safar P, Stone A, van Eys J. The physician's responsibility toward hopelessly ill patients: A second look. N Eng J Med, 1989; 320:844-849.

78. Hill PA. Treating the dying patient: The challenge for medical education. Arch Intern Med 1995; 155:1265-1269.

79. Brody H. Assisted suicide: A challenge for family physicians. J. Fam. Pract. 1993; 37:123 125.

Issues for Pharmacists
in Assisted Patient Death

Michael T. Rupp

SUMMARY. Assisted suicide and euthanasia are explored from the pharmacist's perspective. Legal, operational and clinical issues are described. The assumption that pharmacists will simply fill prescriptions for drugs intended to end the lives of terminally ill patients who wish to do so has not been tested. The position adopted by the Washington State Society of Hospital Pharmacists opposed the proposed Washington Death with Dignity Act. Survey data on pharmacist attitudes about use of drugs to end the lives of terminally ill patients are described. Ethical codes of the profession of pharmacy as they pertain to this issue are discussed. Clinical issues addressed include published criteria for appropriate patients for assisted death. Operational impediments to pharmacists participating in assisted death include the silence on the role of the pharmacist in proposed laws to legalize hastened death. The importance of ensuring good pain and symptom management and control of psychiatric disorders is discussed. The influence of patient centered pharmaceutical care on pharmacists participating in actively ending patients' lives is addressed. *[Article copies available from The Haworth Document Delivery Service: 1-800-342-9678.]*

Michael T. Rupp, PhD, is Associate Professor of Pharmacy Administration at Purdue University.

Address correspondence to: Dr. Michael T. Rupp, Department of Pharmacy Practice, School of Pharmacy and Pharmacal Sciences, Purdue University, West Lafayette, IN 47907.

[Haworth co-indexing entry note]: "Issues for Pharmacists in Assisted Patient Death." Rupp, Michael T. Co-published simultaneously in *Journal of Pharmaceutical Care in Pain & Symptom Control* (Pharmaceutical Products Press, an imprint of The Haworth Press, Inc.) Vol. 3, No. 3/4, 1995, pp. 43-53; and: *Drug Use in Assisted Suicide and Euthanasia* (ed: Margaret P. Battin, and Arthur G. Lipman) Pharmaceutical Products Press, an imprint of The Haworth Press, Inc., 1996, pp. 43-53. Single or multiple copies of this article are available from The Haworth Document Delivery Service [1-800-342-9678, 9:00 a.m. - 5:00 p.m. (EST)].

© 1996 by The Haworth Press, Inc. All rights reserved.

KEYWORDS. Pharmacy practice, assisted suicide, euthanasia, hastened death, symptom control, ethical codes, attitudes towards assisted death

In November of 1994, voters in Oregon approved Ballot Measure 16, the Oregon Death with Dignity Act. The question presented to voters in Measure 16 was, "Shall law allow terminally ill adult Oregon patients voluntary informed choice to obtain a physician's prescription for drugs to end life?" In passing Measure 16, the state of Oregon made it legal for patients to obtain–and physicians to prescribe–prescription drugs for the purpose of ending life.

At the time this article was written, implementation of Measure 16 continued to be delayed by court injunction. However, within six months of its passage in Oregon, supporters of assisted death in at least 12 other states had already introduced similar legislation.[1] As a result of this rapidly accelerating pace, the issues of medically assisted suicide and euthanasia are being examined with a new intensity in pharmacy.

This paper explores assisted suicide and euthanasia from the pharmacist's perspective. Three areas of particular concern regarding the legalized use of prescription drugs for the purpose of assisted patient death are examined: moral and philosophical issues; clinical issues; and operational issues. Suggestions are offered for how the pharmacy profession can appropriately respond to society's increasing demand for empowerment and self-determination and still fulfill the mandate of pharmaceutical care while respecting the deeply held convictions of practicing pharmacists.

Although assisted suicide and euthanasia maintain many similarities, there are important differences between these two activities. Euthanasia (literally, "good death") encompasses a spectrum of circumstances that range from withdrawing life support, to actions that directly terminate the life of an incompetent patient. In all cases, euthanasia implies that someone *other* than a rational and fully competent patient is making the decision and taking the necessary action to terminate life, albeit perhaps with prior explicit or implicit directions from the patient (i.e., "voluntary"). In contrast, assisted suicide refers to the act of providing the means of death (e.g., prescription drugs) in response to a request by a competent and rational patient. This "indirect" assistance is often distinguished by physicians and others–perhaps somewhat artificially–from "direct" assistance in which someone (i.e., the physician) personally performs a procedure that causes the patient's death.[2,3]

But while the distinctions between assisted suicide and euthanasia are recognized, they will not be dealt with here except where they are germane to the pharmacist's perspective. Instead, the focus will be on examining the role of pharmacists and pharmaceutical products in medically assisted patient death.

MORAL AND PHILOSOPHICAL ISSUES

At the core of the societal debate over assisted suicide and euthanasia is a fundamental disagreement over the morality, i.e., the "rightness" or "wrongness," of hastening or otherwise facilitating death. While our understanding of pharmacists' attitudes and beliefs about assisted suicide and euthanasia is still preliminary, they appear to mirror those of society's to a great extent. That is, pharmacists' attitudes about assisted suicide and euthanasia appear to be guided in part by the same internal moral compass that directs the conscious behavior of every person. But in addition to being members of society, pharmacists are also members of a profession whose mission is to meet the health-related needs of patients. Because of this special role, pharmacists–and other health professionals–are also guided by another directive, their professional responsibility to patients.

Ideally, these two influences would parallel and even complement each other. But sometimes the health care professional's personal moral convictions can conflict with what they, or their profession, perceive to be their professional responsibility to the patient. The resulting duality of conscience that can result from these competing forces can create conflict within the health professional who is torn between their duty to themselves and their duty to the patient.

In voicing opposition to Initiative 119–another Death with Dignity Act–a resolution was passed by the Washington State Society of Hospital Pharmacists (WSSHP) in 1991 which was unequivocal in its condemnation of assisted suicide and euthanasia. The resolution stated in part that, "pharmacy professionals, in providing pharmaceutical care, stand for health and compassionate care, not assisted suicide or euthanasia."[4] Thus, the official position was clear: assisted suicide and euthanasia is incompatible with the mission of pharmacy practice and the philosophy of pharmaceutical care.

In contrast to this official position, however, a 1992 national survey of licensed pharmacists by Rupp and Isenhower[5] found most (72.6%) agreed that patients are sometimes justified in wanting to end their lives. Furthermore, almost half (48.6%) approved of physicians' active participation in this process. When asked whether they would ever knowingly participate in assisting the death of a patient, pharmacists were almost equally divided, with those who would participate accounting for 34.3%, those who would not participate accounting for 29.3%, and those who were unsure representing the single largest category at 35.8%.

Referring to the opposition of the WSSHP to Initiative 119, Rupp and Isenhower concluded:

> Our study suggests that many pharmacists–albeit probably a minority–disagree that helping a patient to die is in direct and irreconcilable conflict with the concept of pharmaceutical care.[6]

Similarly, in their study of Michigan pharmacists, Vivian et al.[7] found that most respondents (68%) favored the "legal right" of patients to commit suicide. This approval, however, dropped to 52% when pharmacists were asked whether patients have the "moral or ethical right" to commit suicide. When asked if physicians or other health providers should ever assist the suicide of a patient, 58% replied "yes." When asked whether they would ever participate in a planned patient death, Michigan pharmacists were also split with 37% affirmative, 46% negative, and 17% who were still undecided. In both of the above studies, researchers found age and religious affiliation or conviction to be influential in pharmacists' attitudes.

In addition to these two studies, a 1994 national survey conducted by *Pharmacy Times* found that 56.1% of pharmacists supported medically assisted suicide for patients under some conditions.[8] A 1992 study of oncology health professionals by Anderson and Caddell[9] found that 75% of pharmacists who practice in that setting support euthanasia.

The empirical data on pharmacists' attitudes toward assisted suicide and euthanasia are still preliminary. Moreover, the data that are available must be interpreted with caution as pharmacists' attitudes are probably influenced by the mercurial nature of the issue itself. However, a few tentative conclusions can be made. First, most pharmacists appear to favor the right of patients to end their lives under certain conditions. Second, pharmacists appear to be almost equally split regarding the appropriateness of physicians and other health providers assisting their patients to die. Third, among pharmacists who approve of assisted suicide, most believe that it is an appropriate use of prescription drugs. Fourth, pharmacists' opposition to or support of assisted suicide and euthanasia appears to be influenced by a mix of personal and professional factors including age, religious affiliation/conviction, practice setting and prior experience with terminally ill or severely debilitated patients.

Finally, research suggests that, even where it exists, pharmacists' support for assisted suicide is conditional. Vivian et al.[7] found that 86% of responding pharmacists believed that suicide is acceptable in the case of an adult patient with a terminal illness and a prognosis of less than 30 days to live. However, this figure dropped to 47% for an adult patient with a debilitating, but non-terminal disease. Similarly, Rupp and Isenhower[5] found many pharmacists who approved of assisted suicide and euthanasia *in concept* recognized the need for precise patient eligibility criteria and a reliable means to ensure these criteria are always met. Some of these practical considerations are discussed below under 'Operational Issues.'

ASSISTED DEATH AND ETHICAL CODES

While every individual maintains a personal definition of morality, professions have formalized this concept in the form of ethical codes that are intended to guide members in their professional behaviors and relationships. Both the Hippocratic Oath of physicians, and the Code for Nurses specifically prohibit members of those professions from deliberately terminating the life of a patient.[10] Yet, if anecdotal reports and testimonials are true, significant numbers of both professions routinely violate this provision of their ethical codes.

Timothy E. Quill, M.D., a thought leader and cautious advocate of assisted suicide, has offered an explanation for this apparent contradiction in concluding that "rather than extending *meaningful* life, as the Hippocratic Oath intends, medical interventions sometimes result in the prolongation of a painful death."[11] Thus, Quill has been able to reconcile his support for assisted suicide through his interpretation of the *spirit* of the Hippocratic Oath, if not the letter. It is likely that support for assisted patient death by other health providers is similarly guided by individual conscience, and personal definitions of moral, ethical and professional responsibility, all of which color the individual's interpretation of their ethical code.

Pharmacy's ethical code does not prohibit, or even directly address, the issue of assisted patient death.[12] To the contrary, it can be argued that pharmacists' involvement in assisted suicide and euthanasia is entirely consistent with the mission of pharmacy practice and the philosophy of pharmaceutical care.[13] But regardless of its theoretic defensibility or institutional proscription, available research suggests that deeply held and intensely personal moral and religious convictions influence pharmacists' attitudes toward assisted suicide and euthanasia, particularly those in opposition.[5,6] It is therefore questionable whether its advocacy or opposition in the profession's ethical code would significantly alter the attitudes or behavior of individual pharmacists toward participating in an assisted death.

CLINICAL ISSUES

Moral and philosophical issues aside, the circumstances under which assisted suicide and euthanasia may be considered as a possible course of action also raises a variety of clinical issues for pharmacists. For example, unremitting and/or intractable pain is perhaps the most commonly cited justification for considering assisted suicide and voluntary euthanasia. Consideration of assisted suicide and euthanasia as a legitimate therapeutic alternative, however, presupposes that all possible approaches to managing the patient's pain have been exhausted. Unfortunately, this is too often not the case. Many who practice in the area of pain management would agree with Dr. Quill's assessment of pain management by many of his colleagues:

> [Many physicians] lack the technical skills to provide pain and symptom relief for patients who are dying. Some physicians routinely undermedicate chronic pain even with terminally ill patients, partly because their training in pharmacology emphasizes the risks of overmedication, sedation, and addiction much more than the need to fully assess and relieve pain.[14]

Assuring that patients experiencing severe pain have received an adequate trial of aggressive therapy, particularly narcotic analgesics, would appear to be an appropriate role for the pharmacist. It is likely that some–perhaps many–patients who consider suicide would opt for a more natural passing if their pain were competently managed.

Central to Quill's philosophy of caring for the dying patient, and his reluctant advocacy of assisted suicide (although *not* voluntary euthanasia), are three principles: informed personal choice by the patient, minimizing suffering, and nonabandonment. He has operationalized these principles in seven suggested clinical criteria for physician-assisted suicide. While these criteria are clearly targeted toward physicians, ensuring their presence should be considered a joint responsibility of *all* persons who are involved in the clinical care of the patient:

1. the patient must, of his own free will and at his own initiative, clearly and repeatedly request to die rather than continue suffering;
2. the patient's judgment must not be distorted;

3. the patient must have a condition that is incurable, and associated with severe, unrelenting, intolerable suffering;
4. the physician must ensure that the patient's suffering and the request are not the result of inadequate comfort care;
5. physician-assisted suicide should only be carried out in the context of a meaningful doctor-patient relationship;
6. consultation with another experienced physician is required; and
7. clear documentation to support each condition above is required.[15]

Of particular relevance to pharmacists among these clinical criteria is to assure that the patient is receiving adequate pain management, that (s)he is not suffering from treatable depression or the effects of illness or medication that could distort judgment, that a legitimate doctor-patient relationship exists, and that the patient's decision is not the result of abandonment by the health care system and its providers. Beyond these special considerations, it should be emphasized that the pharmacist's clinical responsibility, and indeed that of all health providers, is to provide the same level and intensity of care to the patient for whom assisted suicide and euthanasia may be considered as that provided to any other patient. While the therapeutic goals of care may differ, the quality of care should not.

OPERATIONAL ISSUES

Perhaps the single greatest shortcoming of the debate surrounding the use of prescription drugs in assisted suicide and euthanasia is the relative absence of operational detail. That is, how, specifically, will it be accomplished? Unfortunately, such practical considerations appear to have been largely ignored in Oregon's Measure 16, the specifics of which end with the physician's generation of a prescription order for a lethal dose of medication. Indeed, since there is no requirement for physician assistance of–or even contact with–the patient beyond this point, Measure 16 is more appropriately described as the legalization of physician *prescripted* suicide. This lack of operational detail beyond the generation of a lethal prescription order by a physician is particularly disturbing to pharmacists, coming as it does at precisely the point where the pharmacist's primary responsibilities begin.

While there are many as yet unanswered operational questions related to the use of prescription drugs in assisted suicide and euthanasia, several tend to capture much of the confusion.

- What will be the nature of the communication between the prescribing physician and the pharmacist?

Far from proposing the ideal model, the authors of Oregon's Measure 16 merely codified existing clandestine medical practice by legalizing a practice that had formerly been carried out covertly between physicians and patients. In so doing, however, many of the shortcomings of the former were maintained. For example, there appears to be no requirement in Measure 16 that physicians inform pharmacists that a prescription is being written for the purpose of assisting a suicide. In his critical review of the law, Campbell has observed that such a practice is "professionally demeaning, for it views the pharmacist simply as the technical arm of the physician's practice."[16]

It has been argued that the physician's failure to inform the pharmacist presents no special concerns in assisted suicide and euthanasia because pharmacists are often unaware of the intended use of the medications they dispense. But while it is true that many pharmacists practice in settings where information is scarce and difficult to obtain, when applied to assisted suicide and euthanasia this argument overlooks an important consideration. As Rupp has observed,

> These assumptions amount to a covenant of faith on the part of the pharmacist that the physician's intended goals of therapy, if they were known, would be acceptable to and supported by the pharmacist. At issue [in physician assisted suicide] is an intended and unstated goal of therapy that is inconsistent with the assumptions–the professional covenant–under which pharmacists implement the therapeutic plans of physicians. Some physicians (and patients) may believe this deception is warranted and even desirable, because it protects the pharmacist from possible legal and moral problems. However, such an act of intentional deceit on the part of a physician would appear to be at least a breach of interprofessional courtesy, if not a clear violation of professional ethics.[13]

Considering the irrevocability of the decision, it is essential that a mechanism be created to ensure fully informed consent by *all* persons who may be substantively involved in assisting the death of a patient. Certainly, the gravity of this situation would seem to call for a different approach to communication between prescriber and pharmacist–both qualitatively and quantitatively–than that which accompanies a standard prescription order.

- How will pharmacists satisfy their prospective DUR and patient counseling requirements?

The pharmacy practice-related provisions of the Omnibus Budget Reconciliation Act of 1990 (OBRA '90) were implemented in January of

1993. The stated goal of this legislation was "to improve the quality of pharmaceutical care by ensuring that prescriptions are appropriate, medically necessary and that they are not likely to result in adverse medical results."[17] Since its implementation, most state pharmacy practice acts have been revised to require pharmacists to perform prospective drug utilization review (DUR) and patient counseling on all new prescriptions.

Assuming for the moment that the pharmacist is aware of the intended use of the prescription, how will they satisfy their prospective DUR responsibilities? It would be absurd to hold pharmacists accountable for ensuring that a prescription that is intended to be used in a suicide is "safe" for its intended use. Moreover, what about "effectiveness?" How will the pharmacist determine that the appropriate drug or dose has been prescribed? The clinical literature related to the proper selection and dosing of a drug to reliably produce a lethal effect cannot be large. Will drug manufacturers seek, and will the FDA grant, approval of drugs for this indication? In the absence of such information the pharmacist is confronted with what is surely the ultimate "off-label use" problem. When coupled with the requirement in most states that a prescription must be issued for a "legitimate medical purpose," it is unclear how the practicing pharmacist will be able to satisfy current legal and professional responsibilities when dispensing a prescription for assisted suicide and euthanasia.

• How should the profession respond to pharmacists who object?

It is clear that many pharmacists are fundamentally opposed to assisted suicide and euthanasia. Moreover, this opposition is unlikely to be altered by any future formal positions that the profession takes in its associations and institutions. For this reason, legalizing the use of prescription drugs for assisted suicide and euthanasia creates the possibility of future dilemmas in pharmacy that pit pharmacists' personal moral beliefs against their professional responsibility, perhaps at the risk of losing their job. How can the deeply held beliefs of these "objectors of conscience" be respected and yet still respond to the needs of patients and the demands of employers?

One answer may be the development of a "conscience clause." For example, it is apparently common for state therapeutic abortion laws to include a "conscience exception" for medical providers whose religious ethical or moral beliefs prevent their participation in abortion.[18] The purpose of such a clause is to ensure that medical providers who have a conscience objection to abortion cannot be held criminally or civilly liable, nor can they be subjected to administrative or disciplinary action.[19] Assisted suicide and euthanasia may require the pharmacy profession to explore development of a similar type of conscience clause to define the rights of pharmacists and employers in circumstances where the pharmacist's moral convictions prohibit participation in a particular job-related activity.

CONCLUSIONS

Historically, the pharmaceutical product represented the social object around which pharmacy practice was organized. Within this narrow scope, pharmacists maintained responsibility for ensuring the integrity of the products they dispensed, but little more. As pharmacy practice evolved, so too did the role and responsibility of the pharmacist. Eventually, the emphasis of pharmacy practice shifted away from the drug product to a greater focus on ensuring its appropriate use by patients. The latest phase in this continuing evolution, pharmaceutical care, expands the pharmacist's role still further to include a shared responsibility for ensuring that patients realize the desired outcomes of their drug therapy.

Using a patient-centered approach, an argument can be made that assisted suicide is not necessarily in conflict with the mission of pharmacy practice. Moreover, available evidence suggests that most pharmacists approve of assisted patient death under certain conditions, and many indicate they would even be willing to participate in such an activity. However, pharmacists who oppose this activity appear to have fundamental objections of conscience. Even among those pharmacists who approve, and who would participate in an assisted death, there exists a recognized need for guidelines and standards to answer the many questions that are raised.

It is a virtual certainty that society will increasingly seek to have a greater role in making decisions regarding their health care, and their death care. Pharmacy, in cooperation with other health professions, must examine the many unresolved issues related to assisted patient death. The goal of this initiative should be to create strategies that meet the needs of patients while at the same time respect the convictions of pharmacists and other health care providers whose moral beliefs place them in opposition to participating in an assisted patient death.

REFERENCES

1. Castenada CJ. Oregon's assisted suicide law a 'catalyst' for 12 other states. USA Today, March 9, 1995, pg. 8A.

2. Wanzer SH, Federman DD, Adelstein SJ et al. The physician's responsibility toward hopelessly ill patients. N Engl J Med 1989; 320: 844-49.

3. Quill TE. Death and dignity. WW Norton & Co., NY, 1993.

4. St. Jean AD. Washington State Society succeeds in opposition to euthanasia measure. Am J Hosp Pharm 1992; 49: 265-6.

5. Rupp MT, Isenhower HL. Pharmacists' attitudes toward physician–assisted suicide. Am J Hosp Pharm 1994; 51: 69-74.

6. Ibid. p. 74.

7. Vivian JC, Slaughter RL, Calissi P. Michigan pharmacists' attitudes about medically-assisted suicide. J Mich Pharm 1993; November: 490-5.

8. Buckley B. Pharmacists offer their views on reimbursement, illicit drugs, suicide. Pharm Times 1994; April: 43-6.

9. Anderson JG, Caddell DP. Attitudes of medical professionals toward euthanasia. Soc Sci Med 1993; 37: 105-14.

10. American Nurses Association (1994). Position statement on assisted suicide. Washington, DC.

11. Quill TE. Death and dignity. New York: Norton; 1993, p. 43.

12. Code of ethics adopted, bylaws amended. Pharmacy Today. 1993; 33(Feb):1.

13. Rupp MT. Physician-assisted suicide and the issues it raises for pharmacists. Am J Hosp Pharm 1995;52:in press.

14. Quill TE. Death and dignity. p. 100.

15. Ibid, pp. 161–3.

16. Courtney CS. When medicine lost its moral conscience: Oregon Measure 16. BioLaw. 1995; Volume II, No.1 Special Section:p. S-11.

17. Medicaid program: drug use review program and electronic claims management systems for outpatient drug claims. Federal Register. Nov. 2, 1992;57 (212): pp. 49397-412.

18. Brushwood DB. Drugs for the intentional termination of pregnancy. Top Hosp Pharm Manage 1990; 10:34-39.

19. Ibid. p. 37.

Nursing Perspectives
on Assisted Suicide and Euthanasia

Betty R. Ferrell
Lynne M. Rivera

SUMMARY. As primary caregivers across settings, nurses are challenged to provide compassionate care to terminally ill patients and their families. The issue of assisted suicide and euthanasia creates unique challenges for the nursing profession. Previous literature related to nurses' attitudes regarding euthanasia and assisted suicide is reviewed in this discussion of the issues central to nursing. These issues include ethical dimensions of nursing care, nursing attitudes regarding suicide, and nurses' unique roles with patients and family caregivers. The unique role of the nurse and professional obligations of the nursing profession are pivotal in addressing this important social issue. *[Article copies available from The Haworth Document Delivery Service: 1-800-342-9678.]*

KEYWORDS. Nursing, assisted suicide, euthanasia, suffering, terminal illness, home care, caring, attitudes of nurses, ethics, physician-assisted dying

Betty R. Ferrell, PhD, FAAN, is Associate Research Scientist and Lynne M. Rivera, RN, MSN, is Research Specialist at the City of Hope Medical Center.

Address correspondence to: Betty R. Ferrell, PhD, FAAN, City of Hope Medical Center, Nursing Research and Education, 1500 East Duarte Road, Duarte, CA 91010.

[Haworth co-indexing entry note]: "Nursing Perspectives on Assisted Suicide and Euthanasia." Ferrell, Betty R., and Lynne M. Rivera. Co-published simultaneously in *Journal of Pharmaceutical Care in Pain & Symptom Control* (Pharmaceutical Products Press, an imprint of The Haworth Press, Inc.) Vol. 3, No. 3/4, 1995, pp. 55-66; and: *Drug Use in Assisted Suicide and Euthanasia* (ed: Margaret P. Battin, and Arthur G. Lipman) Pharmaceutical Products Press, an imprint of The Haworth Press, Inc., 1996, pp. 55-66. Single or multiple copies of this article are available from The Haworth Document Delivery Service [1-800-342-9678, 9:00 a.m. - 5:00 p.m. (EST)].

© 1996 by The Haworth Press, Inc. All rights reserved.

INTRODUCTION

Assisted suicide and euthanasia are controversial and vigorously debated issues in current social and health care arenas. The nursing profession is challenged to provide compassionate and supportive nursing care amidst a highly technological system that has the capability to prolong life. However, prolongation of life is not always compatible with quality of life and promotion of human dignity.[1] Virtually all nurses will, at some time, encounter a clinical situation involving a request for assisted suicide or euthanasia which will challenge both personal beliefs and professional standards.

Traditionally, nursing has been viewed as a caring profession with a goal of preserving life and promoting comfort for both the patient and family. Over the past 30 years, nursing has been increasingly confronted with ethical issues related to care provided to patients, especially in relation to life-extending technology. Often, nurses witness the patient and their loved ones suffer based on the pretense of prolonging life.[2] Nurses, as the primary caregivers for patients, are often the chief witnesses of the impact of such care. As the profession at the bedside 24-hours a day, nurses are often confronted with questions from family members long after other providers have left the bedside. The primacy of nursing in requests to terminate life will increase as care is shifted into the home care setting.[3-5]

The request for assisted suicide is often based on the premise of ending life when quality of life is no longer possible. Quality of life is a multidimensional concept, encompassing psychosocial, physical, social, and spiritual components.[1,6] Requests for assisted suicide are based on current or future threats to one or more of these dimensions of quality of life. Nursing care thus must be focused on not only the present, but also on the patients fears and expectations of the future of the illness and anticipated death.

Suffering is the overall distress of illness encompassing physical symptoms as well as psychosocial and spiritual issues. The alleviation of suffering is frequently cited as a justification for assisted death. Suffering also is experienced by family caregivers in life threatening and terminal illness.[2,4] In formulating a response to a patient's request for assisted death, nurses must synthesize their beliefs about these concepts of quality of life and suffering. This paper addresses the unique perspective of nursing in requests for assisted suicide and euthanasia. This discussion is limited to adult patients. The special nature of suicide in children and adolescents has been described elsewhere.[7-10]

Discussions about assisted suicide and euthanasia challenge nurses to explore their individual values concerning life, death, and the meaning of suffering, to contemplate the philosophical foundations of nursing, and to examine nursing's responsibility to the patient.[11,12] However nurses, similar to other professionals, are divided in their beliefs about the issue of assisted suicide. In a random survey of registered nurses in California conducted by *California Nurse*, no consensus related to assisted death could be identified. Drought reported that approximately one half of the survey's respondents supported the individual's right to request assistance in dying; the remaining one half opposed assisted death.[11] Other nursing literature has also reported discrepant beliefs among nurses regarding issues of suicide and euthanasia.[13,14]

NURSING PERSPECTIVES
ON ASSISTED SUICIDE AND EUTHANASIA

Nursing Ethics

In providing care to the terminally ill, nurses incorporate fundamental ethical principles.[8] The dilemma for nurses begins with the principle of sanctity of life which identifies that life is sacred and should be preserved.[15] Another key concept for nursing practice is the principle of autonomy which states that the patient has the right to make decisions about care including those that affect everyday activities.[16,17] Nurses must also consider the principles of beneficence and nonmaleficence that state that care should be provided in the patient's best interests.[18,19] Also important is the principle of justice that implies that care should be given in a fair manner and that resources are allocated in a just manner.[20] These universal principles, taught in nursing ethics curriculum, establish a basis for the dilemmas nurses face in providing optimum care for the dying patient. However, many schools of nursing have only recently incorporated ethics content into the curriculum and there is limited ethics content in continuing education of practicing nurses.[21]

Nurses are also confronted with ethical principles such as truth-telling, confidentiality, fidelity, and justice. The *Code for Nurses with Interpretive Statements*[22] provides nurses with the guidelines necessary to provide responsible, compassionate, quality nursing care. The Code and the interpretive statements provide nurses with the framework for dealing with end-of-life decisions and the unique role of nursing in this dilemma. As the discussion regarding euthanasia and assisted death continues, the nursing profession is certain to remain on the front line of this public policy debate.

Many authors have suggested that active euthanasia violates professional codes[23] and is difficult to justify in a profession that focuses on caring.[24-26] Other nurses contend that it is reliance on these same ethical principles that support their beliefs in assisted suicide as an act of compassion. Saunders and Valente present an eloquent discussion of these issues in a case report regarding rational suicide in a patient with advanced cancer.[27]

Nurses caring for patients with advanced cancer often find themselves faced with ethical challenges for which they feel unprepared.[17] Nurses may feel unprepared to respond to a patient's expression of wish for suicide and may also feel unprepared to conduct a comprehensive psychiatric evaluation. Nurses care for patients and their families in a variety of settings: acute care facilities on either oncology units or medical-surgical units, nursing homes, hospices, and in the home. Thus, nurses need to be aware of consultation available from other disciplines such as psychiatry yet also be prepared to conduct a basic assessment of psychological status and suicide potential, particularly in environments such as home care when other disciplines may not be routinely involved.[28-30] Health care professionals have a responsibility to provide the patient with accurate information about the disease in understandable terms and to present the information in a caring and supportive manner.

The patient has the right to make decisions based on personal values and regardless of the values of the professional caregiver. While there are situations when a patient is unable to make decisions, the decision making process must be returned to the patient once the patient is again capable of making decisions.[17,31] In situations involving discussion of suicide, nurses often find it necessary to weigh their role as patient advocates in protecting the patient's autonomy with their professional accountability in protecting the patient from ultimate harm.

Nurses spend more time with patients than any other members of the health care team. This is true across all settings but particularly relevant in the home care setting. The nurse-patient relationship is ideally one of genuine caring and mutual respect. As primary care providers, nurses are essential in assessing potential for suicide and identification of unmet needs which may precipitate the wish for suicide. The nursing process, basic to professional nursing practice, emphasizes that care is based on assessment of individual needs.

Philosophical foundations of nursing imply that the nurse should provide a consistent standard of care while appreciating each patient as an individual.[32] It is this recognition of the individual's values and experiences that influence the decision making process. Comprehensive nursing assessment assists patients and family members in making critical decisions and in seeking meaning and purpose in decisions regarding the final stages of life and in death. Nursing assessment is the basis of fact finding to plan and coordinate care. Nurses can act as advocates for the patient and family, assisting them in obtaining and clarifying information, and encouraging collaboration with the physician.

Ethical issues related to end of life care are increasing due to the increase in chronic illnesses. The chronic nature of cancer has increased survival at the expense of increased complications, hospitalizations, and expense. Breitbart identifies several factors influencing suicide risk including pain, mood disturbance, delirium, loss of control, fatigue, depression or hopelessness, preexisting psychopathology, prior suicide attempts, exhaustion, disease site, and advanced stage of disease.[33] Others have reported fatigue, depression, suffering, personality issues, and delirium[34,35] and poorly controlled pain[32,33] as symptoms that increase the patient's risk for suicide. Management of the multiple symptoms encountered in patients with advanced cancer is a challenge for nurses across settings and throughout the illness trajectory.

Nurses' Attitudes Regarding Assisted Suicide

Young and colleagues[9] conducted a descriptive study of oncology nurses' attitudes related to what they termed "physician-assisted dying" for competent, terminally ill patients who requested this assistance. Using vignettes, the investigators described patient care situations and possible responses based on the respondent's beliefs related to physician-assisted dying, and explored the nurses' awareness of organizations and legislation that promote the legalization of physician-assisted dying. Study participants (N = 1,210) were derived from an oncology organization and respondents indicated diverse viewpoints regarding the acceptability of physician-assisted dying. Nurses reported varied beliefs about physician-assisted dying ranging from acceptance of physician-assisted dying as a legitimate choice and support for patients during the process to the belief that physician-assisted dying is wrong and refusal to be involved with physician-assisted dying.

Some nurses (29%) in this study reported a willingness to stay with the patient during physician-assisted dying if they already had an established relationship with the patient. Fewer nurses (23%) would stay with the patient if a relationship had not already been established. Fifty-seven percent of the nurses reported agreement with physician-assisted dying if the patient was suffering. Although many respondents (49%) supported physician-assisted dying, 34% reported a reluctance to administer medication that would cause death. This study, and most of the other published research, has been limited to nurses who are active members of professional organizations and generally those with an oncology focus.

Davis and colleagues[9] interviewed 168 cancer care nurses in seven countries on the topic they described as active voluntary euthanasia in which the patient requested euthanasia and health care professionals, following guidelines, acted on that request. While the majority of nurses could not justify active voluntary euthanasia under any circumstances, 35 nurses could ethically justify active euthanasia. Of these, the most frequently stated reason for justifying the act was related to the severe suffering of the patient. The researchers note that some of the nurses in this study confused passive euthanasia with active euthanasia. This raises the importance for nurses to have a clear understanding of the terminology related to assisted suicide and euthanasia.

While the American Nurses Association (ANA) Code for Nurses[17] states that nurses cannot deliberately terminate the life of any patient, the above studies suggest disparity among nurses in adherence or interpretation of that code. The American Nurses Association has recently developed position statements regarding the issues of assisted suicide and euthanasia in order to provide direction beyond the general code. The Oncology Nursing Society (ONS) has endorsed these ANA Position Statements. The ANA and ONS documents are included in the Position Statements which appear elsewhere in this publication.

Nurses' unique role with patients and family caregivers. Nurses manage symptoms related to treatment and disease, with the goal of improving quality of life for the patient. Nursing care and support extends to family caregivers, such that the family is generally considered to be the unit of care rather than the patient in isolation.[38-40] The nurse frequently acts as an advocate for the patient in relation to other professionals and amidst what is often an overwhelming health care system. Basic values and obligations for nursing practice are listed in Table 1.

In providing care in the home, nurses become intimately involved with family members who also experience suffering. Previous research has identified the experience of pain and terminal illness from the perspective of family caregivers.[2-4,41,42] The family's experience of a loved one's terminal illness unfortunately often is characterized by fears of loneliness, uncertainty about the future, disruption of family life, and a wish for death as a means for ending the suffering.

Patients who request suicide are often supported by family caregivers who have considered assisted suicide or euthanasia due to lack of support and a sense of helplessness.[43,44] Emerging trends in health care have

TABLE 1. Tacit Assumptions (Values) from Which Ethical Principles Governing Nursing Practice Are Derived and Their Associated Obligations

Value	Obligation
Alleviation of suffering	Behavior that seeks to relieve suffering
Preservation of human dignity	Any activity that seeks to preserve and respect human dignity
Existence of meaningfulness	To act in such a way as not to remove or destroy the meaningfulness of any human life but to preserve and enhance the meaningfulness of any life
Sanctity of life	To act to preserve human life
Compassion	To perform all compassionate deeds and not to refuse to perform compassionate deeds.

Source: Coyle N. The euthanasia and physician-assisted suicide debate: Issues for nursing. Oncol Nurs Forum 1992; 19(7): 41-46.

transformed living rooms into intensive care units and delegated the responsibilities of intensive nursing and medical care to family caregivers. Studies of children, adults and elderly have demonstrated that failure to provide adequate family support and optimum symptom management result in requests for hastened death.[2-4,41,42]

Nurses' moral and legal obligations. The nursing profession is struggling with the moral and professional questions that relate to assisted suicide and euthanasia.[32] Assisted suicide and euthanasia are controversial and emotional issues of discussion. At recent professional nursing meetings, discussions have arisen as to whether or not the nursing profession should or should not take a position related to assisted suicide and euthanasia, whether there is an active role for nurses in assisted suicide, and what the boundaries of the role might be. Table 2 includes examples of principles which serve to guide nurses in their care for the patient requesting assisted suicide or euthanasia. Table 3 illustrates what does not constitute euthanasia.

Similar to the dilemmas faced by physicians, nursing involvement in euthanasia spans a wide range of possibilities from passive knowledge of a suicide plan to active administration of the medications used for suicide.

TABLE 2. Requests for Euthanasia and Assisted Suicide

Nursing Management Principles
• Establish a rapport with the patient.
• Know the issues for the individual patient
• Inadequate symptom control
• Depression, hopelessness, spiritual despair
• Being a burden on the family
• Altered quality of life and unacceptable limitations
• Has lived a full life and wants to die while still in control
• Address the issues
• Do not act independently; involve colleagues from other disciplines
• Assess suicide vulnerability factors
• Assess family status and adequacy of support resources
• Know the law

Source: Coyle N. The euthanasia and physician-assisted suicide debate: Issues for nursing. Oncol Nurs Forum 1992; 19(7): 41-46.

TABLE 3

What Does **Not** Constitute Euthanasia
• Giving a patient who is dying, hypotensive, and in pain sufficient opioid to control pain (Principle of "Double Effect")
• Giving a patient who is dying and dyspneic sufficient morphine to control symptoms (Principle of "Double Effect")
• Sedating a patient who is symptomatic or distressed at his or her request (Principle of Autonomy)
• Withholding nutrition or hydration at the request of the patient who is dying (Principle of Autonomy)

Source: Coyle N. The euthanasia and physician-assisted suicide debate: Issues for nursing. Oncol Nurs Forum 1992; 19(7): 41-46.

Position statements or other policy efforts directed toward the role of professionals will need to address the many facets of this issue, rather than exert only simplified positions.

There is a paucity of literature related to nurses' clinical decision making related to assisted suicide. Jansson and Norberg[38] have examined the ethical reasoning or decision making by experienced registered nurses in Sweden related to the feeding of terminally ill cancer patients. Using vignettes to examine the decision making process, it was identified that nurses chose not to feed the terminally ill, mentally alert, old cancer patient who refused food. Nurses reported that they would never use force or violence against their patients. Thirteen nurses in this study reported that they would feed the patient under certain circumstances: the medical director gave an order to feed the patient, not enough time to feed the patient, an entire staff meeting is against you, and the patient had previously stressed that life is sacred. This study clarifies the need for future research on the decision making process related to assisted suicide.

In a retrospective study conducted at Memorial Sloan-Kettering Cancer Center[39] suicide was openly discussed as an option by over one quarter of the subjects. Patients expressing the possibility of suicide had advanced disease with progressive disability. These patients also reported a severe degree of fatigue. The researchers observed that these patients used the discussion of suicide as an opportunity to express the depth of their suffering. The mitigating circumstances identified by the patients included excruciating pain, becoming a burden for family members, losing the ability to think, losing dignity through the loss of bowel or bladder function, and becoming quadriplegic. The ability to discuss their desire for suicide in the context of their unique fears facilitated a communication of their losses.[39] Although some of the patients developed symptoms previously reported as justifying suicide, none of these patients committed suicide. The investigators attribute this to adaptation that occurs due to the provision of support by health care professionals, acknowledgement of the patient's suffering, open communication, and continued monitoring. Similar experiences are cited throughout hospice literature in which patients' previous requests for death were reversed once care became focused on aggressive symptom control and alleviation of suffering.

The American Nurses' Association's *Code for Nurses with Interpretive Statements*[22] advises that when the nurse is aware of an inappropriate or questionable practice in the delivery of health care, that nurse should discuss that concern with the individual who is performing the inappropriate or questionable practice. Nurses are ethically and legally accountable for actions taken in the course of their practice.

CONCLUSION

Nurses are critically involved in the care of the terminally ill and their families and are central to the debate regarding assisted suicide and euthanasia. Previous literature has documented the diversity of opinion regarding these issues by nurses and the clear need for additional education and discussion of these topics. As health care continues to move outside of the institutional setting and into the home environment, nurses are increasingly assuming the primary role of care. As depicted throughout the literature, nurses must not address these issues in isolation but rather must recognize their roles and obligations in concert with other professionals. Previous literature has also demonstrated the critical need to increase education of nurses regarding risk factors for suicide and their role in counseling.

As a caring profession, nursing must seek to provide optimum physical, psychosocial and spiritual care of the terminally ill. Requests for assisted suicide must be heard as critical messages from our patients and society. A request for hastened death is a voice of suffering and nurses, as with other providers of care, have an obligation to respond.

REFERENCES

1. Ferrell BR, Wisdom C, Wenzl C. Quality of life as an outcome variable in the management of cancer pain. Cancer 1989; 63: 2321-2327.

2. Hinds C. Suffering: A relatively unexplored phenomenon among family caregivers of non-institutionalized patients with cancer. J Adv Nurs 1992; 17: 918-925.

3. Ferrell BR, Rhiner M, Cohen MZ, Grant M. Pain as a metaphor for illness. Part I: Impact of cancer pain on family caregivers. Oncol Nurs Forum 1991; 18(8): 1303-1309.

4. Ferrell BR, Cohen MZ, Rhiner M, Rozek A. Pain as a metaphor for illness. Part II: Family caregivers' management of pain. Oncol Nurs Forum 1991; 18(8): 1315-1321.

5. Johnston-Taylor E, Ferrell BR, Grant M, Cheyney L. Managing Cancer Pain at Home: The Decisions and Ethical Conflicts of Patients, Family Caregivers, and Homecare Nurses. Oncology Nursing Forum, 1993; 20(6): 919-927.

6. Padilla GV, Ferrell B, Grant M, Rhiner M. Defining the content domain of quality of life for cancer patients with pain. Cancer Nursing, 1990; 13(2): 108-115.

7. Hendin H. Youth suicide: a psychological perspective. Suicide and Life Threatening Behavior 1987; 17: 151-165.

8. Simons K. Adolescent suicide: second leading death cause. JAMA 1987; 227: 3329-3332.

9. Valente SM. Assessing Families with a Suicidal Teenager. In Leahey M and Wright L (editors), Families and Psychosocial Problems. Springhouse PA, Springhouse, 1987.

10. Valente SM, Saunders JM. High school suicide prevention programs. Pediatr Nurs 1987; 67: 174-177.

11. Drought TS. Assisted death: A CNA dialogue. California Nurse July/August, 1994: 8-9, 16.

12. Saunders JM. Ethical Issues Related to the Care of Persons with HIV. In: J.H. Flaskerud & P.J. Ungvarski (Eds.) HIV/AIDS A Guide to Nursing Care. New York: W.B. Saunders (3rd Edition); 1995.

13. Young A, Volker D, Rieger PT, Thorpe D. Oncology nurses' attitudes regarding voluntary physician-assisted dying for competent terminally ill patients. Oncology Nursing Forum, 1993; 20(3): 445-455.

14. Coyle N. The euthanasia and physician-assisted suicide debate: issues for nursing. Oncology Nursing Forum, 1992; 19(Suppl 7):41-47.

15. Clouser KD. The sanctity of life: An analysis of a concept. Ann Int Med 1973; 78: 119-125.

16. Veatch RM. A Theory of Medical Ethics, New York, Basic Books, Inc., 1981.

17. Scanlon C, Fleming C. Ethical issues in caring for the patient with advanced cancer. Nurs Clin N Amer 1989; 24(4): 977-986.

18. Gillon R. Beneficence: Doing good for others. Brit Med J 1985a; 291: 44-45.

19. Gillon R. "Primum non nocere" and the principle of nonmaleficence. Brit Med J 1985b; 291: 130-131.

20. Gillon R. Justice and medical ethics. Brit Med J 1985c; 291: 201-202.

21. Ferrell BR, & Rivera LM. Ethical Considerations in Oncology Clinical Practice. Cancer Practice, 1995; 3(2): 94-99.

22. American Nurses' Association. Code for Nurses with Interpretive Statements. Kansas City, MO, American Nurses' Association, 1985.

23. Davis AJ, Davidson B, Hirschfield M et al. An international perspective of active euthanasia: Attitudes of nurses in seven countries. Int J Nurs Stud 1993; 30(4): 310-310.

24. Watson J. Nursing: The Philosophy and Science of Caring. Boston, MA, Little Brown, 1979.

25. Benner P, Wrubel J. The Primacy of Caring. Menlo Park, CA, Addison Wesley, 1989.

26. Ledinger MM. (Ed.) Ethical and Moral Dimensions of Care. Detroit, MI, Wayne State University Press, 1990.

27. Saunders JR, Valente SM. Nicole: Suicide and Terminal Illness. Suicide and Life-Threatening Behavior 1993; 23(1): 76-82.

28. Valente SM, Saunders JM, Grant M. Oncology Nurses' Knowledge and Misconceptions about Suicide. Cancer Practice, 1994; 2(3): 209-216.

29. Valente SM. Evaluating suicide in the medically ill. Nurse Pract, 1993; 18(9): 41-50.

30. Saunders JM, Valente SM. Cancer and suicide. Oncol Nurs Forum, 1988; 15(5): 575-581.

31. Saunders C, Baines M. Living with Dying. Oxford, Oxford University Press, 1984.

32. Scanlon C. Nurses discuss profession's role in assisted suicide and euthanasia. Amer Nurse October 1993.

33. Breitbart W. Cancer pain and suicide. In Foley KM editor, Advances in Pain Research and Therapy, Vol 16, New York, Raven Press, 1990.

34. Baile WF, DiMaggio JR, Schapira DV, Janofsky JS. The request for assistance in dying. The need for psychiatric consultation. Cancer 1993; 72(9): 2786-2791.

35. Bukberg J, Penman D, Holland JC. Depression in hospitalized cancer patients. Psychosom Med 1984; 46: 199-212.

36. Levin DN, Cleeland CS, Dar R. Public attitudes towards cancer pain. Cancer 1985; 56: 2337-2339.

37. Breitbart W. Suicide in cancer patients. Oncology 1987; 1: 49-56.

38. Jansson L, Norberg A. Ethical reasoning concerning the feeding of terminally ill cancer patients. Cancer Nurs 1989; 12(6): 352-358.

39. Coyle N, Adelhardt J, Foley K, Portenoy RK. Character of terminal illness in the advanced cancer patient: Pain and other symptoms during the last four days of life. J Pain Symp Manage 1990; 5(2): 83-93.

40. American Nurses' Association. Nursing: A Social Policy Statement. Kansas City, MO, American Nurses' Association, 1986.

41. Ferrell BR, Rhiner M, Shapiro B, Dierkes M. The Experience of Pediatric Cancer Pain. Part I: Impact of Pain on the Family. Journal of Pediatric Nursing, 1994;9: 368-379.

42. Rhiner M, Ferrell BR, Shapiro B, Dierkes M. The Experience of Pediatric Cancer Pain. Part II: Management of Pain. Journal of Pediatric Nursing, 1994; 9: 380-387.

43. Valente SM, Saunders JM, Cohen MZ. Evaluating Depression among Patients with Cancer. Cancer Practice, 1994; 2(1): 65-71.

44. Valente SM, Saunders JM. Management of Suicidal Patients with HIV Disease. JANAC, 1994; 5(6): 19-29.

THE PATIENT'S SITUATION

Suffering and the Dying Patient

C. Richard Chapman
Jonathan Gavrin

SUMMARY. Suffering in the dying patient derives from immediate sources of physical distress, perceived threats to the integrity of the self, and the psychological make up (memory, beliefs, expectations) of the individual at the end of life. The most common causes of somatic distress in dying patients with cancer are: (1) pain, (2) shortness of breath, and (3) nausea and/or vomiting. Other noteworthy problems include confusion, restlessness, itch, disturbed bladder and bowel function, sleep disruption, low energy, sedation and cachexia.

C. Richard Chapman, PhD, is Professor of Anesthesiology, Psychology, and Psychiatry and Behavioral Sciences at the University of Washington School of Medicine and Director of the Pain and Toxicity Research Center at the Fred Hutchinson Cancer Research Center. Jonathan Gavrin, MD, is Assistant Professor of Anesthesiology at the University of Washington School of Medicine and Associate in Clinical Research at the Pain and Toxicity Research Center, Fred Hutchinson Cancer Research Center, Seattle, WA.

Address correspondence to: Dr. C. Richard Chapman, Department of Anesthesiology, University of Washington, Box 356540, Seattle, WA 98195-6540.

[Haworth co-indexing entry note]: "Suffering and the Dying Patient." Chapman, C. Richard, and Jonathan Gavrin. Co-published simultaneously in *Journal of Pharmaceutical Care in Pain & Symptom Control* (Pharmaceutical Products Press, an imprint of The Haworth Press, Inc.) Vol. 3, No. 3/4, 1995, pp. 67-90; and: *Drug Use in Assisted Suicide and Euthanasia* (ed: Margaret P. Battin, and Arthur G. Lipman) Pharmaceutical Products Press, an imprint of The Haworth Press, Inc., 1996, pp. 67-90. Single or multiple copies of this article are available from The Haworth Document Delivery Service [1-800-342-9678, 9:00 a.m. - 5:00 p.m. (EST)].

© 1996 by The Haworth Press, Inc. All rights reserved.

Specific physiological mechanisms foster suffering in dying persons. These include tissue trauma, visceral distention and cardiovascular events. Neurological signals generated by tissue trauma or sensitization during inflammation lead to sensations of pain and also produce emotional arousal in noradrenergically innervated limbic brain structures. In addition, such signals stimulate the hypothalamo-pituitary-adrenocortical axis. This creates a stress response which, if prolonged, disturbs circadian and ultracadian biological rhythms. One can direct preventative and palliative interventions toward such mechanisms. Patients also suffer because of unmet psychological needs or psychosocial problems. Identifying such needs or problems and addressing them can often contribute substantially to patient comfort. Since we have the resources to prevent or largely alleviate pain and other distressing conditions in the majority of cases, and care providers can meet most patients' psychological needs once they identify them, unaddressed suffering need not accompany death from cancer or other prolonged disease. *[Article copies available from The Haworth Document Delivery Service: 1-800-342-9678.]*

KEYWORDS. Suffering, dying patient, pain, shortness of breath, nausea, vomiting, palliative care, euthanasia, assisted suicide, psychological needs, emotion, cancer

INTRODUCTION

Dying is a natural and inevitable aspect of living. When health care providers save a life, they postpone death, but never truly prevent it. While these statements seem to belabor the obvious, the majority of health care practitioners continue to ignore the dying process and, with the notable exceptions of palliative care specialists and hospice programs, medical management of the terminally ill patient rarely involves systematic planning for protecting the quality of dying. Since medicine possesses the resources to prevent or largely alleviate pain and other distressing conditions in the majority of cases, suffering of physiological origin need not accompany death from progressing disease. That patients should suffer needlessly while dying from cancer or other terminal illness is simply unacceptable.

This paper addresses the problem of unrelieved suffering at the end stages of terminal illness. We explore definitions of suffering, review current knowledge about the psychophysiological basis of suffering, and describe common pathophysiological and psychological factors that contribute to suffering in dying patients. We identify and examine several formidable barriers to the medical prevention of suffering in dying patients, and offer an approach that can help surmount them.

WHAT IS SUFFERING?

Most health care professionals have traditionally thought of suffering as a vernacular term for physical and emotional distress of complex or non-specific origin. The term connotes subjectivity, existential crisis and dysphoria. As such, its prevention and control falls outside the boundaries of conventional medical practice. Increasingly, however, health care professionals are recognizing the need for a working concept of suffering and the potential importance of suffering as a therapeutic target. The definitions in Table 1 illustrate the evolution of the concept.

Taken together these definitions indicate that suffering: involves perceived threat to the self that may encompass the body, the psychosocial self or both; is inherently emotional, unpleasant, and psychologically complex; is an enduring psychological state and not a transient or fleeting experience; and not a synonym for pain. However, our concept is still incomplete. Thrill seekers and adventurers often seek out situations involving objective threat to the self and somehow achieve exhilaration rather than suffering. We suggest that perceived helplessness (inability to cope, bankruptcy of physical, psychological or social resources) is a key element in suffering. We also note that the above definitions ignore grief and loss. Grief can ensue when an individual perceives the loss of a psychological or social resource, a body part or desired personal appearance, a prized employment status, or a physical capability for a treasured activity. Loss often equates with perceived threat to self. Finally, we suggest that the sense of separation from social support or alienation that dying persons often experience merits inclusion in the definitions.

We have defined suffering elsewhere as "a complex negative and cognitive state characterized by perceived threat to the integrity of the self, perceived helplessness in the face of that threat, and exhaustion of psychosocial and personal resources for coping.[6] For the purposes of this paper, we underscore that suffering in the dying patient derives from immediate sources of physical distress, perceived threats to the integrity of the self, and the psychological make up (memory, beliefs, expectations) of the individual at the end of life.

BASIC MECHANISMS OF SUFFERING

The psychophysiology of suffering involves both unpleasant sensory awareness and sustained negative emotion. In addition, cognitive processes such as memory, expectation, and meaning-making help shape the experience. Some of the basic mechanisms of both physical and psycho-

TABLE 1. Five Definitions of Suffering

"Suffering may be defined as a negative affective state resulting from an event or situation that is perceived to be physically painful, uncomfortable, or psychologically distressing." *Benedict, 1989[1]*
". . . the global aversive experience sustained over time by multiple aversive negative perceptions including (but not limited to) pain." *Portenoy, 1990[2]*
"Suffering is a state of mind or an experience in the consciousness of a person that is created by many different influences, whereas pain is only one of these influences and its presence does not necessarily produce suffering." *Fishman, 1990[3]*
"I believe suffering to be the distress brought about by the actual or perceived impending threat to the integrity or continued existence to the whole person." *Cassell, 1991[4]*
"Suffering can be described as an aversive emotional experience characterized by the perception of personal distress that is generated by adverse factors undermining the quality of life." *Cherney, Coyle and Foley, 1994[5]*

logical suffering are described below. For simplicity in description, we approach the physiological mechanisms of suffering from the viewpoint of pain. Our purpose is to demonstrate that current knowledge of pain mechanisms leads directly to a rudimentary but growing understanding of the brain mechanisms involved in suffering. Other distressing somatic stimuli such as persisting itch or nausea must activate similar central mechanisms.

Basic Sensory Mechanisms of Pathological Pain

Pain derives from signals of tissue trauma produced by injury-sensitive receptors (nociceptors) or from aberrant peripheral nervous system function associated with neuropathy. Noxious signaling initiates processes in the central nervous system that ultimately produce the perception we call pain. This involves sensory, affective and cognitive processing within the brain. The central sensory processing of noxious transmission is well defined in the literature and involves spinothalamic transmission pathways and somatosensory cortex.[7]

While this is a valuable body of knowledge, clinical pain states rarely follow the classically defined patterns for sensory transduction and processing. Pain in dying patients often arises from sensitization associated with persisting noxious stimulation and/or inflammation. Woolf [8,9] distinguished between physiological pain and pathological pain to emphasize this difference. The former is the "nociception-mediated" transient pain response of everyday life, highly correlated with the flexion withdrawal response. The latter reflects disruption of normal sensory mechanisms. Pathological pain may occur in response to normally innocuous stimuli or ill-defined stimuli and the pain response to noxious stimulation may be exaggerated and prolonged. During pathological pain nociceptor thresholds become lower (sensitization), signals get amplified, and aversive sensations extend beyond the duration of the stimulus that provokes them.

Receptor sensitization typically occurs during inflammation (a common feature of metastatic tumor) because associated chemical changes can alter the transduction properties of nociceptors, causing them to respond to normally inoffensive stimuli. Normally silent receptors, and those that do not normally function as nociceptors, activate in the presence of a sensitizing chemical environment and contribute to the noxious afferent barrage.[9]

The conversion of sensory end organs that are normally mechanoreceptors to sources of noxious signals reflects changes at the dorsal horn of the spinal cord. Spinal cord cells engaging in prolonged noxious signal processing eventually begin to respond in exaggerated or abnormal ways to input from mechanoreceptors and other normally non-noxious sensory endings. Such change, termed central sensitization, develops as a consequence of prolonged, intensive noxious signaling from the periphery, and so tends to appear following extended peripheral sensitization.

These considerations indicate that pathological pain states tend to self-perpetuate. Fundamental sensory mechanisms can function in abnormal, exaggerated ways to produce pain that is disproportionate to the pathology. Two patients with similar tissue trauma may show altogether different patterns of pain, and the same patient may report little pain or severe pain at different points in time when the mechanical cause of the pain has not appeared to change. Although the literature has not yet addressed the possibility, other aversive sensory experiences such as nausea, vertigo and itch may result from peripheral or central sensitization processes in patients. Peripheral and central sensitization probably interact with the affective dimension of pain, contributing to the emotional as well as the sensory distress of the patient.

Basic Emotional Mechanisms of Pathological Pain

Negative emotion is a complex state involving physiological arousal, complex patterns of limbic brain activity, unpleasant feelings, and negative thoughts. From the viewpoint of evolutionary psychology, feeling states such as fear serve a protective function. Philosophers and psychologists have recognized since the time of the ancient Greeks that pain has emotional as well as sensory properties. The key point is that signals of biological threat trigger negative emotional states via well defined sensory pathways.

Spinoreticular Structures

Noxious transmission engages more than sensory pathways: spinoreticular pathways transmit noxious signals to several areas of the brainstem[10] and these areas provide access to central affective processing mechanisms. Spinoreticular axons possess receptive fields that resemble those of spinothalamic tract neurons projecting to medial thalamus. Like their spinothalamic counterparts, these axons transmit tissue trauma information rostrally.[11] Most spinoreticular neurons carry noxious information and many respond preferentially to noxious input.[7]

Central Noradrenergic Mechanisms

From the viewpoint of pain, the locus coeruleus (LC) is among the most important area brain stem excited by spinoreticular transmission. It responds consistently to noxious sensory input; i.e., any input that signals tissue or organ stress. This primarily noradrenergic nucleus is positioned bilaterally near the wall of the fourth ventricle. Three major projections characterize the LC:[12] the ascending projection known as the dorsal noradrenergic bundle (DNB) is the most extensive, reaching throughout limbic brain and to all of neocortex. It accounts for about 70% of all brain norepinephrine. [13]

The LC gives rise to most of central noradrenergic fibers in the spinal cord, hypothalamus, thalamus, and hippocampus and to the projections to the limbic cortex and the neocortex. The LC reacts to afferent messages that signal actual or potential damage to the biological integrity of the individual. For example, nociception inevitably and reliably increases activity in the neurons of the LC, and LC excitation appears to be an inevitable response to noxious stimulation.[13] This response does not require cognitively mediated control since it occurs in anesthetized animals.[14] Also, experimentally induced phasic LC activation produces alarm and apparent fear in primates[15] and lesions of the LC eliminate normal heart rate increases to threatening stimuli.[16] Collectively, these observations indicate that the LC responds to threatening events and that this response normally leads to trepidation, fear or panic.

Various threatening events unrelated to pain also excite this nucleus, for example: (1) distention of the bladder, stomach, colon or rectum and visceral events excite the LC;[13] (2) strong cardiovascular stimulation activates the LC;[17] and (3) while the literature is less definitive, it is probable that various aversive interoceptive signals such as nausea also involve excitation of the LC. It responds to threatening and distressing events of which tissue trauma is a significant subset. Thus, it may well play a role in the emotional distress of suffering. Up to this point, in describing the link between the LC and threatening stimuli, we have characterized its reactive function. However, the LC appears to have a clearly defined proactive (anticipatory) function associated with vigilance and orientation to threatening stimuli. Aversive stimuli lead to hypervigilance and increased emotion as well as an inability to attend to ordinary tasks. Clinically, this state would manifest as chronic debilitating anxiety.

The link between activation of the LC and the DNB and heightened anxiety emerges from animal studies involving direct electrical activation of the DNB and associated limbic structures. Stimulating these structures produces sympathetic nervous system response and elicits emotional behaviors in animals such as defensive threat, fright, enhanced startle, freezing and vocalization.[18] Under normal circumstances, activity in these pathways increases alertness. Tonically activated LC and DNB discharge corresponds to hypervigilance and emotionality.[14] As suffering involves the experience of threat, and the noradrenergic pathways associated with the LC and DNB appear to generate negative emotion, we propose that these noradrenergic pathways account for one of the biological links between pain and suffering.

A second link between central noradrenergic activity and emotional arousal exists in the ventral noradrenergic bundle (VNB), which involves parts of the hypothalamo-pituitary-adrenocortical (HPA) axis. The VNB, like the DNB, is an ascending noradrenergic system; it enters the medial forebrain bundle. Neurons in the medullary reticular formation project to the hypothalamus via the VNB.[19] These are VNB-linked noradrenergic and adrenergic pathways to paraventricular hypothalamus in the rat:[20] (a) the AI region of the ventral medulla (lateral reticular nucleus), (b) the AII region of the dorsal vagal complex (the nucleus tractus solitarius,) which receives visceral afferents and (c) regions AV and AVII (although these make comparatively minor contributions to the VNB).

Central Mechanisms and Stress Response

The control center for the HPA axis is the paraventricular nucleus (PVN) of the hypothalamus.[21] Since this nucleus responds to aversive stimulation, HPA activation may well play a part in central response to sustained pain or other prolonged aversive experience. Nociception-transmitting neurons at all segmental levels of the spinal cord project to medial and lateral hypothalamus and several telencephalic regions.[22] Moreover, neurons in the medullary reticular formation project to hypothalamus via the ventral tegmental tract.[19] The medullary neuronal complexes supply 90% of catecholaminergic innervation to the paraventricular hypothalamus via the VNB.[23] In addition the PVN receives sensory information from several reticular areas including the ventrolateral medulla, the dorsal raphe nucleus, the nucleus raphe magnus, and the dorsomedial nucleus.[20] Other afferents project to the PVN from the hippocampus and amygdala, and most hypothalamic and preoptic nuclei send projections to PVN, including the infundibular nucleus.

HPA Axis, Stress, and Suffering

The HPA axis accommodates the individual's physiology to the demands of biological stressors, coordinates physiology with behavior, and adjusts the circadian and ultracadian rhythms of normal living. Normally, the hypothalamus transforms neurochemical messages from the threatening stimuli into hypophysiotrophic signals, and the adenohypophysis initiates neurohumoral signals, secreting corticotrophin-releasing hormone (CRH) from the hypothalamic median eminence into the portal circulation. This causes the release of adrenocorticotrophic hormone (ACTH) into systemic circulation, which stimulates both the synthesis and secretion of adrenocortical steroids. These hormones exert extensive metabolic effects, and their appearance in systemic circulation completes a feedback loop that regulates ongoing ACTH release.

As the adaptation syndrome progresses to resistance and approaches exhaustion, biological disequilibrium can occur. Biorhythmic dysregulation is one of the prominent features of distress in cancer patients. Those who are suffering rarely sleep well or display normal appetite, for example. For dying patients, sustained pain or nausea, air hunger, and psychosocial difficulties can combine to produce an unrelenting constellation of stressors that drives the adaptation syndrome to the edge of exhaustion, desynchronizing many circadian and ultracadian functions. These considerations implicate prolonged stress in the suffering of patients with life threatening disease. Together with the dysphoria of perceived threat and helplessness, the disequilibrium of sustained stress can produce a condition of profound discomfort.

Common Patterns of Distress in Dying Patients

Certain psychological and biological markers signal impending death in the patient with advanced disease. Cognitive function in many terminally ill patients diminishes markedly in the weeks prior to death, and restlessness, air hunger, pain and delirium often emerge in the final 48 hours.[24-26] Specific observable changes signal when death is imminent, usually a few days before the final event. Not every dying patient manifests all the signs, but knowledge that these are normal human patterns gives solace to patients, family and friends, while guiding caretakers in provision of comfort care (Table 2).

Lichter and Hunt[26] studied the nursing records of 200 patients in their

TABLE 2. Signs of Impending Death

(adapted from Hospice and Home Care of Snohomish County, Washington)[27]

Hypersomnolence

Disorientation

Irregular breathing

Excessive secretions

Visual and auditory hallucinations

Diminished clarity of sight

Decreased urine production

Mottled skin

Cool extremities

Truncal warmth

last 48 hours of life. Thirty-six percent experienced noteworthy distress such as pain, agitation, confusion or restlessness. In contrast to the signs listed in Table 2, these problems merit prevention or intervention. Below, we discuss the major somatic problems that distress dying patients such as pain, nausea and vomiting, and dyspnea in detail.

Pathophysiological Determinants of Suffering

The most common causes of somatic distress in the days or weeks that precede death are: (1) pain, (2) shortness of breath, and (3) nausea or vomiting.[25,26] Other noteworthy problems include confusion, restlessness, itch, disturbed bladder and bowel function, sleep disruption, low energy, sedation and cachexia. The latter is often a greater source of distress to families and caretakers than to patients and is probably a natural part of physiologically preparing to die.[28]

Nonetheless, cachexia has great practical importance because it depletes one's energy, marks malnutrition and decline, and interferes with the ability to socialize at meal times.[29] These symptoms occur in isolation.

Pain

Dying patients usually fear pain above all other problems, and although it is far from inevitable, pain is a common problem in many terminal illnesses, including cancer and AIDS. Often pain exacerbates with disease progression, but it can also emerge as a toxicity of a rescue intervention.[30]

Pain interferes with activity, prevents enjoyment of even simple satisfactions, and can prevent important and nurturing social exchanges near the end of life. It causes psychiatric symptoms in cancer patients with advanced disease, and, when pain and psychiatric pathology such as severe depression coexist, pain control should be the first step.[31]

Pain in the dying patient fits into two broad categories, nociceptive and neuropathic.[32] Nociceptive pain, normal neural activity mediated by healthy intact nerves, signals tissue trauma and/or inflammation. It can be either somatic or visceral in origin, the latter manifesting as diffuse, poorly localized distress or sometimes in patterns referred in characteristic ways to the body surface.

Neuropathic pain results from damage or entrapment of nerves, and it can result from disease progression, surgery, radiation or chemotherapy. In some cancer pain patients it results from central lesions such as damage to the ventral or medial thalamus. Neuropathic pain has peculiar qualities and sometimes resists conventional approaches to pain control.

The most common source of somatic pain in cancer patients is metastasis to bone. The primary causes of pain in metastatic disease are inflammation of the periosteum and increased intraosteal pressure from tumor infiltration.

Not all of the sites that appear on a bone scan hurt, and over time a specific lesion may flare up or quiet down in unpredictable ways.[33] In some cases bone lesions can cause fracture and acutely painful crises such as vertebral collapse. Most patients derive sufficient benefit from systemic analgesics, but palliative irradiation of specific lesions can alleviate intransigent pain and prevent catastrophic fracture.

Visceral pain may indicate direct tumor infiltration, swelling, distention of ducts or obstruction within organs. Inflammation can cause or exacerbate it. Because pain often elicits autonomic reflexes, visceral pain can contribute to nausea, affect bowel and bladder function, and alter appetite. When referred to the body surface, visceral pain can cause skin sensitivity in the area of referred pain and sometimes provoke muscle contracture or spasm in the affected area, thus creating further sources of pain.

Neuropathic pain syndromes include plexopathies, peripheral neuropathies and central pain states. Pancoast's syndrome (a superior pulmonary sulcus tumor), for example, is a brachial plexopathy that causes lancinating deafferentation pain in the affected shoulder and arm. Some neuropathic pain in cancer patients results from central lesions. Neuropathic pain differs in character from somatic pain in that it tends to appear with delayed onset following a causative event (e.g., delayed response to pin prick), its qualities are dysesthetic (burning, "pins and needles," "electricity-like," and sometimes paroxysmal), and its somatic reference tends to follow patterns of sensory loss. Peripheral nerve injury sometimes involves exquisite tissue hypersensitivity in the absence of inflammation; patients complain that light touch and minor temperature changes cause or exacerbate pain (allodynia).

Nausea and Vomiting

Nausea and vomiting are frequent, often severe, sources of distress for patients with life-threatening illness.[34] Sometimes these symptoms are iatrogenic; in other cases they occur because of visceral lesions. They are common during cancer therapy but can emerge secondary to palliative medications, including opioid analgesics. Disease pathology in a variety of organs, including the brain, may cause these symptoms. Nausea interferes with a patient's ability to move about and to engage in the social interactions that are very important to dying persons and it limits the titration of opioid drugs to the level of full pain relief. Vomiting, which does not always accompany nausea, is particularly dangerous since it may promote dehydration, electrolyte imbalance, aspiration pneumonia and malnutrition. As a social event, recurrent vomiting is disastrous. Patients who need the comfort of friends refuse social contact, and family members agonize over the problem.

The mechanisms and mediators of nausea and vomiting are complex and remain incompletely defined. Both central and peripheral factors play a role. The chemoreceptor trigger zone and the nucleus tractus solitarius are located in the area postrema of the brain stem which is highly vascular and devoid of an effective blood-brain barrier. It is rich with opioid, dopaminergic, cholinergic, histaminergic and serotonergic receptors. Investigators hypothesize that activation of these receptors stimulates an emetic center which, in turn, produces nausea and can initiate vomiting. A vestibular component is particularly prevalent with opioid-induced nausea and can severely limit ambulation. Decreased gut motility, associated with diabetes mellitus, chemotherapy-induced autonomic neuropathies, opioid therapy, inactivity and primary gastrointestinal pathology are important causes of nausea or emesis.[35-37]

Dyspnea and Cough

Dyspnea (shortness of breath or air hunger) is an awareness of difficulty in breathing, not necessarily related to exertion, that compels the individual to increase his ventilation or reduce his activity.[38] Dyspnea is not synonymous with respiratory distress, the latter of which implies hypoventilation, hypoxemia, or both, but respiratory distress certainly is associated with, and a common cause of, the subjective feeling of breathlessness. It can manifest as copious secretions, cough, chest pain, fatigue and air hunger. Sustained breathlessness causes great psychological distress. The etiology of air hunger is complex and varied. Head and neck cancers can cause partial upper airway obstruction and often are associated with excessive secretions. Neuromuscular pathology or generalized weakness will lead to restrictive airway disease with secondary buildup of secretions which in turn can lead to obstructive lung disease. Cardiac failure can cause exertional dyspnea, tachypnea, orthopnea, paroxysmal nocturnal dyspnea and cough. If left untreated, cardiac failure will cause pulmonary edema which often imparts a sensation of drowning. Renal insufficiency can cause fluid overload and make cardiac failure more likely. Mediastinal pathology, such as enlarged lymph nodes, can compromise both cardiac and pulmonary function, leading to dyspnea. Intra-abdominal pathology, enlarging mass or ascites, will encroach on lung volumes and capacities, resulting in tachypnea to maintain minute ventilation, a common cause of subjective air hunger. Primary pulmonary pathology of many kinds can lead to dyspnea: chest wall, pleural, airway or parenchymal tumor; infectious or aspiration pneumonitis; pulmonary embolus; broncho-pleural fistula; radiation or chemotherapy induced fibrosis; tobacco related injury.

Breathlessness can progress slowly over the course of a long illness or it can present rapidly in association with acute decompensation and imminent death. It is a common feature in the last days of life.[39] Loved ones and clinicians often feel uncomfortable in the presence a person who is short of breath. This can contribute to the patient's sense of alienation.

Cough may or may not accompany dyspnea. It is often the symptom that brings a patient to medical attention initially and may have frightening connotations to patients and families, particularly if associated with hemoptysis. Heart failure can precipitate dry cough, but more commonly cough results from primary airway or lung pathology, including pharyngeal irritation or restriction from tumor, large or small airway obstruction, reactive airway disease, mucous plugging, pleural effusion, parenchymal disease.

Psychosocial Determinants of Suffering

Dying persons are sometimes physically and emotionally exhausted. The burden of physical symptoms and the specter of death combine to create enormous personal stress. Patients therefore suffer for psychological as well as physical reasons. While the two are not easily separated (e.g., severe persistent pain can cause psychological symptoms), some psychological or psychosocial problems are amenable to intervention.

Psychological Problems in the Dying Patient

Psychological disorders occur with high frequency in dying patients: these include depression, delirium, anxiety adjustment disorders and suicidal ideation.[5] Cherney et al. emphasized the importance of existential distress in dying patients. This manifests as a sense of meaninglessness, remorse for unresolved guilt, hopelessness and futility. In addition, their review of the literature indicates that 50%-80% of dying patients experience death anxiety. Disrupted personal integrity (disintegration of who one is as a person) can be a major stressor for many patients for whom disease has meant the loss of social identity, physical ability or attractiveness or self confidence. Some patients see themselves as physical, emotional, social and financial burdens on family and loved ones and suffer with the sense of burden that they perceive they impose upon others.

Psychological Needs of the Dying Patient

Dying persons have emotional and social needs that often go unrecognized and unaddressed because their physiological burdens are so prominent. However, even when one cannot prevent the progression of the disease or its complications, it is often possible to identify and address the patient's psychosocial needs.

Patients differ notably in the trajectories of their dying processes, across age cohorts, in cultural backgrounds, and across levels of education and socio-economic status. Nonetheless, certain psychological aspects of care recur frequently across individual cases and merit comment.

One common observation is that patients rarely enter the process of dying and progress to death in a unitary frame of mind. Kübler-Ross[40] contended that dying patients go through stages of denial, anger, bargaining, depression, and finally acceptance. Her writings have generated controversy, but the fundamental point remains valid: the psychological needs of dying patients tend to change, and compassionate care requires that the physician tune into these changes and meet new needs as they arise.

Also, patients share risk for specific fears. The most common is the possibility of abandonment or dying alone.[41,42] This includes fears of spending one's last days or hours in a medical technology environment separated from loved ones and dying in the absence of warm human contact. Also, patients often worry that they will be repulsive to others. This is realistic when vomiting goes uncontrolled, when the patient emits loathsome odors, and when patients do not receive adequate symptom relief. When patients cannot control bodily secretions or develop other socially offensive characteristics, it is important to protect them from a loss of self-image and self-worth at the time of death and to ensure that they do not suffer from isolation. Patients also fear the loss of autonomy. To become helpless and dependent on others is odious to some people, and many dread having the disease advance to this stage.[43]

Smith and Maher[44] explored the possibility that patients can take "healthy" attitudes into the dying situation and thereby achieve a "healthy" death. They developed an inventory of questions and submitted these to a national, systematically selected sample of hospice coordinators. They asked each to choose from his or her experience one individual who exemplified a healthy death and to identify attitudes that individual held (using the inventory) that contributed to the healthy death.

Having important people around the dying person proved extraordinarily important in the survey. Nearly all (97.4%) of the respondents indicated that the successful dying patient wanted "to have significant others (family and/or friends) around him/her." In addition, the dying person wanted "to participate in physical expressions of caring such as touching, hugging or kissing" (92%). This corroborates our emphasis above: dying people rarely want to be alone. Fully 96% of the respondents thought that a dying person wanted to "hear the truth even when painful." The authors noted that some patients fear the loss of intellectual integrity at the time of dying. Sometimes family members and health care providers unwittingly collude in creating a pattern of denial and avoidance at a time when the patient needs direct and candid information.

A strong majority of the hospice coordinators (92.4%) perceived an individual experiencing a healthy death as one who "preferred to have as much control as possible in making decisions concerning care." Moreover he or she wanted to discuss the practical issues of dying such as finances, and the family's future (92.1%). Most respondents (87.5%) indicated that the successful dying patient "liked to review past pleasures and pains; accomplishments and regrets." Sometimes review involves a family conference chaired by the dying person or individual conferences between the dying person and significant others. In other cases audiocassettes and videotapes make this possible. For example, a dying mother can leave a videotape for an infant child.

Personal cleanliness and appearance were important to dying patients. An overwhelming majority of hospice coordinators (89.6%) indicated that "his/her appearance and personal cleanliness were of great importance." A patient's appearance and social presentability may seem trivial from the medical perspective at the time of dying, but this has a great deal to do with protecting the dignity of the dying patient. Demonstrating respect for this simple need contributes substantially to the quality of care.

Religion and spirituality were important, but less so than social contact and the exercise of control. Of the hospice coordinators polled, 71.9% indicated that those patients experiencing a healthy death "had a desire to talk about religious/spiritual issues." Fewer than one third (31.3%) indicated that this type of patient "wished to explore the topic of an afterlife." This occurred independently of the patient's involvement in organized religion.

Viewed collectively, these concerns suggest some important principles in the management of dying persons. Those for whom death goes smoothly often have a sense of control and involvement in decisions about care. They exercise opportunities to bring life to closure at a practical level, arranging their affairs and negotiating changes in family roles. They require truth and intellectual integrity rather than denial and evasion. Finally, these "successful" patients are concerned about spiritual issues and the afterlife, but spiritual concerns did not equate with religiosity. This observation supports what hospice workers and chaplains have long known, that it is not necessary to be of the same religious faith as the patient in order to support that patient's spiritual needs.

Psychological Factors in the Family Setting

An ideal dying patient would have a compassionate and supportive family. Since family members serve as care providers for dying persons, they can take important roles in the home setting (medication delivery, hygienic routines, monitoring of signs and symptoms), and they can provide organized and appropriate psychological support. In this ideal case, the family physician would evaluate the situation and organize family care providers, specifying their patient care roles. He/she could, when appropriate, define certain terms of duty for each role, rotating family members through specific roles to minimize burnout and yet giving everyone the chance to feel that he or she has contributed significantly.

Unfortunately, few families fit the ideal situation. In cases where the disease trajectory has involved multiple failed treatments, otherwise healthy family members may progress to "burnout." In many situations both the patient and the family feel that the patient's continuing survival causes everyone to suffer, and they believe collectively that death will resolve this.

BARRIERS TO THE PREVENTION OF SUFFERING

These factors fall into three groupings: (1) Deficits in knowledge and skills among health care professionals; (2) Misguided beliefs and attitudes among care providers; and (3) Public attitudes and patient reticence to bring suffering to the attention of care providers.

Deficient Care Provider Knowledge and Skills

Many care providers lack knowledge of the process of dying and skills to manage the symptoms and pathophysiological changes that accompany the later stages of dying. The scope of this problem is best illustrated by work that targets failure to manage pain in dying patients.

Numerous writers have documented that medical and nursing educations have failed to provide health care professionals with adequate backgrounds for the management of pain in terminally ill patients.[45-49] Consequently, many health care professionals cannot properly assess pain and other complications in dying patients and many possess limited skills for controlling pain. Moreover, care providers tend to underestimate patient pain and distress.[48]

A weak knowledge base on pain compromises quality of care in myriad ways for dying patients. For example, patients differ markedly in morphine requirements for pharmacokinetic reasons. Two patients with identical sources of pain may require notably different doses to achieve the same pain relief. The care provider who fails to understand this may withhold adequate dosage from the patient with the greater dose requirement on the grounds that titrating to relief will foster tolerance or increase risk of respiratory depression.

Fortunately, many health care professionals are aware of their deficits in knowledge and would like to learn more about management of the dying patient. Elliott and Elliott[50] conducted a survey of 243 physicians in Minnesota, asking them how they have learned about cancer pain management and how they would like to learn more. The response rate of 62% indicated that the majority of physicians sampled thought the issue significant. Only 16% indicated that a medical school course had provided a major source of information. Eighty-four percent of the responders indicated a desire for local conferences to update their knowledge.

Of course, insufficient knowledge of other aspects of comfort care also contributes to the barrier. Few physicians are well prepared to deal effectively with nausea and vomiting, air hunger, bowel obstruction or confusional states.

Misguided Attitudes and Beliefs Among Providers

Many physicians, believing that their primary mission is rescuing the patient from lethal disease, pursue this end beyond reasonable expectation for cure and to the exclusion of palliation. In such cases family members and physicians sometimes collude in proffering hope for rescue where none exists while the patient, resigned to the inevitability of death, lacks reassurance that his comfort and functional capability will receive adequate medical attention during his last days or weeks.

Physicians and other providers fear that planning palliative care for the end stages of dying will disturb the protective mechanism of denial and thereby distress the patient and family. Some cultures still espouse the denial of terminal disease. The patient, family and physician actively seek to avoid confronting the patient with the poor prognosis and in some countries frank deception is still the rule. In the United States, these practices have largely disappeared, but other denial patterns have replaced them. Patients and families who unrealistically believe that they will find a cure appear hopeful, and the denial that this affords appears to benefit all concerned. In such cases physicians often find it difficult to introduce the need for worst case planning and palliation.

Finally, some care providers believe that suffering is inevitable for patients with advanced cancer. Because so many patients still suffer so much at the end of life, care providers take suffering to be the norm rather than the exception that it could be.

Public Attitudes and Patient Behaviors

The beliefs that the American public holds about the end stages of life and the likelihood of pain and great distress at the end stage of cancer affect their interactions with care providers. Often patients conceal problems that are subjectively defined such as pain, nausea, sleep disturbance or excessive fatigue. Moreover, many think that the physician's role does not extend beyond rescue from disease and they fear that medical technology, relentless in its obsession to cure, will extend disease into prolonged dying, perpetuate intractable pain, and strip the dying person of dignity. When patients and families fail to appreciate that resources exist for symptom relief or believe that such problems are inevitable and intractable, they implicitly endorse excessively conservative or inadequate comfort care.

Levin, Cleeland and Daut[51] studied attitudes toward cancer pain via a telephone survey in Wisconsin. They obtained an estimated response rate of 66% for 496 interviews. Forty-eight percent of the sample rated cancer as very or extremely painful and 42% felt that cancer treatment was very or extremely painful. Seventy-two percent agreed or strongly agreed with the statement "Cancer pain can get so bad that a person with cancer might consider suicide." Fifty-two percent thought that cancer patients could expect a painful death. This survey suggests that the public associates pain and suffering with cancer.[52]

The Levin et al.[51] survey also determined that approximately 50% of the sample harbored significant concerns about opioid analgesics: development of tolerance, addiction risk, mental confusion and side effects. Foley[53] pointed out that the public and the law view opioid drugs both as lethal weapons (they can be used to terminate life) and as controlled substances characterized by abuse liability restricted by federal and state laws. Public awareness campaigns (Just Say No to Drugs, Drug Abuse Resistance Education [D.A.R.E.]) have not distinguished between narcotic drug abuse and therapeutic drug use in patients with severe pain. Consequently, opioid drugs are universally vilified in the public mind. Many patients therefore view opioids with trepidation and some refrain from complaining of pain for fear of being put on medication that will turn them into drug addicts.

Patient reticence to report personal distress poses a major barrier for the control of suffering. This seemingly simple problem has multiple roots. Some patients believe that the physician's major priority is to cure the disease, and they do not want to risk distracting health care providers from their central mission by complaining of personal distress or troublesome symptoms. Still others feel diminished by complaining and try to maintain a stoic, courageous attitude in dealing with physicians and nurses. Often such patients feel that physical distress and suffering are inevitable and largely uncontrollable. Still others, as noted above, fear the drugs that could relieve symptoms, believing that such medications will distort their personalities, cause excessive sedation and diminish functional capability, cause them to develop drug cravings or other signs of addiction, or cause a tolerance that will prevent pain control at the time of a future crisis.

The acknowledgment of a pain problem or other subjectively defined complication can be difficult for some patients because denial of the cause of the problem is an important coping mechanism. Daut and Cleeland[54] studied 667 cancer patients with pain and determined that those who believed that pain represented a worsening of physical condition also reported that the pain interfered most with normal daily activity. In contrast, those who attributed pain to causes unrelated to cancer were least affected by the pain and reported minimal interference with daily activity patterns and functional capability. This suggests that negative personal beliefs about the meaning of cancer pain determine in part the disease's psychosocial impact. The effective coper, therefore, is the patient who denies or distorts the meaning of his pain. Such patients tend to minimize reporting pain to care providers, and aggressive pain therapy may threaten the psychological defenses of such patients.

Whatever the reason for patients not acknowledging subjective distresses, physicians, nurses and other health care professionals cannot assess problems and intervene effectively if physicians and family members do not communicate about physical or psychological distress.

TOWARDS PLANNING A PEACEFUL DEATH

We must all die, and no one wants an agonizing death for himself or his loved one. Just as it is sensible to plan for the economic viability of one's health care needs through health insurance, it makes sense to plan in advance for the circumstances of one's dying when these circumstances are predictable. Life threatening disease, while sometimes curable, affords the opportunity for such planning. Planning in advance in order to assure control of pain and other discomforts across the therapeutic course, whether to cure or end life, can provide peace of mind for the patient and family.

If this simple message comes from a physician shortly after cancer diagnosis when there is still substantial hope of cure, it is easy for most patients to accept it. Delivered late, the message may connote that there is no longer any hope for a cure or that the physician anticipates a painful, troubled death. One key to effective planning, therefore, is to open the dialogue with patient and family early on, when death is still distant and the patient can derive assurance that, if the worst case comes to pass, he or she will not have to bear unrelieved pain or discomfort.

Working with Patients and Families

Once the dialogue is open, the physician can undertake contingency planning for various discomforts, including worst case planning for the end if therapy does not succeed. The patient and family need not enter into the details of worst case forecasting, but they should know that it is in process. Patient and family involvement should work toward a clear understanding of the various problems that can emerge and the symptom management or palliative options for such problems. The goals of such planning are to (1) anticipate all probable complications and discomforts associated with either treatment or disease progression (this is the physician's task), (2) develop a pain and discomfort management plan (the physician does this with the patient and family), and (3) insure that the patient will report pain and other symptom problems, circadian/ultracadian disruption such as sleep and appetite disturbance, psychological problems such as panic attack or depression, and excessive fatigue. The key point is that patients need to know that comfort and function issues are high priority and that the physician expects to monitor them.

Some patients and/or families will have dire doubts and misconceptions about opioid drugs and other treatments, and it helps to address these concerns early on. The potential use of palliative irradiation, nerve blocks or epidural catheters may help assure some patients that multiple options for pain control exist. Many will want to arrange for advanced directives. Still others will need to learn about hospice care as an alternative, what it attempts to achieve, and when the time is right to seek hospice services. As the disease advances, families often benefit from designating certain family members as care providers for specific tasks, alternating or rotating roles to prevent burn out.

Some families are inherently dysfunctional or minimally functional because of pre-existing psychological problems, drug or alcohol abuse patterns, or poor family dynamics. In such situations, the physician must occasionally act as the patient's advocate. If certain family members tend to stress the patient and contribute to the suffering, it is important to direct the efforts of those individuals away from the patient. Such problems are often subtle. For example, a well meaning spouse, feeling desperate to help and unable to accept the natural cachexia that the patient is experiencing, may insist on preparing elaborate meals and demanding that the patient eat. In this case it is important to identify genuine needs that the patient has and direct the spouse's energy toward meeting them. Sometimes one must simply protect the patient from an unnecessary conflict with a family member.[55]

The end product of early planning with patients and families should be a contingency plan for pain control and symptom management that extends to the end of life in the eventuality that therapy fails. Planning entails patient education. Patients and families should know the basic complications that could occur and what the options for intervention are. In addition, a long range plan documents the joint commitment of the physician and the patient to monitoring the patient's symptoms and complications.

Long Range Contingency Planning

This type of planning considers each case from the perspective of disease, treatment and patient characteristics. One knows, for example, that specific chemotherapeutic interventions are likely to cause severe nausea and vomiting problems and oral lesions. Similarly, as death approaches, one can predict that lung cancer patients are likely to have pain, dyspnea and cough problems. Abdominal tumors are likely to cause nausea and bowel complications. Breast and prostate tumors are likely to produce bone metastasis pain. Older patients will suffer greater fatigue than younger ones and may be more prone to dementia or confusional states. The unique features of the patient define the risks for discomfort that he or she will incur.

There will be certain periods in which severe problems emerge, persist for a time, and subside (e.g., treatment toxicities), and there may be one or more chronic problems such as fatigue or loss of appetite. At the end, in the event that the rescue fails, certain complications are more likely than others to emerge. One can plan in advance for these problems.

By anticipating problems, the physician can prepare for them in advance and in some cases prevent their emergence. Using guides such as the Cancer Pain Guideline[56] published by the Agency for Health Care Policy and Research or the analgesic use guide booklet published by the American Pain Society can greatly assist in optimizing pain control. These sources provide principles for treatment as well as specific information on treatment resources and alternatives.

REFERENCES

1. Benedict S. The suffering associated with lung cancer. Cancer Nurs 1989; 12: 34-40.

2. Portenoy RK. Pain and quality of life: clinical issues and implications for research. Oncology 1990; 4: 172-178.

3. Fishman B. The treatment of suffering in patients with cancer pain. In Foley KM, Bonica JJ, Ventafridda V, editors, Advances in Pain Research and Therapy, Vol. 16, New York, Raven Press, 1990.

4. Cassell EJ. The importance of understanding suffering for clinical ethics [see comments]. J Clin Ethics 1991; 2: 81-82.

5. Cherny NI, Coyle N, Foley KM. Suffering in the advanced cancer patient: a definition and taxonomy. J Palliat Care, 1994; 10(2)57-70.

6. Chapman, CR and Gavrin, JG. Suffering and its relationship to pain. J Palliat Care 1993; 9: 5-13.

7. Willis, WD Jr, ed. The pain system: the neurobasis of nociceptive transmission in the mammalian nervous system. New York, Karger, 1985.

8. Woolf, CJ. Evidence for a central component of post-injury pain hypersensitivity. Nature 1983; 306: 686-688.

9. Woolf, CJ. Generation of acute pain: central mechanisms. Br Med Bull 1991; 47: 523-33.

10. Villanueva L, Bing Z, Bouhassira D, Le Bars D. Encoding of electrical, thermal, and mechanical noxious stimuli by subnucleus reticularis dorsalis neurons in the rat medulla. J Neurophysiol 1989; 61: 391-402.

11. Fields, HL. Pain. New York: McGraw-Hill, 1987.

12. Fillenz, M. Noradrenergic Neurons, Cambridge, Cambridge University Press, 1990.

13. Svensson, TH. Peripheral, autonomic regulation of locus coeruleus noradrenergic neurons in brain: putative implications for psychiatry and psychopharmacology. Psychopharmacology 1987; 92: 1-7.

14. Foote SL, Bloom FE, Aston-Jones G. Nucleus local coeruleus: new evidence of anatomical and physiological specificity. Physiology Review 1983; 63: 844-914.

15. Redmond DE Jr, Huang YG. Current concepts. II. New evidence for a locus coeruleus-norepinephrine connection with anxiety. Life Sci 1979; 25: 2149-2162.

16. Redmond, DE Jr. Alteration in the functions of the nucleus locus coeruleus: a possible model for studies of anxiety. In Hannin I, Usdin E, editors, Animal Models in Psychiatry and Neurology, New York, Pergamon Press, 1977.

17. Elam M, Svensson TH, Thoren P. Differentiated cardiovascular afferent regulation of locus coeruleus neurons and sympathetic nerves. Brain Res 1985; 358: 77-84.

18. McNaughton N and Mason ST. The neuropsychology and neuropharmacology of the dorsal ascending noradrenergic bundle–a review. Prog Neurobiol 1980; 14: 157-219.

19. Sumal KK, Blessing WW, Joh TH, Reis DJ, Pickel VM. Synaptic interaction of vagal afference and catecholaminergic neurons in the rat nucleus tractus solitarius. J Brain Res 1983; 277: 31-40.

20. Sawchenko PE, Swanson LW. The organization of noradrenergic pathways from the brain stem to the paraventricular and supraoptic nuclei in the rat. Brain Res Rev 1982; 4: 275.

21. Lopez JF, Young EA, Herman JP, Akil H, Watson SJ. Regulatory biology of the HPA axis: an integrative approach. In Risch SC, editor, Central Nervous System Peptide Mechanisms in Stress and Depression, Washington, DC, American Psychiatric Press, 1991.

22. Burstein R, Cliffer DK, Biesler GJ. The spinohypothalamic and spinotelecephalic tracts: direct nociceptive projections from the spinal cord to the hypothalamus and telencephalon. In Dubner R, Gebhart GF, Bond MR, editors, Proceedings of the 5th World Congress on Pain, New York, Elsevier, 1988.

23. Assenmacher I, Szafarczyk A, Alonso G, Ixart G, Barbanel G. Physiology of neuropathways affecting CRH secretion. In Ganong WF, Dallman MF, Roberts JL, editors, The Hypothalamic-Pituitary-Adrenal Axis Revisited. Ann NY Acad Sci 1987; 512: 149-161.

24. Bruera E, Miller MJ, Kuehn N, MacEachern T, Hanson J. Estimate of survival of patients admitted to a palliative care unit: a prospective study. J Pain Symptom Manage 1992; 7(2): 82-86.

25. Enck RE. The last few days. Am J Hosp Palliat Care 1992; 9(4): 11-13.

26. Lichter I, Hunt E. The last 48 hours of life. J Palliat Care 1990; 6(4):7-15.

27. Hospice and Home Care of Snohomish County. Signs That Death is Near, 1980.

28. Holden CM. Anorexia in the terminally ill cancer patient: the emotional impact on the patient and the family. Hospice J 1991; 7(3): 73-84.

29. Splinter TA. Cachexia and cancer: a clinician's view. Ann Oncol 1992; 3: 25-27.

30. Foley KM. The treatment of cancer pain. N Engl J Med 1985; 313(2): 84-95.

31. Breitbart W. Psychiatric management of cancer pain. Cancer 1989; 63(11 Suppl): 2336-2342.

32. Bonica JJ, Ventafridda V, Twycross RG. Cancer Pain. In Bonica JJ, editor, The Management of Pain, Volume I, Philadelphia, Lea & Febiger, 1990.

33. Collins D, Eary JF, Donaldson G et al. Samarium-153-EDTMP in bone metastases of hormone refractory prostate carcinoma: a Phase I/II trial. J Nucl Med 1993; 34: 1839-1844.

34. Gralla RJ. Current issues in the management of nausea and vomiting. Ann Oncol 1993; 3: S3-S7.

35. Allan SG. Nausea and vomiting. In Doyle D, Hanks GWC, MacDonald N, editor, Oxford Textbook of Palliative Care, Oxford, Oxford University Press, 1994.

36. Andrews PL. Physiology of nausea and vomiting. Br J Anaesth 1992; 69(7 Suppl 1): 2S-19S.

37. Watcha MF, White PF. Postoperative nausea and vomiting. Its etiology, treatment, and prevention. Anesthesiology 1992; 77(1): 162-184.

38. Ahmedzai. Palliation of respiratory symptoms. In Doyle D, Hanks GWC, MacDonald N, editors, Oxford Textbook of Palliative Care, Oxford, Oxford University Press, 1994.

39. Hsu DH. Dyspnea in dying patients. Can Fam Physician 1993; 39: 1635-1638.

40. Kübler-Ross E. On Death and Dying. New York: The Macmillan Publishing Company, Inc., 1969.

41. Mermann AC. Spiritual aspects of death and dying. Yale J Biol Med 1992; 65(2): 137-142.

42. Sansom A. The fear of dying alone. Nurs Elder 1992; 4(6): 39.

43. Thomasma DC. The ethics of caring for the older patient with cancer: defining the issues. Oncol Huntingt 1992; 6(2 Suppl): 124-130.

44. Smith DC, Maher MF. Achieving a healthy death: the dying person's attitudinal contributions. Hosp J 1993; 9(1): 21-32.

45. Charap AD. The knowledge, attitudes, and experience of medical personnel treating pain in the terminally ill. Mt Sinai J Med 1978; 45(4): 561-580.

46. Cleeland CS, Cleeland LM, Dar R, Rinehardt LC. Factors influencing physician management of cancer pain. Cancer 1986; 58(3): 796-800.

47. Weissman DE. Glucocorticoid treatment for brain metastases and epidural spinal cord compression: a review. J Clin Oncol 1988; 6: 543-551.

48. Grossman SA, Sheidler VR, Swedeen K, Mucenski J, Piantadosi S. Correlation of patient and caregiver ratings of cancer pain. J Pain Symptom Manage 1991; 6(2): 53-57.

49. Ferrell BR, McCaffery M, Rhiner M. Pain and addiction: an urgent need for change in nursing education. J Pain Symptom Manage 1992; 7(2): 117-124.

50. Elliott TE, Elliott BA. Physician acquisition of cancer pain management knowledge. J Pain Symptom Manage 1991; 6(4): 224-229.

51. Levin DN, Cleeland CS, Daut RL. Public attitudes toward cancer pain. Cancer 1985; 56(9): 2337-2339.

52. Cleeland CS. Measurement of pain by subjective report. In Chapman CR, Loeser JD, editors, Issues in Pain Measurement, vol. 12, Advances in Pain Research and Therapy, New York, Raven Press, 1989.

53. Foley KM. Controversies in cancer pain. Medical perspectives. Cancer 1989; 63(11 Suppl): 2257-2265.

54. Daut RL, Cleeland CS. The prevalence and severity of pain in cancer. Cancer 1982; 50(9): 1913-1918.

55. Wellisch DK, Wolcott DL, Pasnau RO, Fawzy FI, Landsverk J. An evaluation of the psychosocial problems of the homebound cancer patient: relationship of patient adjustment to family problems. J Psychosocial Oncol 1989; 7: 55-76.

56. Jacox A, Carr DB, Payne R et al. Management of Cancer Pain. Clinical Practice Guideline, Rockville MD, Agency for Health Care Policy and Research, U.S. Department of Health and Human Services, Public Health Service, 1994.

End of Life Issues
in Patients with AIDS:
Clinical and Research Considerations

Steven D. Passik
Margaret V. McDonald
Barry D. Rosenfeld
William S. Breitbart

SUMMARY. This paper examines some clinical and research considerations that are important in understanding end of life issues in patients with AIDS. Pain and other medical symptoms, neuropsychiatric complications and psychosocial factors are discussed that impact upon the views such patients may have of palliative care, physician-assisted suicide, euthanasia and the desire to hasten death. The importance of increasing physicians' ability to diagnose and treat depression, anxiety, organic mental syndromes, pain and other distressing symptoms is stressed. The possible impact that such

---

Steven D. Passik, PhD, is Assistant Attending Psychologist, Memorial Sloan-Kettering Cancer Center and Assistant Professor of Psychology in Psychiatry, Cornell University Medical College. Margaret V. McDonald, CSW, and Barry D. Rosenfeld, PhD, are Research Associates, Memorial Sloan-Kettering Cancer Center. William S. Breitbart, MD, is Associate Attending Psychiatrist at Memorial Sloan-Kettering Cancer Center and Associate Professor of Psychiatry, Cornell University Medical College.

Address correspondence to: Dr. Steven D. Passik, Department of Psychiatry, Box 421, Memorial Sloan-Kettering Cancer Center, 1275 York Avenue, New York, NY 10021.

[Haworth co-indexing entry note]: "End of Life Issues in Patients with AIDS: Clinical and Research Considerations." Passik, Steven D. et al. Co-published simultaneously in *Journal of Pharmaceutical Care in Pain & Symptom Control* (Pharmaceutical Products Press, an imprint of The Haworth Press, Inc.) Vol. 3, No. 3/4, 1995, pp. 91-111; and: *Drug Use in Assisted Suicide and Euthanasia* (ed: Margaret P. Battin, and Arthur G. Lipman) Pharmaceutical Products Press, an imprint of The Haworth Press, Inc., 1996, pp. 91-111. Single or multiple copies of this article are available from The Haworth Document Delivery Service [1-800-342-9678, 9:00 a.m. - 5:00 p.m. (EST)].

© 1996 by The Haworth Press, Inc. All rights reserved.

treatment may have on obviating the desire to hasten death that stems from unrecognized suffering is discussed. The great social diversity of the AIDS population, and the challenge it poses to palliative care specialists, and a number of social factors that affect end of life issues in our clinical experience and research are described. *[Article copies available from The Haworth Document Delivery Service: 1-800-342-9678.]*

KEYWORDS. AIDS, palliative care, physician-assisted suicide, suicide, neuropsychiatric complications, depression, anxiety, delirium, dementia, pain, suffering, minority, HIV

INTRODUCTION

End of life issues have been the subject of considerable debate in the medical community and general public over the past decade.[1-4] There have been a number of recent legal decisions and state referendums[5-7] that will have a major impact upon the physician-patient relationship at the end of life. Along with this growing public awareness, several researchers have attempted to study attitudes towards euthanasia and physician-assisted suicide among the lay public,[8,9] medical professionals,[10,11] and terminally ill patients.[12,13] However, only one study has been published to date focusing on the attitudes of HIV infected patients towards physician-assisted suicide and euthanasia.[13] This study indicated that relatively healthy ambulatory white, gay men with acquired immunodeficiency syndrome (AIDS) in an academic setting had favorable attitudes toward assisted suicide. It is unclear how the attitudes of this sample represent those of other subgroups within the AIDS population (i.e., women, minorities–a point we return to below).

Our group has been involved in the study of pain and psychosocial correlates in AIDS.[14-16] Pain in AIDS is often severe and is highly prevalent, and affecting between 40-60% of patients. Pain has a deleterious impact upon quality of life in AIDS patients as it has been associated with high levels of psychological distress, depression, suicidal ideation, physical dysfunction and poor social support.

We have recently extended our work on AIDS pain to examine the degree to which pain, psychological distress, depression, demographic and social variables are associated with attitudes favoring euthanasia and physician-assisted suicide in patients with AIDS.[17] The main predictors of the desire for physician-assisted suicide that were identified are: depression and psychological distress, religious observance, race/ethnicity, and experiencing the death of one or more friends or family members due to AIDS. Pain and high rates of physical symptom distress, in this ambulatory sample, perhaps somewhat surprisingly, were not statistically significant predictors of the desire for physician-assisted suicide. These results highlight the need for better recognition and understanding of psychiatric factors and their relationship to the desire to hasten death in AIDS patients on the part of the professionals that care for them.

In this paper, we draw upon the results of this recent empirical work and our clinical experiences as mental health professionals involved in the care of cancer and AIDS patients in highlighting the clinical issues involved in requests for assisted suicide in patients with AIDS. Clinicians involved in the primary or palliative care of patients with HIV and AIDS are, at times, confronted with requests from patients and their significant others for assistance in hastening death. In such situations, the ethical and legal debates are transformed into existential and clinical challenges. We have, in our clinical work, generally regarded requests for hastening death as "distress calls" signifying the need to address psychiatric, symptom management or social aspects of patient care more effectively, but guidelines for assessment are lacking. Organizations such as Choice in Dying and the Hemlock Society have struck a responsive chord in the public. As "Death with Dignity" initiatives are being proposed there needs to be an improvement in the knowledge and understanding of end of life issues to insure that the debate over a patient's right to die does not obscure a patient's right to quality palliative care. In our experience, we have found that the desire for assistance in hastening death is often attenuated by improvements in symptom management and psychiatric care. Below we will explore quality of life issues of terminally ill patients, particularly AIDS patients.

For many reasons, quality of life issues require special sensitivity and assessment in AIDS. AIDS and HIV+ patients are known to have high rates of co-morbid psychopathology in general and depression and suicidality in particular.[18-24] AIDS patients in the United States are unusual as compared to other populations of patients with serious medical illnesses. A large part of the AIDS population is at heightened risk for a number of mental disorders predating positive HIV serostatus. There is evidence that suggests homosexual men and intravenous drug users may have high lifetime rates of psychiatric disorders.[18,25] Patterns of drug use and life circumstances complicate the understanding of association between HIV status and psychopathology. Thus, detailed assessment and treatment of depression is crucial in the understanding of requests for assisted suicide in patients with AIDS. Pain and physical symptom distress are also very prevalent in AIDS,[26-28] are dramatically under-treated[16,29,30] and associated with the presence of depression.[16,24]

Apart from frank psychiatric disorders that require assessment, there are a number of social and emotional factors that are particular to the AIDS population that can influence requests for hastened death. The AIDS population is tremendously diverse. Issues of multiple bereavement, survivor guilt, poverty, disenfranchisement, and patient rights empowerment movements all influence the AIDS patient's view of end of life issues. These factors complicate both the assessment of requests for assisted suicide and the maintenance of acceptable quality of life. In the sections that follow, we discuss the key psychiatric, medical, and social factors that require assessment in AIDS patients in terminal stages of illness, particularly those who desire hastened death.

PSYCHIATRIC CONSIDERATIONS

In our study examining predictors of favorable attitudes toward physician-assisted suicide, depression and psychological distress were the most statistically significant correlates.[17] This points to the need to improve our ability to assess depression and distress in patients with AIDS, including those with far advanced disease, and understand its relation to the desire for assisted suicide. In the section to follow, we review the diagnosis of depression, suicidality, and distress in AIDS.

PREVALENCE OF PSYCHIATRIC DISORDERS IN THE AIDS PATIENT

The patient with advanced disease faces many stressors during the course of his/her illness, including fears of painful death, disability, disfigurement, and dependency. While such concerns are universal, the level of psychological distress is quite variable, depending on personality, coping ability, social support, and medical factors.

There have been several reports of psychiatric diagnoses seen in AIDS patients who were hospitalized and more seriously ill. Barbuto et al.[31] reviewed the psychiatric consultation data collected on 65 hospitalized patients with AIDS. Psychiatric consultations were most frequently requested to evaluate depressive symptoms, suicidal risk, and behavior related to central nervous system impairment by delirium or dementia. In this study, organic mental disorders, adjustment disorders, anxiety disorders, and affective disorders ranked in order of decreasing prevalence. Eighty percent of AIDS patients given a functional psychiatric diagnosis had the diagnosis changed to an organic mental disorder as illness progressed and cognitive impairment became more obvious. Perry and Tross[32] reported on the prevalence of psychiatric disorders seen in medically hospitalized AIDS patients at the New York Hospital. Sixty-five percent of patients were diagnosed with an organic mental disorder, and 17 percent were diagnosed with major depression. The organic mental disorders seen were predominantly AIDS dementia complex and delirium, often in combination.

In an ambulatory sample of 279 patients with AIDS spectrum disorders, Tross and her colleagues[22] reported the prevalence of psychiatric disorders. The study included asymptomatic gay men, gay men with AIDS-related complex, and gay men with frank AIDS. Patients with organic mental disorders or obvious neurological impairment were excluded. Three-quarters of the men with AIDS-related complex, one half of the AIDS patients, and two-fifths of the asymptomatic gay men were diagnosed as having a psychiatric disorder. The most common psychiatric diagnosis was adjustment disorder, seen in two-thirds of AIDS patients and more than half of patients with AIDS-related complex. Depression was present in one-quarter of the entire study population. Interestingly, men with AIDS-related complex showed the greatest distress and frequency of psychiatric disorder. Similar results were demonstrated in another group of gay or bisexual men studied by Chuang et al.[33] While substantially elevated levels of depression, mood disturbance, anxiety, and hopelessness were recorded for all patients with HIV infection, the patients classified with AIDS-related complex were the most distressed. Presumably for these patients, uncertainties about the progression of the illness, fears of suffering, and more general fears of the unknown, are more distressing than finally getting the diagnosis of AIDS. Overall, the key points of increased psychological distress for AIDS patients are time of HIV+ diagnosis, development of new symptoms, and progression to full-blown AIDS. These episodic periods of heightened emotional distress can usually be viewed as appropriate adjustment responses to the cyclical disease process. Reactions to new conditions need to run their course. For a full understanding of requests for assisted suicide, consideration of the fluctuating emotional states of the patient due to the disease cycle is necessary.

For clinical consideration it is important that these high rates of psychological distress are not solely attributed to the pain and suffering of experiencing a terminal disease. Clinicians need to bear in mind that the high rates of psychiatric disorders in patients with AIDS are in part due to the fact that subgroups in the AIDS population have high rates of psychiatric disturbance prior to HIV infection.[18,25,34] There is a higher prevalence of psychiatric disorders seen in homosexual men (with or without HIV infection) as compared to heterosexual men or the general population. Atkinson et al.[18] found that homosexual men had higher lifetime rates of substance abuse, affective and anxiety disorders than the general population. Their report suggests lifetime rates exceeding 40% in both seronegative and seropositive homosexual men. In a study using DSM-III psychiatric diagnosis of opioid addicts, Khantzian and Treece[25] found that 93% of their sample met the criteria for one or more psychiatric disorder(s) other than substance abuse. Just under half of the abusers were clinically depressed at interview. In a more recent study of injecting drug users, Lipsitz et al.[34] found the severity of depressive and anxiety symptoms in both HIV-positive and HIV-negative subjects were greater than in the general community. Many patients with AIDS, who have had lifelong struggles with psychiatric and substance abuse problems, are now being forced to deal with additional serious stressors such as advancing illness and disability, as well as greater financial concerns. The high prevalence of pre-morbid psychological distress in many AIDS patients brings to question the ability to assess whether requests of assisted suicide are really the wishes of a fully competent person. A comprehensive evaluation of the patients' lifetime psychosocial conditions would assist in determining the appropriate intervention for requests of hastened death, but further research is imperative in this area.

DEPRESSION IN PATIENTS WITH AIDS

Depressed mood and sadness can be appropriate responses as patients with life-threatening illnesses face death. These emotions can be manifestations of anticipatory grief over the impending loss of one's life, health, loved ones, and autonomy. At times though, they signal the presence of a major depressive syndrome.

The diagnosis of a major depressive syndrome in a patient with life-threatening illness often relies more on the psychological or cognitive symptoms of major depression (worthlessness, hopelessness, excessive guilt, loss of social interest and suicidal ideation), rather than the neurovegetative or somatic signs and symptoms of major depression.[35-37] The presence of neurovegetative signs and symptoms of depression, such as fatigue, loss of energy, and other somatic symptoms, is often not helpful in establishing a diagnosis of depression in the medically ill.[38] AIDS itself can produce many of these physical symptoms so characteristic of major depression in the physically healthy. The issue is complicated by the association between high rates of AIDS-related symptoms and depression.[39] The strategy of relying on the psychological or cognitive signs and symptoms of depression for diagnostic specificity also needs to be put in context of the reality of a dying person. How is the clinician to interpret feelings of hopelessness in the dying patient when there is no hope for recovery? Typically, our practice is to explore feelings of hopelessness, worthlessness, or suicidal ideation in some detail. While many AIDS patients never have a hope of a cure, they are able to maintain hope that pain can be controlled and quality of life can be maintained. Hopelessness that is pervasive and accompanied by a sense of despair or despondency is more likely to present a symptom of a depressive disorder. Similarly, patients often state that they feel they are burdening their lovers or families unfairly causing them great pain and inconvenience. Those beliefs are less likely to represent a symptom of depression than if the patient feels that their life has never had any worth, or that they are being punished for evil things they have done. Suicidal ideation, even mild and passive forms, is very likely associated with significant degrees of depression in terminally ill cancer and AIDS patients.[40,41]

In our study of interest in physician-assisted suicide and euthanasia, depression and psychological distress were the most powerful predictors of attitudes in favor of these end of life options. Yet, the diagnosis of depression is often missed in patients in the clinical setting[42-44] and the association between depression and requests for assisted suicide has not been well studied empirically.

As noted above, it is a challenge for clinicians to recognize the symptoms of depression as such. Depression is quite undertreated in patients with advanced disease. The impact of treatment for depression on the desire for hastened death has not been examined in the medically ill in general or AIDS patients specifically. The desire for hastened death has been demonstrated to be fluid over time[45] and such fluctuations may reflect changes in mood and mood disorder. Disease progression is cyclical with ongoing symptom distress, treatment, relief, new conditions, etc. Heightened emotional distress at times is a natural adjustment to this cycle and needs time to run its course. If necessary, patients can usually be treated effectively through these difficult periods with psychotropic interventions and/or supportive counseling.

AIDS AND SUICIDE

The desire for hastened death, requests for physician-assisted suicide and euthanasia must be carefully distinguished from suicidality that is a consequence of a psychiatric disorder. This issue can be complicated, especially considering that there is a dramatically increased risk of suicide in persons with AIDS. A study of the rate of suicide in 1985 in New York City residents diagnosed with AIDS revealed that the relative risk of suicide in men with AIDS aged 20 to 59 years was 36 times that of men without AIDS in the same age-range, and 66 times that of the general population.[46] AIDS patients who commit suicide generally do so within 9 months of diagnosis and usually die as a result of falling from heights or hanging. About 25 percent had made a previous suicide attempt, half were reportedly severely depressed, and 40 percent saw a psychiatrist within 4 days of committing suicide. At the time of this study, AIDS was seen primarily in the homosexual population and so it is not surprising that all suicides occurred in males. A 1986 review of our psychiatric consultation data at the Memorial Sloan-Kettering Cancer Center[31] revealed that AIDS with Kaposi's sarcoma was the single most common medical diagnosis amongst our suicidal patients. Patients with AIDS and Kaposi's sarcoma who were suicidal frequently had prominent signs of delirium, often superimposed on AIDS dementia. Poor prognosis, delirium, depression, hopelessness, loss of control, helplessness, preexisting psychopathology, and prior suicide attempts are all factors that help identify and seem to contribute to increased risk of suicide. Rundell et al.[47] report a 16 to 24 times higher rate of suicide attempts in HIV-infected Air Force personnel than in the Air Force in general. Risk factors for suicide attempts in this group of HIV seropositive individuals included: social isolation, perceived lack of social support, adjustment disorder, personality disorder, substance/alcohol abuse, past history of depression, and HIV-related interpersonal or occupational problems.

Suicidal ideation, either lifetime prevalence or current ideation, is also dramatically higher in HIV-infected individuals than in the general population or even in the cancer population.[48-51] In HIV seropositive populations of homosexual males, alcohol or substance abusers and psychiatric out-patients, prevalence rates of lifetime suicidal thoughts ranged from 50 percent to 82 percent.[48-51] HIV-negative individuals in the same at-risk populations had similar rates of suicidal ideation, thus suggesting that it is not HIV status *per se* that accounts for such high rates of suicidal ideation, but rather the psychiatric morbidity found in the at-risk groups. In addition, stage of HIV illness and the presence of such physical and psychiatric symptoms as pain and depression increase rates of current suicidal ideation.

In the Netherlands, where euthanasia and physician-assisted suicide have been recognized as acceptable medical practices, the presence of depression and pathological suicidality are reasons to exclude patients for consideration of these options. The desire for hastened death that is driven by despair and depression is unlikely to qualify as "rational" suicide in many clinicians' views. Yet, these differential diagnoses are often not straightforward. The relationship between suicidality and the desire in hastening death are likely to be different in the various subgroups of the AIDS population (though there is a lack of empirical studies). Minority patients who are depressed may have suicidal thoughts but due to their estrangement from doctors might not consider doctors as potential sources of assistance in dying. Patients who are less estranged from doctors are likely to receive better treatment for depression but might still view their doctors as a partner in the end of life.

ANXIETY IN THE PATIENT WITH AIDS

The patient with life-threatening illness presents with a complex mixture of physical and psychological symptoms in a context of a frightening reality. Thus the recognition of anxious symptoms requiring treatment can be challenging. Patients with anxiety complain of tension or restlessness, or they exhibit jitteriness, autonomic hyperactivity, vigilance, insomnia, distractibility, shortness of breath, numbness, apprehension, worry, or rumination. Often the physical or somatic manifestations of anxiety overshadow the psychological or cognitive ones, and are the symptoms that the patient most often presents.[52] The clinician must use these symptoms as a cue to inquire about the patient's psychological state, which is commonly one of fear, worry, or apprehension. The assumption that a high level of anxiety is inevitably encountered during the advanced phases of illness is neither helpful nor accurate for diagnostic and treatment purposes. In deciding whether to treat anxiety during the advanced illness, the patient's subjective level of distress is the primary impetus for the initiation of treatment. Other considerations include problematic patient behavior, such as noncompliance due to anxiety, family and staff reactions to the patient's distress, and the balancing of the risks and benefits of treatment.[53]

Anxiety, like fever, in this population is a symptom that can have many etiologies. Anxiety may be encountered as a component of an adjustment disorder, panic disorder, general anxiety disorder, phobia, or agitated depression. Additionally, in the terminally ill AIDS patient, symptoms of anxiety are most likely to arise from some medical complication of the illness or treatment, such as organic anxiety disorder, delirium, or other organic mental disorders.[52-54] Hypoxia, sepsis, poorly controlled pain, and adverse drug reactions, such as akathisia or withdrawal states, are specific entities that often present as anxiety. Patients who had been managed for long periods of time with relatively high doses of benzodiazepines or opioid analgesics for the control of anxiety or pain, often become tolerant or physically dependent upon these drugs. During terminal phases of illness, when patients become less alert, there is a tendency to minimize the use of sedating medications. It is important to consider the need to slowly taper benzodiazepines and opioid analgesics in order to prevent acute withdrawal states. Withdrawal states in medically ill patients often present first as agitation or anxiety and become clinically evident days later than might be expected in younger, healthier patients, due to impaired metabolism. Benzodiazepine withdrawal, for example, can present first as agitation or anxiety, though the diagnosis is often missed in terminally ill patients, and especially the elderly, where physiological dependence on these medications is often unrecognized. In the actively dying patient, anxiety can represent impending cardiac or respiratory arrest, pulmonary embolism, electrolyte imbalance, or dehydration.[55]

Despite the fact that anxiety in terminal illness commonly results from medical complications, it is important not to forget that psychological factors related to death and dying or existential issues, play a role in anxiety, particularly in patients who are alert and not confused. Patients frequently fear the isolation and separation of death. AIDS patients in particular have often been intimately involved with the dying process of several friends and loved ones, and their images of these others' deaths can be quite anxiety-provoking when they find themselves in advanced stages of disease. These issues can be disconcerting to clinicians who may find themselves at a loss for words that are consoling to the patient. Nonetheless, one should not avoid eliciting these concerns, listening empathically to them, and enlisting pastoral involvement where appropriate.

Many fears may influence the desire to hasten death in patients with advanced AIDS. Once again, this issue is complicated by the underrecognition and undertreatment of anxiety in AIDS patients, particularly individuals with a history of substance abuse. Anxiety in patients with AIDS often results from their sense of being unable to control aspects of their illness. Fears of prolonged suffering, loss of mental capacity, inability to predict disease course progression are all common. Physicians are often uncomfortable discussing resuscitation and advanced directives with patients for fear it will lead to loss of hope. Yet, such discussions can lower anxiety by increasing the sense of control over these concerns. The effect of having such discussions on the desire to hasten death is not well understood nor empirically studied.

ORGANIC MENTAL DISORDERS IN AIDS

Cognitive failure is unfortunately all too common in patients with advanced illness. The presence of organic mental syndromes in AIDS patients voicing requests for hastened death, assisted suicide and euthanasia, perhaps more than any other psychiatric complication of AIDS, belies the alleged rationality of such requests. The diagnosis of organic mental syndrome is often overlooked. While virtually all forms of organic mental syndromes can be seen in the patient with advanced AIDS, the most common include delirium, dementia, organic mood and organic anxiety disorders. Lipowski[56] categorized organic mental disorders into those that were characterized by general cognitive impairment (that is, delirium and dementia), and those where cognitive impairment was rather selective or limited (amnestic disorder, organic hallucinosis, organic mood disorder). With organic mental disorders where cognitive impairment is selective, limited, or relatively intact, the more prominent symptoms tend to consist of either anxiety, mood disturbance, delusions, hallucinations, or personality change.

Delirium has been characterized as an etiologically non-specific, global, cerebral dysfunction, characterized by concurrent disturbances of level of consciousness, attention, thinking, perception, memory, psychomotor behavior, emotion, and the sleep-wake cycle. Disorientation, fluctuation, or waxing and waning of the above symptoms, as well as acute or abrupt onset of such disturbances, are other critical features of delirium. Delirium is also conceptualized as a reversible process, as compared to dementia for instance. Reversibility of the process of delirium is often possible even in the patient with advanced illness, although it may not be reversible in the last 24 to 48 hours of life. This is most likely due to the fact that irreversible processes, such as multiple organ failure, are occurring in the final hours of life. Delirium occurring in these last days of life is often referred to as terminal restlessness or terminal agitation in the literature on palliative care.

At times it is difficult to differentiate delirium from dementia, since they frequently share such common clinical features as impaired memory, thinking, judgment, and disorientation. Dementia appears in relatively alert individuals with little or no clouding of consciousness. The temporal onset of symptoms in dementia is more subacute or chronically progressive, and the sleep-wake cycle seems less impaired. Most prominent in dementia are difficulties in short and long-term memory, impaired judgement and abstract thinking, as well as disturbed higher cortical functions (such as aphasia and apraxia). Occasionally one will encounter delirium superimposed on an underlying dementia in AIDS. Clinically, we can utilize a number of scales or instruments that aid us in the diagnosis of delirium, dementia, or cognitive failure.[57]

Several factors make organic mental disorders somewhat unique in the AIDS patient. Concomitant substance abuse, as well as neuropsychiatric side-effects of antiviral or chemotherapeutic agents, can cause organic mental disorders, such as organic mood disorder-manic type.[58] But by far the most important issue is the fact that the HIV virus is neurotropic, invades the central nervous system early in infection, and can result in AIDS dementia complex.

AIDS dementia complex is the most common neurological complication (organic mental disorder) of AIDS.[59] The syndrome of AIDS dementia complex is characterized by disturbances in motor performance, cognition, and behavior. It is estimated that two-thirds of AIDS patients will develop clinical dementia during the course of their illness. Patients with AIDS dementia complex clinically exhibit a triad of cognitive, motor, and behavioral disturbances. Cognitive and intellectual impairment is typically subtle in onset and progressive. Progression can be rapid or gradual, and is quite variable. Initially, the presentation is one of memory impairment, mental slowing, and impaired concentration. This can progress to global cognitive impairment with disorientation, confusion, psychosis, and mutism. Motor disturbances can begin with clumsiness, unsteady gait, tremor, impaired handwriting, and can lead to ataxia, paraplegia, myoclonus, incontinence, and seizures. Early behavioral symptoms include apathy, withdrawal, depression, and anxiety. Late behavioral changes include paranoia, agitation, confusion, psychosis, hallucinations, and affective disturbances such as mania or depression.[59]

The earliest symptoms of AIDS dementia are often mistaken for functional psychiatric disturbance. Patients often react with disbelief, denial, numbness, irritability, feelings of hopelessness, and occasionally suicidal ideation. These symptoms are common in major depression, anxiety disorders, and adjustment disorders and are easily misconstrued as an understandable reaction to the diagnosis of a life-threatening illness rather than signs of early encephalopathy.[58] As dementia progresses, the organic nature of psychiatric symptoms becomes more obvious. Formal neuropsychological testing can be quite helpful in accurately documenting AIDS dementia complex and distinguishing it from depression or an adjustment disorder.

The presence of organic mental syndrome complicates the assessment of the desire for hastening death in patients with AIDS. Questions, such as, is the organic mental syndrome transient or permanent? Does it impact upon competence? Are the attitudes expressed by the patient similar to those that were held prior to the development of cognitive problems?–can be subtle and difficult to answer. Our clinical experience suggests that even obvious delirium is often missed in patients with advanced AIDS and treatment is often not initiated. Again, the impact of treatment of organic mental syndrome on quality of life in AIDS has not been examined empirically.

PAIN AND OTHER DISTRESSING SYMPTOMS

Our group has demonstrated that pain in AIDS occurs in the context of multiple distressing medical symptoms[14] highlighting the need for palliative care in this population. Pain is reported in 40-60% of HIV+ individuals. Common pain syndromes are neuropathy, joint pains (arthritis, arthralgia, rheumatic (unspecified)), skin pain (Kaposi's sarcoma, infection), and headaches. Pain in AIDS increases with disease progression, is often severe, associated with functional impairment and produces psychological distress. However pain, like the psychological symptoms mentioned above, is too often unrecognized and dramatically undertreated in this population.[16] Using the Pain Management Index[60] as an index of the adequacy of analgesic medications being provided to patients in pain, we detected inadequate analgesia in 85% of the patients that participated in our study. This undertreatment is worse for injecting drug users and women with AIDS.[61] We have also identified patient-related barriers to pain management in AIDS. These barriers (such as the fear of addiction or of being viewed as drug-seeking) relate to fears on the part of patients that diminish their ability to feel free to seek improvements in pain control. Such estrangement from the medical profession and those who might provide for palliative care can fuel helplessness and the desire to hasten death in this population.

Pain has a profound impact on the level of emotional distress, and psychological factors such as anxiety and depression can intensify pain. In our study of the impact of pain on ambulatory HIV-infected patients,[15] depression was significantly correlated with the presence of pain. HIV-infected patients with pain were more functionally impaired, and this was highly correlated to levels of pain intensity and depression. Those who felt that pain represented a threat to their health reported more intense pain than those who did not see pain as a threat. Patients with pain were more likely to be unemployed or disabled and reported less social support.

We also examined the prevalence of suicidal ideation in this ambulatory HIV-infected population and examined the relationship between suicidal ideation, depression, and pain.[15] Suicidal ideation in ambulatory HIV-infected patients was found to be highly correlated with the presence of pain, depressed mood, and low T4 lymphocyte counts. Whereas 20% of ambulatory HIV-infected patients without pain reported suicidal thoughts, more than 40% of those with pain reported suicidal ideation. As with cancer pain patients, suicidal ideation in AIDS patients with pain is more likely to be related to a concomitant mood disturbance (depression) than to the intensity of pain experienced. The presence of pain, depressed mood, low T4 lymphocyte counts and a diagnosis of AIDS increased rates of suicidal ideation.

One surprising finding in our study of attitudes towards physician-assisted suicide in patients with AIDS was the inverse relationship between pain and positive physician-assisted suicide attitudes. The lay public and medical experts often cite intractable pain as a motivation for physician-assisted suicide requests,[19] yet this study demonstrated the reverse. Although this finding may represent an artifact of the research (since many variables were collected and analyzed and the sample as a whole was extremely symptomatic), the presence of pain as a significant predictor in the multivariate analyses suggests that this phenomenon may warrant further investigation. While few would suggest that increasing pain and disability would reduce interest in physician-assisted suicide, these findings indicate that the relationship between these variables may be more complex than often assumed.

Fatigue is also frequently reported as a distressing symptom in patients with AIDS. Darko and colleagues[62] reported that over 50% of their sample of patients with AIDS had problematic fatigue. Forty-one per cent of the sample of men that Longo and colleagues[63] studied described fatigue as a major physical concern. Yet even with this high prevalence, there are no published reports of any controlled intervention trials for the treatment of fatigue in patients with HIV disease. Interventions using non-pharmacologic (exercise, energy conservation) and pharmacologic (psychostimulants, corticosteroids) therapies for fatigue in multiple sclerosis and cancer are described in the literature yet the practice of using these interventions with HIV-infected individuals has not been widely demonstrated.

Among palliative care specialists, there is the generally held belief that good palliative care will obviate the desire for hastened death in most patients. While this may generally be true in AIDS (i.e., as it is in cancer) the issue becomes more complex because of the undertreatment of symptoms in AIDS patients. Once again, research to investigate these issues is necessary. Some of the social factors related to this undertreatment and potential consequences of not receiving adequate medical care are discussed in the next section.

SOCIAL FACTORS

Sociologically, AIDS patients represent a highly diverse group; some are disenfranchised while others have been empowered. The majority of AIDS patients are members of stigmatized groups within our society (i.e., injecting drug users, gay males, females, low socio-economic status, and minority groups) and as such, they are placed at risk for insufficient connections to medical care in general and poor palliative care in particular. This disenfranchisement can lead to requests for assisted suicide that emanate from the despair and unnecessary suffering that stems from poor palliative care. On the other hand, there are groups of people with AIDS that have been the focus of influential empowerment efforts that have changed the face of the treatment of people with life-threatening illnesses. Patients involved in such efforts may view physician-assisted suicide as a right and make special demands on caregivers even when adequate palliative care is being provided. Thus, AIDS patients present a challenge for the clinician interested in providing sufficient psychiatric support and palliative care.

DISENFRANCHISEMENT AND END OF LIFE ISSUES

Sixty-five percent of ambulatory HIV+ and AIDS patients surveyed in our study favorably endorsed statements supporting physician-assisted suicide. Not only is this proportion lower than might be expected given the growing public awareness and controversy surrounding physician-assisted suicide, it is considerably lower than previously published findings of a sample of gay white HIV+ males, in which over 90% responded that they would personally like to have the option of euthanasia if they were given a life-threatening diagnosis.[13] Our sample was a highly diverse group of gay men, injecting drug users, women and minority patients.

One possible explanation for these findings is the composition of the New York City HIV+ population. Of 260 subjects surveyed in this study, only 42 percent were caucasian, and only 20 percent of the total sample identified themselves as gay caucasian males. Past research has indicated considerably lower rates of physician-assisted suicide approval among minority populations.[64] Some speculation exists that this may reflect an overall greater skepticism of the medical profession in general, possibly generated from an historic lack of access to services. Studies have demonstrated that variation of health care utilization by individuals who are HIV+ can be predicted by looking at socio-demographic variables. Mor et al.[65] found that, when controlling for symptoms and disease stage, minorities and injecting drug users had fewer outpatient visits to primary care HIV clinics than white, gay/bisexual men. Thus, although some of the impetus behind increased public attention focused on assisted suicide has come from the gay community, this may not accurately represent the attitudes of all HIV-infected individuals. While pain in AIDS is almost universally poorly treated, it is patients who are more likely to receive good palliative care at present (i.e., middle-class, gay white males) who are probably more likely to have favorable attitudes toward physician-assisted suicide as they are less alienated from doctors. Patients at greater risk for poor palliative care (i.e., women, minorities, the poor, injecting drug users) may be less likely to favor physician-assisted suicide due to not having close ties to doctors.

EMPOWERMENT AND MULTIPLE BEREAVEMENT

AIDS patients are often multiply-bereaved. McKusick and Hilliard reported on a study in San Francisco that the average gay man with AIDS had lost nine people, with whom he had a close relationship, to AIDS.[66] In our study asking this question of a more diverse sample, the average number of losses was eight. Patients with AIDS live with the burden (guilt, isolation and/or estrangement) of being a potential source of infection to others. Despite their youth, many have participated in the terminal care of multiple friends and lovers and some of those that have outlived their peers feel guilty about their survivorship. Such experiences can lead to strong convictions about how one's own death is to be orchestrated. Patients are likely to have witnessed poorly controlled pain, suffering and loss of physical and mental integrity in these loved ones. They are likely to have experienced the intense burdens of being a primary caregiver to one or more of these losses. Thus, they are likely to be pessimistic about doctors' ability to treat pain and suffering on the one hand while wanting to spare friends and lovers the burden of caring for them. These experiences can lead to attitudes favoring physician-assisted suicide in such individuals (as our study indicated). It is a challenge for palliative care specialists to impact on those strongly held beliefs and gain the trust of individuals who have had experiences that have galvanized their views on end of life issues.

Different religious affiliations are associated with differing levels of favorable physician-assisted suicide attitudes.[8] In the general population Jews have more favorable views of physician-assisted suicide than Protestants and Protestants more than Catholics. In our study subjects who indicated that their religious affiliation was Protestant were more likely to have favorable physician-assisted suicide attitudes than other subjects. One goal of improving palliative care for patients with AIDS and better understanding these views on end of life issues should be improving integration of pastoral counselors and chaplains as members of the palliative care team.

CONCLUSION

There is an increasing likelihood that legislative proposals to legalize euthanasia and assisted suicide as a means of ending the suffering of patients with terminal illness will be accepted in some states. This paper does not attempt to debate whether requests for assisted suicide are rational or ethical, but rather we strive to emphasize the importance of understanding the psychological complexities involved in a request for hastened death. Now that AIDS is the number one cause of death among both men and women between 25 and 44 years of age, end of life issues are clearly going to demand more attention of palliative care specialists. Understanding the desire to hasten death in patients with AIDS demands improved appreciation of a number of psychiatric, social and medical factors. At present, these factors are poorly recognized and treated in the clinical situation and have not been well-studied by researchers. There have been tremendous advances in the treatment of AIDS in the recent past and we are hopeful that improvements in palliative care will soon keep pace.

REFERENCES

1. Quill TE. Doctor, I want to die. Will you help me? JAMA 1993; 270: 870-873.

2. Pellegrino ED. Compassion needs reason too. JAMA 1993; 270:874-875.

3. Caine ED, Conwell YC. Self-determined death, the physician, and medical priorities: is there time to talk? JAMA 1993; 270:875-876.

4. Kass LR. Is there a right to die? Hastings Center Report 1993; 23:34-43.

5. Altman LK. Jury declines to indict a doctor who said he aided in a suicide. The New York Times 1991; July 27:1, 10.

6. Mathews J. Washington State confronts euthanasia. The Washington Post 1991; February 6:A1, 7.

7. Annas GJ. Death by prescription: the Oregon initiative. N Engl J Med 1994; 331:1240-1243.

8. Blendon RJ, Szalay US, Knox RA. Should physicians aid their patients in dying? JAMA 1992; 267:2658-2662.

9. Genuis SJ, Genuis SK, Chang, W. Public attitudes toward the right to die. Can Med Assoc J 1994; 150:701-708.

10. Caralis PV, Hammond JS. Attitudes of medical students, housestaff, and faculty physicians toward euthanasia and termination of life-sustaining treatment. Critical Care Medicine 1992; 20:683-690.

11. Slome L, Moulton J, Huffine C, Gorter R, Abrams D. Physicians' attitudes toward assisted suicide in AIDS. J Acquir Immune Defic Syndr 1992; 5:712-718.

12. Owen C, Tennant C, Levi J, Jones M. Suicide and euthanasia: patient attitudes in the context of cancer. Psycho-oncology 1992; 1:79-88.

13. Tindall B, Forde S, Carr A, Barker S, Cooper DA. Attitudes to euthanasia and assisted suicide in a group of homosexual men with advanced HIV disease [letter]. J Acquired Immune Defic Syndromes 1993; 6:1069-1070.

14. Breitbart W. Suicide risk and pain in cancer and AIDS patients. In Current and Emerging Issues in Cancer Pain Research and Practice, edited by CP Chapman and KM Foley. Raven Press, Ltd., New York, 1993, 49-65.

15. Breitbart W, Passik S, Rosenfeld B et al. Pain in substance abusers with AIDS. [Abstract] American Pain Society, 13th Annual Meeting, Miami, FL, Nov 10-13, 1994.

16. Breitbart W, Passik S, Rosenfeld B et al. Undertreatment of pain in AIDS. [Abstract] American Pain Society, 13th Annual Meeting, Miami, FL, Nov 10-13, 1994.

17. Breitbart W, Rosenfeld BD, Passik SD. Interest in physician-assisted suicide among ambulatory HIV infected patients. (Submitted for publication) 1995.

18. Atkinson JH, Grant I, Kennedy CJ, Richman DD, Spector SA, McCutchan JA. Prevalence of psychiatric disorders among men infected with immunodeficiency virus: a controlled study. Arch Gen Psychiatry 1988; 45:859-864.

19. Williams JB, Rabkin JG, Remien RH, Gorman JM, Ehrhardt AA. Multidisciplinary baseline assessment of homosexual men with and without human immunodeficiency virus infection, II: standardized clinical assessment of current and lifetime psychopathology. Arch Gen Psychiatry 1991; 48:124-130.

20. Perry S, Fishman B, Jacobsberg L, Frances A. Relationships over 1 year between lymphocyte subsets and psychosocial variables among adults with infection by human immunodeficiency virus. Arch Gen Psychiatry 1992; 49:396-401.

21. Brown GR, Rundell JR. Prospective study of psychiatric morbidity in HIV-seropositive women without AIDS. Gen Hosp Psychiatr 1990; 12:30-35.

22. Tross S, Hirsch DA. Psychological distress and neuropsychological complications of HIV infection and AIDS. American Psychologist 1988; 11:929-934.

23. Ostrow DG, Monjan A, Joseph J, VanRaden M, Fox R, Kingsley L, Dudley J, Phair J. HIV-related symptoms and psychological functioning in a cohort of homosexual men. American Journal of Psychiatry 1989; 146:737-742.

24. Belkin GB, Fleishman JA, Stein MD, Piette J, Mor V. Physical symptoms and depressive symptoms among people with HIV infection. Psychosomatics 1992; 33:416-427.

25. Khantzian EJ, Treece C. DSM-III psychiatric diagnosis of narcotic addicts. Arch Gen Psychiatry 1985; 42:1067-1071.

26. Lebovits AK, Lefkowitz M, McCarthy D et al. The prevalence and management of pain in patients with AIDS: A review of 134 cases. Clin J Pain 1989; 5:245-248.

27. Singer EJ, Zorilla C, Fahy-Chandon B et al. Painful symptoms reported for ambulatory HIV-infected men in a longitudinal study. Pain 1993; 53:15-19.

28. O'Neill WM, Sherrard JS. Pain in human immunodeficiency virus disease: a review. Pain 1993; 54:3-14.

29. McCormack JP, Li R, Zarowny D, Singer J. Inadequate treatment of pain in ambulatory HIV patients. Clin J Pain 1994; 9:247-283.

30. Lebovits AH, Smith G, Maignan M, Lefkowitz M. Pain in hospitalized patients with AIDS: Analgesic and psychotropic medications. Clin J Pain 1994; 10: 156-161.

31. Barbuto J, Fleishman S, Holland J. Prevalence of psychiatric disorders in AIDS patients. Current Concepts in Psycho-Oncology and AIDS. Memorial Sloan-Kettering Cancer Center, 17-19 September 1987.

32. Perry SW, Tross S. Psychiatric problems of AIDS inpatients at the New York Hospital: Preliminary report. Public Health Reports 1984; 99:200-205.

33. Chuang HT, Devins GM, Hunsley JH, Gill MJ. Psychosocial distress and well-being among gay and bisexual men with human immunodeficiency virus infection. American Journal of Psychiatry; 146:876-880.

34. Lipsitz JD, Williams JBW, Rabkin JG, Remien RH, Bradbury M, el Sadr W, Goetz R, Sorrell S, Gorman JM. Psychopathology in male and female intravenous drug users with and without HIV infection. Am J Psychiatry 1994; 151: 1662-1668.

35. Clark DC, Cavanaugh S, Gibbons RD. The core symptoms of depression in medical and psychiatric patients. J Nervous and Mental Disease 1983; 171: 705-713.

36. Plumb MM, Holland J. Comparative studies of psychological function in patients with advanced cancer-1. Self-reported depressive symptoms. Psychosomatic Medicine 1977; 39:264-276.

37. Massie MJ, Holland JC. Depression and the cancer patient. Journal of Clinical Psychiatry 1990; 51:12-17.

38. Harker JO, Satz P, Del.-Jones F, Verma RC, Gan MP, Poer HL, Gould BD, Chervinsky AB. Measurement of depression and neuropsychological impairment in HIV-1 infection. Neuropsychology 1995; 9:110-117.

39. Hays RB, Turner H, Coates TJ. Social support, AIDS-related symptoms, and depression among gay men. J Consulting and Clinical Psychology 1992; 60;463-469.

40. Breitbart W. Cancer pain and suicide. Advances in Pain Research and Therapy 1990; 16:399-412.

41. Breitbart W. Suicide in cancer patients. Oncology 1987; 1:49-53.

42. Nielson AC III, Williams TA. Depression in ambulatory medical patients: Prevalence by self-report questionnaire and recognition by non-psychiatric physicians. Arch Gen Psychiatry 1980; 37:999-1004.

43. Knights EB, Folstein MF. Unsuspected emotional and cognitive disturbance in medical patients. Ann Intern Med 1977; 87:723-724.

44. Moffic HS, Paykel ES. Depression in medical in-patients. Br J Psychiatry 1975; 126:346-353.

45. Chochinov HM, Wilson KG, Enns M, Mowchun N, Levitt M. Desire for death among the terminally ill. Proceedings of the annual American Psychiatric Association meeting, 1992 May 2-6; Symposium on euthanasia and suicide in the terminally ill. Washington, DC 1992.

46. Marzuk PM et al. Increased risk of suicide in persons with AIDS. JAMA 1988; 259:1333-7.

47. Rundell JR, Kyle KM, Brown GR, Thomason JL. Risk factors for suicide attempts in a human immunodeficiency virus screening program. Psychosomatics 1992; 33:24-7.

48. Atkinson H et al. Suicide ideation and attempts in HIV illness [Abstract]. VI International Conference on AIDS. 21-24 June 1990, San Francisco, CA.

49. Drexler K et al. Suicidal thoughts, suicidal behaviors, and suicide risk of factors in HIV-seropositive and alcoholic controls [Abstract]. VI International Conference on AIDS. 21-24 June 1990, San Francisco, CA.

50. Gutierrez R et al. Coping and neuropsychological correlates of suicidality in HIV [Abstract]. VI International Conference on AIDS. 21-24 June 1990, San Francisco, CA.

51. Orr D, O'Dowd MA, McKegney FP, Natali C. A comparison of self reported suicidal behaviors in different stages of HIV infection [Abstract]. VI International Conference on AIDS. 21-24 June 1990, San Francisco, CA.

52. Holland JC. Anxiety and cancer: the patient and family. International Journal of Psychiatry in Medicine 1985-1986; 15:75-79.

53. Massie MJ. Anxiety, panic and phobias. In: Holland JC, Rowland J, eds. Handbook of Psychooncology: Psychological Care of the Patient with Cancer. New York, Oxford University Press, 1989: 300-309.

54. Foley KM. The treatment of cancer pain. New Eng J of Med 1985; 313: 84-95.

55. Strain JJ, Liebowitz MR, Klein DF. Anxiety and panic attacks in the medically ill. Psychiatry Clinics of North America 1981; 4:333-48.

56. Lipowski ZJ. Delirium (acute confusional states). JAMA 1987; 284: 1789-92.

57. Smith MJ, Breitbart WS, Platt MM. A critique of instruments and methods to detect, diagnose, and rate delirium. J Pain and Symptom Management 1995; 10:35-77.

58. Perry SW. Organic mental disorders caused by HIV: Update on early diagnosis and treatment. American Journal of Psychiatry 1990; 147:696-712.

59. Brew BJ, Sidtis JJ, Petito CK, Price RW. The Neurological complications of AIDS and human immunodeficiency virus infection. Archives of Contemporary Neurology. New York: P.A.Davis 1988:1-49.

60. Cleeland CS, Gonin R, Hatfield AK. Pain and its treatment in outpatients with metastatic cancer: the Eastern cooperative oncology group's outpatient study. N Engl J Med 1994; 330:582-596.

61. Breitbart W, Passik S, Rosenfeld B et al. Patient related barriers to pain management in AIDS. [Abstract] American Pain Society, 13th Annual Meeting, Miami, FL, Nov 10-13, 1994.

62. Darko DF, McCutchan JA, Kripke DF, Gillin JC, Golshan S. Fatigue, sleep disturbance, disability and indices of progression of HIV infection. Am J Psychiatry 1992; 149:514-520.

63. Longo MB, Spross JA, Locke AM. Identifying major concerns of persons with acquired immunodeficiency syndrome: a replication. Clinical Nurse Specialist 1990; 4:21-26.

64. Caralis PV, Davis B, Wright K, Marcial E. The influence of ethnicity and race on attitudes toward advance directives, life-prolonging treatments, and euthanasia. J Clinical Ethics 1993; 4:155-165.

65. Mor V, Fleishman JA, Dresser M, Piette J. Variation in health service use among HIV-infected patients. Medical Care 1992; 30: 17-29.

66. Hedge B. Psychosocial aspects of HIV infection. AIDS Care 1991; 3:409-412.

LEGAL AND REGULATORY ISSUES IN ASSISTED SUICIDE AND EUTHANASIA

A View of Current Law on Withholding and Withdrawing Treatment at the End of Life

Robert T. Angarola
Gail P. Middlekauff

SUMMARY. Focussing on current law in Washington, California, the District of Columbia, Michigan, and New York as illustrations of

Robert T. Angarola, JD, is a partner in the law firm of Hyman, Phelps & McNamara, P.C. in Washington, DC, Director of the U.S. Cancer Pain Relief Committee and a former General Counsel of the White House Office of Drug Abuse Policy. Gail Middlekauff, JD, is an associate with Hyman, Phelps & McNamara, P.C. and also earned a Masters degree with an emphasis in bioethics at the Virginia Theological Seminary.

Address correspondence to: Mr. Robert T. Angarola, Hyman, Phelps & McNamara, P.C., 700 Thirteenth Street, N.W., Suite 1200, Washington, DC 20005.

[Haworth co-indexing entry note]: "A View of Current Law on Withholding and Withdrawing Treatment at the End of Life." Angarola, Robert T., and Gail P. Middlekauff. Co-published simultaneously in *Journal of Pharmaceutical Care in Pain & Symptom Control* (Pharmaceutical Products Press, an imprint of The Haworth Press, Inc.) Vol. 3, No. 3/4, 1995, pp. 113-125; and: *Drug Use in Assisted Suicide and Euthanasia* (ed: Margaret P. Battin, and Arthur G. Lipman) Pharmaceutical Products Press, an imprint of The Haworth Press, Inc., 1996, pp. 113-125. Single or multiple copies of this article are available from The Haworth Document Delivery Service [1-800-342-9678, 9:00 a.m. - 5:00 p.m. (EST)].

© 1996 by The Haworth Press, Inc. All rights reserved.

113

how states approach medical decision-making, this article exhibits differences among statutory provisions concerning withholding and withdrawal of treatment and in the use of pain-relieving medication. Statutes in some states, while repudiating the hastening of death, acknowledge the individual's right to manage his or her own medical treatment through an advance health care directive or declaration; others have not legislated in this area, and issues are resolved judicially rather than legislatively. *[Article copies available from The Haworth Document Delivery Service: 1-800-342-9678.]*

KEYWORDS. Law, Washington, California, District of Columbia, Michigan, New York, decision-making, withholding and withdrawing treatment, analgesic overuse, pain, natural process of dying, life-sustaining treatment, assisted suicide, euthanasia, living will, declaration, durable power of attorney for health care, Delio, natural death statutes

Under the Constitution of the United States, each state has the power to enact legislation to protect the health and welfare of their citizens. "[T]he protection of a person's *general* right to privacy . . . is, like the protection of his property and of his very life, left largely to the law of the individual States."[1] States can enact legislation pertaining to euthanasia, assisted suicide, and issues of health care. State courts interpret these laws.

Current law does not sanction euthanasia. Much discussion surrounds the concept of assisted suicide. If assisted suicide is introduced into American law, it will most likely come through judicial trends in the nontreatment of incompetent patients.[2]

At the present time, the law distinguishes between assisted suicide and a patient's right to refuse medical treatment. The statutes of most states recognize an individual's right to make medical treatment decisions related to the withholding or withdrawal of medical treatment that will be implemented at the end of life through an advance directive for health care. Typically, the withholding or withdrawal of medical treatment still requires providing palliative care.

This article focuses on recent laws in Washington, California, the District of Columbia, Michigan, and New York as random illustrations of how these states approach medical decision-making. Statutory provisions differ even among the five states reviewed in this article. Washington, California, and the District of Columbia provide for advance directives.[3] Michigan has established a commission to study issues surrounding the voluntary ending of life. New York does not recognize advance directives by statute.

The language of each statute is precise and the conditions for compliance are explicit. In order to convey the unequivocal nature of the legal rights and obligations set forth in these statutes, portions of the laws are quoted.

State statutes consistently undergo revision in response to the evolution of ethical debate. However, the current laws within each state, and the judicial decisions that interpret these laws, establish the conditions of liability of medical personnel when withholding or withdrawing medical treatment. Therefore, medical personnel need to be aware of the laws of the state in which they practice.

WASHINGTON

The Natural Death Act of the state of Washington (the Washington Act) specifically repudiates mercy killing, as well as any affirmative or deliberate act or omission to end life other than to permit the natural process of dying.[4] Promoting a suicide attempt, by knowingly causing or aiding another person to attempt suicide, is a class C felony.[5]

The Washington Act expresses the fundamental right of adult persons to control decisions relating to their own medical care, including the decision to have life-sustaining procedures withheld or withdrawn at the end of life. The statute states that prolongation "of the process of dying for persons with a terminal condition or permanent unconscious condition may cause loss of patient dignity, and unnecessary pain and suffering, while providing nothing medically necessary or beneficial to the patient."[6] However, the Washington Act directs physicians and nurses *not* to withhold or diminish providing pain medication that is intended to alleviate pain and further the patient's comfort.[7]

In recognition of the principle that an individual may decide to have life-sustaining procedures withheld or withdrawn in instances of a terminal condition, the Washington Act establishes the conditions for a legally enforceable written advance directive.[8] However, the statute makes clear that the provision for an advance directive does not sanction mercy killing, physician-assisted suicide, or any affirmative action, or lack of action, to terminate life, other than to allow the natural process to occur.[9]

The Washington Act defines a "terminal condition" as "an incurable and irreversible condition caused by injury, disease, or illness, that, within reasonable medical judgment, will cause death within a reasonable period of time in accordance with accepted medical standards, and where the application of life-sustaining treatment serves only to prolong the process of dying."[10] In determining what is the moment of death, one Washington case held that "death" is both a legal and a medical question. In the view of the court, the law should define the legal standard of death. That standard is brain death. However, the medical profession should decide if brain death has occurred in accordance with accepted medical practices.[11]

A "life-sustaining treatment" is "any medical or surgical intervention that uses mechanical or other artificial means, including artificially provided nutrition and hydration, to sustain, restore, or replace a vital function, which, when applied to a qualified patient, would serve only to prolong the process of dying."[12] A "qualified patient" is an adult patient who has been diagnosed in writing by the attending physician as suffering from a terminal condition, or is a patient who has been diagnosed in writing by two physicians (one of whom is the attending physician) to be in a permanent unconscious condition.[13]

A physician, a health care provider under a physician's direction, or a health facility and its employees who in good faith withhold or withdraw life-sustaining treatment from a qualified patient in accordance with a directive are immune from civil and criminal liability or sanction for unprofessional conduct, absent negligence.[14] Nor will a physician, health facility, or health personnel be criminally or civilly liable for *failing* to give effect to a directive *if* the patient has been informed of any policy or practice that might affect the honoring of the directive.[15]

No health care practitioner may be *forced* against his or her wishes to comply with a directive nor be discriminated against in employment or professional privilege for this reason.[16] Also, no physician, health care facility or provider, or health care service plan may require an individual to execute a directive as a condition for receiving insurance or health care services.[17]

In Washington, an incompetent patient does not lose the right to consent to termination of life-supporting care. The family of the individual may assert the right on the individual's behalf. In addition, if an individual has no family, one Washington case held that the court should appoint a guardian. If the treating physician and prognosis committee unanimously consent to withhold treatment, and the guardian concurs, judicial approval for termination of treatment is then not required.[18]

To summarize, the state of Washington rejects euthanasia and assisted suicide. However, Washington law provides that the direction of an adult to withhold or withdraw life-sustaining procedures when the individual is terminally ill is not an act of suicide or a homicide.[19] Alleviation of pain should continue. No health care provider is civilly or criminally liable for compliance with a directive.

CALIFORNIA

California's Natural Death Act (the California Act) expressly repudiates mercy killing, assisted suicide, or "any affirmative or deliberate act or omission to end life other than to permit the natural process of dying."[20] The statute also provides that a person who aids, advises, or encourages another to commit suicide is guilty of a felony.[21] In 1992, a legislative initiative, Proposition 161, was *rejected* by California voters. The initiative would have provided that death due to a request for assistance in dying would not be considered suicide, and a physician who assisted in a death would not be criminally liable.

California recognizes the fundamental right of an adult to control medical care decisions. The California Act provides for a written declaration that establishes conditions for the withholding or withdrawal of life-sustaining treatment if, in the future, an individual becomes terminally ill or permanently unconscious.[22] Death resulting from the withholding or withdrawal of a life-sustaining treatment under the statute is not a suicide or homicide.[23]

Life-sustaining treatment is "any medical procedure or intervention that, when administered to a qualified patient, will serve only to prolong the process of dying or an irreversible coma or persistent vegetative state."[24] A qualified patient is "a patient 18 or more years of age who has executed a declaration and who has been diagnosed and certified in writing by the attending physician and a second physician who has personally examined the patient to be in a terminal condition or permanent unconscious condition.[25]

A "terminal condition" is "an incurable and irreversible condition that, without the administration of life-sustaining treatment, will, within reasonable medical judgment, result in death within a relatively short time."[26] A "permanent unconscious condition" is "an incurable and irreversible condition that, within reasonable medical judgment, renders the patient in an irreversible coma or persistent vegetative state."[27] In a controversial case, one California court recognized the right of a competent individual to disconnect life-support equipment although the patient did not suffer from a terminal illness.[28]

A declaration is implemented when the patient's attending physician and a second physician, who has personally examined the patient, diagnose and certify that the patient is in a terminal condition or permanently unconscious condition and can no longer make decisions regarding administration of life-sustaining treatment.[29] The provisions for a declaration do not affect the responsibility of the attending physician or health care provider to provide treatment for a patient's comfort or the alleviation of pain.[30]

A physician or other health care provider is not subject to civil or criminal liability, or discipline for unprofessional conduct, for implementing a declaration. However, the physician or other health care provider must act in accordance with reasonable medical standards and in good faith that the action is consistent with the statute and the desires of the patient.[31] A physician unwilling to comply with the directive must transfer care of the patient to a physician or health care provider who is willing to do so.[32] Wilful failure to transfer the care of a patient is a misdemeanor.[33]

A declaration is not valid if the declarant is a patient in a skilled nursing facility when the declaration is executed, unless one of the two witnesses to the declaration is a patient advocate or ombudsman.[34] Further, no one can demand the execution of a declaration as a condition for obtaining insurance or health care services.[35]

Under the California law, a declaration that is in compliance with the law of the state in which it is executed is valid in California.[36] As well, a declaration that is *not* in compliance with the law of the state in which it is executed is valid in California if it substantially complies with California requirements.[37]

One California case held that the declaration is not the exclusive means by which an incompetent person can express legally supportable wishes regarding the withholding of life-sustaining measures. In the court's opinion, the fundamental right of individuals to control their own medical treatment survives incompetence. If an individual is incompetent, a conservator can make a good faith decision regarding treatment that reflects the best interests of the incompetent individual.[38]

In summary, California, like Washington, repudiates euthanasia and assisted suicide. The provisions in the California Act are similar to those in the Washington Act. As in Washington, alleviation of pain continues despite the cessation of life-sustaining treatment. Courts in both states have extended the right to incompetent persons, and recognized legal means for exercising health care decisions outside the scope of the statute. Both Acts absolve health care personnel and providers from civil and criminal liability for giving effect to a declaration.

However, in contrast to the Washington Act, the California Act extends a declaration to a condition of irreversible coma or persistent vegetative state. Also, California law does not qualify the medical procedure as utilizing mechanical or artificial means. California explicitly recognizes declarations valid under other state laws.

DISTRICT OF COLUMBIA

The District of Columbia's Health and Safety Code (the Code) express-ly repudiates mercy killing or any affirmative or deliberate act or omission to end a human life other than to permit the natural process of dying.[39]

The Code is an interesting blend of the Washington and California Acts, along with its own unique provisions. The following discussion highlights similarities and differences between the three statutes.

The Code provides for any person 18, or older, to execute a declaration directing the withholding or withdrawal of life-sustaining procedures in the case of a terminal condition.[40] The definition of "terminal condition" in the Code is identical to that of the Washington Act. The definition of "life-sustaining procedures" is similar to that of Washington's, although the Code does not qualify life-sustaining procedures as mechanical or artificial. Also, the Washington Act speaks of imminent death, whereas the Code uses the phrase "death will occur" whether or not the life-sustaining procedure is utilized.[41]

The duty imposed upon the physician to confirm a terminal condition under the Code is slightly different than that in Washington and California. The Code provides that, if the attending physician has knowledge that a patient has executed a declaration, upon diagnosis of a terminal condition, the physician, must "without delay" provide for written certification. The physician must also obtain confirmation of the patient's terminal condition by a second physician, so that the patient is deemed a qualified patient.[42]

Upon certification, a patient becomes a qualified patient only if the physician verbally or in writing informs the patient of his or her terminal condition and documents the communication in the patient's medical re-cord. However, if the patient is unable to comprehend the communication, the patient becomes a qualified patient immediately upon certification.[43] An attending physician who does not comply with this provision is consid-ered to have committed an act of unprofessional conduct.[44]

As in Washington and California, the withholding or withdrawing of life-sustaining procedures from a qualified patient does not constitute suicide or assisted suicide, and will not subject a physician, health care professional, or health facility acting in accordance with the code to crimi-nal or civil liability.[45] However, under the Code, an attending physician who does not comply with the declaration is guilty of unprofessional conduct if he does not transfer the qualified patient to a physician who will honor the declaration.[46] The Washington Act does not specify a penalty. In contrast, the California Act makes this action a misdemeanor.

Both the California Act and the Code explicitly recognize the decisions of a qualified patient even if the patient has executed a declaration. The

Code specifies that the desires of a qualified patient will supersede the effect of a declaration.[47]

The provisions in the Code for the revocation of the declaration are similar to those in the Washington Act.[48] The restrictions if the declarant is in an intermediate care or skilled care facility is similar to that in the California Act.[49] The Washington Act does not contain such a provision. As in Washington and California, a declaration may not affect life or health insurance.[50]

Unlike Washington and California, the Code explicitly provides that the statutory recognition of a declaration does not obviate any other lawful withholding or withdrawal of life-sustaining procedures.[51] Also, the *absence* of a declaration does not raise a presumption of consent to the use or withholding of life-sustaining procedures if an individual is terminally ill.[52]

MICHIGAN

Much national attention has focused on the state of Michigan due to Dr. Jack Kevorkian, a resident of the state who has assisted in multiple suicides. In 1993, in response to Dr. Kevorkian's activities, the state of Michigan enacted a law making assisted suicide a felony. State courts in Michigan are currently hearing cases that challenge the constitutionality of this law.

The Michigan legislature passed an act to establish the Michigan Commission of Death and Dying, in order to study and develop recommendations pertaining to ethical and public health questions regarding the voluntary ending of human life, with or without assistance.[53] Under the Act, a voluntary termination of an individual's life does not include "the administration of medication or medical treatment intended . . . to relieve . . . pain or discomfort, unless that administration is also independently and specifically intended by the person to cause the end of his or her life."[54]

The Commission was directed to submit recommendations for legislation concerning a wide range of issues surrounding the voluntary self-termination of life. These issues include the proper aims of such legislation, an assessment of the consensus in the state of the morality of both the voluntary ending of life and the assistance of another person in the termination of life.

The Commission will also evaluate the basis for the patient's decision, including apprehension or existence of physical pain, disease, or disability. In addition, the Commission will consider any differentiation between physical as opposed to psychological conditions, terminal as opposed to nonterminal conditions, and the withdrawal or withholding of medical treatment in contrast to the administration of medication, if both are in furtherance of voluntary cessation of life.[55]

In regard to a person assisting in another's voluntary attempt to end life, the Commission will evaluate the nature of the assistance, which may range from inaction to participation that incurs immediate risk to the person assisting. As well, the Commission will consider issues of the motivation of the person assisting, and the patient's awareness of his or her true condition.[56]

Further issues under consideration are the legal status of suicide, living wills, durable powers of attorney for health care, the common law right to refuse medical care or treatment, and constitutional freedoms bearing on the voluntary ending of an individual's life. The Commission will also study methods of preventing the voluntary ending of life if prevention becomes an aim of the legislation.[57]

Effective at the same time is a provision that makes assisted suicide a felony. If an individual knows that another person intends to commit suicide, an individual is guilty of criminal assistance to suicide if the individual intentionally provides the physical means for the other's suicide or participates in a physical act by which the other person attempts suicide.[58] However, this provision does not apply to the withholding or withdrawal of medical treatment.[59] Also, it does not apply to the administration of medications or procedures with the intent to relieve pain or discomfort, even if this increases the risk of death.[60]

NEW YORK

New York's criminal statute makes promoting a suicide a class E felony. Intentionally causing or aiding another person to attempt suicide constitutes promoting a suicide.[61] Aiding a suicide attempt by the use of force or deception constitutes an attempt to commit murder.[62]

New York's Public Health Law provides a right to control the course of medical treatment by codifying conditions of consent.[63] There is, however, no statutory recognition of a written directive containing decisions respecting life-sustaining treatment.

In the absence of state legislation pertaining to requests to terminate life-sustaining treatment for incompetent patients, the New York Supreme Court, Appellate Division, in *Delio v. Westchester County Medical Center*,[64] reviewed the question of whether the common law right to decline medical treatment encompasses a right to remove or withhold artificially-delivered nutrition and hydration to an individual in a persistent vegetative state. The Court described the issues involved in the case as moral, ethical, philosophical, social, and legal.

Daniel Delio was a 33-year-old exercise physiologist with a doctor of philosophy degree in exercise physiology. Complications from routine surgery left him in a chronic vegetative state with no cognitive awareness and no hope for improvement. He could breathe spontaneously, but could not chew food or swallow. Two artificial devices provided nutrition and hydration. However, he was not terminally ill. Although he had not executed any type of "living will," in the course of his adult life he had expressed the clear and emphatic opinion that, if he became comatose, he did not wish the prolongation of his life through artificial means.

To reflect her husband's wishes, Julianne Delio applied for an order appointing her as conservator in order to direct the discontinuance of all medical treatment provided to her husband. The Medical Center, which provided Daniel Delio's care, opposed the application because termination of treatment was contrary to its commitment to preserving life. The Medical Center also resisted direction compelling it to act against this interest.

Even though Daniel Delio was relatively young, not terminally ill, and was kept alive by a feeding tube, not a respirator, the Court held that Daniel Delio's wife, as conservator, was authorized to direct discontinuance of nutrition and hydration, in compliance with directions made to her by her husband while he was competent. Rather than force the Medical Center to act contrary to its perceived ethical duty, the Court directed the Medical Center to comply with Daniel Delio's wishes, or to transfer him to a facility that would do so. The Court reiterated the established common law right to refuse medical treatment. The Court cited extensive legal precedent for extending this right to incompetent patients.

The Court also held that withholding artificial nutrition and hydration is not distinguishable from other artificial devices used to sustain life. Further, the right to refuse medical treatment is not limited by age and medical condition, such as the absence of a terminal illness. In fact, in the opinion of the Court, the absence of a terminal illness in an individual in a chronic vegetative state may reinforce the decision to discontinue life-sustaining treatment because of the potentiality of an extended period in this state.

Further, the Court held that, absent traditional countervailing state interest, the court should honor the patient's wishes. The interest in preventing suicide was not relevant. In the opinion of the Court, suicide requires a specific intent to die, whereas a desire for termination of artificial life-support systems signified only an intent to live free of mechanical devices. Also, there were no innocent third parties to protect.

In the opinion of the court, medical intervention at all costs is no longer the ethical standard in medicine, so the decision to refuse treatment in this case did not jeopardize the integrity of the medical profession. A physician who follows the choice of a competent adult patient to refuse medical treatment has not violated his professional responsibilities as long as he advises the patient of the risks of foregoing the treatment.

To conclude, New York is a state that does not provide statutory recognition of a written directive regarding life-sustaining treatment at the end of life. Therefore, the right of a competent adult, or surrogate for an incompetent individual, to terminate life-sustaining treatment is based upon common law and judicial precedent. The *Delio* case reflects a holding compatible with other cases reviewing similar issues.

CONCLUSION

Many state statutes have addressed issues surrounding medical decisions at the end of life. States, such as Washington, California, and the District of Columbia, while repudiating the hastening of death, acknowledge the individual's right to manage his or her own medical treatment through an advance health care directive or declaration.[65] Legislation, such as Natural Death Statutes, sets forth the legal requirements for these rights. This establishes a basis for decision-making.

Other states, such as New York, have not legislated in the area of advance directives for health care. Therefore, the determination of issues surrounding medical care decisions in the state are resolved judicially rather than legislatively. Characteristically, legal decisions reflect individual fact situations, drawing upon legal precedent where applicable.

Issues of decision-making at the end of life are not static, but are constantly evolving. It is essential for every individual, as well as physician, health care personnel, and health care provider to have knowledge of the current law and new developments in the law of the state in which each practices his or her profession.

REFERENCES

1. *Katz v. United States*, 389 U.S. 347, 350-51 (1967).
2. Rosenblum and Forsythe, "The Right to Assisted Suicide: Protection of Autonomy or an Open Door to Social Killing?" 6 Issues in Law & Medicine, 3, 12 (1990).
3. The paper will not discuss durable powers of attorney for health care.
4. Wash. Rev. Code Ann. § 70.122.100.

5. Wash. Rev. Code Ann. § 9A.36.060.

6. Wah. Rev. Code Ann. § 70.122.010.

7. *Id.*

8. Wash. Rev. Code Ann. § 70.122.030(1). The statutory directive is not the one only method for the withholding or withdrawing life-sustaining treatment. See In the Matter of Guardianship of Hamlin, 102 Wash.2d 810. 689 P.2d 1372 (1984).

9. Wash. Rev. Code Ann. § 70.122.100.

10. Wash. Rev. Code Ann. § 70.122.020(9).

11. *In re Welfare of Bowman*, 94 Wash.2d 407, 617 P.2d 731 (1980). The case did not decide whether a persistent vegetative state, in which some brain functioning exists, is included within brain death.

12. Wash. Rev. Code Ann. § 70.122.020(5).

13. Wash. Rev. Code Ann. § 70.122.020(8).

14. Wash. Rev. Code Ann. § 70.122.051.

15. Wash. Rev. Code Ann. § 70.122.060(2) and (3).

16. Wash. Rev. Code Ann. § 70.121.060(3).

17. Wash. Rev. Code Ann. § 70.122.070(3).

18. *In the Matter of Guardianship of Hamlin*, 102 Wash.2d 810, 689 P.2d 1372 (1984).

19. Wash. Rev. Code Ann. § 70.122.070(1).

20. Cal. Health & Safety Code § 7191.5(g).

21. Calif. Penal Code § 401.

22. Cal. Health & Safety Code § 7185.5.

23. Cal. Health & Safety Code § 7191.5(a). The opportunity to execute a directive does not supersede any other lawful right that an individual may have to make medical care decisions. *Barber v. Superior Court of State of Cal.*, 195 Cal.Rptr. 484(Cal.App. 2 Dist. 1983).

24. Cal. Health & Safety Code § 7186(d).

25. Cal. Health & Safety Code § 7186(h).

26. Cal. Health & Safety Code § 7186(j).

27. Cal. Health & Safety Code § 7186(e).

28. *Bartling v. Superior Ct. (Glendale Adven. Med.)*, 209 Cal.Rptr. 220 (Cal.App.2 Dist. 1984).

29. Cal. Health & Safety Code § 7187.5.

30. Cal. Health & Safety Code § 7189.5(b).

31. Cal. Health & Safety Code § 7190.5.

32. Cal. Health & Safety Code § 7190.

33. Cal. Health & Safety Code § 7191(a).

34. Cal. Health & Safety Code § 7187.

35. Cal. Health & Safety Code § 7191.5(c).

36. Cal. Health & Safety Code § 7192.5.

37. Cal. Health & Safety Code § 7193.5.

38. *Conservatorship of Drabick*, 245 Cal.Rptr.840 (cal.App.6Dist. 1988).

39. D.C. Code Ann. § 6-2430.

40. D.C. Code Ann. § 6-2422.
41. D.C. Code Ann. § 6-2421.
42. D.C. Code Ann. § 6-2425(a). The Code's definition of "qualified patient" is similar to that of Washington's. D.C. Code Ann. § 6-2421(5).
43. D.C. Code Ann. § 6-2425(b).
44. D.C. Code Ann. § 6-2425(c).
45. D.C. Code Ann. § 6-2427(a), 6-2428(a).
46. D.C. Code Ann. § 6-2427(b).
47. D.C. Code Ann. § 6-2426.
48. D.C. Code Ann. § 6-2424.
49. D.C. Code Ann. § 6-2423.
50. D.C. Code Ann. § 6-2428(b) and (c).
51. D.C. Code Ann. § 6-2429.
52. *Id.*
53. Mich. Compiled Laws Ann. § 752.1021.
54. Mich. Compiled Laws Ann. § 752.1022(f).
55. Mich. Compiled Laws Ann. § 752.1024.
56. *Id.*
57. *Id.*
58. Mich. Compiled Laws Ann. § 752.1027(1).
59. Mich. Compiled Laws Ann. § 752.1027(2).
60. Mich. Compiled Laws Ann. § 752.1027(3).
61. N.Y. Penal Law § 120.30.
62. N.Y. Penal Law § 120.35.
63. N.Y. Public Health Law § 2504.
64. 516 N.Y.S.2d 677 (A.D.2Dept. 1987).
65. Wash. Rev. Code Ann. § 70.122.030, Cal. Health & Safety Code § 7186.5, D.C. Code Ann. § 2422.

Is Physician Aid-in-Dying
a Constitutional Right?

Kathryn L. Tucker

SUMMARY. A majority of states, including Washington and New York, have statutes that prohibit aiding suicide. This article presents the argument employed in a constitutional challenge to Washington's statute. By prohibiting mentally competent, terminally ill patients from hastening death by self-administering drugs, the state intrudes into and controls a profoundly and uniquely personal decision, one that is properly reserved to the individual, to be made in consultation with his or her doctor. This argument rests on *Casey* and *Cruzan* concerning constitutional liberty interests, and addresses the issue of equal protection. A case concerning aiding suicide in terminal illness will eventually reach the U.S. Supreme Court; if a federal constitutional right is recognized, states will likely be allowed to regulate but not prohibit physician-assisted death; if not, litigation will move to states' courts, and activity will increase in state legislatures. *[Article copies available from The Haworth Document Delivery Service: 1-800-342-9678.]*

Kathryn L. Tucker, JD, is an attorney with the firm of Perkins Coie in Seattle Washington. Ms. Tucker is lead counsel in *Compassion in Dying et al. v. Washington*, the first federal challenge to the constitutionality of a state statute prohibiting assisting suicide, and in *Quill et al. v. Koppell*, a similar challenge pending in New York. Ms.Tucker served as counsel to the sponsors of Initiative 119, the first effort nationwide to legalize physician aid-in-dying for mentally competent, terminally ill patients.

Address correspondence to: Kathryn L. Tucker, Perkins Coie, 1201 Third Avenue, 40th Floor, Seattle, WA 98101-3099.

[Haworth co-indexing entry note]: "Is Physician Aid-in-Dying a Constitutional Right?" Tucker, Kathryn L. Co-published simultaneously in *Journal of Pharmaceutical Care in Pain & Symptom Control* (Pharmaceutical Products Press, an imprint of The Haworth Press, Inc.) Vol. 3, No. 3/4, 1995, pp. 127-137; and: *Drug Use in Assisted Suicide and Euthanasia* (ed: Margaret P. Battin, and Arthur G. Lipman) Pharmaceutical Products Press, an imprint of The Haworth Press, Inc., 1996, pp. 127-137. Single or multiple copies of this article are available from The Haworth Document Delivery Service [1-800-342-9678, 9:00 a.m. - 5:00 p.m. (EST)].

© 1996 by The Haworth Press, Inc. All rights reserved.
127

KEYWORDS. Law, Washington, constitutional issues, liberty, privacy, terminal illness, suicide, assisted suicide, physician-assisted suicide, *Casey, Cruzan,* refusal of treatment, withdrawal of treatment, equal protection, abortion, nutrition and hydration

INTRODUCTION

A majority of states, including Washington and New York, have statutes that prohibit aiding suicide. These statutes are understood to prohibit physicians from assisting their mentally competent, terminally ill patients to hasten death. The assisted suicide statutes in Washington and New York have recently been challenged in federal court under the Fourteenth Amendment to the United States Constitution.[1] In addition to these federal cases, the Michigan State courts have confronted similar issues in various challenges to Michigan laws prohibiting assisted suicide. In December 1994, the highest Michigan State court ruled that the Constitution provides no right to physician-assisted death. The United States Supreme Court declined to review this case.

Until November 1994, legislative efforts to establish the right to physician aid-in-dying had not succeeded. A number of states, including Washington (in 1991) and California (in 1992), considered, but narrowly failed to approve, initiative measures permitting physician aid-in-dying. Oregon passed such a measure in November 1994. A lawsuit attempting to prohibit the Oregon law from taking effect was immediately filed by anti-choice activists.[2] Several states have appointed "Blue Ribbon" Task Forces to analyze the issue and make recommendations to the state legislatures. The Task Forces have split on the issue: New York's recommended against legislative reform; Michigan's favored legislative reform.

Plaintiffs in the federal cases maintain that the Constitution protects the right of mentally competent, terminally ill persons to choose to hasten their death by self-administering drugs prescribed by their doctor for that purpose–a manner that is sure to result in death, is nonviolent, and preserves dignity.[3]

SUMMARY OF THE CONSTITUTIONAL CHALLENGE

The Fourteenth Amendment Protects Individual Liberty and Equality

The United States Supreme Court has consistently recognized that the protection afforded by the Fourteenth Amendment on protection of liberty extends to important personal decisions that individuals make about their lives and how they will live them. The challenged statutes, which make aiding a suicide a criminal act, prevent mentally competent, dying citizens from choosing to shorten the period of suffering before death by self-administering drugs prescribed for the purpose of hastening death. The state thus intrudes into and controls a profoundly and uniquely personal decision, one that is properly reserved to the individual, to be made in consultation with his or her doctor. These statutes thereby abridge the liberty guaranteed by the Fourteenth Amendment.

Equal Protection

A somewhat unusual aspect of the challenged laws is that they do not seek to punish suicide, or attempted suicide, itself; citizens have the right to refuse, or direct the withdrawal of, life-sustaining treatment with the intent to hasten death. Physicians who comply with such requests are immune from prosecution under the challenged statutes. Some terminally ill patients, thus, are able to choose to hasten their inevitable death with medical assistance. This distinction between terminally ill patients whose condition involves life-sustaining treatment and those whose condition does not violates the Equal Protection Clause of the Fourteenth Amendment.

THE CONSTITUTIONAL RIGHT
TO CHOOSE A HUMANE, HASTENED DEATH

Competent, Terminally Ill Adults Have the Right to Choose to Hasten Inevitable Death with Physician-Prescribed Medications

Competent, Terminally Ill Adults Have a Liberty Interest in Making End-of-Life Decisions Free of Undue Governmental Interference

> The Fourteenth Amendment provides that the state may not "deprive any person of life, liberty, or property, without due process of law." In *Planned Parenthood v. Casey,*[4] the Supreme Court recognized the right of the woman to choose to have an abortion before viability and to obtain it without undue interference from the State. Before viability, the State's interests are not strong enough to support prohibition of abortion or the imposition of a substantial obstacle to the woman's effective right to elect the procedure.

The Court stated:[5]

> Constitutional protection of the woman's decision to terminate her pregnancy derives from the Due Process Clause of the Fourteenth Amendment. It declares that no State shall "deprive any person of life, liberty, or property, without due process of law." The controlling word in the case before us is "liberty." *Casey* reiterated that the liberty protected by the Due Process Clause encompasses more than the rights guaranteed by the express provisions of the first eight amendments. *Casey* stated resoundingly: It is a promise of the Constitution that there is a realm of personal liberty which the government may not enter.

Plaintiffs challenging assisted suicide statutes assert that end-of-life decisions for competent, terminally ill adults occur within that realm. The district court in Washington agreed, as did the dissenting judge on the Ninth Circuit panel. The district court in New York rejected this argument, as did the majority on the Ninth Circuit panel.

Casey recognizes that "[o]ur law affords constitutional protection to personal decisions relating to marriage, procreation, contraception, family relationships, child rearing, and education."[6] *Casey* noted that "[i]t is settled now, as it was when the Court heard arguments in *Roe v. Wade,* that the Constitution places limits on a State's right to interfere with a person's most basic decisions about family and parenthood, as well as bodily integrity."[6] The protection of basic personal decisions from state intrusion limits the state's power to interfere with end-of-life decision-making, the doctor-patient relationship, and the joint selection and implementation of appropriate treatment.

There is no sound basis to exclude end-of-life decisions from the protection defined by *Casey*. Indeed, the Court's discussion of why decisions in these situations are protected applies with full force to end-of-life decisions:

> These matters, involving the most intimate and personal choices a person may make in a lifetime, choices central to personal dignity and autonomy, are central to the liberty protected by the Fourteenth Amendment. At the heart of liberty is the right to define one's own concept of existence, of meaning, of the universe, and of the mystery of human life.

As noted in *Casey*,[7] "[b]eliefs about these matters could not define the attributes of personhood were they formed under compulsion of the

State." *Casey* recognizes that where the suffering of an individual is involved, the state's ability to insist that the individual endure the suffering is limited.

Recognizing the right of competent, terminally ill persons to hasten death unquestionably raises religious implications, just as does abortion; yet, as recognized by *Casey*,

> that cannot control our decision. Our obligation is to define the liberty of all, not to mandate our own moral code. The underlying constitutional issue is whether the State can resolve these philosophic questions in such a definitive way that a woman lacks all choice in the matter. . . .

In the case of dying,[6] competent patients, the question is whether the state can resolve the philosophic questions relating to the end of life in such a definitive way that competent, terminally ill adults lack all choice in the matter. The answer, consistent with *Casey*, must be no. To hold otherwise would necessarily mean that the state's religious or philosophic preference outweighs the competent individual's control over his or her own suffering and method of dying.

The Court in *Casey* observed the doctrinal affinity between *Roe*'s rule of personal autonomy and bodily integrity and cases recognizing limits on governmental power to mandate medical treatment or bar its rejection. Indeed, the Court noted that cases since *Roe* accord with *Roe*'s view that "a State's interest in the protection of life falls short of justifying any plenary override of individual liberty claims."[8]

Casey permits the state to enact rules governing abortion so long as they do not impose an undue burden on the woman's ability to make her decision. An undue burden exists where regulation "has the purpose or effect of placing a substantial obstacle in the path of a woman seeking an abortion of a nonviable fetus."[9] The undue-burden/substantial-obstacle rule of *Casey* adequately protects any state interests in this area as well.

The Liberty Interest in Refusing Unwanted Medical Treatment in Order to Hasten Death Is No Greater Than That in Choosing to Hasten Inevitable Death with Medical Assistance

In the only "Right to Die" case yet decided by the United States Supreme Court,[10] the Court acknowledged that competent persons have the constitutional right to direct the removal of life-sustaining medical treatment and thus hasten death, and that the liberty to make this end-of-life decision is uniquely and "deeply personal."[11] *Cruzan* addressed the question of the level of evidence Missouri could require as to the wishes of a presently incompetent person that life-sustaining treatment be withdrawn. The Court made it clear that a state's interest in this area is in ensuring a voluntary decision, not in interfering with one.

The dissents in *Cruzan* differed as to the limitations that the state could impose to ensure voluntariness, but emphasized the personal nature of end-of-life decisions and the limited state interest in such decisions:

> Dying is personal. And it is profound. For many, the thought of an ignoble end, steeped in decay, is abhorrent. A quiet, proud death, bodily integrity intact, is a matter of extreme consequence. . . .
>
> Although the right to be free of unwanted medical intervention, like other constitutionally protected interests, may not be absolute, no state interest could outweigh the rights of an individual in Nancy Cruzan's position. Whatever a State's possible interests in mandating life-support treatment under other circumstances, there is no good to be obtained here by Missouri's insistence that Nancy Cruzan remain on life-support systems if it is indeed her wish not to do so. Missouri does not claim, nor could it, that society as a whole would be benefited by Nancy's receiving medical treatment.

Justice Stevens' separate dissent states his view that:[12]

> Choices about death touch the core of liberty. Our duty, and the concomitant freedom, to come to terms with the conditions of our own mortality are undoubtedly "so rooted in the traditions and conscience of our people as to be ranked as fundamental . . . ."
>
> The more precise constitutional significance of death is difficult to describe; not much may be said with confidence about death unless it is said from faith, and that alone is reason enough to protect the freedom to conform choices about death to individual conscience.

Where the patient is competent,[13] as in both the Washington and New York challenges to assisted suicide statutes, *Cruzan's* recognition of the extremely personal nature of the decision to refuse medical treatment, even where that refusal will cause death, strongly supports the plaintiffs' position. Having recognized that the decision to refuse treatment and thus hasten death is protected and uniquely personal, it cannot reasonably be distinguished from the decision to seek medical assistance in hastening death. Indeed, from the patient's perspective, the decision to refuse artificial nutrition and hydration is different in no material respect from the decision to choose to otherwise hasten death: "Patients request physician-assisted suicide for the same reasons that they refuse life-saving treatment: they want control over when they die, where they die, and their physical and mental state at the time of their death."[14-16] Thus, the constitutional principle behind recognizing a right to refuse artificial life support applies equally to the choice to hasten inevitable death by other means.[17,18]

Forced continuation of a life ravaged by pain and suffering for a competent, terminally ill adult who has a voluntary and informed desire to hasten his or her own death is a cruel and demeaning invasion into basic rights of liberty, privacy, and self-determination.

THE CHALLENGED STATUTES DENY EQUAL PROTECTION TO COMPETENT, TERMINALLY ILL ADULTS WHO ARE NOT ON LIFE SUPPORT

Even before *Cruzan*, both Washington and New York courts (as have many other state courts nationwide) recognized the right of a competent, terminally ill adult to hasten death by directing that life-sustaining medical treatment be suspended.[19-23] The courts effectively exclude from the facial coverage of the assisted suicide statutes those who assist in such decisions.

The Washington Natural Death Act explicitly recognizes the patient's interest in avoiding "loss of patient dignity, and unnecessary pain and suffering."[24] The statute protects "the fundamental right to control the decisions relating to the rendering of [adult persons'] own health care," "individual autonomy," and "dignity and privacy." These interests and rights apply equally to all terminally ill adults. The statute, however, specifically allows only those terminally ill adults who are on life-sustaining treatment to direct their doctors to withdraw such treatment,[25] and it protects such doctors from criminal prosecution.[26,27] Similar statutes exist in many other states.

Thus, many states, including Washington, recognize a significant liberty interest in the right to control the decisions relating to the rendering of heath care, and then distinguish between those competent, terminally ill adults whose condition involves life-sustaining treatment and those whose condition does not. The first group has the right to direct the course of treatment with the specific purpose and result of hastening inevitable death. The second group does not, and must suffer the very same pain and suffering and loss of dignity and privacy from which the statute protects the first group. As discussed above, the decision to request termination of life-sustaining treatment is different in no material respect from requesting other means of hastening inevitable death. This fact, and the equal protection implications, has been recognized:

> In essence, the distinction between physician-assisted suicide and the withdrawal or refusal of treatment is grounded in the policy-based categorization of suicide by withdrawing treatment as legal and suicide with physician assistance as illegal. Despite claims to the contrary, courts created exceptions to laws against "aiding suicide" when they permitted patients to demand withdrawal of life-sustaining treatment.[14,28]

The right of competent, terminally ill adults to choose to hasten inevitable death with physician-prescribed medications is a choice protected by the Liberty Clause of the Fourteenth Amendment and is a fundamental right. Where governmental action burdens the fundamental rights of some more than those of others, the disparity is subject to strict scrutiny.[29]

By prohibiting competent, terminally ill adults whose treatment does not include life support from exercising the right to choose to hasten death that is recognized in *Cruzan* and Washington and New York law, access to this choice is unequally distributed. The choice made by such persons to hasten inevitable death is different in no material respect from the choice of terminally ill persons on life support to request its termination for the purpose of hastening death. No compelling state interest supports such a discriminatory classification.

THE PRACTICAL IMPLICATIONS OF JUDICIAL RECOGNITION OF A CONSTITUTIONALLY PROTECTED RIGHT TO CHOOSE TO HASTEN DEATH WITH PHYSICIAN ASSISTANCE

Physicians Can Prescribe Drugs for the Purpose of Hastening Death

If a constitutionally protected right to choose to hasten death with physician assistance is ultimately established, physicians will be able to prescribe drugs for the purpose of hastening death to their competent, dying patients, consistent with their professional judgment. Of course, physicians will be responsible to assure that such patients are competent and acting voluntarily. In light of the severity resulting from a mistake, doctors and hospitals will need to develop protocols to assure that these standards are met and that the patient's privacy is protected.

State Regulation of Assisted Dying

It is likely that a court recognizing the patient's right to choose to hasten death will also recognize that the state may regulate the practice. Physicians, physician organizations, and others involved in providing health care services can and should play an active role in the development of regulations in this area. Clinical criteria will need to be established.[30,31] Regulations might require a waiting period; the provision of information regarding alternative care options (e.g., hospice); a treating relationship between doctor and patient; reporting by facilities where assistance occurs; and various other measures.

Challenges to State Regulation Can Be Anticipated

Regulation by the state will be subject to scrutiny under the *Casey* undue burden standard. It can be anticipated that regulation of this practice will be controversial and may result in litigation challenging the provisions, akin to the reproductive rights cases, as the issue of what regulation is permissible (i.e., does not unduly burden) versus what is not (i.e., constitutes an undue burden) is resolved. Interestingly, it would appear that the Oregon Death with Dignity Act is vulnerable to an undue burden challenge. That law requires, for example, a 15-day waiting period. Such a lengthy waiting period might well constitute an undue burden.

CONCLUSION

There can be little doubt that the question of whether dying patients have a constitutionally protected right to choose to hasten inevitable death with physician assistance will ultimately reach the United States Supreme Court. Should that Court determine that such a right exists, the effect will be similar to that of *Roe v. Wade* in the reproductive rights context. States will be permitted to regulate, but not prohibit, physician-assisted death. Alternatively, if a federal constitutional right is not recognized, litigation may move to state courts under state constitutions that are often more protective than the Constitution. Another alternative means to afford patients the right to choose physician-assisted death is through legislative means. Should judicial relief prove elusive, the pressure for legislative reform will likely increase.

REFERENCES AND ENDNOTES

1. *Compassion in Dying v. State of Washington*, 850 F. Supp. 1454 (W.D. Wash. 1994) (summary judgment granted to plaintiffs holding that mentally competent, terminally ill patients have a constitutionally protected right to choose to hasten death with physician assistance. Washington's assisted suicide statute is unconstitutional under both the Liberty and Equal Protection Clauses of the Fourteenth Amendment), *rev'd*, 49 F.3d 586 (9th Cir. 1995) (petition for rehearing en banc pending); *Quill v. Koppell*, 870 F. Supp. 78 (S.D.N.Y. 1995) (state's motion to dismiss granted; physician-assisted death is not constitutionally protected), *appeal docketed*, No. 95-7028 (2d Cir. 1995).

Compassion in Dying, the lead plaintiff in the Washington case, is a nonprofit corporation based in Seattle, Washington, that provides information and counseling to mentally competent, terminally ill adult patients who are considering hastening their own deaths in order to alleviate suffering, including offering personal presence and emotional support at the time of death.

2. *Lee v. State of Oregon*, No. 94-6467-H (D. Or.).

3. The need for physician involvement is most readily apparent to the medically and/or pharmacologically educated. Terminally ill persons are generally consuming a variety of drugs to mange their condition. Determining the correct drugs(s) to effect a humane death, and the amount and manner of consumption, is a complex medical pharmacological task. *See generally* R. Ogden, *Euthanasia, Assisted Suicide and AIDS* (1994). Physicians' attitudes about assisting death have been surveyed in some states. *See, e.g.*, R.W. Wood, M.D., *Attitudes Toward Assisted Suicide and Euthanasia Among Physicians in Washington States*, 331 N. Eng. J. Med. 89(1994) (reflecting that a majority of Washington State physicians favor permitting patients to choose physician aid-in-dying).

4. *Planned Parenthood v. Casey*, 112 S. Ct. 2791 (U.S. 1992), *aff'g Roe v. Wade*, 410 U.S. 113 (1973), the Supreme Court recognized.

5. 112 S. Ct. at 2804.

6. *Id.* at 2806.

7. *Id.* at 2807.

8. *Id.* at 2810 (citing *Cruzan v. Director, Mo. Dep't of Health*, 497 U.S. 261, 278 (199)).

9. *Id.* at 2818-20.

10. *Cruzan v. Director, Missouri Department of Health*, 497 U.S. 261 (1990).

11. *Id.* at 281.

12. *Id.* at 310-12 (Brennan, J., with Marshall & Blackmun, dissenting).

13. *Id.* at 343.

14. *Physician-Assisted Suicide and the Right to Die With Assistance*, 105 Harv. L. Rev. 2021, 2026 (1992).

15. Cornwell JR., *Wrongful Life and the Problem of Euthanasia*, 23 Gonz. L. Rev. 573, 583 X1988) (distinction between "hastening death" and "not prolonging dying" or between "killing" and "letting die" is meaningless from a volitional standpoint).

16. Young HH. *Assisted Suicide and Physician Liability*, 11 Rev. Litig. 623, 633 (1992).

17. The decision to refuse treatment is seen from the medical profession's perspective as "assisting in a patient's wish to die." *See* Steven I Addelstone, Book Note, Liability for Improper Maintenance of Life Support: Balancing Patient and Physician Authority, 46 Vand. L. Rev. 1255, 1262 (1993).

18. This right includes necessary medical assistance. Medical assistance is involved when treatment is refused, for example, in removing a feeding tube, ventilator, or dialysis machine. Similarly, medical assistance is necessary to permit implementation of this choice. In this case, assistance would consist of the doctor prescribing appropriate medications.

19. *In re Guardianship of Grant*, 109 Wn.2d 545, 747 P. 2d 445. (1987).

20. *In re Guardianship of Hamlin*, 103 Wn.2d 810, 689 P. 2d 1372 (1984).

21. *Rivers v. Katz*, 67 N.Y.2nd 485, 504 N.Y.S. 2d 74, 78 (1986).

22. *Fosmire v. Nicoleau*, 75 N.Y.2d 218, 551 N.Y.S.2d 876 (1990).

23. *Grace Plaza of Great Neck Inc. v. Elbaum*, 82 N.Y.2d 10, 623 N.E.2d 513 (1993).

24. RCW 70.122.010.

25. RCW 70.122.030.

26. RCW 9A.36.060.

27. RCW 70.122.051.

28. *Loving v. Virginia*, 388 U.S. 1 (1967).

29. Tribe LH. American Constitutional Law. § 16-6. At 1451-54, § 16-12, at 1464 (2nd ed., 1988).

30. Miller FG et al. Regulating Physician-Assisted Death. N Eng J Med 1994; 331:119.

31. Quill T. Clinical Criteria for Physician-Assisted Suicide. N Eng J Med 1992;327:1380-84.

Current Law
on Physician-Assisted Suicide
for the Terminally Ill

Cheryl K. Smith

SUMMARY. The subject of physician-assisted suicide for the terminally ill is becoming a major topic of public policy discussion. The state of the current law–what the law is, how it is enforced, and changes throughout the United States–as well as recent challenges or changes to the law and the actual incidence of the practice are discussed. Situations in which the author concludes that such practices should be legalized and needed safeguards for abuse are described. Other issues which must be addressed, including improved communication by physicians, better medical management of terminal illness, recognition of depression and limitations on access to handguns are discussed. *[Article copies available from The Haworth Document Delivery Service: 1-800-342-9678.]*

KEYWORDS. Physician-assisted suicide, terminally ill, ethical arguments, public policy, law, safeguards

The right to die has become a major issue in the last decade. While a majority of Americans believe in the right to make end of life decisions,[1]

Cheryl K. Smith, JD, is an attorney and writer who was one of the drafters of Measure 16, Oregon's Death with Dignity Act.

Address correspondence to: Cheryl K. Smith, P.O. Box 2422, Eugene, OR 97402.

[Haworth co-indexing entry note]: "Current Law on Physician-Assisted Suicide for the Terminally Ill." Smith, Cheryl K. Co-published simultaneously in *Journal of Pharmaceutical Care in Pain & Symptom Control* (Pharmaceutical Products Press, an imprint of The Haworth Press, Inc.) Vol. 3, No. 3/4, 1995, pp. 139-149; and: *Drug Use in Assisted Suicide and Euthanasia* (ed: Margaret P. Battin, and Arthur G. Lipman) Pharmaceutical Products Press, an imprint of The Haworth Press, Inc., 1996, pp. 139-149. Single or multiple copies of this article are available from The Haworth Document Delivery Service [1-800-342-9678, 9:00 a.m. - 5:00 p.m. (EST)].

© 1996 by The Haworth Press, Inc. All rights reserved.

139

they do not always agree on where to draw the line. Should assisted suicide or active voluntary euthanasia be allowed? What safeguards are necessary? Who can choose? Under what conditions may a person choose to have physician-assistance? These and other questions will eventually be answered by the laws being proposed throughout the world, which will determine and set limits on an activity that is already being practiced.

The first law in the world to legalize assisted suicide was passed in the state of Oregon, in November of 1994. The Oregon Death with Dignity Act, Measure 16, passed by 51-49% of the vote on November 8, 1994, despite the fact that opponents of the measure outspent proponents by three to one.[2] Prior to that, similar laws that would have also allowed voluntary active euthanasia, as well as physician-assisted suicide, just barely failed in Washington state and California, both by 46% to 54%.[3] Since 1990, legislators in 17 states have proposed legislation that would legalize assisted suicide or physician aid-in-dying for people with terminal illnesses, and the number of proposals is increasing each year.[4]

Although the Oregon Death with Dignity Act was to be effective 30 days after its passage, it was temporarily stopped by a federal judge after a group of physicians and patients, represented by an Indiana attorney, filed a complaint asking that it be enjoined. In that complaint, the plaintiffs argued that the law, which would allow competent adults with a terminal disease to obtain a prescription for the purpose of ending their life, is unconstitutional and unlawful. They argued, first, that the law deprives terminally ill Oregonians from protection of certain laws, i.e., the law that provides a criminal prohibition against assisted suicide and the law that provides for commitment of mentally ill persons. The complaint also stated that the law violates the Americans with Disabilities Act, the Religious Freedom Restoration Act, the First Amendment right to freedom of association, and the Equal Protection and Due Process clauses of the 14th amendment to the U.S. Constitution.[5]

A hearing on the complaint was held on December 19, 1994 and an opinion was handed down on December 27, 1994. That opinion further postponed the implementation of Measure 16. Measure 16 was judged unconstitutional by the federal district court in August, 1995. Appeal is pending; the matter is not yet resolved. Rather than wait for legal reform that may come about too late, a growing number of people are enlisting the assistance of friends, family or physicians and acting outside of the law in not only the United States but other parts of the world, as well.[4]

Physicians should not have to risk their professions and futures by helping patients who are suffering and ask for assistance in dying; instead, carefully drafted laws legalizing physician aid-in-dying must be passed and allowed to become effective throughout the United States.

CURRENT STATUTORY LAW ON ASSISTED SUICIDE

Suicide is defined as the deliberate termination of one's existence.[6] It is not currently illegal under any state statute, although it may arguably be a crime in a few states under common law.[7] While neither suicide nor attempted suicide are criminal acts in most states, a failed attempt at suicide may lead to involuntary psychiatric commitment. Under the laws in most states, a person who is a danger to self or others may be committed for evaluation, usually for at least 48 hours. In fact, in at least one reported case, an individual who simply confided to her physician that she had read *Final Exit* and requested sleeping medications, was committed for two days to a local mental hospital.[8]

Assisted suicide may be defined as conduct that is affirmative, assertive, proximate, and direct, such as furnishing a gun, poison, knife, or other instrumentality of usable means by which another could physically and immediately inflict some death producing injury on himself.[9] However, neither this definition nor other similar definitions have been tested as they apply to current laws against assisted suicide. Assisted suicide is generally considered to be a criminal act, despite the fact that suicide is not. The state of Louisiana recently passed a law making assisted suicide a crime, bringing the total to 34 states that have specific statutes on the subject.[4] While the types of cases for which these statutes were intended is in most cases not known, at least one was passed with the specific purpose of preventing assistance in the suicides of terminally ill individuals.[10] On the other hand, such laws passed in the 1990s were likely a reaction to Dr. Kevorkian's activities, and meant to apply to assisted suicide for people who are terminally ill.

In those states that do not specifically criminalize assisted suicide, the act may fall under murder or manslaughter statutes. Because most cases are handled on the trial court level and therefore are not reported, one can only speculate on the outcome in an individual case of assisted suicide where no specific statute exists.

CASES WHERE ASSISTANCE IN SUICIDE WAS REQUESTED

The majority of cases regarding the right to die are refusal of medical treatment cases and, as such, may be distinguished from assisted suicide cases.[11] In several cases, however, assisted suicide is explicitly discussed, providing some elucidation as to how courts view this issue.

The most well-known opinion favoring the right to assisted suicide is that of *Bouvia v. Superior Court*.[9] Elizabeth Bouvia was quadriplegic from cerebral palsy and lived in a state hospital. She was totally dependent on others and required intermittent pain medication. She petitioned the court, seeking removal of a feeding tube being maintained against her will. The California Court of Appeals ultimately ruled that Ms. Bouvia had the right to refuse medical treatment, stating that the decision to live or die belongs to the patient rather than the state.

While the majority distinguished the refusal of medical treatment from suicide, a concurring opinion written by Justice Compton treated the case as one of requesting assisted suicide. Justice Compton wrote:

> The right to die is an integral part of our right to control our own destinies so long as the rights of others are not affected. That right should, in my opinion, include the ability to enlist assistance from others, including the medical profession, in making death as painless and quick as possible.

Although characterized as assisted suicide, the facts of the Bouvia case are quite different from those in the case of *Donaldson v. Van De Kamp*.[12] In that case, Thomas Donaldson, who suffered from brain cancer and was expected to die within five years, petitioned the court to be allowed assistance in his suicide so that he could be cryogenically preserved until a cure was found and, he hoped, his body returned to life.

The court referred to relevant state interests (preserving life, preventing suicide, protecting innocent third parties, and maintaining the ethical standards of the medical profession) that must be balanced against an individual's interest. It also added an unqualified general interest in the preservation of human life. However, the court failed to articulate whether Donaldson's interest in choosing death outweighed the state's interest. Instead it based its conclusion that Donaldson not be allowed assistance in suicide on the state interest in maintaining the social order through enforcement of the criminal law.[14] The court reasoned that this interest outweighs any interest in Donaldson in ending his life and having a third party assist him in doing so. The court also reasoned that evaluating the assister's motive and potential undue influence is difficult. The implication here is that if an assisted suicide law did not exist, there would be little reason to disallow Mr. Donaldson's request despite the court's determination that no constitutional right existed.

In the case of *Zant v. Prevatte*,[13] a Georgia prison had petitioned the court to be allowed to force-feed inmate Prevatte, who was attempting to starve himself to death, arguing a compelling state interest in preserving his life. Although acknowledging that the state has a duty to keep prisoners safe from harm, the court ruled that the duty does not justify force-feeding of this former death row prisoner. It reasoned that a prisoner does not relinquish his constitutional right to privacy because of his status as a prisoner. The court observed that the fact that Prevatte was competent and had no dependents weighed in favor of his right to privacy from such intrusions on his person; ergo the state interest in preserving life was insufficient to justify forced feeding.

Although Zant did not deal with a terminally ill individual requesting assisted suicide, the factors mentioned, i.e., competency and lack of dependents, are relevant to such cases when weighing the right to privacy against state interests in maintaining life.

Despite the fact that Judge Compton's opinion in the *Bouvia* case was a concurrence and not part of the majority opinion, these cases and others indicate that courts are willing to accept that, in some cases, competent patients have a right to choose death and that medical assistance in such cases is not always inappropriate.

CHALLENGES TO ASSISTED SUICIDE STATUTES

In 1994, Compassion in Dying, a right-to-die organization in Washington, began a series of challenges to state laws that make assisted suicide a crime, arguing that, as applied to mentally competent, terminally ill adults, they violate the U.S. Constitution.[14] Although initially they succeeded with that claim in Washington, the Ninth Circuit Court of Appeals overturned the decision. Similarly, in a case brought by Compassion in New York, the District court also found the state statute to be constitutional. Ultimately, one of these cases will end up in the U.S. Supreme Court, where a definitive conclusion may be reached.

Interestingly, in the Ninth Circuit Court of Appeals opinion, the court identified some unique state interests that it felt outweighed a liberty interest in suicide. In addition to the usual interest in preventing suicide, the court also mentioned an interest in preserving the integrity of the physician's practice; an interest in not subjecting elderly or infirm persons to psychological pressure to consent to death; the interest in protecting poor and minority persons from exploitation; an interest in protecting people with handicaps to society's indifference and antipathy; and an interest in preventing abuse (referring to reports of the Netherlands).[15] While these may be valid state interests, they are less likely to be applicable to a statute that legalizes assisted suicide as opposed to those that make it a crime.

RECENT ASSISTED SUICIDE CASES

Very few assisted suicides come to the attention of authorities; of those that do, few are prosecuted and even fewer result in convictions. The Hemlock Society USA, which compiles information on assisted suicides from newspapers, reported only 53 assisted suicides from 1980 through 1994.[16] Eighty-five percent of these cases occurred in the 1990s. Whether this increase in occurrences is due to improved reporting or an actual increase in assisted suicide is unclear. Some cases typical of those occurring across the U.S. follow.

On August 20, 1994, Tony Winik, who had AIDS, died after taking an overdose of sleeping pills in Austin, Texas. His wife, Marion, publicly admitted to having assisted him by mixing the pills with yogurt, and preparing the house for him. Marion Winik was not prosecuted, despite the existence of law against assisted suicide in Texas.[17]

In Auburn, California, Jesse James Quinn, age eighty-seven, was arraigned on January 23, 1992, for helping his wife commit suicide by leaving a gun on her nightstand. The case was resolved by the judge without a guilty or innocent plea; Mr. Quinn agreed to undergo counseling for a year and give up his firearms in return for eventual dismissal of charges.[18] In a similar case two years later, a sixty-seven year old Oklahoma man used a gun left in his room by a relative to end his life. He had been suffering from terminal abdominal cancer. No one was prosecuted for the crime, which was declared a suicide.[16]

On July 16, 1991, forty-nine year old Dick Bauer of Cripple Creek, Colorado, got his mother her gun, at her insistence, so that she could end her suffering. Wanda Bauer was in excruciating pain from what was believed to be terminal liver and pancreatic cancer and had been discharged from the hospital with no pain medication or care plan. Wanda, who shot and killed herself, was found on autopsy to have an infected liver, pancreas, and peritoneum. Physicians at the trial testified that she was dying.[19]

Dick Bauer was charged with assisted suicide under the Colorado statute and, after four days of trial, was found not guilty by a jury of his peers. They believed that Mr. Bauer lacked the requisite intent for the crime. Had a statute that allowed physician-assisted death for terminal patients been in place at the time of Wanda Bauer's death, she might have had more incentive to undergo the definitive diagnostic test and receive treatment, rather than ending her life and putting her son through the prosecution.

Since 1990, Dr. Jack Kevorkian has been involved in 24 assisted suicides in Michigan. In the first case, Dr. Kevorkian assisted Janet Adkins, an Alzheimers patient from Portland, Oregon, to end her life with his suicide machine. Although he was initially charged with murder, the charges against him were eventually dismissed.[20]

Since then, Kevorkian has been charged with either aiding in suicide or open murder at least five more times; four of those charges were dismissed and in the one that went to trial, Kevorkian was acquitted. Most recently Kevorkian opened an obitorium, a suicide clinic for his patients.[21] After only one suicide, by a woman with amyotrophic lateral sclerosis, Kevorkian's landlord gave him a month's notice to vacate the building, voicing concerns regarding media pressure. At the time of this writing, Kevorkian still faces possible murder charges in two cases and assisted suicide charges in three others.

In August of 1990, Bertram (Bob) Harper and his stepdaughter flew with his wife, Virginia Harper, from California to Michigan, where he assisted his wife in ending her life with pills and a plastic bag. Mrs. Harper was dying of liver cancer. Mr. Harper was charged with open murder but ultimately found not guilty by a jury.[22]

In a case that typifies the current, but usually secret, practice of some doctors, Dr. Timothy Quill reported his assistance in the suicide of a terminally ill cancer patient, with whom he had a long-term physician-patient relationship.[23] His patient, Diane, was diagnosed with leukemia and decided to forgo treatment after learning that she had only about a 25% chance of survival, even with the treatment. Quill described Diane as a confident and independent person who exercised control over her life. Her decision was fully informed–she knew her prognosis, benefits of treatment, and risks of nontreatment. Although he was aware of the use to which she might put a prescription, Dr. Quill was willing to give her that choice, which she ultimately exercised. After an investigation, the prosecutor in Rochester, New York, decided not to charge Dr. Quill, despite the fact that he had admitted having a part in Diane's suicide.

A case that is illustrative of the reality that people attempt suicide in an effort to end their suffering of involuntary commitment is that of Alice Marks, of the Los Angeles area.[24] The eighty-one year old Marks, who suffered from degenerative bone disease, injected an overdose of morphine, while her son stood by her side. Believing that she was dead, Christopher Marks called paramedics, who revived her. In the hospital, Marks was deprived of further pain medication and then transferred to a locked psychiatric unit as a danger to herself. Her son, in the meantime, may be indicted for assisted suicide, which is a crime under California law.

PHYSICIAN POLLS

In addition to cases that come to public attention, physician polls are also instructive in regard to assistance in dying by doctors. In a Center for Health Ethics and Policy at the University of Colorado at Denver poll, 4.2% of the licensed physicians responding indicated that they had assisted a patient to stockpile a lethal dose of medication, aware that it might be used for suicide.[25]

In a New Hampshire physician poll, 22 of 597 anonymous physicians admitted that they had assisted in a patient's death by granting requests for medication by dying patients; eleven had given lethal injections to dying patients.[26]

A recently reported 1993 study of Michigan oncologists' attitudes toward and experiences with physician-assisted death showed a substantial number of physicians reporting that they had participated in physician-assisted death. In that study 18% of respondents indicated that they had provided the means or instructions by which a patient could take his or her own life; 4% indicated that they had administered medication with the intent to cause the death of a patient.[27]

Despite these survey results showing that a small percentage of doctors are acting to assist their patients despite the law, the present legal situation in most of the United States (and much of the world) regarding assisted suicide chills free discussion between patient and doctor regarding certain end of life decisions. Patients fear involuntary commitment and physicians fear criminal prosecution. This situation leaves many patients to join in quiet conspiracy with their loved ones.

SCOPE OF LEGALIZED ASSISTED SUICIDE

The right to refuse medical treatment is well established in law. All U.S. states have some sort of advance directive law; a number of states also have laws governing the right to refuse resuscitation. As can be seen by the cases previously discussed, in which patients who were not dying were authorized by courts to refuse medical treatment, the line between treatment refusal and suicide may be fuzzy.

Two basic problems exist in the use of treatment refusal or abatement when applied to most incurable or dying persons. First, most are not dependent on life support, so refusal of treatment, other than food and water, is not applicable. Second, even if they choose to refuse food and water, it may not be the most humane way to die, even with sedation and pain control.[28] In his recent book, *A Chosen Death,* Lonny Shavelson recounts the attempted death by fasting of a thirty-five year old man with quadriplegia. After forty-eight days, the vomiting and pain became too much for him and he resumed eating.[29]

Under the current state of the law, even though assisted suicide is in most cases a crime, cases of such assistance are not treated uniformly, giving an unclear message to citizens. While some individuals openly flaunt the law and still avoid prosecution, others may lose their liberty, at least temporarily, and have to finance an expensive defense for acting out of compassion and loyalty.

For those who are still concerned that a zealous prosecutor may become involved, secrecy in assisting a loved one becomes key, further obscuring the actual number of cases in which dying or incurable individuals choose to end their lives early and limiting the possibility that medical professionals might be able to suggest a less drastic alternative. Such a shroud of secrecy also allows less than altruistic individuals or those stressed by the patient's illness to coerce or encourage the patient to commit suicide, or even worse, to cross the line from assisted suicide to mercy killing.

Other risks of unregulated assisted suicide for incurable or dying persons include inaccurate reporting of cause of death, emotional suicides brought on by undetected depression or mental illness, and botched or violent suicides brought about by a lack of knowledge of lethal drugs and dosages or by using the only available method, usually a firearm.

Laws permitting assisted suicide must be limited to a narrow class of people and contain appropriate safeguards to prevent the potential abuses previously discussed. At a minimum, safeguards should include the following:

> the patient must be a mentally competent, incurably ill adult, with no other reasonable alternative available; the patient must be informed regarding his or her condition, prognosis and treatment; the request must be persistent and voluntary, and made without outside pressure or duress; where mental illness or depression causing impaired judgment exist, counseling must be obtained; consultation with at least one other physician, preferably a specialist, must be obtained; all of these must be documented; and a requirement of reporting must be in place, with prosecution penalties for failure to obey the law.

Much criticism has been made of the situation in the Netherlands, and allegations of abuse are often cited. However, assisted suicide is not legal there, and physicians still face possible prosecution. With a specific law, reporting requirements, and penalties for failure to obey these requirements, the possibility of abuse will be substantially reduced, if not eliminated.

CONCLUSION

Although assisted suicide for persons who are terminally ill may seem an extreme solution for an extreme problem, recent polls indicate that many Americans support this option, and a number of physicians are already helping their patients to die. Narrowly drawn laws, with necessary safeguards, should be passed and allowed to become effective so that physicians may help people who are suffering and terminally ill to end their lives when other alternatives fail.

REFERENCES AND ENDNOTES

1. 1991 Roper Poll of the West Coast. Hemlock Quarterly 1991: 44: 9. Americans favor euthanasia, according to new Harris Poll. Elmira (NY) Star-Gazette, Apr 5, 1993.

2. Smith CK. Oregon's Measure 16: Once more to the ballot box. Last Rights 1994; 42-43.

3. Ogden RD. Euthanasia Assisted Suicide and AIDS, British Columbia, Perreault Goedman, 1994.

4. Conversation with Kris Larson. Hemlock Society USA, 1995.

5. Lee v. Harcleroad et al. Complaint for Declaratory and Injunctive Relief. Cause No 94-6467-TC.

6. Black's Law Dictionary, Fifth Ed. 1979.

7. See, e.g., State v. Willis, 121 S.E.2d 854(N.C. 1961).

8. Billings N. Final Exit reader sent to mental hospital! Hemlock Quarterly, April 1992.

9. Bouvia v. Superior Court, 225 Cal.Rptr. 291(Cal.Ct.App. 1986).

10. CONN. GEN.STAT.ANN. '53a-56(a) (West 1985).

11. Smith CK. What About Legalized Assisted Suicide? Issues in Law & Med 1993; 8(4): 503-519.

12. 4 Cal. Rptr. 2d 59 (Cal. Ct. App. 1992).

13. 286 S.E.2d 715 (Ga. 1982).

14. Compassion in New York. Last Rights 1994; 13: 22-24.

15. U.S. Ct App (9th Cir.) slip op. 94-35534.

16. National Hemlock Society, Cases of Euthanasia, murder and assisted suicide. 1994.

17. Herman K. Austin writer admits breaking law by helping husband take own life. Houston Post, December 10, 1994.

18. Sacramento Bee, Jan. 24, 1992.

19. Personal observations by author at trial of Richard Bauer, Feb. 12, 1992.

20. Lewin T. Judge Clears Doctor of Murdering Woman with a Suicide Machine, N.Y Time, Dec. 14, 1990.

21. Landlord to shut down Kevorkian's obitorium Eugene Register-Guard, June 28, 1995.

22. Angel C. I Knew . . . What I Did was Right. Detroit News & Free Press, May 11, 1991.

23. Quill TE. Death and Dignity: A Case of Individualized Decision Making. N Eng. J Med 1991; 324(10): 691-4.

24. Moehringer JR. Mother's Wish to Die Leaves Man in Legal Limbo. Los Angeles Times, April 30, 1995.

25. Center for Health Ethics & Policy, U. Colo. at Denver, Licensed Physician Questionnaire 5. 1988.

26. Gianelli D. American Medical News. Oct. 10, 1994.

27. Doukas DJ, Waterhouse D, Gorenflo DW & Seid J. Attitudes and Behaviors on Physician-Assisted Death: A Study of Michigan Oncologists. J Clin Oncol 1995: 13(5): 1055-1061.

28. Docker C. The Art and Science of Fasting. in Beyond Final Exit, Victoria, The Society for the Right to Die of Canada, 1995.

29. Shavelson L. A Chosen Death, New York, Simon & Schuster, 1995.

Pharmacists' Response
to Oregon's Death with Dignity Act

Kristine Carlson Marcus

SUMMARY. The responses of Oregon pharmacists to Measure 16, the Oregon Death with Dignity Act, are discussed. The process through which a ballot measure can establish law in the state of Oregon is described. The passage of Measure 16 by a small majority of voters in 1994 was rapidly followed by a federal district court injunction which delayed implementation of the new law. Issues and concerns which pharmacists have identified relative to their role in Measure 16 are described. The pharmacist's right to refuse to participate in the processing of a Measure 16 prescription is discussed. *[Article copies available from The Haworth Document Delivery Service: 1-800-342-9678.]*

KEYWORDS. Oregon Ballot Measure 16, Death with Dignity Act, pharmacy practice

INTRODUCTION

Measure 16 is a 1994 Oregon Ballot Initiative entitled the Death with Dignity Act. This initiative was intended to prevent legal sanctions against

Kristine Carlson Marcus, RPh, is a practicing pharmacist in Portland, OR and chairs the Professional Affairs Council of the Oregon Society of Hospital Pharmacists and serves on the Statewide Pharmacy Task Force on Measure 16.

Address correspondence to: Kristine Carlson Marcus, c/o Oregon Society of Hospital Pharmacists, P.O. Box 3997, Salem, OR 97302-0997.

[Haworth co-indexing entry note]: "Pharmacists' Response to Oregon's Death with Dignity Act." Marcus, Kristine Carlson. Co-published simultaneously in *Journal of Pharmaceutical Care in Pain & Symptom Control* (Pharmaceutical Products Press, an imprint of The Haworth Press, Inc.) Vol. 3, No. 3/4, 1995, pp. 151-157; and: *Drug Use in Assisted Suicide and Euthanasia* (ed: Margaret P. Battin and Arthur G. Lipman) Pharmaceutical Products Press, an imprint of The Haworth Press, Inc., 1996, pp. 151-157. Single or multiple copies of this article are available from The Haworth Document Delivery Service [1-800-342-9678, 9:00 a.m. - 5:00 p.m. (EST)].

© 1996 by The Haworth Press, Inc. All rights reserved.

practitioners who prescribe lethal drugs for patients with advanced disease for the purpose of ending their lives. Many opponents of the initiative and many health care practitioners were as alarmed by what the initiative did not define as by its intended purpose. Liability issues for pharmacists were not addressed. The initiative was passed by a vote of 51% to 49% on November 8, 1994.

The Official 1994 General Election Voters' Pamphlet entitled *Statewide Measures: Summary of Ballot Measure 16* describes the proposed law as providing a terminally ill adult patient voluntary informed choice to obtain a physician's prescription for drugs to end life. Written "safeguards" in the measure include waiting periods, a required second medical opinion, and the need for two oral and one written request. The patient would then have the option of authorizing next of kin to act on the patient's behalf. Measure 16 would hold health care providers immune from civil and criminal liability if they act in good faith. However, Measure 16 is silent with regard to what happens after a "lethal dose, legally prescribed" is prescribed. Pharmacists are not mentioned in the ballot measure, and one might question whether the drafters even considered the role of the pharmacist. Rather, the authors of the proposal appear to have thought that pharmacists simply act as agents of physicians.[1]

In Oregon, the ballot initiative process is begun when the petitioners draft the proposed "law." This can be an amendment to a current law, a new law, or a constitutional amendment. The proposed petition is submitted to the Secretary of State who determines if the petition meets the requirement of addressing a single subject and then to the Attorney General who writes a Ballot Title for the proposed petition. There is a seven business day period during which the petition can be challenged. If the petition survives the challenge period, it then returns to the Secretary of State who approves the next step: collecting of signatures. Signatures of registered voters are collected and are due the July prior to the November general election. If the signatures are acceptable, the petition goes on the General Election docket as a Ballot Measure. A measure which passes normally takes effect 30 days after the election as a new law or a constitutional amendment.

United States District Court Judge Michael Hogan ordered a preliminary injunction on the implementation of Measure 16 on December 27, 1994. Hearings were scheduled for February and April, 1995, to hear complaints. The complaints centered around perceived conflicts between Measure 16 and the Americans with Disabilities Act and with religious freedom concerns. Judge Hogan indicated that he would make a decision in April 1995 on all issues. In August, 1995, the court ruled that the law is unconstitutional. Appeal is anticipated. Measure 16 is not scheduled to be addressed by the legislature during the 1995 legislative year.

Many Oregon pharmacists have viewed the delay in implementing Measure 16 as providing an opportunity to discuss issues surrounding the measure and to plan for its implementation. Useful discussion has been limited, however, by a lack of answers to questions posed by the language of Measure 16 and which the measure does not explicitly address. Annas' pre-election prediction, published in the *New England Journal of Medicine* rings true: "Even if (Measure 16) does pass, it will be some time before either the people of Oregon, or their physicians, will know what it means."[1]

PHARMACIST DISCUSSION ISSUES

Several important issues which have been proposed for discussion by pharmacists include the following.[2]

Issue: What constitutes "a lethal dose of medication"?
- There is a lack of data in the medical literature that clearly defines a consistently lethal dose.[3]
- Will the use of non-oral routes of administration be allowed under Measure 16?
- Should co-ingestants and other concurrent treatments (e.g., antiemetics) be advocated?

Issue: Can a humane and dignified death be accomplished under the provisions of Measure 16?
- The Dutch experience has shown that one in four patients who take an oral "lethal dose" do not die immediately, but die sometime in the next four days.[3] Will this be considered acceptable by patients and their health care providers?[4]
- Is a humane and dignified death possible if Measure 16 does not allow for parenteral medications to be prescribed for a patient or used by a practitioner to hasten death if the patient's attempt fails?
- What are the likely outcomes of a patient's failed attempt to end their life?

Issue: Could a pharmacist who participates in providing a lethal dose of medication be held liable for the consequences of that action?
- While it appears that the intent of Measure 16 was to shield "health care providers" from liability, it is unclear if pharma-

cists are included in the Measure 16 definition of "health care provider." Pharmacists are not specifically mentioned in Measure 16.[7]

- Even if pharmacists are found immune from liability, they are not protected against the costs of litigation. Therefore, it is still prudent to maintain professional liability insurance since it may cover the costs of a legal defense.[7]

Issue: What will be the pharmacists' roles in the implementation of Measure 16?

- As drug experts, pharmacists may be consulted to answer questions concerning lethal doses, expected side effects, reliability of prescribed medications to produce desired effects, and how best to deliver a lethal dose. How will pharmacists obtain this kind of drug information?
- How much information will be provided to the pharmacist related to the patient's medical history and request for a lethal dose of medication?
- How will conflicts between patient counseling requirements and preservation of patient confidentiality be resolved if the patient's agent (e.g., family member, friend) picks up the prescription?
- How will the pharmacist's "right to choose" to participate be protected if the patient or prescriber is not required to inform the pharmacist of the intent of the prescription?[5]
- What occurs if the pharmacist's "right to choose" to participate is in conflict with their employer's wishes?

PHARMACISTS' RIGHT TO CHOOSE

Pharmacists' "right to choose" may be defined as the pharmacists' right to decide if they are willing to participate in filling a Measure 16 prescription, i.e., do they have a legal "right" to refuse to fill a Measure 16 prescription? This right could be based on personal religious or moral beliefs or on professional ethics and duty grounds. A pharmacist's opinion may vary from patient to patient. Availability of patient information, or how well the patient is known to the pharmacist, may affect the pharmacist's willingness to participate. One of the greatest concerns of pharmacists is that they could be put in a position in which they might unknowingly fill a Measure 16 prescription because the intent of the prescription was not disclosed to them.

There is no mention in the measure of outcomes from a pharmacist refusing to fill a Measure 16 prescription. Oregon pharmacy regulations do not provide explicit protection for the pharmacist who refuses to fill a Measure 16 prescription. Statute ORS 689.025(2) Practice of Pharmacy Act states that it is the purpose of ORS 689.005 to 689.995 to promote, preserve, and protect the public health, safety and welfare by and through the effective regulation of the practice of pharmacy. No provision is made for prescriptions intended to do harm to a patient, i.e., end the patient's life. The Board of Pharmacy is unable to find any specific mention of the pharmacist's responsibility to fill or not to fill a prescription under Oregon Pharmacy Law.[8] Measure 16 does contain language regarding health care providers being immune from liability for refusal to participate in Measure 16, but pharmacists are not mentioned anywhere in the measure.

THE RESPONSE OF OREGON PHARMACISTS TO MEASURE 16

On October 6, prior to the November, 1994 General Election, the Oregon State Pharmacists Association (OSPA) House of Delegates voted to unanimously oppose Measure 16. This action was reportedly taken because of the manner in which OSPA was incorrectly portrayed in the Oregon Voters Pamphlet and the fact that pharmacists were dragged into this subject against their will. The OSPA noted that pharmacists were not consulted in the drafting of the initiative. Moreover, the Board of Directors of OSPA is of the opinion that Measure 16 would result in a Direct contraindication of their professional training and expertise. Pharmacists are educated in the healing arts to prolong life in the treatment and healing of illness and injuries. Measure 16 was seen as being in opposition to that end.

Following the November passage of the measure, OSPA went on record to say that it would work with the Oregon Board of Pharmacy to establish protocols for the lethal drugs to carry out the will of the people. The OSPA president appointed a Task Force of interested pharmacists to provide guidance and direction to the profession.[9] OSPA continues to fund the Statewide Pharmacy Task Force on Measure 16 and to inform its members about Measure 16 through its publications and educational meetings.

The Oregon Society of Hospital Pharmacists (OSHP) voted to remain neutral on Measure 16 prior to the November, 1994 election.[10] Following the election, the OSHP published a position statement which reads:

> . . . The citizens of the State of Oregon have decided through the initiative process that they want the ability to choose physician-assisted suicide as an alternative to traditional therapy. As a profession,

we believe it is up to each individual pharmacist to determine if they are willing to participate in this therapy. The highly moral and ethical nature of this decision is something each will have to weigh in their own professional practice . . . We as a profession need to work with other organizations to develop administrative rules which protect the needs of all involved.

The Statewide Pharmacy Task Force on Measure 16 was established with the following statement of purpose and scope:[10]

. . . The Task Force is comprised of individuals from all branches of pharmacy practice across various regions of Oregon including: community pharmacy, hospital and health systems, academia, long term care and hospice. The Task Force has the primary goal to honor the trust patients have placed in pharmacists to ensure quality pharmaceutical care. The Task Force will accomplish this goal by ensuring that pharmacists are equipped with the knowledge they need to respond to a 'lethal dose, legally prescribed' prescription in an appropriate manner based on their professional judgement. The Task Force will also work through legislative, legal and professional channels to ensure that every step is taken to inform and protect the patient who is facing a terminal illness. Members of the Task Force have different personal views on Measure 16; however, everyone strongly believes in their professional obligation to the patient and for the health care community to provide compassionate pharmaceutical care to the terminally ill.

The three main purposes of the Statewide Pharmacy Task Force on Measure 16 are:

1. to explore and develop implementation guidelines and standards of practice parameters;
2. to investigate, develop, format and propose legislative and executive action or amendments deemed necessary;
3. to develop a resource for pharmacists requesting information on this measure and to develop and manage press/media statements that will be presented by this Task Force on behalf of the collective profession.

CONCLUSION

Discussion among pharmacists on the meaning of Measure 16 and how it may affect their practices if the measure becomes effective continue.

Both the Statewide Pharmacists Task Force on Measure 16 and the Oregon Pharmacists Association Media and Information Dissemination Committee continue to address the issue. A pharmacist opinion survey was developed for distribution to all registered pharmacists in Oregon. That survey was endorsed by the OSPA, OSHP, Statewide Pharmacy Task Force on Measure 16 and Oregon Board of Pharmacy. The survey incudes questions on willingness of pharmacists to participate and attitudes toward physician-assisted suicide, active euthanasia and passive euthanasia.

It is clear that drafters of future laws such as Oregon's Measure 16 should consider all of the health care practitioners who are impacted by the proposal and define how the new law would impact upon their practices, prerogatives and liability.

REFERENCES AND ENDNOTES

1. Annas GJ. Death by prescription: the Oregon initiative. N Eng J Med 1994;331(18):1240-43.

2. Marcus KC. Oregon Society of Hospital Pharmacists Interactions, 1994;19:7.

3. In the Netherlands, nine grams of a fast acting barbiturate in an elixir of alcohol and orange juice has been used and parenteral drugs may be used to hasten death if the first treatment provides unsatisfactory results.

4. Humphry D. Suicides not botched. Eugene Register-Guard, Jan 7, 1995. Letter.

5. Oregon Senate Bill (SB) 1069, which is sponsored by Senator Shannon, includes amendments to Measure 16 that would allow a pharmacist to refuse to prescribe or dispense any drug "the sole purpose of which is to cause death." How the pharmacist will be informed of the prescription's intent is not addressed in SB 1069.

6. Oregon Senate Bill (SB) 907, which is sponsored by Senator Sorenson (at the request of the Oregon State Pharmacists Association), contains language to include pharmacists and pharmacies in the definition of "health care provider."

7. Personal communication with Magginis & Associates, the company which underwrites the majority of malpractice insurance policies of Oregon pharmacists, have revealed mixed responses as to whether these policies will cover pharmacists' actions related to Measure 16.

8. Personal communication with the Oregon State Board of Pharmacy.

9. Gress C. Assisted suicide initiative passes. Oregon Pharmacist 1994;42:6.

10. Statewide Pharmacy Task Force on Measure 16. Letter to every licensed Oregon pharmacist, December 1994.

Regulatory Issues in Euthanasia, Palliative Care and Assisted Suicide

William L. Marcus

SUMMARY. This paper addresses regulatory concepts which affect how regulators may approach euthanasia and assisted suicide in the context of professional discipline. To frame this discussion, brief background information on the history of licensing and the basic framework of discipline is presented.

While each state will determine its own approach to such cases, the discussion will help provide practitioners with some idea of how licensing boards are likely to handle euthanasia and assisted suicide. *[Article copies available from The Haworth Document Delivery Service: 1-800-342-9678.]*

KEYWORDS. Regulators, euthanasia, assisted suicide, licensing, law

HISTORY AND PURPOSE
OF REGULATING HEALTH CARE PROFESSIONALS

Licensing and regulation did not start as a consumer protection movement. It was really fostered, particularly by the legal and allopathic medi-

---

William L. Marcus, JD, is Deputy Attorney General in the California Department of Justice, Liaison Counsel for the California State Board of Pharmacy, and Assistant Clinical Professor, School of Pharmacy, University of California at San Francisco.

Address correspondence to: William L. Marcus, California Department of Justice, 300 South Spring Street, 5th Floor, Los Angeles, CA 90013.

[Haworth co-indexing entry note]: "Regulatory Issues in Euthanasia, Palliative Care and Assisted Suicide." Marcus, William L. Co-published simultaneously in *Journal of Pharmaceutical Care in Pain & Symptom Control* (Pharmaceutical Products Press, an imprint of The Haworth Press, Inc.) Vol. 3, No. 3/4, 1995, pp. 159-176; and: *Drug Use in Assisted Suicide and Euthanasia* (ed: Margaret P. Battin, and Arthur G. Lipman) Pharmaceutical Products Press, an imprint of The Haworth Press, Inc., 1996, pp. 159-176. Single or multiple copies of this article are available from The Haworth Document Delivery Service [1-800-342-9678, 9:00 a.m. - 5:00 p.m. (EST)].

© 1996 by The Haworth Press, Inc. All rights reserved.
159

cal professions, to protect their rights–their exclusivity–at the expense of competitors. It certainly, especially as to physicians, also was meant to deal with charlatans, but control was the primary purpose. By the early 20th century attorneys and allopathic physicians, among others, had achieved nearly total control.

Protection of the public from incompetents and quacks may have been a stated reason for licensing and regulation, but, in fact, it was, at least initially, an afterthought or a veneer put forward to justify exclusionary licensing schemes. Only in the last thirty years has consumer protection begun to play a significant role in state regulation of licensees.

In recent years, others have made inroads on what had become a monopoly. Pharmacists have begun to reassert greater responsibility for pharmacological and clinically-related decisions; nurses, and not just nurse practitioners, and physician assistants have become front-line practitioners, especially for rural, economically-deprived, and, often, prepaid or HMO populations; osteopathic physicians have been put on an equal footing with allopaths; chiropractors are no longer health care pariahs. Many additional categories of health professionals have been recognized in the last 20 years, partly as their education and training has been upgraded or broadened or both and partly due to third party reimbursement issues.

Until quite recently–primarily the last 15-20 years, licensees were disciplined for doing things out of the mainstream; for fraud; for acts which offended society (usually characterized as those involving "moral turpitude"); for "over" prescribing or knowingly or callously issuing or dispensing illegitimate prescriptions; or based on a criminal conviction. Very few actions were taken against licensees for issues related to quality of care–what is usually called negligence, malpractice, gross negligence, incompetence, or something similar.

The honesty or good faith of the particular licensee or, often, even the demonstrated or potential scientific or medical validity of the practice involved was far less significant than whether those who dominated the profession or the particular licensing authority or those who dictated public morality liked or accepted the practice.

Today, licensing boards tend to focus on establishing and enforcing more reasonable standards for initial and continuing licensure. Frequent attention from the legislature, public interest groups, and the public, often coupled with increased public membership on the boards, has moved them away from self-protection and towards consumer protection.

Typical Bases for Discipline

Licensing boards today typically take disciplinary action against a licensee for (1) criminal convictions, (2) failure to comply with specific statutory or regulatory provisions, (3) acts demonstrating dishonesty, fraud or corruption, (4) other acts which can be related to some aspect of the licensing activity or the qualifications for it,[1] (5) professional misconduct committed in the course of practicing the profession or, (6) acts of gross immorality or moral turpitude. In addition, most health-related professional licensing boards provide for discipline for drug-related misconduct, including both drug-related criminal convictions, and drug-related conduct (even without a conviction), such as illegal drug possession, abuse of drugs, or violation of state or federal laws governing prescription drugs or controlled substances.

It is very important to understand that, as to discipline for incompetence or negligence or malpractice, only very recently have boards and the courts begun to recognize the diversity of professional practices. In other words, for what a licensee does to be a basis for discipline, it must be significantly at variance from that which most practitioners do (or approve), have some credible potential for harm to individuals or the public generally, or involve matters such as fraud or inadequate disclosure to the patient.

How Is Licensing and Regulation Related to the Issues of Euthanasia, Assisted Suicide, and Palliative Care?

As the pressure grows to allow a person, especially a terminal patient or one in unrelenting pain to end his or her life with professional medical assistance, those who regulate health care professionals–especially licensing boards–will be faced with some very difficult questions.

For example, it has been suggested by some that palliative care amounts to (or can be intended as) assisted suicide or euthanasia and is really a euphemism for suicide or euthanasia. Because that belief persists, perhaps even among a few in the pain community, pain management practitioners who are involved in palliative care may be at risk for disciplinary action by licensing boards or even criminal prosecution.[1]

But the threshold issue is *whether* regulators have any place in this arena. The secondary issue is, assuming regulators do have any role, what should be regulated and according to what standards.

Scenarios: Where a Patient Asks to Die

The following illustrate some of the different circumstances under which a physician, nurse, or pharmacist may be faced with a difficult choice.[1]

The primary purpose of these scenarios is to illustrate some of the situations which can present a problem for a health care practitioner, either under disciplinary provisions or under criminal statutes.

1. A person who wants to die and *asks* a physician to (1) provide the means or (2) kill her. The patient (1) has no ailment or injury or (2) has a severe, unrelieved psychological condition or illness or (3) is a concert violinist who lost her bow arm in an accident.
2. A person or patient has a condition or illness, but is not in imminent danger of death or in significant pain and asks a physician to (1) provide the means to die or (2) kill him. The condition or illness might be such as Alzheimer's, HIV(+), AIDS, or cancer. The provider or providers may have tried numerous modalities or the person (or patient) simply does not want to deal with the condition or illness or its likely or eventual effects and simply wants to die now.
3. A patient has a disease or condition which results in some pain, at least occasionally severe. Her pain state is not relieved by available treatments and cannot be improved or will worsen. The patient is *not* immediately facing death, but asks a physician to (1) provide the means to die or (2) kill her. Examples might be some patients with advanced multiple sclerosis or advanced cancer.
4. A patient is in great, virtually constant pain and will die soon. The patient asks a physician to (1) provide the means to die or (2) kill him. Alternatively, the patient is no longer coherent, conscious or otherwise able to communicate his wishes and (1) previously gave those instructions to the physician or other health care provider or (2) his family or significant other says the patient gave such instructions or (3) the physician "believes" the patient intended the physician to kill him in such a situation or (4) the physician believes it would be merciful.
5. A patient, as in No. 4, except that the patient has Alzheimer's and is not suffering significant pain.

There are obviously many other scenarios. The above are simply illustrations, often based on recent, newsworthy cases, of the kinds of situations with which practitioners, particularly those in pain management, have been or soon will be faced. They allow us to give a context to the grounds for which a licensee might be disciplined (or prosecuted) as well as the basic issue of whether (or when) a health care provider should be subject to discipline or prosecution.

Discipline for Crimes: Where the Conduct (Assisted Suicide; Euthanasia) Is Illegal

Traditionally, conviction of a crime has been a major basis for discipline, if for no other reason than the ease of justifying discipline where a court has already criminally convicted the licensee (the case is usually shorter, goes faster, and is harder to contest).

Has There Been a Criminal Conviction for Performing Euthanasia or Assisting in a Suicide?

If suicide is illegal in a jurisdiction, and a physician (or other health professional) assists a person in committing suicide and there has been a criminal conviction, the physician can be disciplined. This is probably true even if no professional skills or knowledge were employed and the licensee did not use his or her authority as a licensed professional to aid in committing the crime.

Similarly, the killing of another person is also a homicide–a felony–unless it is justifiable homicide (such as where self-defense is involved) or the killer is found to be mentally incompetent at the time of the killing.[1]

In many, if not most, jurisdictions, a board can take action against a licensee for assisting in a suicide or for actually committing a homicide, even *without* a criminal conviction, especially if the licensee employed professional knowledge or skills to do so, or if the decedent was, at the time, a patient. Effectively, this was the basis for revoking Dr. Kervorkian's license in both Michigan and in California. In general, boards do not rely solely on a successful criminal prosecution and often do file for violation of a criminal statute *without* a prior criminal conviction. This is both because many prosecutors cannot or do not prosecute every case they could and because, even in the case of an unsuccessful criminal prosecution, the standard of proof in disciplinary cases is easier to meet than that in criminal cases.[4] Under most existing laws euthanasia would also be a crime–premeditated murder–and grounds for discipline for any licensee involved in carrying it out. The only time either euthanasia or assisted suicide would not be a crime is if (1) the state did not ban suicide and (2) the conduct engaged in by the person assisting in the suicide or performing euthanasia either was expressly authorized by law or did not fall within the state's definition of homicide.[1]

Discipline for Violation of Statutes or Regulations

Even where something is not a crime, it may be a violation of a specific statutory or regulatory requirement or restriction. They may be very general requirements–such as keeping records of all prescription drug transactions–or those specific to a particular procedure or practice setting.

Assuming assisted suicide or euthanasia were legal, one would have to ask whether the law or regulation which was violated is constitutional? Does the law or regulation infringe on a person's right of privacy, of control of one's own life and body? Is the law or regulation too vague for the professional (or patient) subject to it to understand and follow?[1] If the standards or requirements are constitutionally valid, did the professional comply with them? Is failure to comply with those standards specifically a ground for discipline? If not, is there some broader standard–professional misconduct, violation of laws governing the practice of the profession, etc.–which can be a basis for taking action because of the failure to follow such laws or regulations? Even if the agency has the authority to proceed, should it exercise the authority?[2]

Nevertheless, any licensee must be aware that a board can take action in such cases, particularly where there is a violation of a provision of the board's own practice act or of regulations adopted by the board. This means the licensee must be intimately familiar with such laws and regulations and, unless the licensee is prepared to risk violating them, in full compliance.

Discipline for Acts of Dishonesty, Fraud or Corruption

Acts of "dishonesty, fraud or corruption" would not ordinarily apply to assisted suicide or euthanasia, unless the licensee tried to hide his or her involvement by lying to others or by falsifying or altering medical, death or other records, such as prescriptions. In most, if not all, jurisdictions making false records or signing false documents in connection with one's professional practice is a separate, specific ground for discipline; in many it is also a criminal act.

Did the licensee have a motive other than the patient's relief? Was there some monetary motive, such as insurance? Was there an organ sale involved? These are obvious (and unlikely) horror stories, but they illustrate acts of corruption.

Discipline for Gross Immorality or Moral Turpitude

Gross immorality or moral turpitude is a much more difficult concept and a more dangerous one. It is not readily susceptible to close definition, but has been broadly used to justify action against a licensee for acts which offend either current or historical moral (frequently religious) values. This can include such clearly improper misconduct as crimes of violence (murder, rape, etc.), crimes against property (arson, etc.), or crimes against the public (treason being a prime example), which we would all probably agree are immoral. But it has also included homosexuality, "disloyalty," abortion, and other either highly political, ethnocentric, or religion-based concepts which were, at some time, reflective either of community or religious standards or those of the dominant majority in the legislature, the courts, the profession or on the licensing board.

Because the whole subject of euthanasia and assisted suicide is so much in flux, changing from month to month and varying from state to state, the above examples, particularly abortion,[2] may provide some guidance as to how the role of regulators should or will develop in the near and long-term future.

For example, there is no law of which the author is aware which specifically makes the Hippocratic Oath legally binding in a jurisdiction, but the Oath does provide:

> . . . I will prescribe regimens for the good of my patients according to my ability and my judgment and never do harm to anyone. *To please no one will I prescribe a deadly drug, nor give advice which may cause his death.* Nor will I give a woman a pessary to procure abortion. . . . In every house where I come I will enter only for the good of my patients, keeping myself far from all intentional ill-doing and all seduction . . .

This 2500 year old ethical guide for physicians is often cited as a moral imperative which, regardless of statutes, bars a physician from either performing euthanasia or assisting in suicide or abortion. Suicide is also considered immoral by many of the leaders of the dominant strains of Christianity and Judaism. They say that because life is given by God, it is a sin to end life, including, for a significant minority, that of the unborn as well as of those in great suffering or with no hope of recovery, no matter what the stated justification.

At the same time, there are equally strong obligations for health care practitioners, perhaps also dating back to Hippocrates, that pain should be relieved. The difficulty of using such "moral" obligations as a basis for discipline, as opposed to more specific, clearer standards, is that while some morals are fairly constant, others are changeable, if not ephemeral, and may even subject a licensee to the particular prejudices of a board as it exists at a particular moment in time.

Discipline for Inadequate Care

A major basis for action against a licensee involves inadequate care. This typically includes significant carelessness in practicing one's profession (often called professional negligence, gross negligence, or malpractice) or incompetence in practicing one's profession.

Actionable carelessness (negligence, malpractice, etc.) typically involves poor judgment in deciding whether to perform an act–including euthanasia or assisted suicide–or in the manner of performing an act (although the licensee might well, in fact, be *capable* of making and carrying out a proper medical judgment). It can include a failure to act as well.[3]

A key question would be the standard against which the licensee is to be measured. Would it be that of the general practitioner or of a specialist? If of a specialist, which specialty? Would it be of a certified pain management specialist? An oncologist? A thanatologist? And who would (or even could properly) serve as an expert? Expert opinion is usually required to establish incompetence or negligence. If someone styles herself as a thanatologist, can someone who does not qualify himself as one render an opinion on her competence or the quality of care she rendered?

Is there anyone currently qualified to judge such a practitioner on the decision to euthanize or to assist in a suicide? In most states, the licensing board will proceed, where it believes it is warranted, employing the most qualified expert available, but this still leaves the question whether a licensing board *should* be determining whether a licensee did a professional job in causing or assisting in a death, unless the Legislature has specifically said the board can.

Perhaps just as importantly, who determines *whether* the licensee, for legal purposes, actually did euthanize or assist in the patient's death? How should it be determined?

Incompetence generally means one lacks the present ability or knowledge necessary to practice one's profession. A finding of incompetence might result from a determination a licensee lacked the medical knowledge or skills needed to perform an act or decide whether to perform an act. A major question would be, as with the quality of care, who could opine that there was incompetence.

Expert opinion always involves analysis of how a patient *was* treated, which always means the use of hindsight–second-guessing. And anytime a new field develops or a new treatment or procedure emerges within a profession, establishing fair standards by which to measure competence is difficult and at least somewhat arbitrary at first.

Licensing boards do not generally set the standards for specialties within a practice (such as neurosurgeons, orthopedists, or oncologists). They leave the substantive standards for specialties to the professions, including specialized medical organizations and certifying bodies. In general, the boards simply apply general, baseline standards to whatever act or omission of health care is involved and determine if the licensee met standards for the profession or specialty within the profession (and complied with specific statutory or regulatory provisions).

Those on the cutting edge of pain management in general and especially palliative care are already often deeply concerned about the scrutiny and second-guessing of their actions or their judgments by government or by others who do not fully understand the nature of pain, the standards for pain management, the rights of individuals to influence or control their medical care, and the proper, often extremely aggressive use of powerful opioids in the management of many patients. Opioid phobia has already substantially inhibited adequate pain management for decades. The line between palliative care and euthanasia or assisted suicide *can* be a fine one; if the actions of licensees are scrutinized too closely, will it prevent patients from receiving essential care?

Discipline for Related Conduct

This is a concept that a licensee can be disciplined for conduct not specified in the licensing law or regulations.

Although the conduct is not committed in the course of professional activities, and there is no criminal conviction, the conduct is considered sufficiently related to the practice that it can be a basis for discipline. Not all state laws reach such conduct; not all states allow discipline for conduct not specified in a board's law or regulations. But many do.

Where the authority to discipline for such conduct exists, it must be shown that there is at least some plausible connection between the conduct and either the qualifications, functions, or skills necessary to safely and honestly practice the profession. The same kind of analysis is often made to determine whether conviction of certain crimes, especially those not involving major felonies, do, in fact, have some bearing on one's fitness to practice a profession.

This would have little relevance to euthanasia or assisted suicide, except, perhaps, where the professional used no professional skill, knowledge, or authority in performing euthanasia or assisting a suicide.

Relevance of the Specific Facts in Any Given Situation

Sometimes as to the issue of whether disciplinary action is justified, and always as to the issue of the seriousness of the conduct in a particular case, the issue of under what circumstances the procedure was performed is highly relevant. So are the licensee's education, training, general methods and standards of practice.

If euthanasia is illegal, performing euthanasia will almost certainly be grounds for discipline of a licensee. But the circumstances are still highly relevant to the issue of the appropriate punishment or discipline for the conduct. If assisted suicide is illegal, it is just as simple (assuming one can prove the health care professional actually did assist the suicide).

Palliative care is clearly legal. But if palliative care isn't *really* just palliative and was really *intended* to enable–or cause–a patient to die, it may be assisted suicide or euthanasia (and homicide), at least in some jurisdictions. It depends on the facts.

IF EUTHANASIA OR ASSISTED SUICIDE IS LEGAL

But assume euthanasia or assisted suicide is legal[4] or its legality is unclear. Then the circumstances of the death are paramount, and a number of questions may need to be asked. Was euthanasia or assisted suicide discussed with the patient in advance? Was the reason for assisting in or causing death discussed with the patient or patient's representative?

Were any underlying medical reasons thoroughly discussed with the patient? Depending on the law of the jurisdiction, were appropriate additional consultations from specialists obtained? Was a psychological evaluation indicated (because there was some question about the patient's fitness to make the decision)? If so, was it performed?

Was the patient's desire to die supported by objective, competent medical opinion that the patient's situation was hopeless (either terminal, hopelessly in pain, or in a debilitated, irreversible state)? If the patient is in a health facility (or a home health or hospice setting), did facility protocols exist, were they adequate–and were they followed?

These and similar questions are those which might well be asked by someone–such as a regulator or law enforcement official and any expert retained by the agency–assessing an assisted death or euthanasia case. For that reason, the *practitioner* should also ask such questions of his or her own practice or of actions as to a specific patient. This goes to a principle health care professionals have become unpleasantly familiar with–"medico-legal" considerations. It is preventative medicine only in the sense that it is aimed at preventing or limiting potential liability (as to prevention of illness or disease), but it is part of current practice of medicine in this arena as in so many others.

How Regulators Evaluate a Case

Those who set and apply the rules for professional discipline (including legislators, board members, and agency staff) prefer certain, immutable, black and white standards. It is far easier, as licensing boards usually did in abortion cases before *Roe* v. *Wade,* to await criminal prosecution and then revoke or otherwise severely discipline a licensee for the *fact* of criminal conviction for performing an abortion or to proceed, even without a criminal conviction, because the mere act of performing an abortion was, itself, criminal.

Before *Roe* v. *Wade,* boards could ignore on whom the abortion was performed, the judgment used in deciding whether to perform the act, the facility and equipment used, and the skill with which the abortion was performed, even the issue of patient consent. The mere fact it occurred was all the proof needed for discipline to be imposed.

Regulators and legislators simply do not like situations which force them to evaluate highly sophisticated concepts–especially developing concepts or standards–and second-guess professional decisions; they don't like gray areas. They worry about open-ended standards, in large measure because there is a much greater possibility of losing (as well as the possibility of spending time on the wrong case). They also worry about what will be justified next where standards are open-ended.[4] They worry about what is sometimes called the slippery slope–that eventually everything will be so wide open that there will be no standards, no prohibitions.

BUT WHAT OF PATIENT CHOICE?

Today, the focus is on whether to allow a physician to assist in the death of any patient–terminal or otherwise–in great, ongoing pain which has virtually destroyed the patient's quality of life and for which pain no solution has been (or apparently can be) found. And, somewhat less, the issue is whether a physician should–or even can ethically–euthanize a patient who cannot recover from a totally disabling condition which has left him unable to exist in any real sense.[4]

What if, tomorrow, it means the Alzheimer's patient–or wheelchair bound patient who feels he is becoming a progressively greater burden on his family–who doesn't want to face the end-stages (or to have a loved one do so)? The patient who has a condition with which he or she doesn't want to live (the violinist with the amputated arm) or face (the HIV+, ARC, or early stage AIDS patient)? The rational person, not necessarily a patient, who simply wants to die?

In this discussion, the role–the rights–of the patient cannot be ignored. What if, no matter how much a legislature, a regulatory body, or the regulator actually reviewing a case may disagree or be offended by an assisted suicide or euthanasia, the patient fully participated in the evaluation which led to her death, was clearly in full control of her faculties at the time, and absolutely wanted to die, either at that time or if her condition deteriorated to an agreed-upon point?

Does government–or, more broadly, society–have any business in preventing death in such a situation? Even if others, such as family members are affected? Suppose the family members have been consulted and agree with and are at peace with the decision? Suppose it is only "society" (or a licensing board) which thinks there is an offense?[4]

WHAT WERE THE CIRCUMSTANCES?

Using the abortion issue as an analogy, the issue is not simply whether the abortion was performed, but the circumstances of the abortion. Was the abortion performed according to state law? Was any requirement for a waiting period observed? Was information provided to the patient, and was informed consent obtained? Did the facility have required equipment and supplies? Were any records required by law kept?

Beyond the legal requirements, were adequate records kept (adequate to meet professional standards, as opposed to any specific law)? Were the equipment and supplies adequate under the circumstances (again, to meet professional standards, as opposed to any law)? Was the procedure safely and properly performed? Did the physician, in fact, adequately discuss the procedure, including possible alternatives, with the patient? Put another way, did the patient provide documented, adequate, truly informed consent?

These are just a few of the questions which must be asked today when determining whether a licensee who performed an abortion is subject to disciplinary action. And they–or similar ones–will be necessary in evaluating how assisted suicides or euthanasia were decided upon and performed, if such acts are more clearly legalized in the future.

And possibly the most important factor is that the abortion is presumed legal, if the person who performed it was a licensed physician and surgeon (and, depending on the state, it was performed early enough in the pregnancy and met other requirements or restrictions imposed by state law). Until the last 25 years, in most states *illegality* was not only presumed, it was often absolute.

THE HISTORY OF ABORTION LAW IS INSTRUCTIVE

The history of how abortion was treated by legislatures, the courts, law enforcement, and licensing agencies and how it is treated today by those agencies may well be instructive in evaluating the current and likely future regulatory response to physician-assisted suicide and euthanasia. In most states, abortion remained strictly illegal until one of a number of legal challenges led to *Roe* v. *Wade* and its direct recognition of the right of bodily privacy.[4]

Many legislatures then broadly legalized abortions; some legalized it only to the extent absolutely mandated by *Roe*. Others drafted the most restrictive laws possible and left it to the courts to decide just what restrictions or requirements could still be imposed. That process is still ongoing.

Assume that assisted suicide (leaving euthanasia for the moment) is legalized in a state, either by the legislature, by the courts, or, perhaps, by initiative of the people. As with abortion, it is likely that statutory restrictions and requirements will be imposed. It will be fairly easy for a licensing board (or law enforcement, where violation of the restrictions or requirements is made a criminal act) to take action based on failure to follow statutory provisions.

In addition, a licensing agency can, as with any other act, look to issues of disclosure, violation of legal or regulatory provisions, consent, fraud, negligence or malpractice or incompetence.

Euthanasia is still illegal in all states (because it is murder, in the absence of statutory provisions to the contrary), as is assisted suicide (either because suicide is illegal, which makes aiding and abetting one illegal, or because aiding or abetting suicide is specifically considered a homicide). So any practitioner who performs euthanasia or assisted suicide, as we have defined it, is presumptively guilty of a crime and misconduct; in some cases, there is no legal defense.

The standard defenses which can be used to excuse a homicide do not apply in cases of euthanasia or assisted suicide. It can't be called "self defense." The mental incapacity defense does not apply, nor does the "necessity" defense (necessity has not generally been interpreted to include to stop further suffering of an individual, but to refer to a public health need so great as to justify violating a law). So what defense can there be in a jurisdiction in which either euthanasia or assisted suicide is still illegal? "Mercy" is not a legal defense, although any capable, thorough attorney will make sure the evidence a killing was merciful gets before a jury, and an increasing number of "mercy" defenses are either succeeding or resulting in minimal sentences.

What about privacy issues? Or the right to pursue life, liberty and happiness? The United States Supreme Court sodomy case suggests that government will be able to continue to restrict or ban assisted suicide or euthanasia over a constitutional privacy argument, although it is hard to predict where court members will stand on such an intensely personal issue or where the court will move as its membership changes.

As to the right to pursue life, liberty and happiness, the courts–including the Supreme Court–have tended to see those rights (which come from the Declaration of Independence, a document predating, but not part of, the Constitution) in terms of rights expressly (freedom of speech; freedom of religion; right to bear arms; right against unwarranted search and seizure) or implicitly (the right of privacy intuited from the "penumbra" of rights guaranteed by the Constitution and the Bill of Rights) recognized in the Constitution. If the courts do not find it in the relatively recently recognized right of bodily privacy, they are unlikely to find it elsewhere in the Constitution, Bill of Rights, or the Declaration of Independence.

It is also important to distinguish between euthanasia and assisted suicide. Assuming the patient has truly consented, assisted suicide is, by definition, a choice made by the patient. If we were to recognize the patient's legal right and ability to control his or her own time of death, at least where the patient is in a grave, irreversible state (whether because of terminal or irreversible illness or extreme, unrelieved–and unrelievable–pain), would it be so wrong (the Hippocratic Oath aside) for a physician to assist a patient who is determined to die in a rapid, relatively simple, painless manner while the patient still has the will and the ability to make and act on that choice?

More importantly, unless there is a criminal conviction *does a professional licensing board want to be in the position of deciding which circumstances justify the physician's decision to provide assistance?*

Euthanasia, by contrast, is fraught with images of killing the defective, the derelict, and the aged, and of genocide, although its basic definition is "mercy killing." There is a basic fear of allowing government or any individual to have the power to authorize the death of persons. Some are concerned that it is just a short step from authorizing a patient to decide what efforts will be made to maintain him or her or under what circumstances his or her life will be terminated to a committee–or an individual–to deciding, without any prior authorization from the patient, that the patient should be put to death.

At the same time, we are beginning to truly accept that a person has the right to decide when enough efforts to treat a terminal or progressively debilitating illness or disease are enough. Should we then deprive that patient of the right to die with dignity at a time of his or her choosing simply because he or she is no longer physically able to kill himself or herself or make the choice?

We once found it unacceptable to "no code" a patient; now we have Living Wills. We once thought it was immoral to desecrate the dead body by removing organs; now society encourages everyone to donate them. In these situations, as well as with abortion, moral imperatives gave way to new moral imperatives, personal rights, practical considerations. Where in this stream of ongoing change does the current debate fall? And if it is difficult, if not fundamentally wrong, for society to play God with people's lives and their control of their life–or death–choices, it is just as difficult, and probably basically ill-advised, for the regulator, to second-guess the decision of a practitioner to perform euthanasia or aid in a suicide.

WHEN SOMETHING NEW IS NOT PROGRESS

Cases on the cutting edge–here, death caused or aided by professionals–must be approached carefully and with respect for innovation–even in such a sensitive area as making life and death decisions. But while new developments should not be held back by the "old guard" or medical "establishment," some "new developments" are actually dangerous, stupid, fraudulent, not justified by accepted research or scientific or medical analysis and evaluation.

Just because someone claims she is on the cutting edge of ethical medicine does not make it so. Regulating the practitioner who engages in fraudulent or dangerous practices clearly is a fundamental obligation of licensing boards. The regulator often cannot know the difference between cutting edge care and fraud or dangerous practices without thoroughly examining and investigating it.

If the concept of either euthanasia or assisted suicide is legalized, when a physician is involved in the act, the performance of the act–the how, the when and the where–will usually involve the licensee's medical judgment. Medical judgment is *clearly* the province of the licensing board, which is, as we have discussed, supposed to monitor the competence, prudence, and honesty of its licensees.

While some might suggest that regulators simply stay out of the area while the issues and standards are worked out by legislatures, the public, and the courts, this is not going to happen. The sorting out may take many years. Even if regulators stay away from cases where the issue is the mere fact there was euthanasia or assisted suicide in which a licensee was involved, the regulators must still examine how the professional handled the process (again meaning information gathering, disclosure and consent, evaluation, adequacy of resources, quality of actual care rendered).

And if the licensing board is to discipline a licensee, will it or could it ever be grounds for discipline for a licensee to *refuse* to perform euthanasia or assist a suicide, no matter how strongly the patient wants it and no matter how painful or hopeless her condition is? It has been relatively rare for licensing boards to discipline licensees for failure to provide treatment. The medical profession and medical schools are currently struggling with the issue of whether a medical student can refuse that portion of his or her *education* which relates to abortion. Could a practitioner who specializes in pain management be forced to euthanize or assist in a suicide where he has ethical or religious objections? Could that refusal, at some point in the future, be a deprivation of the patient's right to full medical care and constitute grounds for discipline?

CONCLUSION

If preserving life is a fundamental tenet of medicine, it must be reconciled with physicians putting patients to death or assisting them in dying. And it is increasingly recognized that life inherently includes *quality*, not just the mere fact of cardiac and respiratory action. If not allowing patients to suffer is also a fundamental tenet of medicine, then the goal of preservation of life must be balanced with the right of a patient in a hopeless condition, in severe, continuous and unrelenting pain, or where the quality of life is otherwise absent or substantially so, to choose whether to remain in that state.[4] At the same time, physicians already make life and death decisions. They perform abortions. They already decide to withhold potentially lifesaving or life prolonging treatment when they "no code" a patient or comply with a Living Will. Surveys show that a high percentage of medical practitioners whose practice includes the severely or terminally ill have made the decision to terminate at least one patient's life. Practitioners sometimes must select among otherwise terminal patients, including patients who are candidates for organ transplants.

Health care facilities and systems–private and government–must make such decisions now and will have to make them more frequently in the near future. It seems inevitable for virtually all Americans that physicians and health care facilities will have to ration health care even more than some do now, including weighing whether to provide extremely low odds, expensive, life-saving treatments, especially to infants or the elderly. Medical economics and, probably, federal law, will require physicians to withhold such treatment for those who cannot pay for it. As this is written, major limits on Medicare and Medicaid are being proposed over the next 7-10 years. Managed care or prepaid plans are limiting coverage, increasing annual premiums, increasing charges for covered visits or prescriptions, or a combination of all three. This will only accelerate rationing for many Americans who will simply be unable to afford excluded care.

And are euthanasia and assisted suicide really new or unique? Are they just a logical–even if potentially frightening and threatening to some–extension of medicine? A reflection of modern technology and changing understanding and definitions of life and death? Closely tied to emerging issues of individual rights and patient control of their lives and medical care? And of the entire field of medical or bioethics?

The regulators of professionals must be part of the ongoing dialogue to help establish workable standards and definitions, to ensure those standards will neither be misapplied by regulators nor ignored, and to avoid imposing requirements or restrictions which cannot–or should not–be enforced or used as a basis for discipline. What that regulator does can greatly influence or even control the future of euthanasia and assisted suicide.

Today the regulator must simply decide whether euthanasia or assisted suicide occurred and then decide *whether* to take action. In the future, it will be a hopeless and inappropriate task for regulators to try to determine whether it is right, in principle, to perform euthanasia or assisted suicide.

Where laws forbid euthanasia and assisted suicide, licensees cannot legally do it and, if a licensee is prosecuted and convicted–especially where it involves his or her license or medical knowledge and skills, licensing boards should take action based on the conviction. When and where laws do not forbid it, the only proper questions for a licensing board may be (1) whether the patient was truly informed what was to happen and consented to it and (2) whether the licensee followed adequate, appropriate medical procedures in causing or aiding in death.

Government agencies are obligated to carry out the laws which govern them. Where those laws reflect a society's morals, the agency, including a licensing board, is charged with enforcing them. This includes pursuing disciplinary actions for clear violations of those laws. But the agency itself should not determine what is moral and then impose those morals, particularly in retrospect, on professionals who are simply trying to do their human best for their patients.

NOTES

1. These issues will–ultimately–have to be decided by the courts, especially the United States Supreme Court.

2. As discussed below.

3. Although, to date, actions for failure to provide adequate pain management have been rare, in a number of contexts there has been discipline for failure to be

aggressive in treating a patient. One example might be failure to perform adequate evaluation or to order or conduct adequate tests for a patient to properly diagnose and treat him; another would be abandoning a patient, either entirely or by simply not bothering to see or evaluate her. It seems likely that as the level of knowledge and of practice improves in pain management in each state, a substantial failure to provide adequate pain management will be a basis for discipline.

4. The standard of proof in a criminal case is evidence beyond a reasonable doubt; the standard in disciplinary cases is generally the same as in civil cases—preponderance of the evidence, although it may be higher in some states (e.g., clear and convincing evidence to a reasonable certainty).

DRUG USE IN ASSISTED SUICIDE AND EUTHANASIA

Lethal Drugs for Assisted Suicide: How the Public Sees It

Derek Humphry

SUMMARY. The author of *Final Exit* describes some of the ways in which terminally ill patients obtain, store, and use drugs in seeking a painless, dignified death, as well as his observations of the drugs most effective in producing death. *[Article copies available from The Haworth Document Delivery Service: 1-800-342-9678.]*

Derek Humphry is a journalist and author who, after the international impact of *Jean's Way*, founded the Hemlock Society in 1980 and was its executive director until retiring in 1992. He then founded the Euthanasia Research & Guidance Organization (ERGO!) to formulate guidelines for assisted death and provide information for the dying and their families.

Address correspondence to: Mr. Derek Humphry, ERGO, 24829 Norris Lane, Junction City, OR 97448-9559.

[Haworth co-indexing entry note]: "Lethal Drugs for Assisted Suicide: How the Public Sees It." Humphry, Derek. Co-published simultaneously in *Journal of Pharmaceutical Care in Pain & Symptom Control* (Pharmaceutical Products Press, an imprint of The Haworth Press, Inc.) Vol. 4, No. 1/2, 1996, pp. 177-182; and: *Drug Use in Assisted Suicide and Euthanasia* (ed: Margaret P. Battin, and Arthur G. Lipman) Pharmaceutical Products Press, an imprint of The Haworth Press, Inc., 1996, pp. 177-182. Single or multiple copies of this article are available from The Haworth Document Delivery Service [1-800-342-9678, 9:00 a.m. - 5:00 p.m. (EST)].

© 1996 by The Haworth Press, Inc. All rights reserved.

177

KEYWORDS. Assisted suicide, terminal illness, drugs, dying, death, euthanasia, AIDS lethal drugs, Compassion in Dying, Hemlock Society, Oregon Death with Dignity Act, plastic bag

Dear Hemlock, please send me one of your little red pills for me, and one for my friend Mary. I enclose $2. (Signed . . . Name withheld)

This little note which reached me one day back when I was national executive director of the Hemlock Society typifies–with only slight exaggeration–the attitude of much of the general public to the availability of fatal drugs for release from suffering from a terminal illness. Some people feel that there must be on the market instant, painless 'drop dead' drugs, or, if there is not, then there ought to be. I tell them that they've been brainwashed by James Bond movies, and spy thrillers, which give an impression that governments hand out these fatal pills liberally. I also tell them that, in cases where it is true, the poison is almost certainly cyanide, which, although extremely lethal, is in fact usually unacceptably painful, and you would not want to die in this shocking way in front of your family.

The whole purpose of the pro-euthanasia movement is to make accessible a type of death–only for those who need and want it–which is painless, dignified, lawful, justifiable and rare. It must be able to take place in front of the family, even in front of the children. To secure this option, which I count as the ultimate civil liberty, laws must be changed, old taboos dropped, and health professionals–most notably physicians, nurses, and pharmacists–become acclimatized to occasionally being involved in a euthanasia death. Modern caregivers (and I include pharmacists) must cease being merely body technicians, operating at a distance, and start practicing humanity at closer quarters. The poet John Donne wrote:

No man is an island. The death of any man diminishes me.

Thousands and thousands of people have stored away in dark recesses of their homes caches of lethal pills against the day when they might be suffering from an unendurable terminal illness. If you pried apart hundreds of old shoe boxes pushed into the back of closets you would find hoards of widely assorted sleeping pills, pain-killers and anti-emetic pills, never opened, lovingly packed away in an even temperature, gloomy hidey-hole, the location of which only the householder knows. "How long will they keep?" is the most frequent question I receive.

These precious treasures are left-overs from an illness, snatched from the bedside of a dead relative, or 'hand-me-downs' from a dear departed friend. Or they may have been bought during a holiday in Mexico or Switzerland, although those sources have mostly dried up in recent years: popularity spread the welcome word and consequently nervous authorities have tightened up the availability. A few desperate people go as far as Bangkok and Hong Kong where barbiturates can be bought without a prescription and smuggle them back in holiday luggage. One woman I knew paid a small fortune for lethal drugs in Hong Kong but in a panic in front of the Customs barrier slipped back and flushed them down the toilet. (She later became a client of Dr. Kevorkian.) Another woman of my acquaintance traveled to Mexico and purchased a lethal quantity of Darvon without a prescription and on return jubilantly told her doctor. He responded, "You just needed to ask. When the time comes, I'll give you a prescription for Seconal, which is much better." He did and she used it.

In the gay communities in the big cities there is an underground network of persons who pass around lethal drugs so that a patient dying of AIDS can 'self-deliver.' More often than not these are drugs which are left over, or not used, by another patient. Usually money does not change hands for the exchange of these drugs. But this itinerant traffic means that some of the drugs are not as lethal as the owners believe they are: there is a big difference between drugs which produce quick death and those which are potentially lethal but take huge quantities and perhaps days to bring about the desired effect.

The most common method of acquiring lethal drugs is by stockpiling over several years. Some people become adept at convincing their physician of the desperation of their insomnia and get small, non-lethal prescriptions of a barbiturate, say ten, and in a year or so have accumulated the 40-50 required (when taken judiciously). A good many physicians are aware that their patient is fooling them. But, given the state of the law, they don't mind. Very, very few physicians will give a prescription for a fatal amount of drugs to a healthy patient no matter how well the patient argues, offers guarantees, and so on. But now that the taboo against assisted suicide as an option for the dying has largely disintegrated in the past ten years, even though the legal prohibition remains, more and more will quietly and discreetly give a prescription to a terminal patient with whom they sympathize, know, and trust. A patient with AIDS is rarely refused.

For instance, Compassion in Dying, a Washington state organization which provides counseling to the terminally ill who seek their services, has at the time of this writing helped seventeen persons with assisted suicide but never once had to provide the drugs. In every case the primary care physician was eventually convinced of the justification (and his safety) in writing a prescription. If the patient wishes, a physician provided by

Compassion will usually supervise the on-the-spot ingestion to ensure its desired effect.

I wish I had received that type of backup in 1975 when I helped my terminally ill wife, Jean, to die. Whilst I had secured the drugs openly–but illegally–from a willing physician, in those days I knew nothing about what I like to call 'self-deliverance.' Jean swallowed the drugs in a mug of coffee, and quickly passed out. But after twenty minutes she vomited because I did not then know that we should have added an anti-emetic. For another thirty minutes I was terrified that what she had taken was not enough. Nobody wants to wake up from that intended last sleep, and as the carrier of the drugs it was my responsibility. Fortunately, after a total of fifty minutes she died as she had wished, ending two years of suffering from bone cancer.

Since the citizens of Oregon shook the world on November 8, 1994, by approving Ballot Measure 16 permitting physician-assisted suicide under a new Death with Dignity Act (it is being challenged in the courts at the time of this writing), there has been considerable controversy about (a) the correct lethal dosage for oral ingestion (the only method sanctioned by the Oregon law); and (b) the position of pharmacists in operating this law. My own work in self-deliverance in starting the Hemlock Society and writing two well-known and widely-used 'how-to' books on the subject[1,2] has provided me with extensive feedback over 15 years about the efficacy of drugs in accelerating the death of a dying person.

Several points stand out from my observations:

1. The drugs must be ingested quickly or else the person is likely to fall asleep before a fatal dose is consumed;
2. It should always be done in the presence of a physician, or at the very least a good friend, so that mistakes are not made, there are no interruptions, and there is a comforting and supportive presence;
3. An anti-emetic must always be taken and the contents of the stomach should be light but not empty;
4. If the drugs are not fast-acting barbiturates (because a physician refuses to help) and are merely sleep-aids or some other concoction, then a plastic bag should also be carefully used. In a desperate situation to escape hopeless suffering there is no need to worry about what the neighbors think. To the healthy individual, the plastic bag method sounds appalling, but you would be surprised how many intelligent people when wishing to die use this technique as a fail-safe.

What is the most effective lethal dose to be taken by mouth? This can be answered from the experience of physicians in The Netherlands, where some 400 people a year request and get assisted suicide. About 2,000 dying people in that country request and get a lethal intravenous injection or infusion because that is unquestionably the quickest and most effective method. For those few who wish to do it themselves, some physicians have used the following formulation:

Pentobarbital Sodium	9 g
Alcohol	20 ml
Purified water	15 ml
Propylene glycol	10 ml
Orange syrup	50 ml

Other physicians regard this formulation as outmoded and rely on the simpler formulation of pentobarbital in orange juice. Secobarbital sodium could also be used, of course, but Dutch physicians feel that pentobarbital gets into the human system a little bit faster. Over the last twenty years Dutch physicians and pharmacists have tried numerous other drugs and 'cocktails' of drugs, including orphenadrine, which was thought for a while to be effective, but today are pretty unanimous in using barbiturates.

Nobody survives taking 9 grams of pentobarbital properly ingested. But in about 25 percent of cases, for all the curious conditions to which the human body is heir, the dying person lingers for between two hours and four days more. Of course, in The Netherlands lethal injections are permitted in certain conditions, so the patients are helped to die after several hours that way–except, of course, for the 90 people who were part of a controlled study which produced the above statistic.

My own experience in North America gives about the same rate of delayed death. Plus, of course, if an insufficient amount of drugs is taken, there is a disturbing failure to die as intended. There can be fewer more terrible emotional experiences than waking up when you had intended to die. That is why, unaesthetic as it sounds, I recommend the use of a plastic bag in the borderline cases where the drugs might not be precisely lethal. Used according to the special techniques which have been developed in The Netherlands and America, the plastic bag technique is not as fearsome as it might seem.

Nevertheless, lawful physician-assisted suicide using an effective prescription professionally made up by a licensed pharmacist should always result in a quick and easy death without resorting to a plastic bag, provided the aforementioned guidelines are observed.

The Oregon Death With Dignity Act specifies that a physician may only write a prescription for a lethal dose, and may not give an injection. This ban on injections is going to be distressing for those patients who cannot do it for themselves, for they are often those most in need of this escape from terminal suffering. But at least the Oregon statute permits other persons, including the physician, to be present at the moment of self-deliverance. This will much reassure the patient and family at a time of tremendous stress.

The evidence from rising memberships of euthanasia organizations, sales of books, the viewership of movies and television specials on the subject, and the volume of votes in the citizen's ballot initiatives (4.5 million in California for example) suggests that a large proportion of the population expects the health professions (which includes pharmacists) to move towards accommodating their wishes for an accelerated death in a lawful and thoughtful manner.

REFERENCES

1. Humphry D. Let Me Die Before I Wake: How Dying People End Their Suffering. ERGO books, 1981.

2. Humphry D. Final Exit: The Practicalities of Self-Deliverance and Assisted Suicide for the Dying. Dell Paperbacks, 1991.

Observations Concerning Terminally Ill Patients Who Choose Suicide

Thomas A. Preston
Ralph Mero

SUMMARY. Observations on the outcomes of 46 terminally ill patients who voluntarily elected suicide to hasten death and who met the guidelines of Compassion in Dying (Compassion), a Seattle, Washington based organization, are presented. Compassion does not promote suicide, but does provide counseling and advice for patients who seek it to hasten death in the presence of terminal illness and suffering. The guidelines that Compassion has developed and the results of the organization's first 13 months of operation are described. Patient inquiries about suicide, participation of the patients' personal physicians and methods used to hasten death are discussed. *[Article copies available from The Haworth Document Delivery Service: 1-800-342-9678.]*

Thomas A. Preston, MD, Professor of Medicine at the University of Washington and Chief of Cardiology at the Pacific Medical Center in Seattle, is a member of the medical advisory board of Compassion in Dying. Ralph Mero, MDiv, DD, is Executive Director of Compassion in Dying.

Address correspondence to: Dr. Thomas A. Preston, Pacific Medical Center, 1200-12th Avenue South, Seattle, WA 98144.

[Haworth co-indexing entry note]: "Observations Concerning Terminally Ill Patients Who Choose Suicide." Preston, Thomas A., and Ralph Mero. Co-published simultaneously in *Journal of Pharmaceutical Care in Pain & Symptom Control* (Pharmaceutical Products Press, an imprint of The Haworth Press, Inc.) Vol. 4, No. 1/2, 1996, pp. 183-192; and: *Drug Use in Assisted Suicide and Euthanasia* (ed: Margaret P. Battin, and Arthur G. Lipman) Pharmaceutical Products Press, an imprint of The Haworth Press, Inc., 1996, pp. 183-192. Single or multiple copies of this article are available from The Haworth Document Delivery Service [1-800-342-9678, 9:00 a.m. - 5:00 p.m. (EST)].

© 1996 by The Haworth Press, Inc. All rights reserved.

KEYWORDS. Suicide, assisted suicide, suffering, antiemetics, barbiturates, cancer, AIDS, starvation, comfort care, reconciliation, Washington state

Compassion in Dying, or Compassion, a Seattle non-profit organization, was formed in April, 1993, to help terminally ill patients who choose rational suicide after reaching the limits of benefit from medical therapy. This is a report of our observations, made during Compassion's first 13 months of service, of 46 terminally ill patients who met our guidelines for rational suicide and who sought to hasten death through this means.

Members of Compassion are operating in an uncertain legal environment. However, we are not violating a Washington state statute, RCW 9A.36.060, which reads:

1. A person is guilty of promoting a suicide attempt when he knowingly causes or aids another person to attempt suicide.
2. Promoting a suicide is a class C felony. There have been no prosecutions under this statute. Compassion, four physicians and three patients are plaintiffs in a federal challenge to the constitutionality of the law. In May, 1994, the U.S. District Court for Western Washington found the statute unconstitutional; but this finding was reversed by the U.S. Court of Appeals for the Ninth Circuit.

We do not suggest, encourage, or promote suicide, but are willing to provide professional counseling and comforting for patients with terminal illness who voluntarily seek to hasten death as a last resort for relief of suffering. Members of Compassion who volunteer their services include clergy, mental health counselors, attorneys, physicians, a hospice nurse, and persons experienced in dealing with terminally ill patients. We consider our work a demonstration that mentally competent, terminally ill adult patients can hasten death in a voluntary, safe and humane manner.

We provide patients with information about alternatives to suicide, including conventional medical treatment and hospice care. If patients meet our guidelines and choose rational suicide, we accept that decision and offer our continued counseling and presence at the time of dying. We do not provide the agents of dying, and no physician representing Compassion prescribes or provides drugs. We arrange spiritual support upon request and provide emotional support to the patient and/or family as death occurs, and ongoing emotional support for the survivors, upon request.

GUIDELINES

Our guidelines for involvement of Compassion are as follows:

The patient's regular physician and at least one other physician must confirm the patient's condition as terminal and that it will result in death in less than six months, regardless of continued treatment. The patient's condition must cause severe, unrelenting suffering which the patient finds unacceptable and intolerable. The patient must understand the medical condition, prognosis, and types of comfort care which are available as alternatives to suicide.

It must be clear that the patient's suffering and request for assistance are not the result of inadequate comfort care, and that the patient's intent of suicide is not substantially motivated by inadequate health insurance or other economic concerns.

The request for assistance of Compassion must originate with the patient. The request must be made in writing or on videotape on three occasions, with an interval of at least 48 hours between the second and third requests. All requests and records are confidential. Requests for our involvement may not be made through advance directives or by a health-care surrogate, attorney-in-fact, or any other person. We will not provide assistance if there is expressed disapproval by any member of the immediate family.

RESULTS

During the first 13 months of operation, Compassion received approximately 300 serious and repeated requests for counseling from patients in the Seattle area who expressed a desire for rational suicide. Most of these patients did not meet our guidelines because they did not have an incurable medical condition or because they were not in the terminal stage of dying. Members of Compassion had extensive working contact with 46 patients who met our guidelines and died during this period (see Table 1). Twenty-two of these 46 patients had cancer (bone, breast, lung, ovarian, pancreatic, prostate), 16 had AIDS, three had chronic lung disease, and five had neurological diseases (ALS, multiple sclerosis). Twenty-seven were male; 19 were female. Ages ranged from 31 to 88. All patients were white.

Of the 46 patients who fulfilled our criteria and whom we counseled, nine were in institutions (hospice, nursing home, hospital) and were unable to obtain medicines necessary to hasten death. Five of these patients

TABLE 1. Activity of Compassion over First 13 Months

<u>11,000</u>* requests for information

<u>300</u>* inquiries from Seattle area of patients who expressed desire to hasten dying

<u>46</u> terminally ill patients who met guidelines and subsequently died

    <u>9</u> deaths in institutions

        <u>5</u> "natural" deaths

        <u>4</u> deaths by starvation

    <u>37</u> deaths at home

        <u>10</u> "natural" deaths

        <u>2</u> deaths by starvation

        <u>1</u> death by violent means (gunshot)

        <u>24</u> deaths with prescription drugs

*approximate

died "naturally" from their diseases and four starved to death. We estimate that these nine patients lived from one to six weeks longer than if they had been able to obtain medicines for hastening death.

Thirty-seven of the 46 patients died at home. Eight of these 37 patients asked their physicians for medicines necessary for suicide, but the physicians refused. We do not know the physicians' exact reasons for refusal, but in each case the physician acknowledged the patient's terminal status. Three of these eight patients subsequently committed suicide, two by starvation and one by gunshot. The other five died slowly of their diseases. An additional five patients who were able to obtain the necessary medicines died "naturally" before deciding on suicide.

We counseled 24 patients who fulfilled our criteria for rational suicide and who hastened death at home with prescription drugs. Thirteen were male, eleven were female. Ages ranged from 31 to 84. Eleven of these 24 patients had cancer, ten had AIDS, two had neurological diseases, and one had pulmonary disease. These patients had 15 to 40 hours of face-to-face contact with members of Compassion over an average of five weeks (range two weeks to three months) prior to dying. No suicide attempt was unsuccessful.

In 20 of the 24 cases the patients' personal physicians prescribed the drugs with explicit knowledge of the patients' intention to use them to end life. In the remaining four cases the patients did not state their intention explicitly, and their physicians did not ask, but prescribed the medicines.

Seven of the 24 patients also obtained some drugs (quantity unknown) from relatives or friends. Compassion maintains absolute confidentiality of all patients and their physicians. Members of Compassion did not supply drugs, and no physician associated with the organization wrote a prescription for or altered the medical care of any of these patients.

All of these 24 patients were confined to bed or chair, with the ability to walk only a few steps at most. In every case the patient's personal physician considered the patient as terminal with no chance for significant extension of life. The primary symptom was severe dyspnea in eight patients, nausea, vomiting and loss of excretory function in four patients, and extreme weakness, inanition and dependency in 12 patients. All patients had adequate, comprehensive palliative care, with maximal treatment of symptoms such as dyspnea or nausea. Fourteen patients had chronic pain, adequately controlled by narcotics in all cases. In no patient was pain the primary reason for suicide, although several patients required continuous high doses of narcotics for adequate pain relief.

Fifteen patients did not request a member of Compassion to be present but had the supportive presence of family and/or close friends at the time of dying. One or more Compassion members were present with nine patients at the time of dying.

The lethal medicines included barbiturates, benzodiazepines, and narcotics. Anecdotal reports from observers of these patients suggest that the combination of a hypnotic and a narcotic provided the quickest death. Death ensued at an average of about three hours with a range of 25 minutes to 10 hours after ingestion of the lethal drugs. (Ten hours was the maximum duration of the dying period during our first 13 months of experience, which this report covers. In subsequent experience, there has been one case in which death occurred in 24.5 hours.) Our clinical experience demonstrates that three times the standard dose of antinausea medication effectively inhibits nausea and vomiting of oral medications used for the purpose of intentionally hastening death. The antinausea tablets are taken simultaneously with three beta blockers such as Inderal, 80 mg, and followed by the powder from 60 to 90 capsules of 100 mg of Seconal or Nembutal suspended in a cup or more of applesauce, and made more palatable by the powder from three packets of artificial sweetener. We have had no instances of vomiting of the barbiturates or other medications in these situations, thus there has been no diminishment of potency of the barbiturates for their intended use. Drinking two ounces of an alcoholic beverage (whiskey, vodka, champagne) after ingesting the barbiturates appears to potentiate the barbiturates and result in speedier death, although approximately half of the patients, whether because they were nondrinkers or for other reasons, wished to forgo this part of the protocol.

All the terminally ill patients we have observed using this protocol to end their lives, or whose deaths have been described to us by family members in cases where we were not present, have fallen deeply asleep within five minutes, and then peacefully died within 25 minutes to 10 hours. The vast majority of patients have died in four hours or less (average, about three hours), with the longer death processes experienced by younger patients. Respiration slows quickly, dropping to four breaths per minute, then becoming more and more shallow until breathing ceases, along with heartbeat. There are no signs of struggle, respiratory distress, pain, or discomfort.

We are aware of other cases in which attempts to hasten death have been considered "failures" by family members or others present because death did not occur within a short time. People who have formed a mental impression of how death occurs from representations in cinema or television may be surprised that the process of dying from a lethal quantity of barbiturates may require many hours. They may even feel it necessary to try to administer other medications to the comatose patient, or even end the dying process through asphyxiation by using a plastic bag. It is important that terminally ill patients considering a barbiturate-hastened death, and others who may be involved, are thoroughly counseled about the details of such a process of dying and have realistic expectations in advance.

While injected medications are commonly more powerful in lower doses, we believe that when self-administered in the proper manner, six to nine grams of barbiturates taken by mouth can result in an easy and tranquil death for almost all terminally ill persons who have decided that hastening death is preferable to continued suffering.

All the deaths with which we are familiar have been attributed by the patient's primary physician to the patient's underlying disease. Local medical examiners have not questioned these determinations in an effort to turn up cases of suicide.

DISCUSSION

Although the majority of physicians in the state of Washington now favor legalization of physician-assisted suicide under some circumstances,[1] medical societies in general have taken a position against deliberate assistance in the suicide of even a terminally ill and suffering patient. Such activity, they feel, is interdicted by "professional ethics" and the proper role of the physician.[2] Also, many physicians consider physician-assisted suicide medically unnecessary and preventable by better access to medical care and particularly to better comfort care.

Nevertheless, despite comprehensive medical care some patients suffer intolerably before death. Suffering for these patients encompasses myriad symptoms during the terminal stages of dying, including pain, breathlessness, inanition and weakness, nausea, vomiting, loss of excretory control, and hallucinations. Others would rather die than remain heavily sedated or rendered nearly unconscious by continuous medication, or linger with adequate comfort care but with what they consider an unacceptable quality of life, a loss of dignity and resources, and emotional anguish of loved ones.

The results of our first 13 months' experience show that most persons who make inquiry about rational suicide do so early in the course of their terminal disease and are interested in the availability of the option if they should come to need it. This is in keeping with the widespread notion that patients fear prolonged technological dying more than death itself. It also conforms to the data from the Dutch experience with euthanasia, which show a small proportion of patients who ultimately follow through after initial request for physician-assisted dying.[3] In our experience, only about eight percent of patients who made serious inquiries about rational suicide met our criteria and hastened death with prescription drugs, but knowing the option existed under proper safeguards gave others reassurance and comfort.

We believe our work enables some persons to postpone suicide. Many patients expressed a fear of discussing their plans with loved ones or their physicians, lest they be institutionalized or stripped of their stockpile of medicines. In about half the cases we facilitated discussions between patients and loved ones or physicians which had not previously occurred. Once patients had the explicit support of family and physician they felt secure in waiting until suffering became unbearable before taking the pills, and five patients who planned rational suicide died naturally before feeling the need to do it. Moreover, none of those who acquired prescription drugs used violent suicide or starvation. Of the 17 patients in institutions or at home who were unsuccessful in obtaining the necessary drugs, one shot himself with a handgun and six starved to death.

Time from beginning of starvation to death ranged from 10 to 24 days. In a recent publicized report, a physician recommended starvation as an alternative to drug-induced death after his mother died peacefully following six days of no food or liquids.[4] However, that patient was in a hospital and received supplemental morphine to control symptoms. By our observations, without these aids starvation is a slow and lengthy ordeal, and we do not recommend it.

Our patients who committed rational suicide did so despite having adequate comfort care. All had maximal medical treatment, but this was not sufficient to eliminate dyspnea, loss of excretory function, nausea, or extreme weakness. Of the 24 patients who hastened death at home with prescription drugs, 14 had chronic pain but in all cases this was adequately controlled with narcotic analgesics. Our experience contradicts the argument that better comfort care or pain management could obviate assistance in dying for the terminally ill. Adequate pain control was not an issue.

These patients who chose termination of life did so because of what they characterized as unbearable suffering. They expressed their suffering in physical and emotional or spiritual forms. In most cases extreme dyspnea, or inability to move within a chair or bed, was apparent to any observer. These patients spoke of weakness and dependency so extreme and demeaning that continued existence meant nothing but extended agony, and they rejected the concept of spiritual benefit or salvation from suffering until "natural" death. We could find no single objective standard by which they defined when life became more burdensome than death, but they were all resolute in that conclusion.

All patients expressed a strong aversion to drifting into a semi-comatose or comatose condition, and many were particularly vehement about not wanting drug-induced coma, which one patient described as "an indignity worse than death." None expressed a desire for, nor could we detect a need for, better general medical care. No patient expressed financial concerns as a factor in choosing rational suicide, and in no case could we detect underlying financial considerations on the part of a family member or physician. About one-fourth of our patients had home-hospice care, which they said was excellent and fulfilled their needs as much as was possible. All patients understood but rejected the option of inpatient hospice because they did not want to leave home and feared drug-induced stupor or unconsciousness as a means of symptom control. We believe the medical community greatly underestimates the growing desire of many patients to avoid a prolonged technological death, particularly in an institution or in a sedated or "drugged" state.

Although some of these patients were of limited financial means, we had no factual analysis of their resources other than whether they had medical insurance. The patients who learned of our organization and sought our services were savvy in using medical services in general. The total absence of minority patients suggests strong cultural influences in seeking or avoiding rational suicide. Patients less able to access and use the medical system may be more susceptible to financial influences, but such patients are also probably more wary of medical intrusions of any sort and less assertive in seeking non-traditional help of this kind.

No suicide is easy. Of the nine suicides one or more Compassion members observed, one was marked by delays and complexities of medical management.[5] In one case the spouse was fully supportive but displayed fear of potential criminal prosecution for acquiescence in the dying patient's act, and has continued with pastoral counseling for feelings of guilt. The pervasive taboo against suicide in general, and the presence of a law making "promotion" of suicide a criminal offense, made some anxiety inevitable for all persons associated with the events. Nevertheless, family members were overwhelmingly appreciative of the peacefulness of their loved ones' deaths.

Dying can take many forms, and frequently entails suffering of patient, family and friends. In an expression of idealized dying, Callahan, who does not favor assisted suicide, has described what he terms a "peaceful death."[6] Of the nine suicides at which one or more members of Compassion were present, two were preceded by delays related to meeting our guidelines and safeguards, and three were prolonged (death 5-7 hours after induced sleep), but all were successful and all met Callahan's criteria for a "peaceful death."

We do not know whether these patients found spiritual meaning in death, but they were reconciled to it. They were treated with respect and sympathy by family, friends and physicians, and found in their dying a physical and spiritual dignity. Their deaths mattered to others, were seen in a larger sense as a loss and a rupturing of the human community, understood to be preferable to a prolonged and excessive suffering, and understood as a part of the biological nature of humans. They were not rejected by their physicians or psychologically ejected from the community because of impending death. The people they loved were with them in the days before they died, and with them in the same room at the time of their deaths.

These dying patients accepted dependency on their families for an extended time, but were not undue burdens on others in their dying. Their dying was not the financial or emotional ruination of other lives. Those around them did not dread their deaths, they comforted them in their dying, and, after death, they and members of Compassion comforted each other. These patients were conscious very near to the time of their deaths, with mental and emotional capacities intact. They died quietly in their sleep. The pain they had during the months before dying they bore well.[7] Theirs were the most peaceful deaths any of those with them have ever witnessed.

To those of us who knew these patients, the most unanticipated benefit was the reconciliation of patient with family and loved-ones in the weeks or days before dying. Such reconciliation, sometimes expressed with a simple "I love you," but often with frank reminiscences of shared conflicts and joys, may well be possible only in the brief period prior to a predictable or known time of death. In the typical case of intentionally hastened death, family and friends gather for a day or more preceding the death, in an atmosphere akin to "goodbye parties" some dying patients arrange. A former spouse traveled over 2000 miles to be present at the dying of one patient, 12 years after they had last seen each other.

Such goodbyes are unlikely or inappropriate in "natural" dying when duration of life is unknown, are impossible after unexpected death, and grievously absent before violent suicide. Similar peaceful deaths occur in hospices, although the time of dying is not known in advance, and patients are often heavily sedated. With a planned death, the occasion for apology, forgiveness, and completion of unfinished business comes to the present. The expression of unrestricted love for the patient, and reconciliation with loved ones who in turn avert lifetimes of guilt, misunderstanding, and unresolved enmity, is a gift of incalculable value over and beyond peaceful dying.

REFERENCES

1. Cohen JS, Fihn SD, Boyko EJ et al.: Attitudes toward assisted suicide and euthanasia amoung physicians in Washington State. N Eng J Med 1994; 331: 89-94.

2. Decisions near the end of life. Council on ethical and judicial affairs, American Medical Association. JAMA 1992; 267:2229-33. See also, Preston TA: Professional norms and physician attitudes toward euthanasia. J Law, Med & Ethics 1994; 22:36-40.

3. van der Mass PJ, van Delden JM, Pijnenborg L, Looman, CWN: Euthanasia and other medical decisions concerning the end of life. Lancet 1991; 338:669-74.

4. Eddy DM: A conversation with my mother. JAMA 1994; 272:179-81.

5. Belkin L. There's no simple suicide. The New York Times Magazine, Nov 14, 1993, pp. 50-75.

6. Callahan D. Pursuring a peaceful death. Hastings Cen. Rep.1993; 23:33-8.

7. The characterization of peaceful death is based on that of Callahan; see reference 6.

Euthanasia and Euthanizing Drugs in The Netherlands

Gerrit K. Kimsma

SUMMARY. In The Netherlands euthanasia and physician-assisted suicide are legally pardoned if certain conditions are met. After portraying the development of euthanasia as a public and legal issue, this paper describes the pharmaceutical aspects of euthanasia and physician-assisted suicide. In 1977, 1980, 1987, and 1994, information on means to end life has been formulated, revised, and made available to physicians and pharmacists; this information is summarized and analysed here. In spite of the reality of this practice in The Netherlands and the expanded knowledge of euthanatic drugs now available, there are some remaining dilemmas concerning legality, choices between euthanasia and physician-assisted suicide, unrequested ending of life, and practical medical issues of communication with patients. *[Article copies available from The Haworth Document Delivery Service: 1-800-342-9678.]*

KEYWORDS. Physician-assisted suicide, euthanasia, ethics, The Netherlands, euthanzing drugs, euthanatica, law

---

Gerrit K. Kimsma, MD, MPhil, is a member of the Department of Family and Nursing Home Medicine and the Medical Faculty at the Free University, in Amsterdam.

Address correspondence to: Dr. Gerrit K. Kimsma at the Department of Family and Nursing Home Medicine, Faculty of Medicine, Free University of Amsterdam, Van der Boechorststraat 7, 1081 BT Amsterdam, The Netherlands.

[Haworth co-indexing entry note]: "Euthanasia and Euthanizing Drugs in The Netherlands." Kimsma, Gerrit K. Co-published simultaneously in *Journal of Pharmaceutical Care in Pain & Symptom Control* (Pharmaceutical Products Press, an imprint of The Haworth Press, Inc.) Vol. 4, No. 1/2, 1996, pp. 193-210; and: *Drug Use in Assisted Suicide and Euthanasia* (ed: Margaret P. Battin, and Arthur G. Lipman) Pharmaceutical Products Press, an imprint of The Haworth Press, Inc., 1996, pp. 193-210. Single or multiple copies of this article are available from The Haworth Document Delivery Service [1-800-342-9678, 9:00 a.m. - 5:00 p.m. (EST)].

© 1996 by The Haworth Press, Inc. All rights reserved.

INTRODUCTION

The Netherlands figures centrally in the issue of euthanasia. It is the only country in the world where euthanasia is legally pardoned if certain conditions are met. Public support, judicial recognition of the right of self determination in the face of death and, most important, professional support and advocacy are all elements contributing to a law-based procedure that essentially maintains the criminal nature of ending someone's life but makes allowances in exceptional cases. What counts as 'exceptional' is described in *Rules of Care*, and, since all non-natural deaths have to be reported, the determination of what is exceptional is tested on a case-by-case basis. This means that several aspects of medical decisions at the end of life, so-called MDELs, have been analysed and accepted while others are still very much in a state of flux. These limits are also tested by the Dutch courts in 'new' cases.

Until quite recently, however, the pharmaceutical aspects of euthanasia and physician-assisted suicide had received little attention. These aspects are the main focus of this paper. First, I shall describe the Dutch position on euthanasia; then, secondly, describe activities to disseminate pharmaceutical information over the years past and shifts in this information; third I shall focus on recent research on the actual application of the pharmaceuticals used in euthanasia, and fourthly, I shall mention some issues that we still have to deal with.

EUTHANASIA IN THE NETHERLANDS

In spite of widespread suggestions that 'euthanasia and the Dutch' have a common ancestry within a liberal tradition, history shows that the subject of euthanasia in The Netherlands, compared to Great Britain, Germany or the United States of America, has little or no tradition at all.[1] Both Lindeboom and van der Sluis conclude that before 1930 interest in euthanasia was small to almost non-existent, compared to the surrounding countries.[2,3] At a time when euthanasia societies were founded in other countries, for example in England in 1935 and in the US in 1938, legal and medical journals in The Netherlands hardly contain any articles on this issue. This gap between suggestion and historical reality becomes even more apparent in the area of actual law proposals. In the US, the first (defeated) proposal to legalize euthanasia was put before the Ohio State Legislature in 1906. Other earlier attempts that failed likewise were tried in Nebraska in 1937 and in New York in 1947.[4]

Contrary to these early signs of interest elsewhere, the Dutch Society for Voluntary Euthanasia was not founded until 1973, after a case of euthanasia that apparently crystallized ideas and emotions sufficiently to become a public and organized cause.[5,6] This case concerned the active ending of the life, in 1971, of a 78-year old widowed woman by her physician-daughter, after repeated requests, through injection of an over-dose of 200mg morphine. The prosecution of this case received wide-spread public attention and unexpected support from the medical profes-sion and ministry all over the country. The Court in Leeuwarden accepted medical standards permitting the use of medication to end suffering through progressive doses of pain medication, taking into account the risk of death. Since the defendant had used just one dose, without progression, that led to death, rather than progressive doses, the court found the means unreasonable with respect to the effect. Although the court had no choice but to sentence the daughter, it gave a clear message: she was given a suspended sentence of one week in prison.

From that date on, euthanasia became a public issue within the medical profession, in the churches and in the media in The Netherlands. Both advocates and opponents claim that it is possible to prevent unnecessary and undesired suffering in hopeless situations. The cases that are brought to the courts have shaped the final acceptance of euthanasia: even though the law still prohibits the intentional taking of someone's life and killing remains a criminal act, taking a life is pardoned in situations of conflicting duties. These duties are to protect life and to relieve suffering.

Both the Royal Dutch Medical Society and the courts after 1973 seem committed to establishing guidelines that allow for the practice of actively ending life. The discussions within the medical and legal professions result in typically Dutch definitions and a new professional awareness of the area of death and the end of life. A novel terminology has been developed under the umbrella of medical decisions at the end of life, the so-called MDELs. This group has four distinct and separate areas:

1. non-treatment decisions (NTD), either because of refusal by the pa-tient or because of futility of the potential goals,
2. alleviation of pain and suffering (APS),
3. euthanasia and physician-assisted suicide (PAS),
4. life-ending action without explicit request (LAWER).

The Dutch definition of euthanasia has become: *the intentional ter-mination of life by someone other than the patient at this patient's request.* Elsewhere this may be called active euthanasia: in the Dutch concept, euthanasia is active by definition and the term active has lost its intended specificity. The term passive euthanasia is no longer used. Although elsewhere this term defines a practice that results in a patient's death due to stopping treatment, in The Netherlands the reasoning is that a treatment that has no clear medical benefit to a patient constitutes futile treatment, and since no patient should be subjected to useless medical interventions, not offering such interventions can hardly be called euthanasia.

The same holds for the terms direct or indirect euthanasia. Unintended shortening of life in the course of treatment of suffering, elsewhere called indirect euthanasia, does not come under this heading in the Dutch discussion. In The Netherlands, this practice is called alleviating pain and is considered a physician's duty. The chance that a seriously ill patient may die as a result of this treatment does not constitute euthanasia. The same holds for the terms voluntary and involuntary euthanasia. According to the Dutch concept, euthanasia can only be voluntary, by its very definition. Involuntary euthanasia is a contradiction in terms, since a request is essential for the action to qualify as euthanasia. Involuntary ending of a life falls under the heading of murder and must be reported and investigated as such. The LAWER group, Life-ending Actions Without Explicit Request, actually consists of terminal patients without treatment options, without possibility of communicating, where comfort care is failing and only suffering remains. Ending the life of these patients elsewhere is called 'involuntary euthanasia,' in recognition of the humane nature of the act. However, since the Dutch definition of euthanasia stresses the presence of a request, this group emerged as a separate entity only as a result of the change in the definition of euthanasia.

Even though several attempts have been made to legalize euthanasia and decriminalize the act by introducing bills in Parliament, disagreement on this issue among political parties of the coalition government has prevented a majority vote in favor of legalization. In 1993 this process resulted in an agreement between the Christian Democratic and Socialist coalition to keep euthanasia a crime, but to allow physicians to end lives under very specific conditions, where each physician must report the unnatural ending of a life and each case is tested after the event by public prosecutors. Doctors are legally bound to report any case of unnatural death, including euthanasia, physician-assisted suicide, and unrequested termination of life. There are penalties for not reporting.

INFORMATION ON DRUGS

Over the past 20 years the practice of euthanasia has taken shape morally, legally and medically. However, in spite of the widespread public and professional support, exact knowledge of the pharmaceutical means by which euthanasia is performed has been scant. Nevertheless, on four separate occasions, information on means to end life has been formulated and made available to physicians and pharmacists: in 1977, 1980, 1987 and again in 1994. In 1977, Dr. Pieter Admiraal, anesthesiologist, wrote the first article with information on drugs used in a hospital in a book on euthanasia that appeared in a medical series.[7] In 1980, in order to improve knowledge of these means, the so-called 'euthanatica,' the Dutch Voluntary Euthanasia Society sent this material in a small manual, called *Responsible Euthanasia*, to all Dutch physicians. The unrequested distribution of this manual caused quite an uproar and was met with resentment from opponents of euthanasia. This upheaval was probably one of the reasons why the next report, the 1987 *Technical Report on Euthanatica*, was made available to physicians and pharmacists on request only and, due to the potentially deadly advice, was designated 'confidential.' This same restriction applied to the 1994 report, entitled *Application and Preparation of Euthanatica*. A comparison of these reports reflects increased experience and sophistication, both in describing the professional conditions of a 'good death' and identifying the necessary qualities of the lethal drugs recommended.

Professional Conditions and Norms

In 1980 Admiraal, the author of the manual, advised discussing the speed of the dying process with the family, but takes the position that the act of euthanasia should not prolong the suffering of either the patient or the family. He maintains that a physician should aim for a quick, soft death, preferably by taking an agent orally, by the patient himself or, if that is not possible, administered by the parenteral route. No specific timespan for the process of dying is mentioned as a norm, only that the physician should be aware of possible foul-ups of ineffective means.[8] The 1987 report spells out more in detail the requirements that should be applied to 'the ideal euthanaticum, a substance whose administration by the various routes should cause a quick and gentle death.' The substances must be:

1. usable through simple administration,
2. the separate applications must be quick, effective and available,
3. its volume should be small enough to work with,
4. the substance must cause an irreversible coma within 30 minutes and death within hours,
5. the drugs should be available only on prescription through pharmacists,

6. there should not be unwanted mental or physiological side-effects,
7. potentially vomiting-inducing effects should be preventable,
8. the lethal effect should be guaranteed.

These requirements involve a mixture of medical-ethical norms, practical details and public safeguards. The 1994 report does not mention any specific additional condition; it is mainly an analysis of a survey of actual acts of euthanasia, identifying the drugs that were used and their effects.

The Drugs and Their Justification

Knowledge of the drugs that are used for euthanasia has increased dramatically over the past 15 years. Admiraal's manual of 1980[8] stated that his choice of drugs was based on personal experience; the 1987 report was based on critical analysis of available drugs by a larger committee of physicians and pharmacologists; and the report of 1994 is based on the empirical facts established in the survey. This increased experience has resulted in a narrowing down of the list of advised drugs and routes. This survey reflects a selected sample, based on returned questionnaires of physicians who actively requested the 1987 report and sent back their survey; in a statistical sense these physicians form a 'biased' group.

Knowledge of what really has been taking place in the area of pharmaceuticals used for euthanasia was expanded by the work of the Investigation Committee on the Medical Practice of Euthanasia (the 'Remmelink Committee'), the thesis on euthanasia by former family physician Gerrit van der Wal, and research by the Department of Family and Nursing Home Medicine at the Vrije Universiteit (Free University), Amsterdam.[9,10] A description and comparison of some of the results of these investigations follows.

Drugs, Routes and Time Span for Death to Occur

The 1980 manual states the potential applicability and use of four groups of drugs: curare-like agents, barbiturates, morphine and morphine-like drugs, and insulin. It is also suggests that the patient drink alcohol to strengthen the intended effect. The methods Admiraal calls preferable are the oral ingestion of barbiturates, combined with alcohol or a tranquillizer, and the use of a combination of barbiturate and curare-like substance through intravenous application by a physician. The time between application and death is described as between 10 to 15 minutes for the combination of barbiturate and curare-like substances, and hours to days for all other substances. There is no concrete advice on the most desired timespan, but there are several warnings about potentially ineffective choices; the report describes and evaluates (other) available drugs and recommends avoiding them. The 1987 recommendations are as follows:

1. barbiturates: effective for oral and intravenous use,
2. benzodiazepines: to be avoided, because of the uncertain effect,
3. neuromuscular curare-like relaxants: not for oral or rectal use; usable only after coma has been induced with a barbiturate,
4. morphine and other narcotic analgesics: uncertain because of the chance for tolerance and ineffectiveness,
5. orphenadrine: potentially effective in combination with barbiturate,
6. ketamine: ineffective to induce a sufficiently deep coma because of the high quantity needed for intramuscular injection,
7. insulin: to be avoided, because of its unpredictable outcome,
8. others, such as digitalis, beta-blocking agents, potassium chloride: to be avoided.

The concluding 1987 advice offers three choices:

a. the oral administration of 3 g of dextropropoxyphene hydrochloride followed by 9 g of sodium secobarbital or sodium pentobarbital preceded by an antiemetic (metoclopramide) for a day. In the presence of tolerance to dextropropoxyphene, the recommendation was to use 3 g of orphenadrine hydrochloride.
b. for parenteral use, the advice was to induce a coma through intravenous injection of 1 g (or 1.5-2 grams) of thiopental or pentobarbital, followed by intravenous injection of 45 mg of alcuronium or 18 mg of pancuronium.
c. rectal administration was recommended only as a last resort with a suppository containing 1 g sodium pentobarbital or sodium secobarbital, three doses every hour, up to 15 grams; this may require terminating life by a neuromuscular relaxant if the patient does not die after 15 suppositories.

Empirical Findings

The evaluation of available questionnaires after the 1994 report allows a number of conclusions. Of the 165 inquiries, the route of administration was oral in 87 cases, parenteral in 73 cases, and rectal in 5 cases. In the oral group, all but one physician used barbiturates with or without dextropropoxyphene or orphenadrine. In 59 cases an antiemetic was given, usually with the desired effect. Two patients who did not receive the antiemetic vomited the deadly drugs. For over three quarters of the patients, death occurred within hours, at most after five hours. But in 20% of the patients who received a barbiturate, a muscular relaxant was needed to end life after the 5 hour time period.

With parenteral administration, contrary to the advice, benzodiazepines or other medications were used to induce coma in 23.3% of cases, usually resulting in the need for repeated and higher doses and sometimes resulting in reawakening with the need for a second attempt. In all other cases the combination of thiopental with a muscle relaxant was used. In those cases patients sometimes died before the muscle relaxant could be given.

Rectal application, used in 5 cases, led to death for two patients within three hours; in the other three cases administration of muscle relaxants was required up to five hours after administering the suppositories with barbiturates.

The extent of measures to end life became clear in the research of the Remmelink Report and the van der Wal and Muller et al. investigations (Table 1). The Remmelink Report was primarily intended to describe the extent of medical decisions at the end of life, especially the number of cases of euthanasia and the medical situations involved. The findings proved very surprising and covered a broad range. In the area of alleviating pain and suffering, for example, 82% of the physicians interviewed acknowledged that they had used morphine or morphine-like preparations with the result that lives were shortened. In 6% of the interviews, physicians stated that ending a life was the intended aim. In about 40% of these cases, patients had been involved in discussing the possibility of hastening death: in about three quarters of the remaining 60%, patients had been unable to participate in such a discussion.

The means used in euthanasia and physician-assisted suicide were:[10]

sedation (excluding morphine)	19%
sedation and muscular relaxants	47%
morphine	13%
morphine combined with other agents	13%
others	7%

A more detailed extent of drugs and procedures to end life was mapped out by the van der Wal research on 1042 family physicians' involvement in euthanasia in the years between 1986 through 1989.[12,13] Later, the same research profile was used with nursing home physicians, whose discipline is a distinct medical specialty in The Netherlands.[9]

Additional information was provided by van der Wal through analysis of the cases that had been reported and the legal documents that followed

TABLE 1. Drugs Used for Euthanasia

DRUGS	Remmelink data 94 general practitioners (GPs) 87 hospital physicians (HPs)– 187 cases		van der Wal data 388 GPs 367 cases	Muller et al. Data 69 nursing home physicians 69 cases
	GPs	HPs		
benzodiazepines	20%	15%	34%	29%
morphine	11%	22%	29%	11%
morphine combinations	13%	16%		2%
barbiturates	–	–	49%	60%
muscle relaxants	50%	38%	55%	53%
other drugs	6%	11%	9%	13%

from references 9, 11, 12, 13

from reporting. These formed a rich source of information, though they came from a statistically biased and nonrepresentative group. What has become exceptionally clear is that in spite of the openness in the public discussion of euthanasia, there still is a taboo within the medical profession concerning the question of reporting euthanasia. In the years for which the research was conducted, less than half of the cases were in fact reported. This fact is reflected in the means that are used. Not reporting means a choice for secrecy, and hence the chance that less effective means were used that needed no accounting for.

In the 187 euthanasia cases of the van der Maas/Remmelink investigations, sedatives were used alone in 19% of the cases, sedatives in combination with neuromuscular relaxants in 55%, morphine alone was used in 13%, morphine in combination with other drugs in 13%, and other drugs in 7%. In 367 cases of euthanasia examined in the van der Wal investigations, the drugs, applied singly or in combinations, can be divided into five groups:

1. neuromuscular relaxants   55%
2. barbiturates   49%
3. benzodiazepines   34%

4. morphine   29%
5. others   9%, e.g., insulin, alcohol, potassium chloride, digoxin, chloroquine, hexapropymate.

In 23% of cases, for example, a benzodiazepine was combined with a muscular relaxant; in 20% a barbiturate was used in combination with a muscular relaxant. Muscle relaxants thus were used in 55% of the cases. Insulin and alcohol apparently were still used during these years, but they did not appear in legal accounts in the reported cases. In a majority of these cases, the agents were given intravenously: 61%. In 20% the application was oral, mainly consisting of barbiturates. In 10%, mainly using muscle relaxants and morphine, the intramuscular route was chosen. There was a large range of doses used, e.g., 20 to 320 mg of morphine and 200 to 3,000 mg of thiopental. A similar pattern was found for each of the drugs.

The Muller et al. investigations of nursing home physicians' medication choices provides the following results for drugs used singly and in combinations:[9]

1. barbiturates   60% of the patients
2. neuromuscular drugs   53%
3. sedatives   29%
4. morphine   13%
5. other drugs   13%

These figures show a certain consistency and reinforce one another.

The justification for this large variety in means was also surveyed. The reasons offered included effectiveness, speed, slow induction, and specific intended effect such as a coma or depression of the breathing center or muscular relaxation. Half of the physicians in the van der Wal investigations chose guidelines or advice from colleagues as a basis to work from: 12% mentioned personal experience as the main reason for choosing a certain drug. Only 8% mentioned the Manual of 1980 and 1% mentioned the Guidelines of 1987 as a reference source.

TIME BETWEEN APPLICATION OF DRUGS AND DEATH

The time between the administration of drugs for euthanasia and the actual occurrence of death also varied greatly, as shown in Table 2.

In the van der Maas investigation, two thirds of the patients took less

TABLE 2. Time Lapse Between Application and Death

Time	van der Mass et al. n = 186	van der Wal n = 367	Muller et al. n = 60 accumulated
< 1 minute	5%	3%	8%
< 5 minutes			30%
< 10 minutes	33%	43%	37%
< 15 minutes			50%
< 30 minutes			65%
(> 10 min) < 1 hr	64%	63%	68%
> 10 min − < 1 hr			
> 1 hr − < 6 hrs		82%	87%
> 1 hr − < 24 hrs	92%	96%	95%
> 24 hrs − < 48 hrs		100%	100%
> 24 hrs − < 1 wk	99%		
> 1 wk − < 4 wks	100%		

than one hour to die and in a small number the dying process took longer than one day. In this survey, about 30% of the family physicians stated that they had experienced cases in which the time lapse between drug administration and death differed from that intended. The hospital based physicians stated in similar situations that the process had been longer than intended. The median time required for death to occur after administering drugs in the van der Wal research was 3.8 hours; the range was less than one minute to three days. Three percent of the patients died within one minute, 40% within 10 minutes, and 63% within the hour. For 23%, death required between one and six hours, for 14% longer than 6 hours, for 4% longer than a day.

REFLECTING ON THE USE OF DRUGS

Van der Wal has reflected extensively on the use of the available drugs to hasten death. Over 40 different drugs were used by family physicians, but those mainly used were confined to 10 drugs. Most of the general practitioners follow the advice of Admiraal from 1980 or the report from 1987. But ineffective drugs, or combinations of drugs also were used. In spite of the 1987 report, a number of physicians still used morphine and morphine-like substances, routes of administration that were less effective, and doses that were too low. Insulin was still used in 4% of the cases, even though its use had been banned in the 1987 report.

Based on the available figures, the 1994 report offers the current standard advice:

a. The intravenous route should be preferred, due to its effectiveness and reliability, using 1-2 grams of sodium pentothal (Nesdonal[R]) in 10 ml of saline solution, followed by an intravenous muscle relaxant such as 20 mg pancuronium dibromide (Pavulon[R]) or vecuronium bromide (Norcuron[R]).

b. The use of oral agents can be effective. If oral agents are used, physicians need be to aware of the possibility that active termination using a muscular relaxant may be necessary. It is suggested that the muscle relaxant be used about five hours after ingestion of the oral drug, or earlier if the need is felt when the patient did not or could not drink it all. The recommended drug is 9 grams of sodium pentobarbital or secobarbital in 100 ml of liquid, with an antiemetic used for one day prior to the administration of the euthanatic drug.

c. The rectal route should be used only as the last resort when other possibilities are not realizable. Then 1 gram of sodium pentobarbital or secobarbital in a suppository can be used; this must be repeated hourly. Monitoring the patient's body temperature in order to check the melting process is mandatory. Here also the physician must be ready to end life actively if death has not occurred within five hours.

In 1995 Admiraal added a clear personal recommendation to wrap up several discussions of the drugs that he considers preferable or undesirable.[14] Drugs that should not be used any more are: benzodiazepines, morphine, combinations of brallobarbital and morphine, dextropropoxyphene and orphenadrine, besides the already mentioned insulin. Benzodiazepine use is risky because patients can wake up and morphine is unsuitable because its application often fails, resulting in a dying process of long and torturing duration, sometimes lasting days on end. Rectal administration should be considered only as a last resort, because the hourly need for additional suppositories is cumbersome and difficult for both physician and family. In cases of physician-assisted suicide by rectal drug administration, a physician always must be aware of the possibility of failure and be ready and willing to end life actively after a certain number of hours so as not to cause additional harm and grief to all those involved.[14]

REMAINING DILEMMAS

In spite of the reality of this practice in The Netherlands and the expanded knowledge of 'euthanatica' drugs now available, it would be superficial and untrue to state that 'all is well' concerning medical decisions at the end of life. In the area of euthanasia there still are legal, moral and medical-practice problems. However, there are no economic problems. Euthanasia is not an option in a financial sense: people do not ask for it or consider it when financial resources are drained, since in The Netherlands there is universal health insurance. Neither is old age a reason to fear unrequested termination of life. The facts clearly show that euthanasia is a rare event in nursing homes, and the median age of patients who receive euthanasia is in their sixties, less in their seventies and rarely in their eighties, in conformity with the malignant and serious pathology of these age brackets.

Legal Aspects

For some, the current illegality of euthanasia under Dutch law, and the required legal procedure for reporting euthanasia, are philosophically unacceptable because this presents an oxymoron: something is either forbidden by law or it is not. If it is forbidden, then there should be punishments: if it is accepted, there is no need to review it on a case-by-case basis as is the current practice. Legalization still is a possibility that some, like the Dutch Society for Voluntary Euthanasia and the Royal Dutch Medical Society, strive to accomplish. Behind this wish is a divided opinion about the essential nature of euthanasia, whether it is criminal or not. On this issue there is a sharp difference between physicians and lawyers. For physicians, euthanasia is not considered a crime, but medical care–very difficult care at that, and one of the reasons why they do not wish to report it. For lawyers, euthanasia is not medical care but a criminal act, forbidden under the Penal Code and to be checked as to its acceptability. For them, each physician is considered guilty until determined otherwise.

The more concrete legal problem is the fact that there is underreporting by physicians. In 1994, the number of cases reported was greater than 1,300 or 50% of the estimated actual number of cases. This is an increase from 10% in 1983, but still far from full reporting. Here also one can note a legal peculiarity: although ordinarily, under Dutch law, no one has to incriminate himself in the face of the law, physicians are expected to report their own crimes and be subjected to questioning by functionaries in a judicial capacity.[15]

Between this concrete legal fact and the quality of this medical practice is a clearcut relation. Given the underreporting, there is reason to suspect that both fear of prosecution and a desire for secrecy lead some physicians to choose less effective means, since prescribing barbiturates and neuromuscular relaxants would 'betray' their actions and force them to come 'out of the closet.'[16] From the aspect of impact on the family, this secrecy could potentially lead to more difficult grieving because essential facts about the death and the dying process cannot be shared with others lest the physician be placed at risk of prosecution. This inability to share and the need to disguise the facts are essential ingredients for inhibited and disrupted processes of grieving. [17,18]

EUTHANASIA VERSUS PHYSICIAN-ASSISTED SUICIDE

In The Netherlands, the discussion of the choice between physician-assisted suicide and euthanasia has evolved differently from the United States and other countries in Europe. Assisting suicide, like euthanasia, is legally forbidden, although the physician who assists may be protected from prosecution. From a medical-ethical point of view, the two ways of ending a life were seen almost as equals, in spite of the clear legal difference in punishment. In recent years, however, an increasing inclination to prefer physician-assisted suicide over euthanasia has slowly emerged, mainly based on two arguments. The first is a psychological argument: the duress for physicians in performing euthanasia sometimes causes physicians to become temporarily dysfunctional. The second is that some people think that being assisted in committing suicide by drinking a lethal potion rather than being given an injection by a physician is more in conformity with the right of self determination and the right to choose death. Of course, this latter point presupposes that patients are capable of drinking a potion. Thinking that physician-assisted suicide is the entire answer to the question of ending the life of a suffering patient, nevertheless, is a fantasy. There will always be patients who cannot drink, or are semiconscious, or prefer that a physician perform this act. Experience has taught us that there are many cases of assisted suicide in which the suicide fails. Physicians need to be aware of the necessity to intervene before patients awaken.

Based on this history it may become understandable that, from a Dutch point of view, the stress on the advancement and acceptance of physician-assisted suicide, as opposed to voluntary euthanasia (as it is called elsewhere) seems one sided and insufficient. Many, though not all, attempts to legalize physician-assisted suicide, both in America and Australia, are limited to just physician-assisted suicide and do not allow euthanasia. From the above facts, it should be abundantly clear that this limitation is headed for disaster if physicians are forbidden by law to end life actively in cases of failure of the chosen route for assistance.

UNREQUESTED ENDING OF LIFE

One of the realities that van der Maas' investigations uncovered was the existence of a thousand cases of active ending of lives without request. For the opponents of euthanasia this was the definitive proof of a slippery slope: for the advocates it was a source of embarrassment. Of what is known of these cases, at least the majority of the patients involved were terminal and no longer competent, and many had expressed in some distant past some idea about not wishing to have their lives continued without chances for recovery.[19]

Two issues, at least, are relevant. One is the issue of changing a definition and expecting reality to follow suit. The other concerns the time of discussing the end of life within the medical relationship. The first refers to the fact that the change in defining euthanasia as 'ending the life of someone else upon his or her explicit request' presupposes a type of relationship close to the ideal of equals in communication, in which communication between physician and patient is on an open basis. Often medical reality does not answer this ideal: a disease or the disease process does not stop if there is no adequate communication or if one of the partners is not up to discussing the end of life. Sometimes patients are afraid to discuss euthanasia, as is my own experience also: does this mean that their suffering should be ending beyond the point of endurance for them and their families?

Sometimes communication about euthanasia starts too late: one cannot be more blunt about it. Does that mean that suffering should be unending and more extensive than is humane and humanly necessary? I realize that in many medical places the answer would be to increase the morphine dose delivered by an infusion pump as an answer, but we are not trying to evade the question but to confront it with honesty and integrity. This means that if the intention exists to end the life of a patient when there is no request to do so from the patient, there should be consultations and an open decision with a report to the legal authorities as the law presently requires.

MEDICAL PRACTICAL ISSUES

Some of the practical issues I had to learn myself as a physician as my euthanasia cases occurred and I interviewed family members and those of other physicians years later.[18] The main lesson has been that one cannot be careful enough about paying attention to all the aspects of euthanasia, including those that later interviews uncover as potentially problematic.

a. One should start discussing euthanasia earlier rather than later so as not to run the risk of being too late. The main question is: 'have you formed any ideas about the end of your life and how it will be?'
b. Preparing the stage must be based not only on the patient's preference but also must take into account the process of grieving by the family that remains behind. This position results in very open and concrete questions such as:

   1. to the patient:
      • 'given the fact that medicine cannot heal you, do you want to discuss the final phase of your life?'
      • 'if you want to decide when the end of your life is here, have you formed ideas about euthanasia or assisted suicide?'
      • 'if euthanasia is an option, have you formed ideas about the manner in which to end your life, by taking a potion or receiving an injection?' (in conformity with the value of self determination)
      • 'who do you wish to be present when you die?'
      • 'are there people you wish to see before you die?'
      • 'at what time do you wish to die?' (to help the dying patient and be supportive for the process of grief afterward)
      • 'do you wish to die quickly or slowly?' (an important fact for choosing the appropriate drugs but also making the process of death acceptable for the patient and the family)

   2. to the spouse:
      • 'do you wish to be in the room when your husband/wife gets an injection/takes a deadly drink?' (to prevent feelings of guilt, of desertion at an important time)
      • 'how do you want to prepare for this moment?'
      • 'who do you wish to be there to support you?'

It is very important to be sensitive to the family members who remain behind and their acceptance of the active intervention: sometimes it helps to hold a family meeting with the patient and discuss the feelings of each one. If there is opposition to the euthanasia by one close relative, attempts can be made to reconcile the differences, but in the end the patient's decision is the major factor. One should keep in mind, however, that problems may arise. One colleague decided, on the request of the wife of a patient, to perform euthanasia in secret in order not to inform a child who was opposed to it. The net result is that between mother and child a secrecy exists up to this day that makes communicating difficult.

Other practical issues concern the drugs, including procurement, handling and storage. In a professional court, one Dutch physician recently was accused of neglect after leaving the drugs for euthanasia at the house of a patient who decided at the last minute to postpone taking the potion. The patient's husband than committed suicide with the same drugs. As a result, the professionalization of euthanasia has ordered a new rule: that a physician personally obtains the drugs from the pharmacist and is present when the drugs are taken or injected. In case of postponement of the euthanasia, the physician should take the drugs out of the house and to the medical office.

CONCLUSION

This paper focuses on developments in euthanasia in The Netherlands, especially issues related to the use of drugs to accomplish a rapid and easy death. Even though in The Netherlands some of the issues are dealt with in an open fashion, there are still subjects that need improvement and further development. One of the ways to accomplish that goal is education of the public and teaching medical students, be they advocates or opponents, the aspects of a professional approach to euthanasia.[20]

REFERENCES

1. Meerman D. Goed doen door dood te maken, Kok, Kampen, 1991: 107.

2. Lindeboom GA. Euthanasie in historisch perspectief, Amsterdam, 1978.

3. van der Sluis I. Het recht om grootmoeder te doden. Amsterdam, 1978.

4. Persels J. Forcing the issue of physician-assisted suicide; Impact of the Kevorkian case on the euthanasia debate. The Journal of Legal Medicine 1993;14: 93-124.

5. Kimsma GK, van Leeuwen E. Euthanasia: background, practice and present justifications. Cambridge Quarterly of Health Care Ethics 1993;2: 19-31.

6. Kimsma GK. Euthanasia and physician-assisted suicide in the Netherlands, in: Kampits P (ed): Medizin, Ethik und Recht, Krems an der Donau, 1994:161-169.

7. Admiraal PV. Euthanatica, In: Muntendam P (ed): Euthanasie, De Nederlandse Bibliotheek der Geneeskunde, Stafleu, Leiden, 1977.

8. Admiraal PV. Verantwoorde Euthanasie. Nederlandse Vereniging voor Vrijwillige Euthanasie, Amsterdam, 1980.

9. Muller MT, van der Wal G, van Eijk JthM, Ribbe MW. Voluntary active euthanasia and physician assisted suicide in Dutch nursing homes: are the requirements for prudent practice properly met? J Am Geriatr Soc 1994;42:624-629.1.

10. van der Wal GA. Unrequested termination of life: is it permissible? Bioethics 1993;7:330-339.

11. van der Maas PJ, van Delden JJM, L Pijnenborg, Looman CWN. Euthanasia and other medical decisions concerning the end of life. Lancet 1191;338: 669-674.

12. van der Wal GA, Eijk JThM, Leenen HJJ, Spreeuwenberg C. Euthanasia and assisted suicide; I: How often is it practiced by family doctors in the Netherlands? Fam Prac 1992;9:130-134.

13. van der Wal GA, Eijk JThM, Leenen HJJ, Spreeuwenberg C. II: Do Dutch family doctors act prudently? Fam Prac 1192;9:135-140.

14. Admiraal PV. Toepassing van Euthanatica. Ned Tijdschr Geneeskd 1995; 139(6):265-268.

15. Kimsma GK. Clinical Ethics in assisting euthanasia: avoiding malpractice in drug application. Journal of Medicine and Philosophy 1992;17:439-443.

16. van der Wal GA. Euthanasie en hulp bij zelfdoding door huisartsen. Rotterdam, Wyt Uitgeefgroep, 1992.

17. Kimsma GK, Carlucci-Chiesielski C. Euthanasie: rapporteren of niet. Medisch Contact 1993:48:328-332.

18. Carlucci-Chiesielski C, GK Kimsma. The Impact of Reporting Cases in Holland: A Patient and a Family Perspective. Bioethics 1994;8:151-158.

19. van der Maas PJ, van der Delden, JJM, Pijnenborg L. Medische Beslissingen Rond Het Levenseinde, SD Uitgeverij, Den Haag, 1991.

20. Kimsma GK, van Duin B. Teaching Euthanasia. The Integration of the Practice of Euthanasia into Grief, Death and Dying Curricula of Post Graduate Family Medicine Training. Submitted for Publication.

Toxicological Issues
with Drugs Used to End Life

Barbara Insley Crouch

SUMMARY. Several publications contain euthanizing recipes to aid terminally ill individuals who seek to actively end their lives. Unfortunately, there are few objective data on the lethal doses of most drugs and chemicals in humans. A number of factors may influence the toxicity of individual drugs including underlying illness, other medications and food. Published lethal doses that appear in many aid-in-dying publications may underestimate or overestimate the true lethal doses. Terminally ill individuals who are considering ingesting drugs to hasten death and persons forming opinions on such acts should understand that many factors may affect the toxicity of various drugs and chemicals used to end life and that published euthanizing recipes may be unreliable and lead to prolonged suffering. *[Article copies available from The Haworth Document Delivery Service: 1-800-342-9678.]*

KEYWORDS. Poisoning, suicide, euthanasia, euthanizing recipes, toxicology, lethal drugs and chemicals, lethal doses, physician-assisted suicide, *Final Exit*

Barbara Insley Crouch, PharmD, MSPH, is Director of the Utah Poison Control Center and Assistant Professor of Pharmacy Practice, College of Pharmacy, University of Utah Health Sciences Center, Salt Lake City.

Address correspondence to: Dr. Barbara Insley Crouch at Utah Poison Control Center, 410 Chipeta Way, Suite 320, Salt Lake City, UT 84108.

[Haworth co-indexing entry note]: "Toxicological Issues with Drugs Used to End Life." Crouch, Barbara Insley. Co-published simultaneously in *Journal of Pharmaceutical Care in Pain & Symptom Control* (Pharmaceutical Products Press, an imprint of The Haworth Press, Inc.) Vol. 4, No. 1/2, 1996, pp. 211-222; and: *Drug Use in Assisted Suicide and Euthanasia* (ed: Margaret P. Battin, and Arthur G. Lipman) Pharmaceutical Products Press, an imprint of The Haworth Press, Inc., 1996, pp. 211-222. Single or multiple copies of this article are available from The Haworth Document Delivery Service [1-800-342-9678, 9:00 a.m. - 5:00 p.m. (EST)].

© 1996 by The Haworth Press, Inc. All rights reserved.

211

INTRODUCTION

A number of publications containing pharmacologic recipes to actively end human life are available through right-to-die organizations, the Internet and in bookstores. The intent of many of these publications is to permit comfortable death for individuals suffering from terminal illness; however, a number of factors may interfere with this outcome. This paper discusses some of the factors that may influence the toxic properties of some of the drugs noted in the published recipes. However, it is not the intent of this paper to pass judgement on the relative effectiveness of the published recipes.

The United States death rates from suicide have remained essentially constant at 11.9-12.9 deaths/100,000 for the past 10 years.[1] According to the National Center for Vital Statistics, death from suicide ranked eighth among all causes of death in 1990.[1] The majority of these deaths were a result of violent means. Poisoning with a liquid or solid substances accounted for only 10% of these suicide deaths.[1]

Data on deaths from suicide and suicide attempts are also available from the American Association of Poison Control Center's Toxic Exposure Surveillance System (TESS). This voluntary poisoning surveillance system receives data from participating poison control centers throughout the United States. In 1993, 1,751,476 poisoning exposures were reported to TESS, including 132,788 (7.6%) suspected suicides.[2] Only 338 (0.3%) of the exposures suspected to be suicide attempts resulted in fatality. The death rate from suicide reported by poison control centers remained constant from 1990 through 1993 at 0.3% of attempted suicides resulting in death.[2-5] The substance categories involved in the largest number of deaths were analgesics, antidepressants, stimulants and street drugs, and cardiovascular agents. These are quite different than the substance categories most frequently involved in human poisoning exposures, which are cleaning substances, analgesics, cosmetics and personal care products, cough and cold preparations, and plants.

The frequency of physician-assisted suicide of terminally ill individuals is unknown.[6] The age distribution of individuals seeking physician assisted suicide has not been characterized. A recent study documented that older Americans have a much higher rate of suicide than the general population.[7] Suicides in adults aged 50 and older were more likely to be from violent means (64%) and the most common stressor precipitating the suicide was physical illness. Cancer is more prevalent in older individuals and is probably the most common reason people seek to actively end their lives. However, younger individuals may suffer from permanently disabling conditions or terminal illness that may reduce their functional capacity. The overall reason for seeking active end of life may better relate to physiologic or functional age of the individual rather than actual chronological age.

There are several reasons that suicide is less likely to occur with ingested substances than by violent means. In order to produce a toxic reaction, such as death, a sufficient quantity of a substance, or its toxic metabolite, must reach the site(s) of action in a significant concentration and a sufficient length of time to produce death or toxicity. Interference with the absorption, distribution, biotransformation (metabolism), or elimination of drugs and chemicals may have a pronounced effect on their toxic effects. In addition, prompt medical intervention before a sufficient amount of a substance has reached the target organ will likely result in a much diminished toxic reaction. For most drugs and chemicals, early intervention and good supportive care result in survival of the patient.

LETHAL DOSE INFORMATION

There are few objective data about the lethal doses of drugs/chemicals in humans. The majority of lethality data come from toxicity studies performed in laboratory animals that are conducted during preclinical trials or from case reports. The Lethal Dose$_{50}$ (LD$_{50}$) is an experimentally derived dose that causes death in 50% of a sample of animals which receive the agent. This is one of the first tests performed when evaluating the usefulness of a new drug or chemical and provides a crude measure of the relative toxicity of the substance. There are many factors that affect the calculated LD$_{50}$ such as species, ages and genders of the animals studied, and environmental factors such as temperature, other chemicals, and diet.

Extrapolation of LD$_{50}$ data from animal research to estimate the lethal dose in humans is problematic. Humans may have marked differences from animals in the absorption, distribution, metabolism and excretion of the substances. Additional studies are performed in laboratory animals to determine the effective dose for 50% of a sample of animals receiving the agent (ED$_{50}$). This test evaluates whether a given compound produces the desired therapeutic benefit(s). Two common ways of comparing the relative toxicity of drugs and chemicals are the therapeutic index (LD$_{50}$/ED$_{50}$), and the margin of safety (LD$_1$/ED$_{99}$). With both tests, the larger the ratio, the greater the safety profile of the compound. As with the LD$_{50}$, there may be problems in directly extrapolating this information to humans.

Another source of data about lethal doses of drugs and chemicals are case reports in the medical literature. One of the primary problems with case reports of human self-poisoning is that they are often based on subjective information. Data on the substances ingested and the amounts ingested may come from histories provided by the patients, friends or relatives. Many studies have demonstrated the unreliability of subjective histories and self report of substance use.[8,9] Survival of the individual following a self-poisoning depends on substance(s) ingested, quantity taken, health of the individual, other medications the individual may have taken, time to medical intervention and the quality of medical care received. Since case reports often do not address many of these issues, fatal dose data derived from case reports may underestimate or overestimate the actual lethal dose of a given substance.

Confirmation of the history in poisoned patients is sometimes obtained by laboratory analysis. Laboratory results may be used to estimate the dose ingested; however, toxicology screens vary in scope and sensitivity. Many laboratories test for only 40 to 50 selected drugs and chemicals. More than 10,000 drugs are available. For example, cardiovascular drugs, (such as beta-sympathetic blockers and calcium channel blockers) are associated with a large number of fatalities reported to poison control centers,[2] however, these drugs are not routinely detected in hospital laboratory toxicology screens. Post mortem toxicology analysis may encompass more drugs and chemicals, but this too varies by laboratory.

EUTHANIZING DRUGS

There are a number of publications that provide euthanizing recipes to the lay public. The book *Final Exit,* written by Derek Humphry, is the best known of these publications.[10] It contains a table of specific drugs and drug doses to use for individuals seeking active end of life along with information on how to obtain the medications. The categories of drugs listed in this table include the barbiturates, benzodiazepines, other sedative/hypnotic agents, and opioid analgesics. *Beyond Final Exit* is a new publication published by the Right to Die Society of Canada. This publication contains nine chapters that address various medical and non-medical means to end life as well as a guide to other suicide manuals. Information is provided on the relevant evidence in support of lethal potential of the various means of suicide, a discussion of unpleasant side effects, as well as other pertinent information.[11] *Departing Drugs, an International Guidebook to Self-Deliverance for the Terminally Ill* describes several methods involving drugs to end life. It has an expanded list of medications that may be used to end life as compared to *Final Exit.*[12] Other publications are available in the United States and other countries.[13]

Barbiturates may be divided into two groups, short acting and long acting (Table 1). These drugs are primarily used for their sedative-hypnotic and anticonvulsant properties, however, they have largely been replaced by the safer benzodiazepines. Barbiturates depress central nervous system function and have general anesthetic properties when administered in high doses. Initially, patients become drowsy, but will respond to painful stimulation. As the dose is increased, deep tendon reflexes are lost, patients no longer respond to painful stimulation and respiration is slowed. With large doses, cardiac output and respiration become unstable and will cease without appropriate medical intervention. Individuals who take barbiturates on a daily basis develop pharmacodynamic and pharmacokinetic tolerance. Pharmacodynamic or functional tolerance refers to the need for larger doses to produce the desired pharmacologic effect. Tolerance to the effects of sedation and hypnosis is higher than its effects on lethality. Pharmacokinetic tolerance refers to the ability of the drugs to enhance their own metabolism through induction of hepatic microsomal enzymes. Chronic administration of these agents will not only increase their own metabolism, but will also increase the metabolism of other drugs which are metabolized by the same microsomal enzymes.

The differences among the barbiturates are largely due to differences in chemical structure. In general, short-acting agents are more toxic than long acting agents. Of the barbiturates listed in Table 1, amobarbital is currently available only in an injectable form in the United States. Butabarbital is not commonly used and no data appear in the literature about its toxic or fatal dose in humans. The majority of barbiturate deaths reported in the literature involve pentobarbital or secobarbital. Deaths have been reported with as little as 2 grams, yet patients have survived much larger ingestions.

TABLE 1

BARBITURATES LISTED IN *FINAL EXIT*
SHORT-ACTING
Amobarbital
Secobarbital
Pentobarbital
Butabarbital
LONG-ACTING
Phenobarbital

Phenobarbital is commonly used as an anticonvulsant and the mortality rate from phenobarbital overdoses alone is low. Estimates of the lethal dose vary. One source indicated that 1.5 g of phenobarbital was lethal, while another indicated 6 to 9 g were lethal.[14,15] It is reported that one individual survived the ingestion of 25 g.[15]

Benzodiazepines have sedative, hypnotic, anxiolytic and anticonvulsant properties. Benzodiazepines produce qualitatively similar pharmacologic and toxicologic profiles, however, the individual drugs in this class are quantitatively different. With increasing doses, these agents can have profound depressant effects on the central nervous system leading to respiratory and myocardial depression, and eventually death. However, benzodiazepines are considered relatively safe sedative and anxiolytic agents; the therapeutic index is quite large. Few deaths have been reported from the ingestion of benzodiazepines without other drugs or chemicals. The majority of deaths have occurred when alcohol or other drugs are taken concurrently with benzodiazepines.

Final Exit suggests several other sedative-hypnotic agents: glutethimide, chloral hydrate, meprobamate and methyprylon. These drugs have similar pharmacologic activity to the barbiturates and benzodiazepines, and like the barbiturates, they have been largely replaced in clinical practice by the safer benzodiazepines. Chloral hydrate is indicated for nocturnal sedation and is also used for preoperative sedation, especially in children. In addition to the sedative/hypnotic effects, increasing doses of chloral hydrate produce cardiac and gastrointestinal toxicity. Chloral hydrate has a direct effect on the ability of the heart muscle to contract and may produce cardiac arrhythmias.[16] Chloral hydrate has been reported to cause hemorrhagic gastritis, intestinal necrosis and esophagitis with stricture formation.[16,17] In addition, hepatotoxicity and renal toxicity have been attributed to this agent. Death has been reported following the ingestion of 35 to 40 g, however, survival has been noted following the ingestion of 38 g.[18]

Methyprylon has never been widely used and reports of fatalities have been rare. The toxicity of methyprylon is similar to that of the barbiturates. Meprobamate is primarily used as an antianxiety agent although it does have skeletal muscle relaxant properties. It produces central nervous system depression like the other sedative-hypnotic agents. Toxic doses are variable; death has been reported with as little as 12 g, yet survival has been reported following the ingestion of up to 40 g.[19] Glutethimide is primarily used as a hypnotic agent. In addition to its central nervous system depressant effects, it also has anticholinergic properties and may produce a prolonged and cyclic coma. The lethal dose has been reported to be 10 to 20 g, although individuals have survived ingestion of 45 g.[19] Following chronic administration of chloral hydrate, methyprylon, meprobamate and glutethimide, pharmacodynamic tolerance does develop to therapeutic effects. In addition, cross tolerance among all of the sedative-hypnotic agents does occur. Chloral hydrate, meprobamate and glutethimide are known to stimulate the hepatic mixed-function oxidase system and increase their own metabolism. Tolerance to the lethal effects of all of the sedative-hypnotic agents is minimal.

Opioid analgesics account for one-fourth of the drugs listed in *Final Exit*. Agents in this class that are listed in the book include codeine, hydromorphone, meperidine, methadone, morphine and propoxyphene. The toxic effects of the opioids are primarily on the central nervous system and gastrointestinal tract. Increasing doses of these agents lead to respiratory depression which is the primary cause of death. Noncardiac pulmonary edema is present with severe intoxication. In therapeutic and toxic doses these drugs may cause significant nausea, vomiting and constipation. Certain opioid analgesic agents have additional toxicologic considerations. Seizures may occur after chronic use of meperidine due to the accumulation of a toxic metabolite. Propoxyphene may cause both seizures and cardiac arrhythmias following acute overdoses. Terminally ill patients often receive opioid analgesics for pain management. Tolerance develops to some of the effects of these drugs and extremely high doses may be needed and, indeed are appropriate, for pain control in some terminally ill patients. The acute toxic dose is markedly different for individuals who have not had continual exposure to opioids. Lethal doses, therefore, are difficult to define.

The last compound listed as a euthanizing drug in *Final Exit* does not fit into any of the pharmacologic categories listed above. This is orphenadrine, which has anticholinergic and some antihistaminic properties. The chemical structure of this agent is similar to that of diphenhydramine. Anticholinergic toxicities at high doses include hypertension, tachycardia, dilated pupils, hallucinations, dry and flushed skin and possibly seizures. Large doses will also slow movement through the gastrointestinal tract which can result in delayed or decreased absorption of both this and other drugs and chemicals. Orphenadrine is used as an adjuvant treatment for Parkinson's disease and to reduce skeletal muscle spasm. However, it does not have direct skeletal muscle activity. The lethal dose of orphenadrine is reported to be between 2 and 3 g, however, survival after the ingestion of 5 g has been reported.[20]

Final Exit recommends ingestion of alcohol with many of the drugs listed. Alcohol enhances the central nervous system depressant effects of the sedative-hypnotic and opioid drugs. However, it is not known how much alcohol is necessary to do so with each individual drug. It is also not known whether increasing the alcohol dose will proportionally reduce the amount of drug needed to cause toxicity. Large doses of alcohol are irritating to the gastrointestinal tract and may cause spontaneous vomiting.

There are several limitations to the euthanizing potential of the drugs listed in *Final Exit*. For example, the book does not include some of the more lethal categories of drugs and chemicals such as tricyclic antidepressants, beta-blockers and calcium channel blockers, cyanide, and carbon monoxide. Tricyclic antidepressants are the most common cause of suicide death by poisoning reported to poison control centers. Calcium channel blockers and beta-blockers are also involved in a large number of deaths reported to poison control centers (Table 2). The primary toxic effects of the tricyclic antidepressants are on the cardiovascular and the central nervous system. However, rapid development of seizures make these agents unpleasant means of suicide.

A second limitation is that some of the agents included on this list may also cause unpleasant effects prior to death. Orphenadrine is an anticholinergic agent. Large amounts of this drug will produce hallucinations, flushing, elevated body temperature, racing heart, increased blood pressure and possibly seizures. Seizures also may occur following large overdoses of

TABLE 2

REPRESENTATIVE EXAMPLES OF DRUGS ASSOCIATED WITH DEATHS THAT HAVE BEEN REPORTED TO POISON CENTERS
TRICYCLIC ANTIDEPRESSANTS
amitriptyline   Elavil, Endep, generics
doxepin   Sinequan, Adapin, generics
imipramine Tofranil, Janamine, generics
BETA SYMPATHETIC BLOCKERS
propranolol Inderal, generics
CALCIUM CHANNEL BLOCKERS
verapamil Calan, Isoptin, Veralan, generics
diltiazem   Cardizem, Dilacor, generics
nifedipine   Procardia, Adalat, generics

propoxyphene or meperidine. Chloral hydrate is extremely irritating to the digestive tract and vomiting is quite common following an overdose.

A third limitation is that the ability to obtain the drugs listed in *Final Exit* and other publications depends on the willingness of physicians to prescribe large quantities of the medications and the pharmacists' willingness to fill potentially lethal prescriptions. A number of drugs listed in *Final Exit* have been largely replaced by safer, more effective agents in clinical practice. Therefore, pharmacists are likely to question the validity of prescriptions for many of the drugs listed, regardless of the quantity prescribed.

One of the major limitations of *Final Exit* and other suicide manuals that attempt to provide lethal dosage data estimates, is that underlying disease states and chronic drug therapy may affect the absorption, distribution, metabolism and excretion of substances ingested. Factors that may influence the absorption of drugs and chemicals include physical properties of the preparation, solubility of the compound, dissolution rate, gastric emptying time, intestinal motility, tissue perfusion, first-pass hepatic metabolism and surface area for absorption. These factors influence both the rate and extent of absorption. The opioid analgesics, e.g., codeine, hydromorphone, meperidine, morphine, methadone, as well as drugs with anticholinergic properties, e.g., glutethimide and orphenadrine, impede gastrointestinal motility. Such agents may actually delay their own absorption and may delay the absorption of other compounds. This delay in absorption occurs because the primary site for drug absorption is the small intestine. When motility in the gastrointestinal tract is slowed, more drug remains in the stomach for a longer time before reaching the normal site of absorption. Other conditions which may delay absorption include hypotension, changes in the pH of the stomach and intestine, and spasm of the pylorus. The pylorus is the opening between the stomach and the intestine. The actual extent of absorption is usually not affected.

Another reason for a delay in absorption is the formation of a mass or bezoar. Meprobamate is known to form a pharmaco-bezoar; a concretion of tablets in the stomach or intestine that form due to poor solubility characteristics of the drug. This occurs when a large number of tablets is ingested at the same time. Certain drugs used as antiemetics, e.g., metoclopramide, cisipride, may shorten gastric emptying time. Although theoretically rapid passage through the digestive system may move certain drugs past the site of absorption and therefore decrease absorption, this effect has not been documented in humans. Cathartics also increase gastrointestinal motility which might also decrease the extent of absorption of certain drugs. The use of cathartics in the treatment of the poisoned patient have not by themselves proven to be effective at preventing absorption. Hypotension, shock and other disease states that may result in a diminished blood flow to the stomach and intestines may limit absorption of drugs from the gastrointestinal tract. Chronic gastrointestinal diseases may also affect the absorption of certain drugs and chemicals.

After a drug is absorbed, several factors may influence the rate and extent of distribution of the drug to its site(s) of action. Tissue perfusion, pH, protein binding, tissue binding and lipid solubility are the major factors influencing distribution. These factors may enhance or diminish the toxic effects of a given drug.

The liver is the primary organ for detoxifying drugs and chemicals. Certain drugs and chemicals when administered chronically may induce liver microsomal enzymes which, in turn, may enhance detoxification of the compound. Barbiturates and chloral hydrate induce hepatic enzymes; they may induce their own metabolism and therefore enhance their own elimination from the body.

Elimination of drugs from the body may also be affected by tissue perfusion and pH as well as liver and kidney function. Hypotension, shock and other disease states may also result in diminished blood flow to the liver and kidneys, causing a decrease in the distribution and elimination of the drug or chemical. The acid-base balance (pH) in the blood also will affect the distribution and elimination of susceptible drugs. For example, phenobarbital is a weak acid. If an individual's blood is on the acidotic side, more drug is likely to distribute into the brain resulting in an increase in toxic effects. If the urine is alkalotic, more drug will be eliminated resulting in a decrease in toxicity.

Drug interactions with foods are also important considerations when interpreting toxic doses of drugs. Interactions between two or more drugs may result in a number of types of reactions. Certain drugs and foods may affect the rate and extent of absorption of other drugs. For example, food may decrease the rate of absorption of benzodiazepines. Antacids are known to decrease the rate and extent of a number of drugs (Table 3). In addition, interactions may reduce or enhance the effects of a drug at the receptor site or may affect the metabolism or elimination of the agent. For example, cimetidine, a common ulcer medication, can block the metabolism of a number of drugs such as theophylline, resulting in increased toxicity. Carbamazepine, an anti-seizure medication, can increase the metabolism of cyclic antidepressants, reducing their effectiveness and possibly their toxicity. Such drug interactions may enhance or reduce the toxic effects of any given drug.

No good data exist on fatal doses of drugs taken alone by humans or

TABLE 3

DRUGS AFFECTED BY CO-ADMINISTRATION OF ANTACIDS	
DRUG	**EFFECT**
propranol (beta-blocker)	extent of absorption affected
chloroquine	extent of absorption affected
diazepam	rate of absorption affected
ciprofloxacin (antibiotic)	extent of absorption affected

when one considers the many potential confounding factors. Because of this, reliance on these recipes may result in an unsuccessful suicide. Consequences of unsuccessful suicides are hard to predict. Individuals have recovered completely; others have been left with significant residual disability. According to the 1993 report of TESS, 2% of those poisonings that produced life-threatening signs and symptoms had permanent sequelae.[2]

In summary, reliable data on the consistently fatal doses of drug in humans are lacking. Individual factors such as underlying disease states, other medications, and food also may affect the toxicity of a given compound making it difficult to determine the toxic doses. The recipes provided in books such as *Final Exit* may produce fatal outcomes for some individuals, but it is probable that not all individuals who follow these instructions will have the intended outcomes.

REFERENCES

1. National Center for Health Statistics. Vital Statistics of the United States 1990, vol II, mortality, part A. Hyattsville, MD:DHHS Publication No. 95-1101.

2. Litovitz TL, Clark LR, Soloway RA. 1993 Annual Report of the American Association of Poison Control Centers Toxic Exposure Surveillance System. Am J Emerg Med 1994;12:546-584.

3. Litovitz TL, Bailey KM, Schmitz BF, Holm KC, Klein-Schwartz W. 1990 Annual Report of the American Association of Poison Control Centers National Data Collection System. Am J Emerg Med 1991;9:461-509.

4. Litovitz TL, Holm KC, Bailey KM, Schmitz BF. 1991 Annual Report of the American Association of Poison Control Centers National Data Collection System. Am J Emerg Med 1992;10:452-505.

5. Litovitz TL, Holm KC, Clancy C, Schmitz BF, Clark LR, Oderda GM. 1992 Annual Report of the American Association of Poison Control Centers Toxic Exposure Surveillance System. Am J Emerg Med 1993;11:494-555.

6. Conwell Y, Caine ED. Rational suicide and the right to die: reality and myth. N Eng J Med 1991;325:1100-1103.

7. Conwell Y, Rotenberg M, Caine ED. Completed Suicide at Age 50 and Over. J Am Geriatric Soc 1990; 38:640-644.

8. Wright N. An Assessment of the Unreliability of the history given by the self-poisoned patient. Clin Toxicol 1980;16:381-384.

9. Brett AS. Implications of Discordance Between Clinical Impression and Toxicology Analysis in Drug Overdose. Arch Intern Med 1988;148:437-441.

10. Humphry D. Final Exit: The Practicalities of Self-Deliverance and Assisted Suicide for the Dying. Dell Paperbacks, 1991.

11. Smith CK, Docker CG, Hofsess J, Dunn B. Beyond Final Exit. Victoria, British Columbia:The Right to Die Society of Canada;1995.

12. Smith, CK, Docker CG. Departing Drugs, An International Guidebook to Self-Deliverance for the Terminally Ill. Vess, Edinburgh: Christopher Grant Docker and Cheryl K. Smith;1993.

13. Docker CJ. Self Deliverance Guides: A History. DIDMSNJ 1994;1:4-7.

14. Dreissbach RH. Handbook of Poisoning. Eleventh edition. Los Altos, CA, Lange Medical Publications, 1983.

15. Gosselin RE, Smith RP, Hodge HC. Clinical Toxicology of Commercial Products. Fifth Edition, Baltimore, MD: Williams & Wilkins;1984.

16. Gleich GJ, Mongan ES, Vaules DW. Esophageal stricture following chloral hydrate poisoning. JAMA 1967;201:266.

17. Vellar IDA, Richardson JP, Doyle JC, Keating M. Gastric necrosis: A rare complication of chloral hydrate intoxication. Br J Surg 1972;59:317.

18. Poisindex® Editorial Staff. Chloral Hydrate and Related Agents. In: Poisindex Vol 85. Denver, CO: Micromedex Inc;1995.

19. Seyffart G. Antihistamines and Other Sedatives. In: Haddad LM, Winchester JF, eds. Clinical Management of Poisoning and Drug Overdose, 2nd edition. Philadelphia: Saunders;1990:820-861.

20. Poisindex® Editorial Staff. Anticholinergic Poisoning. In: Poisindex Vol 85. Denver, CO: Micromedex Inc;1995.

When Drugs Fail:
Assisted Deaths
and Not-So-Lethal Drugs

Stephen Jamison

SUMMARY. One hundred and sixty interviews with family members, partners, and friends who participated in 140 cases of non-physician-assisted death reveal a number of problems that surround assisted dying. These observations describe events in cases in which an assisted death did not occur as planned, often due to the less-than-fully lethal nature of the drugs used. Of 140 deaths, only 15 were designated as suicides; in 41 of these remaining 125 deaths, physicians knowingly provided lethal prescriptions, were fully aware of their patients' plans to end their lives, and signed their death certificates claiming "natural" causes. Self-enacted and assisted death in terminal illness is far more common than has been previously suspected. While self-enacted or assisted death can be important for those involved, it can also produce regrets when drugs fail. The case descriptions related here describe what happens when drugs fail, and how partners and family of the dying person turn to more desperate

Stephen Jamison, PhD, is a former faculty member in social psychology and family studies at the University of California at Davis where he taught courses in death and dying, a former regional director of the National Hemlock Society and Director of Life and Death Consultations.

Address correspondence to: Dr. Stephen Jamison, Life and Death Consultations, P.O. Box 570, Mill Valley, CA 94942.

Some of the material in this paper appears in a different form in S. Jamison, *Final Acts of Love*, New York, Jeremy Tarcher/Putnam, 1995.

[Haworth co-indexing entry note]: "When Drugs Fail: Assisted Deaths and Not-So-Lethal Drugs." Jamison, Stephen. Co-published simultaneously in *Journal of Pharmaceutical Care in Pain & Symptom Control* (Pharmaceutical Products Press, an imprint of The Haworth Press, Inc.) Vol. 4, No. 1/2, 1996, pp. 223-243; and: *Drug Use in Assisted Suicide and Euthanasia* (ed: Margaret P. Battin, and Arthur G. Lipman) Pharmaceutical Products Press, an imprint of The Haworth Press, Inc., 1996, pp. 223-243. Single or multiple copies of this article are available from The Haworth Document Delivery Service [1-800-342-9678, 9:00 a.m. - 5:00 p.m. (EST)].

© 1996 by The Haworth Press, Inc. All rights reserved.

means, often in haste and with inadequate emotional preparation, rapidly escalating from "merely being present" to "doing anything necessary" to ensure death. Frequent failure due to lack of adequate information leads to frequent over-involvement by significant others. *[Article copies available from The Haworth Document Delivery Service: 1-800-342-9678.]*

KEYWORDS. Suicide, assisted suicide, drugs, lethal dose, physician-assisted suicide, death, dying, euthanasia, failure of drugs

In 1991, I began a research project to investigate the behavior of family members, partners, and friends in cases of non-physician assisted death.[1] In particular, I was interested in the circumstances of these deaths, the motives of those who engaged in this practice, and the effects of such actions on participants. By mid-1994, I had completed 160 interviews with participants in 140 deaths.[2]

This paper focuses on some of the problems that surround assisted dying, especially those that occur when significant others attempt to help a loved one die in the absence of potentially lethal prescriptions. Although the cases I describe in the following pages are not unusual, the reader needs to be aware that I have purposefully excluded discussion of cases where an assisted death was accomplished as planned and where nothing unexpected occurred.

THE EXTENT OF ASSISTED DEATH

In the absence of legal opportunities for assisted dying, those with life threatening conditions have three options. The first is to follow the course of their illness to a natural death either at home with home nursing or hospice care or in a medical or convalescent facility. This is the typical way that most of us die. A second option is a death enacted by a patient after he or she has secured potentially lethal means. The third option is a death assisted in some way by one's partner, family members, or friends. Of particular interest here are the second and third options, where a person's choice has been made possible because of "assistance" by others. Such assistance may range from help in securing the lethal means to ensuring the death through further involvement at the end.

No one knows the extent to which these latter two options are used by those with life threatening conditions. This is because both self-enacted and assisted deaths by the terminally ill are often masked by the nature of their medical condition. Especially when this is combined with lack of evidence to the contrary (i.e., there are no suicide notes, no empty bottles of potentially lethal prescriptions, etc.), the official label of "suicide" is seldom applied. Partners, family members, and friends often cover up the actual cause of death to eliminate the "stigma" of suicide for religious, familial, or social purposes, or to protect themselves or physicians from any suspicion of involvement. In terms of the former, one interviewee told me that he removed all evidence of a physician-assisted and self-enacted death from his partner's home because "this was a self-deliverance, not a suicide." He went on to say that: "There's a huge difference, and I wasn't going to let them apply that label."

This occurred quite frequently in my own sample. For example, in the 140 cases of assisted deaths that comprised my research, only 15 were designated as suicides. None were considered to be assisted deaths, though all were aided in some fashion. Moreover, in these 15 instances, "suicide" as an official cause of death was planned for–in advance–to protect others from any suspicion of involvement. In nearly every case, this became necessary because the individuals were not suffering from a condition where death was imminent. In one case a man's prostate cancer had metastasized to his hip, and was extremely painful, but had not yet spread to his vital organs.

Similarly, in the case of several other individuals, their multiple sclerosis (MS), amyotropic; lateral sclerosis (ALS, Lou Gehrig's Disease) and AIDS-related conditions had not yet reached critical, life-threatening stages. Any attempt to make these assisted deaths look anything other than suicide would have increased the risk for family members, who indeed were quite involved at the end. In a great number of cases it also was apparent that physicians knowingly participated in this secrecy. This can be seen in the fact that in 41 of the other 125 deaths I studied, physicians knowingly provided potentially lethal prescriptions, were fully aware of their patients' plans to end their lives, and signed their death certificates claiming "natural" causes. As one physician told me:

> This was private. It was between the two of us. He was dying, and suffering greatly, and he just decided to eliminate the last few ugly days. He wouldn't have done this had he not been dying. Sure his death was accelerated, but so too are many others in hospital settings that no one would ever claim were anything less than natural.

And even where physicians do not knowingly participate in such assistance, and whether or not they harbor suspicions, they will often sign such certificates due to the terminal nature of a patient's illness. This occurred in the 84 other cases where the deaths came unexpectedly but could be explained by an underlying physical cause. All of this suggests that self-enacted and assisted death by those with life threatening conditions is far more common than has been previously suspected.

SELF-ENACTED VERSUS ASSISTED DEATH

Leaving aside questions of the morality of assistance and the rationality of particular actions, self-enacted and assisted deaths each have their own benefits and drawbacks. Self-enacted deaths, for example, protect others from the possibility of further involvement by excluding them. On the negative side, however, this exclusion eliminates the potential for them to voice their last minute opposition or to achieve final closure. Moreover, it can leave survivors especially upset that a loved one died alone, and always wondering if the last minutes were emotionally or physically painful and if the final act was truly symptom-driven or was motivated by something else.

Other drawbacks also exist, especially if the act occurs without warning. These include the shock of discovery, the regret of not being able to say goodbye, and the possible burden of an "official suicide"–unless someone acts at the time of discovery to cover up this feature of the death. Most importantly, lone efforts by individuals to end their lives pose a significant risk for failure and, depending on the methods used, can increase the potential for physiological damage should they survive these attempts.

By contrast, a death assisted by a partner, family members, or friends provides the benefit of not dying alone, which can also be important for those who might otherwise regret not being with a loved one at this critical time. The presence of others provides the opportunity for a final closure or for words that can change a person's mind. In addition, it also gives others the opportunity of being present and participating in rituals honoring a life and its end. Most importantly, such a presence can also ensure that a death is completed as it was intended. The latter, however, can also be a serious drawback, and errors can and do occur when others are present–even with the best made plans. Drugs often fail, and partners and family, who may be unprepared emotionally and practically, may hesitantly come to use whatever means are left at their disposal to ensure a dying person's last request. Other failings that can occur include the rush for final action, lack of adequate planning, the intrusion of time into the dying process, the selection of settings that fail to guarantee others with a sense of comfort, attempts by the dying to coerce the attendance of unprepared family members and friends, and less than proper motives for participation.

WHEN DRUGS AND SITUATIONS FAIL

Most participants who expressed regrets to me about their involvement in an assisted death did not oppose the dying person's plans to end his or her life, but attached these feelings to the nature of the event itself. This usually was because their expectations of "helping" in only benign, supportive ways were seriously altered due to the failure of the drugs to work.

Too often, out of perceived necessity, their roles gradually escalated from observers "merely being present" to actors "doing anything necessary" to ensure the death of another. As a result, the character of the event shifted from an expectation of a positive and peaceful death in the presence of loving family and friends to a situation fraught with fear, uncertainty, disorder, and an unwanted concentration on the need to complete a task–to fulfill the other's last wish to die. In this way, earlier expectations of a death, with features of minimal participation, limited risk for participants, opportunities for mutual farewell, and even aesthetic orchestration of final rituals, were often shattered. The act of completing and covering up the actual cause of death took precedence.

Many blamed their problems on the failure of the means, that is, the selection of the "wrong" drugs. This was based on the assumption that if one pill can help you sleep, then a hundred will ensure your death, or that if secobarbital works then so will pentobarbital. In the end, drugs that were used did not cause death in the time anticipated and, as the possibility of death began to appear more remote, others present saw no choice but to intervene. Time also became a factor; most simply, the drugs failed to work within a comfortable time period, and either time or patience ran out. At that moment intervention seemed "far easier than waiting any longer." As one man told me:

> At least I had an idea of what to do when he died. I had a vague understanding of what would happen and had the phone numbers of who to call. But I was totally unprepared for failure. This would mean that it would officially become a suicide attempt and could implicate the doctor who gave us the prescription. Plus, I didn't know if the overdose would cause serious damage when he recovered. I didn't want to see him in worse shape afterwards than he'd been in before.

In this case other factors came into play. These included: lack of practical preparation, elevated expectations of success, and the inability of all parties to communicate about realistic possibilities. In this case, and in nearly every other instance of failure that I documented, the result was further involvement by participants than they expected or desired. This occurred both where drugs were obtained from non-medical sources and in a few cases, like Jessica's, where physicians deliberately provided medications they believed would be adequate to cause death.

This type of mistake occurred most frequently when physicians were not brought into the equation, and when the person who was dying and his or her partner or family members used themselves as sources for drugs, and assumed that an arsenal of medications had to work because of their sheer volume and variety.

This occurred in Bill's death. As his health deteriorated from AIDS to where he was told that he had but weeks to live, Bill began his planning. He set a date to die after he obtained a new prescription for duragesic patches of a synthetic narcotic analgesic. He then invited his family to his house for the weekend, and used this time to say goodbye. After spending a second full day with his family, he went to his bedroom with his brother and partner. Selecting from a storehouse of medications, he filled six syringes with Demerol, which were to be injected later after he was unconscious. He then took a hot shower, and applied twenty duragesic patches to his body.

Finally, he swallowed more than two hundred tablets of Soma, Valium, Halcyon, and various other pain relievers, including morphine in the form of MS Contin. Within minutes he was unconscious, and the family, gathered in the next room, began what they felt would be a short wait. After three hours, Bill's brother injected the syringes of Demerol into a muscle on Bill's thigh. Some ten hours after Bill began his journey, a cry was heard coming from his room. Bill's father, brother, and partner rushed in only to find him sitting up, conscious, and vomiting. The drugs Bill had taken had not been assimilated. A physician friend later told Bill's father that he believed the morphine "must've paralyzed his gut." Someone else told his partner that "it was probably the Soma." Bill's brother blamed himself for not giving the injections intravenously, because he was "afraid of contact with his blood." Whatever the cause, Bill fell back into a light sleep, while his family debated what to do next. His brother argued that it was too late, that they had failed, and that Bill would probably need to be hospitalized. Bill's father suggested that they use a plastic bag. Bill had prepared for this possibility by leaving a kitchen trash bag and rubber bands on the bedside table. His brother argued that Bill would awaken and "fight it." His father disagreed, and said: "He won't fight; he wants this more than anything." In resignation, his brother agreed to try. Although Bill was asleep, he was not unconscious. As a result, when his brother placed the bag over Bill's head he briefly awakened.

His father and partner told him to "just relax." In response, Bill managed one last word, "okay." He died minutes later, without a struggle.

The family looked upon his as a "good death" and were prepared for the final act of involvement, but the uncertainty about his near-conscious state, and the possibility of his "fighting the bag," created an atmosphere of stress and indecision. Bill's brother told me later that this was "the longest night" of his life.

WHEN TIME RUNS OUT

A doctor once told me that "the only way you can die from Valium is to get run over by the truck delivering it." I was reminded of this when I was told about Peter's death. In his case a mixture of 500 milligrams of Valium with bourbon was followed eight hours later with a similar decision to use a plastic bag. This was motivated not by obvious failure, but by a concern for time. At nearly 11:00 p.m., the participants knew that Peter had but two hours to die. His wife, who wanted to know nothing about the death until after his body was gone, was due home at 1:00 a.m. Although Peter had set aside a plastic bag and rubber bands for this purpose, "his eyes opened instantly" when they placed the bag over his head. "He wasn't conscious, and he didn't say anything, but he "raised his hands to his face to remove it." A split second of confusion was followed by the unspoken joint silent decision by two of the participants to hold down Peter's arms until his death. Doing so, they met their deadline; Peter's body was gone when his wife got home. Nevertheless, one participant told me later that it wasn't what he expected: "If he wasn't dying, and if he didn't want this so badly, I'd call it murder." He then said: "Still, it hasn't been very comfortable living with the images."

This situation developed in Peter's case solely because of his lack of preparation. Two years before he died, he talked openly about getting his "self deliverance kit together." Reading *Final Exit*, he assumed that Valium would work, especially if he also used alcohol. He had failed to read the small print, and found it easier to slowly set aside the same drug he'd been using for years, than to approach his physician or start a search for other drugs. He also failed to think clearly about the time factor. As a result, his friends, who were practically and emotionally unprepared, found themselves being forced to act in ways that weren't in the original script.

This factor of time had another dimension. It became more of a problem when friends were involved instead of family members, and where individuals were isolated in their role as "helpers," and had feelings of exhaustion, locational discomfort, or wanted to be elsewhere. As another man explained:

I don't want to sound callous, because I really cared for him, but I had my own family, and my own plans, and I was scared, and I didn't want to be there any more, I was tired, and I wanted it over with and to go home.

WEAK DRUGS AND STRONG IMAGES

In an episode similar to that in Peter's case, Sheila described what happened when she and her sister helped their brother die in front of their parents. This case exemplifies what could've happened with Bill, and what his brother feared most but did not materialize. Sheila and her family knew that the plastic bag would be necessary, and were prepared for it emotionally, because they were certain that "the drugs would never do it." Nevertheless, the drugs were "all he had, and he'd run out of time to get any more." What they weren't prepared for was having to "hold his hands down" when her brother "began to fight" against the bag. She then said:

I just smiled and pretended I was just holding his hand, but this was all for my parents benefit, because I was using all the strength I had. Behind my smile, inside I was screaming. I looked over to my sister and saw that she was doing the same thing. She was using all her strength to hold his arm down, all the while looking into my eyes. Neither of us said anything. We just listened to his breathing and waited several minutes, hours it seemed, until it was over.

She explained to me that she didn't want her brother's death, which was horrible enough, to "become something horrific," a memory her parents would never be able to erase. When her sister asked about what had happened, Sheila said, "Oh it was just a natural response." However, inside she wondered, "Did I just kill somebody? Did he still want to die or was he changing his mind?" Sheila continued, "I had to tell myself, 'He was unconscious, this was just his body trying to get air.' My brother and I had talked about this forever and he never once wavered. If he had I would've thought 'My God, this is all a mistake.' So I came to accept that–although it was unpleasant–it was necessary and okay."

Sheila also explained to me that she desperately wanted to talk with someone about the event, but knew that this couldn't be her sister. "I didn't trust my friends' reactions, so I kept it in." She didn't want to talk to her sister and raise doubts in her mind about her role in their brother's death. "I didn't want her to be burdened as I'd been."

One of the key problems is that no one wants to talk about a possible failure. Both the dying and those who assist don't usually want to think about drugs not working, or talk graphically about such a scenario. This can occur even when a plastic bag is present by the bedside. When Bill brought up the topic, for example, his father commented, "The drugs will work, son; you've got enough to kill an army." Nevertheless, Bill did talk briefly with his partner and brother and gave it special thought, leaving it on the table next to his bed. Similarly, a friend of Peter's said that he had mentioned it "but briefly." He explained: "I didn't want to listen to this, because I just knew the combination of Valium and bourbon would work, especially since Peter hadn't had a drink in more than ten years." He added, "If I'd known this would happen I wouldn't have agreed to be there; I only wanted to give him support." And even where the use of additional methods was planned for, full discussion of possibilities was kept to a minimum. This happened in the case of Sheila who said, "The bag was our primary method, but I never thought he'd put up a fight."

YOU HAVE TO TRUST YOUR SOURCE

One man I interviewed said that he would do anything–but use a plastic bag–to help his partner die. He explained that his partner, Daryl, feared suffocation because of a recent hospitalization for pneumocystis pneumonia. Instead, he decided to obtain street heroin, which the two of them could inject directly into Daryl's "central line," a catheter surgically implanted into his chest to ease the infusion of drugs as part of his treatment for an AIDS-related condition. Because of this central line, Allen believed a lethal injection of heroin to be a "technically simple" matter. The plan was devised due to Daryl's inability to keep food down. Allen's assistance became necessary because Daryl wasn't able to "do it himself with one shot of heroin before he went unconscious. Both knew that further injections would be necessary. After informing an acquaintance who "dabbled" in street drugs about their situation, Allen secured "a balloon with enough heroin to kill four people."

Allen then told me his story. The saga began on a Sunday afternoon. At 2:30 pm Daryl took four sleeping pills, waited ten minutes, and then injected himself with one dose of heroin. He then asked Allen to help him get to bed. He soon became unconscious, and Allen immediately gave him a second injection and followed with four shots of liquid oral morphine. For Daryl, death did not come quickly. Over the next several hours Allen gave him two more shots of heroin, more than sixty shots of liquid oral morphine, and even ten injections of vodka. None of this worked. He went on to explain:

> At ten he was still alive so I slipped a plastic trash bag over his head and held it around his neck with my hands. It only seemed to take about four minutes before he finally stopped breathing. As soon as he was dead, I called the answering service to locate his doctor.

Although Daryl's physicians had agreed to sign his death certificate, they could not be reached, and Allen was eventually connected to another backup physician. This man told Allen that he "wouldn't sign anything," but that Allen should call 911. Not knowing what else to do, he did. Allen told them that he thought Daryl was dead, but they arrived in full force.

> I hopped in [the ambulance], and they began working on him. One turned to the other and said: 'I think I got a pulse.' That did it. I began to cry, and I said: 'Please, just let him die.' They looked at me, stopped working on him, and slowed down all the way to the hospital.

Allen finished his story by saying that this was "the longest day" in his life. "I'd been there for more than ten hours without a break; I had no one to talk to, and no one to relieve me." He added that giving the injections was the most difficult thing he'd ever done in his life. I'll never forget dulling all those needle points and tearing up his line with all those injections. His last words were, " 'Don't let me wake up.' So I didn't." Allen's situation was intensified by the excessive nature of the act–by giving more than seventy injections, and then still having to use the plastic bag, something he'd been trying to avoid all along. The negative nature of the death was accentuated by his extreme isolation, constant feelings of failure, and fear of discovery. He summed up his experience by saying: "I'd use a .38 before ever going through this again; It would have been quicker and a lot easier."

WHEN GOOD DRUGS FAIL

When Florence asked her daughter, Helen, to help her die, it didn't come as a surprise. This occurred back in 1979, before the birth of the Hemlock Society. Nevertheless, as a nurse practitioner, Helen knew what to do. She supplied her mother with a large amount of pentobarbital.

There was nothing imminently wrong with Florence. She'd had a mastectomy and partial hysterectomy in the early 1950s, and was left with a permanent disability in one arm due to her surgery. Because of the breast cancer she was unable to take estrogen following the removal of her ovaries. This left her with an insidious depression for twenty five years. Her mother had been an active member of the Christian Science Church, which Helen had rejected. Still, one part of this philosophy rubbed off on her. According to Helen, this was to "not hang around and inch out life." As the general effects of aging also set in, the two of them talked about her philosophy and about how she would do it. Florence's husband had died some ten years earlier, and in addition to Helen, Florence had another daughter and son.

Florence perceived that at 80 years of age "things were not getting any better." She had recently fallen and now needed care. Her son offered to set her up in her own apartment adjacent to his house, but she refused. Florence had other ideas. Florence's first attempt to die came without warning. She had held onto the pills Helen had given her for about five months. She failed and went into a deep coma. When she was found by a nurse's aide, she was unconscious "supposedly from a thrombosis at the base of the brain." The doctors who had hospitalized her told Helen that her mother "had apparently suffered a stroke," but she knew better. "When I was told that 'Mom's unconscious with a stroke.' I said 'Uh-huh, oh yeah, right.' I went to her house and sure enough I found the empty bottle under the bathroom sink, where she had stored her pills."

At the hospital Florence was placed in the ICU and the physician told Helen and her siblings that she'd had "a massive stroke at the base of her brain." After a while Florence finally began to respond to pain. As a result, Helen told them to "just let her go and keep her comfortable." Helen had other plans. After everyone left the room and Helen was alone with her mother in a single room at the hospital, she realized that she "was the only one who could appreciate" what Florence had done. "They hadn't seen this for what it was, a suicide attempt." Helen continued:

> When I knew I was completely alone with her I took an extra pillow and began to smother her with it. Suddenly I could hear noises in the hallway and recognized my sister's voice, and I knew that she and whoever she was with were going to be coming through the door any second. I instantly hid the pillow and in walked my sister and the nurse. As they did I called out 'Oh my goodness, I don't know what's happening to her.' I don't know if the nurse suspected anything, and I didn't care, because I knew I could get away with it without a problem. However, I now knew that something else was going to have to be done.

Helen immediately took her siblings aside and told them that they needed a family conference. When they met, away from the hospital, Helen told them "what really happened to their mother, about her taking the pills." Helen's sister, who lived in another state, complained about her mother's decision to act without her, without saying good-bye. In response, Helen told her: "She wasn't doing it for you or me and David. She was doing it because she had to do it for herself. Mom was angry and frustrated with life." Helen's sister calmed down, and then said that her mother had a living will. Grasping this as justification, they decided to help her die, that "this was what her living will really meant." There were some other arguments, "but not about this."

Taking charge, Helen first decided to gently approach her mother's doctor, but changed her mind once she discovered he was Catholic. "We talked about not using heroic measures, and he said that he had no trouble with this, but I decided not to talk with him further about helping."

> During the next three days Helen made her plans. Another medical professional helped her get what she needed, "something like curare." She then went to the hospital and waited for the nurses to make their rounds. With me I had a syringe of sleeping medication and two vials of this muscle paralyzer. I gave her the sleeping medication and then injected her with the other. I knew there would be no post-mortem autopsy. I stayed with my mom a little while then went into the waiting room. An hour after I gave her the drugs my sister made the discovery. Unfortunately, mom began to show some signs, and I think they knew that something had happened, but they wouldn't have done anything. After all, my father had been a prominent physician at the same hospital.

After Helen and her sister finally left the hospital, they gathered with the rest of the family. Helen told them what she'd done. "My husband was totally sympathetic, and we all laughed and cried." Helen and her husband have never told their own children, who were in their early twenties at the time. And Helen's sister never told her own husband, as "his own brother committed suicide" and Helen's sister "didn't think that it was appropriate to burden him with this information, that it might bring up his own grief." Helen added that: "We didn't want to mess with his defense mechanisms." As a result, Helen, her sister and brother, and two of their spouses hold the secret.

Helen "considered it an honor to help." She'd had a special relationship with her mother, and the two shared a "great deal of humor, trust, and honesty." One time, for example, her mother had even told Helen that, though she loved her, she "would've aborted her had it been legal at the time." However, this level of honesty didn't seem to apply to all things, especially her mother's final decision to die. As Helen told me: "I regret that I couldn't have talked to her more directly about the issues before she died, but whenever I tried to bring up the topic, mom would say, 'Don't be maudlin.'" After her mother's death, Helen did go in for counseling, twice, some three months after her death, "just to talk about it with someone because I knew this was important." She said, "You have to understand that I had no problem with Mom's death, but as a medical professional I decided that I needed it; it was on my agenda from the very start." Although she suggested the same for her siblings, no one else followed suit.

> Until now, I've never talked about it with anyone except for those two visits with the therapist. It was quite something. I was crying and he was crying and the therapist then told me 'I want you to know that we had a similar situation in our family.' I had sat on it for three months before I went to the therapist. We're not all alike. My husband has never initiated communication about this and I was too distant to bring it up. I wanted to talk with someone about it.

Five years later, Helen found out about the Hemlock Society from another healthcare professional. Helen picked up a copy of *Let Me Die*, and then joined. Looking back, Helen has had no remorse over giving her mother an injection. Nor was she afraid of discovery. As she said, "My own status in the community was quite high. We were an important family. No one would've prosecuted me, it would never have gotten that far." And in looking at other losses, and the impact of this event on her grieving process, she has seen no difference. Instead, "my only grief was over the lack of knowledge of ways to make her more comfortable during life."

The event has had one effect on her, however: Helen and her husband have made a pact. She has told her husband, a physician, that "If I need help, you bloody well better do it." He knows what she expects to be done and that, "if the drugs don't work, he'll help with the plastic bag." In addition, his own mother is infirm, and they've talked about the possibility of his eventual Alzheimer's. Helen's husband has asked that if this should happen, she should take him out "for a walk on a cold night." She explained, "You don't leave tracks in falling snow, if you know what I mean." Even with her experience, which she has defined as positive, she still believes that "legalization without strong controls would be wrong," and thinks that "old age abuse by adult family members would be a problem." Her brother's wife has taken a different approach. "She took this all very hard," Helen told me. "She went back to her town and actually started a hospice program there, partly because of mom, and partly because of the death of her own father."

WHEN DOCTORS FAIL

In a seemingly significant number of cases, physicians who decide to help a patient die are either unaware of what might work, or are reticent to prescribe the truly lethal means to do so. This hesitation may well be out of fear that because drugs such as barbiturates are tracked by government agencies, the death of a patient might be investigated. As a result, some doctors provide what turn out to be the "wrong" drugs. The consequences of this can often be even worse than when partners, families, and friends take matters into their own hands and pool their own pharmaceutical resources. This is because, if physicians are involved, the expectations of failure and potential family involvement are lessened; a patient and their significant others may place too high a level of trust in both the physician's knowledge and in their prescription.

This happened in the case of Jessica, whose physician-assisted death failed because her attempt was discovered in progress. Her physician had assured her that the large number of Percocet tablets would be effective for this purpose. Instead, the attempt left her in extreme physical pain with near fatal liver damage. Now hospitalized with but days to live, her doctor was afraid to prescribe her any further drugs, because of her now known suicide attempt. As a result, Jessica's daughter "hit the streets" in search of heroin with which to inject her mother.

This lack of medical knowledge as to "what works" was similarly shown to me in what happened with Mark and his mother. In this case, the physician's help did not come in the form of a prescription, but from his own personal supply. Like Jessica's doctor, he felt that this was safer than leaving behind a lethal paper trail. Mark's mother's diagnosis of stomach cancer came as a shock. "In just a matter of weeks, she went from feeling fine to surgery to never eating again to quickly wasting away." This made her decision easier about "when to die." Mark explained that: "She probably would've died in another week if she hadn't taken her own life at that point." During these weeks Mark's mother, a long-time member of the Hemlock Society, began asking physician friends if they could assist her, or help her obtain what she'd need to die comfortably and safely. Over the years, she had worked closely with many doctors, and it took little effort before one man, a personal friend, agreed to help. After making a fairly rapid final decision, Mark's mother called her friend who immediately came with a quantity of liquid morphine. The physician then explained that he could not take an active role, but would "provide the medication" and be "willing to stay in the house in case of an emergency." He told Mark and his father that they should be the ones to actively assist, but that they should come to this decision together. They agreed. Their plan was to help her fulfill her last wish "to have something to drink." The cancer had crept up her throat and she couldn't swallow due to the pain. If they could deaden the sensation with morphine, "there might be a little period where she could have a couple of last sips and nibbles. More than anything they wanted her to be able to take a few last sips of ginger ale. This was not to be. "The bottom line is that nothing worked that day." Mark continued: "We injected the morphine into the heart catheter and were very surprised that she was instantly made unconscious. We thought that there'd be a period of grogginess during which time we could say our good-byes. Then she would pass into unconsciousness. Well, we injected it and she was gone."

They kept trying to offer her ginger ale, but it was too late and "there was no more communication." But they rationalized that "it was okay" because "she got to slip away easily." He added: "After all, we'd been saying good-bye for weeks anyway." After an hour there was no change in her heartbeat or respiration. They consulted with the physician, who said, "Well I was worried about this; that morphine was something I'd been keeping around for myself for several years and maybe it wasn't potent anymore." At that point the doctor suggested that he could obtain a quantity of insulin, and that a large dose "injected in the heart catheter should induce death." He returned an hour later with several syringes which Mark's father took charge of, injecting them each one after another. They waited, and again nothing happened. As a last resort, the physician had also brought over a very large syringe, which could be used to inject air and induce heart failure.

> We ended up having to repeatedly inject air. It was . . . nightmarish, horrific, how this process seemed to keep on and on. But it finally worked and she passed on. It took at least five hours from when we started. I stayed with her all of that time. This felt very important to be right there holding her hand and to be present with her to the very end.

THE EFFECTS OF LIMITED INVOLVEMENT

Sometimes even if drugs eventually work without further planned involvement of others, the circumstances surrounding the death can lead to dissatisfaction and regret, and family members or partners can be left feeling that they "didn't do enough" or that they "could've done better." This was the situation that followed Julie's participation in her brother Jerry's death. Jerry had been suffering for years from progressive multiple sclerosis, and Julie, a nurse, "was the only member of her family who could talk to him about his dying." After discussing it for four years, Julie finally supplied him with what she believed would be a lethal dose of Demerol. Jerry kept the drugs for several months, and Julie became increasingly worried that he was taking so long, and that he'd soon lose the capacity to swallow. Without warning, he made his decision on Julie's next visit. In the early hours on the day after she arrived, Jerry took forty Demerol tablets. In the morning he was discovered unconscious by his mother. About noon, with Julie and his mother by his bed, he awoke. Now aware that his attempt had failed, they called Jerry's doctor. He told them that, most likely, the pills had lodged in a pocket in his throat and hadn't dissolved. Jerry was upset and confused, but the physician told them all to "let nature take its course," and do nothing until the next day. During this time only Julie, her mother, and the physician knew what was occurring. No other family members had been informed of the attempt. As a result, Julie had to leave late in the afternoon to join her father for a family dinner, "as if nothing was happening." Julie's mother remained with her son and fed him more food, which "washed down the pills." Jerry ended up dying only two hours later. When the authorities were informed of his death, they arrived in force and "asked questions about a possible suicide" until they discovered that he'd been sick a long time.

In looking back, what affected Julie the most was that Jerry "had to go through that horror of awakening after he'd gathered the courage to finally make the attempt." For Julie, "the horror of those hours and the look in his eyes" was something she couldn't forget. In retrospect, Julie regretted that her brother had to do this alone, and that no one was at his bedside when he took the pills. As Julie said: "I've really struggled with how could I have left him and how awful for him to be left." For Julie, this "secrecy" prevented his death from being the special event it might otherwise have been, and kept the full family from knowing of his plans and achieving closure. Instead, it required that they proceeded "as though nothing was happening."

THE EFFECTS OF ISOLATION

In some instances, those who are dying seem only concerned about their desire to die, and others only see the need to help, regardless of the consequences. This type of co-dependency can be accentuated by the private relationship that caregiving often entails, and can especially be intensified by the privacy and secrecy that often develops when two individuals begin planning an assisted death.

This can be seen clearly in the case of Michael and his father. Michael became his father's caregiver after his father was diagnosed with colon cancer and had a mass removed from his liver. At that point Michael's father asked him to secure the drugs, to "someday" help him die, and to keep this a secret from the rest of the family. For the next year Michael worked to obtain "the right drugs," and eventually secured a large amount of Dilaudid. As his father required more care, Michael moved back home, feeling that he was the only one his father could rely on. "This became our secret pact," Michael said, and as a result, he felt a mixture of pride and a heightened sense of awareness and duty, but still resented the fact that "this wasn't the loving act" he wanted to do.

As his father's death drew near, Michael reached burnout. Due to a lack of continuity of care with "day attendants changing every few days," he took on the sole responsibility of caring for his father. His workload increased and, to be able to fulfill his final duty, he began excluding others. As he saw it, he "couldn't take the risk of others getting in the way." Eventually, his father's cancer spread to his liver, which began to press on his diaphragm, causing uncontrollable hiccups. The oncologist "didn't know what to do" to ease his father's discomfort. One night, as a result, his father took several of the Dilaudid. They failed.

In the next two weeks the choices diminished, and Michael's sense of isolation and despair increased. Finally, one night his father fell and was badly cut. Michael got him bandaged and into bed. The next afternoon his father announced, "Today's the day." Michael pleaded with him to wait, but his father said "No!" Michael finally agreed, got the medications, ground them up, and mixed them into his father's pudding. Michael explained that he was in a "profound and heightened state of consciousness." At that moment, after his father had taken the drugs, he finally began to ask him all the questions for which he wanted answers. Michael, exhausted from caregiving, had not taken the time to ask him these questions earlier. He wanted to know how his father had made it through life, and if he had any advice for him. But it was too late, the drugs had taken effect, and his father shared no secrets.

As in so many other cases, however, death didn't come. Michael repeatedly entered his father's room in disbelief that the 200 milligrams of Dilaudid "weren't working." His fear and isolation built. This especially became apparent later that evening when Michael's former girlfriend called. She had known that Michael was home and caring for his father. Needing someone with whom he could share his anxiety, he immediately told her what was happening in the next room. Later, at 1:30 a.m., he then called his business partner and asked his advice. Finally, two hours later, he made his decision. He got two dry cleaning bags and placed them inside one another.

> I didn't think I could do it. It took me a couple of minutes before I could go ahead. But I forced myself. I felt I had no choice. I said some kind of prayer that it would be okay.

This was clearly a loving act, but it seemed like forever. After he removed the bags, he put them in the garbage behind the local supermarket then returned to call the mortuary. They called the coroner, who came with a sheriff's detective. After talking with the doctor, they determined that it was a natural death.

After this, Michael went into "a state of shock" until the funeral was over. A sleep disorder, which began months earlier, continued, and he began to second guess his decision to help. In all of this, he wasn't helped by the secret he carried. Now suffering from insomnia and depression, Michael entered a treatment facility a month after his father's death. Although he was put on medication, the effects continued, and he kept "replaying the event over and over again."

DISCUSSION

These cases exemplify several of the features of what can go wrong in a non-physician assisted death, or even in one assisted by a physician. Most significantly, we can see how patients often fail to talk honestly with their physicians about their desire to die and, as a result, fail to secure the most effective means by which to do so. Instead, they depend on valium, oral morphine, or other substances prescribed to deal with the symptoms of their physical conditions. We also can see how even drugs effective for this purpose can be thwarted when lone attempts are unknowingly discovered in progress by family members and friends, who similarly have been left uninformed of a person's final plans for such an act. This especially can become a problem for family members who find themselves morally bound to carry out a loved one's desires, but who may not be emotionally prepared for the consequences. This shows an inherent problem with "prescription-only" legislation in support of assisted dying.

Without some form of mandatory notification of someone charged with discovering the death, the potential exists for interruption and emergency resuscitation. I have yet to see this dealt with directly and realistically by anyone supportive of such legislation. We further can see the effects of exhaustion from caregiving, absence of support from others for the decision, fear of discovery, and differences about closure and the final timing for a death.

Obviously, part of what goes wrong in assisted deaths is that the very nature of its illegality often raises barriers to positive experience in the form of inadequate drugs and knowledge, fear, and lack of appropriately trained practitioners. But the question that is raised is: How does one accomplish an assisted death in the most "efficient" and yet emotionally positive manner unless one has done it before or has well-developed models to use for this purpose? In this way, the lack of models, experience, and training makes this an act that must be constantly reinvented. Every experience is new, fraught with its own fears, hesitancy, and ignorance, and nearly every one who participates is an actor with an unrehearsed script. This, more than anything else, perhaps, creates the potential for errors, fear, dissatisfaction, and a focus more on methods of death and a concern for secrecy than on a sense of respect for what is actually occurring. For example, when I asked one man, Randy, what he remembered most about his partner's death, he didn't say, "The loss of my partner and closest friend." Instead, he said, "shooting the rubber bands out the window, and wondering if they could be fingerprinted." Similarly, others told me about the "fear of discovery," the "quiet long night," the "isolation," and "wondering when to leave" and "where to dispose of the plastic bag." Others have told me of their apprehension of a last minute autopsy, or of being stopped on the way home by the police while carrying "extra drugs," or even something so mundane as a "plastic bag." Such thoughts are normal, given the illegality of the act and the secrecy represented. However, they also provide us with an insight into what might make for a better death. Drugs and knowledge are key here, but so too are set and setting. Although the latter are not my concern in this paper, they obviously can be assisted by discussion among all significant others of a patient's desire and intent, the full acceptance of the patient's decision to die, the exploration of every alternative, and planning for all contingencies. In this way, a death without secrecy would appear to hold several advantages. But these still don't eliminate the problem of drugs and knowledge, which raise several issues for consideration.

Most important is the question of whether those with life threatening conditions, under certain restrictive conditions, should have access to potentially lethal medications. Reform in this area, of course, follows the prescription-only model of legislation (as in the case of Oregon's Measure 16), which, in principle, would allow terminally ill patients to request and receive lethal prescriptions from physicians. The common ethical questions about euthanasia apply. These include: whether it's ever right to actively help rather than allow to die, whether this violates the long standing traditional role of physicians as healers, whether such a request can be rational, and whether the "right" to receive assistance would soon be expanded to ever larger populations of non-terminally ill or would become an "expectation" and subject to abuse.

The issue of knowledge raises other ethical questions. Although books like Derek Humphry's *Final Exit* have been protected by First Amendment guarantees, it is obvious that the public still lacks accurate knowledge of what works and what doesn't. And it also is obvious that even those who do read such books don't always read them with care. The question this raises is whether healthcare professionals, with help from pharmacists, should provide terminally ill patients with this type of information upon request—even if they still refuse to provide patients with the lethal means to actually end their lives. In this regard, can the provision of information be justified if the intent is to reduce harm to others rather than to cause a patient's death?

This new "double effect" argument follows the model of needle exchange programs used to reduce the risk of HIV exposure among IV drug users, that is, one is not condoning IV drug use, but attempting to slow the spread of HIV infection. In this case, however, the reduction of harm would apply to partners, families, and friends who otherwise might stand a greater risk of becoming directly involved in assisting another to die. As can be seen in the stories presented here, this risk involves a range of criminal actions, including assisting in a suicide, mercy killing, and evidence tampering. The effects also include long-lasting questions of one's role in a death which, in some instances, can affect the grief and post-mortem adjustment processes. Such a program of public information would, of course, be problematic to those supportive only of the healing role of physicians and pharmacists, as well as to advocates of suicide prevention for all categories of individual, even the terminally ill.

Nevertheless, a program of public information about assisting in dying would seem to fall well within First Amendment protections, and could be designed as only a small part of an overall public outreach program of education aimed at preventing rather than encouraging assisted deaths at inappropriate stages in the dying process, or without counseling and consultation with specialists in the area of palliative care. Although I am not here proposing such a program be implemented, I am saying that my findings point to frequent failure in the case of assisted death as well as frequent over-involvement by significant others. And it is obvious that these findings have both ethical and public policy implications.

NOTES

1. I began this project by using a snowball sample in the San Francisco Bay Area, and made initial interviews through contacts with health professionals and right-to-die activists I had made as regional director of the National Hemlock Society. I then expanded my project by eventually announcing a call for interviews in publications of the local chapter of the Hemlock Society and in the National Hemlock Society's *Hemlock Quarterly*. In 1992, I expanded my research to Great Britain, and received assistance from both the Voluntary Euthanasia Society of Great Britain and the Voluntary Euthanasia Society of Scotland. Combining telephone and in-person interviews, I used a narrative approach and allowed each person to tell me their story. I followed up with a set of open-ended questions covering: relationships among the parties involved, the decision-making process, discussions prior to the assisted death, alternatives considered, motives for dying and for helping, expectations about the experience, methods of assisted death, type and source of drugs, the nature and setting of the death, the "official" cause of death, knowledge among friends and family about the actual circumstances, and both the initial and delayed effects of participation. These interviews lasted as long as ten hours over multiple meetings. Where possible, interviews were tape-recorded. Whenever possible, I also interviewed other parties who were involved in these deaths. To protect my sources, I applied pseudonyms to each case, and erased all tape-recordings after transcription. At the end of the project, I also destroyed all written records bearing names, phone numbers, return addresses, or other indicators of identity. Although my respondents were self-selected, and usually obtained by contacts from right-to-die groups, more than half were not members of such organizations. And most who were members only joined after they assisted in the deaths of partners, family members, or friends.

2. These do not include cases where individual details were lacking or could not be accurately described. Nor do they include cases where interviews could not be completed, or the substantiated case of one woman who claimed that she had been present at some thirty assisted deaths, of which she directly assisted in twenty.

COMMENTARIES

Position Statements
on Euthanasia and Assisted Suicide

coordinated by Arthur G. Lipman

Various professional societies and other organizations have developed position statements relating to the legalization and practice of assisted suicide and euthanasia. Most medical and nursing societies that have published positions strongly oppose legalization of these practices, while some recognize that the practices do occur. Pharmaceutical societies have been noticeably absent in publishing statements on these issues while nursing societies have been most active in publishing positions. Several national and state medical societies have published articles relating to these issues, but most have not published position statements, *per se*. The Michigan State Medical Society statement is reprinted as being representa-

Arthur G. Lipman, PharmD, is Professor of Clinical Pharmacy in the College of Pharmacy and Pain Management Center, University Hospitals and Clinics, University of Utah Health Sciences Center.

Address correspondence to: Dr. Arthur G. Lipman at College of Pharmacy, University of Utah, Salt Lake City, UT 84112.

Position statements reprinted with permission.

[Haworth co-indexing entry note]: "Position Statements on Euthanasia and Assisted Suicide." Lipman, Arthur G. Co-published simultaneously in *Journal of Pharmaceutical Care in Pain & Symptom Control* (Pharmaceutical Products Press, an imprint of The Haworth Press, Inc.) Vol. 4, No. 1/2, 1996, pp. 245-289; and: *Drug Use in Assisted Suicide and Euthanasia* (ed: Margaret P. Battin, and Arthur G. Lipman) Pharmaceutical Products Press, an imprint of The Haworth Press, Inc., 1996, pp. 245-289. Single or multiple copies of this article are available from The Haworth Document Delivery Service [1-800-342-9678, 9:00 a.m. - 5:00 p.m. (EST)].

tive of positions that have been adopted by physician associations. It is understandable that the Michigan Society developed a formal statement in the light of Dr. Jack Kevorkian's actions in that state. Numerous right-to-die organizations have published papers, but these are most commonly instructions on how to actively end one's life. The paper published by Compassion in Dying, an organization in Washington state is included as representative of those types of statements.

Perhaps the most thought provoking and scholarly paper on this topic is that developed by the Society for Health and Human Values (SHHV) which recognizes that neither simple condemnations nor endorsements of actively ending life effectively address the issues. SHHV has posed a series of questions which we believe readers will find helpful in forming their own opinions on these difficult issues. The statements which follow are a representative, not an exhaustive, sample of those that have been published.

The following position statements are reprinted with the written permission of the originating organizations. Statements are included from the American Academy of Hospice Physicians, American Cancer Society, American Nurses Association, Compassion in Dying, Michigan State Medical Society, National Association of Social Workers, National Hospice Organization, Oncology Nursing Society and the Society for Health and Human Values.

POSITION STATEMENT ON EUTHANASIA AND ASSISTED SUICIDE THE ACADEMY OF HOSPICE PHYSICIANS

We stand in fellowship with all those who are striving to diminish the pain and suffering of the dying.

As hospice physicians involved in the compassionate care of the terminally ill, we have observed that competent palliative care relieves the pain and suffering of terminally ill persons and their families.

In the current debate we oppose legalization of euthanasia (mercy killing) and assisted suicide. We call instead for public policy changes that ensure genuine access to comprehensive hospice services for all dying patients–regardless of socioeconomic status, age or diagnosis.

Approved July 13, 1991

POSITION STATEMENT ON ASSISTED SUICIDE
AND EUTHANASIA
AMERICAN CANCER SOCIETY

The American Cancer Society is the nationwide community-based voluntary health organization dedicated to eliminating cancer as a major health problem by preventing cancer, saving lives and diminishing suffering from cancer, through research, education, advocacy, and service.

To accomplish its mission, the American Cancer Society is devoted to the prevention, detection and treatment of cancer. We recognize, however, that for those not cured of this disease and for many who are undergoing treatment, needless suffering may occur. Although suffering takes many forms, we are particularly concerned about the pain that can be associated with cancer.

The American Cancer Society believes that pain is not a reason to consider life terminating approaches to end suffering. We advocate an aggressive, thorough approach to relieving pain that is associated with cancer. With current information and careful attention to the use of drugs and other types of pain relief techniques, the majority of individuals with cancer pain can find relief. For those who remain in pain despite the application of standard treatment regimens, we recommend additional consultation with acknowledged experts in the field.

We respect the right of patients to refuse therapy, and we respect their right to request that treatments be withheld or withdrawn if too burdensome. The care of the dying must include attention not only to the needs of the patient, but to the family and care givers. We encourage patients to express their wishes for end-of-life care in the form of advanced directives. We encourage the use of living wills, the use of Do Not Resuscitate orders, and the appointment of health care proxies to serve as patient surrogates.

The American Cancer Society strongly supports the integration of palliative care for all advanced cancer patients and hospice services for comprehensive and compassionate end-of-life care. This care should include the treatment of physical pain, alleviation of suffering, control of symptoms other than pain, and the appropriate assessment and attention to psychological, social, and spiritual concerns.

We do not support assisted suicide and euthanasia. We believe that these acts are contrary to the ethical traditions and threaten the moral integrity of health care professionals. We assert that it is the responsibility of all organizations concerned with cancer care to work to improve care at the end of life, and to undertake broad educational programs for patients, families, and health care professionals concerning care at the end of life.

Approved June, 1995

POSITION STATEMENT ON ASSISTED SUICIDE
AMERICAN NURSES ASSOCIATION

Summary

Nurses, individually and collectively, have an obligation to provide comprehensive and compassionate end-of-life care which includes the promotion of comfort and the relief of pain, and at times, foregoing life-sustaining treatments. The American Nurses Association (ANA) believes that the nurse should not participate in assisted suicide. Such an act is in violation of the *Code for Nurses with Interpretive Statements (Code for Nurses)* and the ethical traditions of the profession.

Background

There is a continuum of end-of-life choices that encompasses a broad spectrum of interventions from the alleviation of suffering, adequate pain control, do-not-resuscitate orders, withdrawing/withholding artificially provided nutrition and hydration, to requests for assisted suicide, and active euthanasia. Throughout this continuum nurses can respond to patients with compassion, faithfulness and support. Yet, nurses must understand the subtleties and distinctions of these issues in order to respond in a reasoned and ethically permissible manner.

Terminology

In discussion of any controversial issue, one set of problems arises over definitions. Nurses and others interpret terms in vastly different and perhaps contradictory fashion. Thus, clarification of language is essential. The first important distinction to make is that there are some end-of-life decisions that are fully consistent with the *Code for Nurses* and others that are not.

Assisted Suicide: Suicide is traditionally understood as the act of taking one's own life. Assisting in suicide entails making a means of suicide (e.g., providing pills or a weapon) available to a patient with knowledge of the patient's intention. The patient who is physically capable of suicide, subsequently acts to end his or her own life.

Assisted suicide is distinguished from active euthanasia. In assisted suicide, someone makes the means of death available, but does not act as the direct agent of death.

Withholding, Withdrawing and Refusal of Treatment: Honoring the refusal of treatments that a patient does not desire, that are disproportionately burdensome to the patient, or that will not benefit the patient is ethically and legally permissible. Within this context, withholding or withdrawing life-sustaining therapies or risking the hastening of death through treatments aimed at alleviating suffering and/or controlling symptoms are ethically acceptable and do not constitute assisted suicide. There is no ethical or legal distinction between withholding or withdrawing treatments, though the latter may create more emotional distress for the nurse and others involved.

For the purpose of this statement, the term active euthanasia refers to those actions that are inconsistent with the ANA *Code for Nurses* and are ethically unacceptable, whether the euthanasia is voluntary, involuntary or nonvoluntary.

Background

Among the most controversial, vigorously debated and, at times confusing issues within contemporary society is assisted suicide. The nursing profession is also struggling with the complex moral and professional questions surrounding this issue. Scientific and technological advances have made it possible to extend life and prolong the dying process. These advances have not necessarily provided for the enhancement of human dignity, personal control or improvement in care.

Nurses witness firsthand the devastating effects of debilitating and life-threatening disease and are often confronted with the despair and exhaustion of patients and families. At times, it may be difficult to find a balance between the preservation of life and the facilitation of a dignified death. Nurses need to recognize their own feelings of sadness, fear, discouragement and helplessness and realize the influence of these feelings on clinical decision making. These agonizing tensions may cause a nurse to consider intentionally hastening a patient's death as a humane and compassionate response, yet the traditional goals and values of the profession mitigate against it.

The ANA *Code for Nurses with Interpretive Statements (Code for Nurses)* explicates the values and ethical precepts of the profession and provides guidance for conduct and relationships in carrying out nursing actions. It is within the framework of the *Code for Nurses* and professional standards that nurses make ethical decisions and discharge their responsibilities. The central axiom that directs the profession is respect for persons. This respect extends to and encompasses patients, families, nurse colleagues and team members. The principles of autonomy (self-determination), beneficence (doing good), nonmaleficence (avoiding harm), veracity (truth-telling), confidentiality (respecting privileged information), fidelity (keeping promises) and justice (treating people fairly) are all understood in the context of the overarching commitment of respect for persons. Nurses are challenged to uphold these principles as they confront the realities of professional practice.

Historically, the role of the nurse has been to promote, preserve and protect human life. The *Code for Nurses* states that respect for persons "extends to all who require the services of the nurse of the promotion of health, the prevention of illness, the restoration of health, the alleviation of suffering and the provision of supportive care of the dying. The nurse does not act deliberately to terminate the life of any person."

The profession of nursing is dominated by an ethic of care, an ideal that permeates and underscores all of nursing practice. The essence of caring takes place in the context of the nurse-patient relationship, the respectful and genuine presence of one human being to another. The perspective of care is a crucial and valuable dimension of ethical deliberation. From the perspective of care, nurses appreciate the emotional and contextual dimensions of ethical discernment. The uniqueness of individuals and the particular dynamics of relationships are recognized as integral components of the discernment process. The nurse's caring approach assists patients and families in finding meaning or purpose in their living and dying and furthers the attainment of a meaningful life and death.

Rationale

The profession's response to nurse participation in assisted suicide is grounded in the ethical traditions and goals of the profession, and in its covenant with society.

- The profession of nursing is built upon the Hippocratic tradition "do no harm" and an ethic of moral opposition to killing another human being. The ethical framework of the profession as articulated through the *Code for Nurses* explicitly prohibits deliberately terminating the life of any human being.

- Nursing has a social contract with society that is based on trust and therefore patients must be able to trust that nurses will not actively take human life. The profession's covenant is to respect and protect human life (Nursing: A Social Policy Statement). Nurse participation in assisted suicide is incongruent with the accepted norms and fundamental attributes of the profession.
- Though there is a profound commitment both by the profession and the individual nurse to the patient's right to self-determination, limits to this commitment exist. In order to preserve the moral mandates of the profession and the integrity of the individual nurse, nurses are not obligated to comply with all patient and family requests. The nurse should acknowledge to the patient and family the inability to follow a specific request and the rationale for it.

Acceptance of assisted suicide practices has the potential for serious societal and professional consequences and abuses.

- While there may be individual patient cases that are compelling, there is high potential for abuses with assisted suicide, particularly with vulnerable populations such as the elderly, poor and disabled. These conceivable abuses are even more probable in a time of declining resources. The availability of assisted suicide could foreseeably weaken the goal of providing quality care for the dying.
- Nurses must examine these issues not only from the perspective of the individual patient, but from the societal and professional community perspective. Involvement in community dialogue and deliberation will allow nurses to recommend and uphold initiatives, and provide leadership in promoting optimal end-of-life care.

Discussion

Assisted suicide is not to be confused with ethically justified end-of-life decisions and actions.

- The moral objection to the nurse's participation in assisted suicide does not diminish the nurse's obligation to provide appropriate interventions throughout the process of dying. Nurses must be vigilant advocates for humane and dignified care, for the alleviation of suffering and for the non-abandonment of patients.
- The withholding or withdrawal of life-sustaining treatment such as mechanical ventilation, cardiopulmonary resuscitation, chemotherapy, antibiotics and artificially provided nutrition and hydration can

be ethically acceptable. Patients have the right to exercise their decisional authority relative to health care decisions, including foregoing life-sustaining treatments.

- The provision of medications with the intent to promote comfort and relieve suffering is not to be confused with the administration of medication with the intent to end the patient's life. "The nurse may provide interventions to relieve symptoms in the dying client even when the interventions entail substantial risks of hastening death" (*Code for Nurses*).

Nurses should seek to understand the meaning of the request for assisted suicide and continue to demonstrate respect for and commitment to patients.

- It is not uncommon for patients to think about suicide during the course of illness. Requests for assisted suicide can be related to numerous factors including unrelieved pain and other symptoms, depression, feelings of loss of control, fear of isolation, concern for family and a sense of hopelessness. Nurses should avoid judgement of patients or their experience and recognize that only the suffering person can define that suffering.
- There are positive obligations to ascertain the patient's concerns, fears, needs and values, to discuss health care options and to provide counsel and support. Discussion of suicidal thoughts does not increase the risk of suicide and may actually be therapeutic in decreasing the likelihood. The relationship and communication between the nurse and patient and diminish feelings of isolation and provide needed support.
- Nurses have an opportunity to create environments where patients feel comfortable to express thoughts, feelings, conflict and despair. The issues that surround a request for assisted suicide should be explored with the patient, and as appropriate with family and team members. It is crucial to listen to and acknowledge the expressions of suffering, hopelessness and sadness. When possible, factors that contribute to such a request should be alleviated, and existing patient strengths and resources promoted and relied on.
- Nurses must identify and seek opportunities to demonstrate their lasting commitment to patients and families within the confines of professional practice. Efforts should be directed at the implementation of programs of palliative care to better manage chronic, severe bio-psycho-social and spiritual distress that limit quality of life and increase suffering.

- Nurses are obligated to listen compassionately to patients' requests, but must recognize the boundaries of acceptable ethical practice. Nurses can be honest with patients and acknowledge that they can not participate in assisted suicide, yet still have a commitment to non-abandonment.

Acknowledging the prohibition against participation in assisted suicide does not necessarily lessen the distress and conflict a nurse may feel when confronted with a patient's request.

- Nurses may encounter agonizing clinical situations and experience the personal and professional tension and ambiguity surrounding these decisions. The reality that all forms of human suffering and pain cannot necessarily be removed except through death is not adequate justification for professional sanctioning.
- Nurses need to be aware of their own sense of suffering, discomfort, confusion and inadequacy. Acknowledgment of care giver struggle and vulnerability can connect nurses deeply with the experience of the patient and family.
- Nurses should seek the expertise and resources of others including nurse colleagues, team members, pastoral services, hospice specialists and ethics consultants/committees when confronting the complexity of these issues.
- The willingness to consider participation in assisted suicide is generally motivated by mercy, compassion, promotion of patient autonomy and quality of life considerations. It is recognized that the nurse's views about participation in assisted suicide may be different than the official position of the nursing profession. Regardless of the opinion of the nurse, it is a breach of the ethical traditions of nursing, and the *Code for Nurses,* to participate in assisted suicide.

Recommendations

The debate and controversy surrounding assisted suicide has highlighted the shortcomings of the health care system, in particular, care of the dying. Nurses and the nursing profession can take an active stance to create health care environments that provide humane care.

- Advance the precepts of *Nursing's Agenda for Health Care Reform,* one of which calls for careful assessment of the "appropriateness of providing high-tech curative medical care to those who simply require comfort, relief from pain, supportive care of peaceful death."

- Engage in professional and public dialogue and decision making around assisted suicide. Encourage the participation of nurses in discussions of this issue at the local, state and national level.
- Collaborate with other members of the health professions and citizens to advance and ensure the availability of quality end-of-life care.
- Provide education for health professionals and the community on ethical and legal rights and responsibilities surrounding health care decision making, treatment options, pain control, symptom management and palliative care.
- Support the use of outcome measurements and further research to ensure more scientifically based, responsible and ethically sensitive end-of-life treatment.
- Advocate for the removal of barriers to the delivery of appropriate end-of-life care through legislation and changes in restrictive regulatory and institutional practices.
- Promote patient and family participation in treatment decision making and the use of advance directives.

Conclusion

Nurses need to remain in the forefront as leaders and advocates for the delivery of dignified and humane end-of-life care. Nurses are obliged to provide relief of suffering, comfort and, when possible, a death that is congruent with the values and desires of the dying person. Yet, nurses must uphold the ethical mandates of the profession and not participate in assisted suicide.

Knowledge of the ethical foundations and parameters of professional practice provides guidance and support to nurses both individually and collectively. Such an undertaking will better prepare nurses to deal with the difficult moral and professional challenges surrounding the issue of assisted suicide.

Effective December 8, 1994

POSITION STATEMENT ON ACTIVE EUTHANASIA
AMERICAN NURSES ASSOCIATION

Summary

Nurses have an obligation to provide timely, humane, comprehensive and compassionate end-of-life care. The American Nurses Association believes that the nurse should not participate in active euthanasia because such an act is in direct violation of the *Code for Nurses with Interpretive Statements (Code for Nurses)*, the ethical traditions and goals of the profession and its covenant with society.

Terminology

Active Euthanasia: The term euthanasia is defined and characterized in many ways, thus clarification of language is important. Euthanasia is often called "mercy killing" and has been taken to mean the act of putting to death someone suffering from a painful and prolonged illness or injury. Active euthanasia means that someone other than the patient commits an action with the intent to end the patient's life, for example injecting a patient with a lethal dose. Sometimes euthanasia is subdivided into a situation in which a patient consents to euthanasia (voluntary) or a situation in which a patient refuses euthanasia (involuntary) or a situation when a patient is unable to consent to euthanasia (nonvoluntary). Active euthanasia is distinguished from assisted suicide. In active euthanasia someone not only makes the means of death available, but serves as the direct agent of death.

Withholding, Withdrawing and Refusal of Treatment: Honoring the refusal of treatments that a patient does not desire, that are disproportionately burdensome to the patient, or that will not benefit the patient is ethically and legally permissible. Within this context, withholding or withdrawing life-sustaining therapies or risking the hastening of death through treatments aimed at alleviating suffering and/or controlling symptoms are ethically acceptable and do not constitute assisted suicide. There is no ethical or legal distinction between withholding or withdrawing treatments, though the latter may create more emotional distress for the nurse and others involved.

Discussion

The ANA *Code for Nurses* provides guidance for ethical conduct and explicates the values and precepts of the profession. It is within the context of the *Code for Nurses* that nurses make ethical judgements and discharge their responsibilities. The principal axiom that directs the profession is respect for persons, and this respect is extended to patients, families, nurse colleagues and team members.

Historically, the role of the nurse has been to promote, preserve and protect human life. The *Code for Nurses* asserts that respect for persons "extends to all who require the services of a nurse for the promotion of health, the alleviation of suffering and the provision of supportive care of the dying. The nurse does not act deliberately to terminate the life of any person." This ethic of moral opposition to actively taking a human life prohibits the nurse form participating in active euthanasia.

The profession's opposition to nurse participation in active euthanasia does not negate the obligation of the nurse to provide proper and ethically justified end-of-life care which includes the promotion of comfort and the alleviation of suffering, adequate pain control, and at times, foregoing life-sustaining treatments.

Conclusion

Nurses must be vigilant advocates for the provision of humane and dignified care. Nurses can demonstrate their respect, support and lasting commitment to patients and families without participating in active euthanasia.

Effective December 8, 1994

ACCUMULATING DRUGS AND PROCEDURE FOR HASTENING DEATH A STATEMENT OF COMPASSION IN DYING

Accumulating Drugs

Many terminally ill patients wish they had an alternative to a prolonged process of dying. Increasingly, persons are saying, "I don't fear death as much as suffering and losing control."

Those of us who have witnessed the prolonged dying of a close friend or family member hope that we do not have to face that exhausting and dehumanizing situation. This can be a tragedy and ordeal for both the patient and the family. Many people would choose to die a few weeks or months early, rather than linger on and lose the ability to make their own decisions and be trapped in a hopeless situation.

A man struggling with cancer for the past year called recently and said, "It's time to begin thinking about how I can end this." Unfortunately, by then it was already too late for him to obtain the prescriptions for a more gentle death. In desperation, he eventually resorted to violent means to end his life.

When rational suicide is being considered, it is important for terminal patients to contact their physician(s) for prescriptions which they can accumulate before it is too late.

The best medicines for this purpose are the barbiturate drugs–Seconal (generic name secobarbital) or Nembutal. The quantity for both drugs is 60 capsules, 100 mg. each. However, barbiturates are difficult to obtain in the quantity needed because they are so lethal that doctors hesitate to prescribe them.

Terminal patients nearing the end are likely to be refused by their physicians if they ask for a single prescription of barbiturates sufficient to cause death. For example, 60 capsules of Seconal or Nembutal constitute a very effective means of causing one's own death, especially when taken with 2 ounces of a distilled alcohol. However, this would be a large number for a physician to authorize in one prescription. Many doctors fear that such a large prescription would come to the attention of the state medical disciplinary board if written for a patient who committed suicide shortly after obtaining the drugs. It could be interpreted that the doctor was intentionally aiding the suicide, which is a serious offense.

Some patients are successful in asking for a series of four prescriptions over a period of time, each for 15 capsules of Seconal. One capsule is a strong sleeping aid which a person would usually take only at bedtime. Thus, a prescription for 15 would be sufficient for two weeks and would not raise any suspicion. The capsules are accumulated until a total of 60 has been obtained. Not all pharmacies sell barbiturates, so it may be wise to phone ahead to ask if they are in stock.

Steps for a Hastened Death

When a terminal patient decides to hasten death using barbiturates, the following steps should be followed: (This outline assumes the patient is at home, not in a hospital or institution, and is able to swallow.)

1. Eat a small amount of food (custard, toast, applesauce, etc.). Wait 30 minutes.
2. Take 1 to 3 *antinausea tablets* to prevent vomiting (Dramamine, Compazine, or Marezine), along with three *beta-blocker tablets* (Inderal 80 mg.). Wait 30 minutes (or less, if patient shows signs of drowsiness).
3. Add the white powder from *60 Seconal or Nembutal capsules* to one-third to two-thirds of a cup of applesauce or pudding sweetened with 3 packets of artificial sweetener, 3 teaspoons of sugar, or honey to counteract bitterness. Stir well.

4. The patient immediately eats *all* of the mixture *without stopping.*
5. If the patient can tolerate alcohol, drinking 2 ounces of vodka, whiskey, or any other alcoholic drink is advisable.

The patient will fall into a deep sleep within 5-20 minutes and will expire within two to eight hours. (Occasionally, some patients with a strong cardiopulmonary system may take longer to die.) Any consideration of changing plans must take place before eating the barbiturates and drinking alcohol.

Before death, there will be a period of heavy breathing or snoring, but there should not be any physical movement or signs of distress. The book *Final Exit* by Derek Humphry is a good source of additional information about this process.

Procedure After Death

If the patient has been receiving hospice care at home, the hospice organization should be notified after death has occurred. They will call the funeral home and notify the county medical examiner. In most cases, the cause of death is entered on the death certificate by the patient's private physician and is attributed to the underlying disease (cancer, AIDS, emphysema, etc.). In such situations, there is no need for an autopsy, and arrangements for cremation or preparation for burial can commence. If the patient has not been receiving hospice care, call the funeral home.

This means of hastening death is put forth for consideration only by adult persons who are terminally ill and mentally competent, and who have informed their families and have their support. Persons considering ending their lives for other reasons are urged to seek help from a crisis line, counseling center, mental health professional, clergy person, or other source of assistance in a crisis.

November, 1994

STATEMENT ON PHYSICIAN ASSISTED SUICIDE
MICHIGAN STATE MEDICAL SOCIETY

The enclosed statement on physician assisted suicide was first developed by the Michigan State Medical Society Committee on Bioethics as requested by the MSMS Board of Directors shortly after assisted suicides were performed in Michigan. These points of consensus were the result of

16 public forums containing hundreds of hours of thoughtful debate over a period of 18 months.

Members of the Michigan State Medical Society's House of Delegates first adopted these consensus points as an organizational statement on physician assisted suicide in May, 1993, and reaffirmed this statement in May, 1994.

In summary, the statement does not endorse physician assisted suicide, but endorses alternatives that, when followed properly by physicians and patients, would result in very few requests for physician assisted suicide. This strongly pro-active statement leaves all medical decisions up to the physician and patient, where they belong.

In this statement, the physician members of the Michigan State Medical Society have reaffirmed their Hippocratic Oath to support their patients to the fullest; not to abandon them during their terminal illness, but to relieve their pain and suffering; to withdraw and/or withhold futile treatment if so requested; and to ease their final passage.

This statement allows nothing to come between Michigan physicians and their patients.

Definitions

Three terms used to discuss the role of physicians in the deaths of patients require definitions to avoid confusion regarding the scope of this statement.

"Allowing a patient to die" refers to discontinuing or withholding life-prolonging medical procedures or treatments when requested or consented to by the competent patient or by the appropriate advocate for the incompetent patient. For example, a patient bleeding from an advanced malignancy requests no further blood transfusions or intravenous fluids. The physician orders these treatments discontinued and morphine administered for pain. The patient dies six hours later.

"Physician assisted suicide" refers to the physician providing the patient with a substance or device with the understanding that the patient intends to use those means to cause his or her own death. For example, a patient with advanced malignancy, who has an indwelling intravenous line, wishes to die because of physical weakness and the inability for self-care. At the patient's request, the physician supplies a syringe with 500 milligrams of morphine, which the patient uses at a later time to self-inject and cause death.

"Active euthanasia" refers to the physician administering the means to cause the patient to die. For example, a patient with advanced malignancy, who has an indwelling intravenous line, wishes to die because of physical

weakness and inability for self-care. At the patient's request, the physician injects 500 milligrams of morphine into the intravenous line, and the patient dies.

Allowing a patient to die is ethically and legally acceptable and is, indeed, mandatory in many cases. Active euthanasia violates laws against homicide although voluntary euthanasia within strict guidelines is advocated by a thoughtful minority of physicians. This statement does not deal further with active or voluntary euthanasia.

Points of Consensus

1. The medical profession in Michigan should strive to provide the following strategies to enhance patient control over the dying process: (a) improved pain and system control; (b) assurance of the right of competent patients to refuse treatment; (c) utilization of advanced directives, both written and verbal. Full utilization and emphasis on the above may reduce the number of patients expressing an interest in assistance in suicide.

2. Providing a patient with sufficient medications to relieve pain even if it ends up shortening life, is neither assisting a suicide nor performing active euthanasia. Such provision is an essential of compassionate care.

3. The so-called "right to die," for example, the right to refuse unwanted or burdensome medical treatment, does not extend to or embrace a right to die with a physician's assistance through assisted suicide or active euthanasia.

4. A physician should never suggest or recommend suicide to a patient. The medical profession should not create nor allow a practice or specialty focused on or limited to assisting in suicide nor the development of specialized facilities for effecting assisted suicide. These could have the effect of advocating assisted suicide as a preferred or routine option.

5. Even if there are theoretical arguments which deny the existence of morally relevant differences among allowing a patient to die, assisting a patient's suicide and active euthanasia, there are strong prudential and clinical reasons to maintain these distinctions as a matter of policy.

6. A patient's mention of an intent or desire to commit suicide, or of a request for assistance, should result in a concerted effort to ascertain and ameliorate any factors contributing to the patient's suffering.

7. The physician's reluctance to assist in or to cause the death of a patient is rooted in the very basic principles of professional integrity

having to do with healing and relief of suffering for the purposes of extending the life of the patient. Only the most pressing circumstances, if any at all, can justify abandoning this position.

8. Legal prohibition of (physician) assisted suicide would be difficult if not impossible to enforce, and it is likely to have undesirable effects upon medical practice.

9. Societal changes to improve the quality of life and the perceived value of the life of the ill and/or elderly and to eliminate financial barriers to medical (including hospice and comprehensive long term) care may serve to limit patient requests for assisted suicide.

Additional MSMS policy states that MSMS opposes any legislation regarding physician assisted suicide, one way or the other.

RESOLUTION ON VOLUNTARY EUTHANASIA AND ASSISTED SUICIDE NATIONAL HOSPICE ORGANIZATION

WHEREAS, The National Hospice Organization is considered the voice of the nation's hospice community; and,

WHEREAS, The National Hospice Organization is often requested to provide comment to the Congress, the Administration, the Courts, and the media and the general public; and,

WHEREAS, The National Hospice Organization is on record supporting a patient's right to palliative care, a patient's right to refuse unwanted medical intervention including the provision of artificially supplied hydration and nutrition; and,

WHEREAS, There has been increased public attention and focus on the issue of voluntary euthanasia and assisted suicide; and,

WHEREAS, We believe hospice care is an alternative to voluntary euthanasia and assisted suicide; therefore,

RESOLVED, That the National Hospice Organization reaffirms the hospice philosophy that hospice care neither hastens nor postpones death.

RESOLVED, That the National Hospice Organization rejects the practice of voluntary euthanasia and assisted suicide in the care of the terminally ill.

Approved by the Delegates of the National Hospice Organization
at the Annual Meeting
November 8, 1990

STATEMENT OF THE NATIONAL HOSPICE ORGANIZATION OPPOSING THE LEGALIZATION OF EUTHANASIA AND ASSISTED SUICIDE

The National Hospice Organization (NHO) was formed in 1978 to promote the principles and concepts of the hospice program of care for terminally ill patients and their families. Over the past decade, NHO has championed the ideals of relief and suffering, freedom of choice, and death with dignity. NHO currently represents more than 1,800 hospice programs providing compassionate, terminal care to more than 275,000 patients and families each year. In November 1990, NHO adopted a resolution rejecting the practice of voluntary euthanasia and assisted suicide. This paper is offered as background information in support of this position.

NHO defines hospice as a coordinated program of palliative and supportive services provided in both the home and the inpatient settings that provides for physical, psychological, social, and spiritual care for dying persons and their families. Services are provided by a medically directed, interdisciplinary team of professionals and volunteers. Hospice recognizes dying as part of the normal process of living and focuses on maintaining the quality of remaining life. Hospice affirms life and neither hastens nor postpones death. Hospice exists in the hope and belief that through appropriate care and the promotion of a caring community sensitive to their needs, patients, and families may be free to obtain a degree of mental and spiritual preparation for death that is satisfactory to them.

The concept of hospice care was imported into this country in response to the unmet needs of dying patients and their families for whom traditional medical care was no longer effective, appropriate, or desired. Hospice has become an effective alternative to there being "nothing else to do." Skilled, intensive palliative care controls physical symptoms and facilitates the relief of the psychological, social, spiritual, and financial pain of terminal illness. Hospice is unique in its focus on the patient/family as the unit of care. Hospice care helps assure patients and families that everything possible has been done to control the patient's disease and its symptoms. Hospice care legitimatizes respite care for the patient so that the family can be revitalized. Effective hospice care supports the opportunity of the anticipatory grief work that aids the bereavement process. Hospice care continues as bereavement support for the patient's family after the patient's death to normalize their grief so that they may return to leading full and productive lives.

For the purpose of this paper, the term euthanasia will mean an act which intentionally and directly causes a patient's death. This definition of euthanasia encompasses active euthanasia, voluntary euthanasia, aid-in-dying, and in some settings, physical-assisted suicide. The term "assisted suicide" is most commonly used to represent an act in which a patient is given the means and specific instructions to take his or her own life. Withholding or withdrawing life-sustaining therapies or unintentionally hastening death through treatments aimed at controlling symptoms does not constitute either euthanasia or assisted suicide. The purpose of these acts is comfort of the patient, not ending the patient's life; thus these acts neither intentionally nor directly cause a patient's death. The position taken in this paper against the legalization of euthanasia applies to both euthanasia and assisted suicide.

The ethical pitfalls in legalizing euthanasia are evident in all aspects of medical ethics: autonomy, beneficence, justice, and integrity of the health care professional. Patient autonomy/self-determination is the most touted rationale for the legalization of euthanasia. Indeed, patients must have the right to choose their own care. They must be allowed to accept or refuse therapy based on informed consent. Central to all good health care, informed consent implies that the patient has been told of the care alternatives available and of the probable consequences of the choice they make.

One must question whether the choice of euthanasia is fully informed or truly voluntary. The choice between euthanasia and a painful, suffering death presented by euthanasia proponents is far different from the choice between euthanasia and a peaceful, comfortable death supported by appropriate hospice care.

Family members, health care providers, and society frequently exert subtle or overt pressures upon terminally ill patients to consent to excessive disease-oriented therapy which can be discontinued should the patient so desire. Terminally ill patients may similarly be pressured to consent to euthanasia if it becomes an acceptable legal option. There is no return from the choice of euthanasia.

Physicians have the right and the responsibility to advise patients whether the therapy they request is beneficial. Euthanasia lacks beneficence in many ways. An act which directly kills the patient, by definition, causes the most basic form of medical harm, death. Since its primary effect is death and only secondarily the relief of suffering, euthanasia does not allow for the inaccuracies in diagnosis and prognosis commonly experienced with patients labeled as "terminal." Patients who choose euthanasia rather than aggressive palliative care forfeit the opportunity to correct errors in prognosis or to benefit from skilled, intensive symptom control. Aggressive palliative care can improve the quality and quantity of remaining life. Previously unobtainable goals may become attainable, and some patients can even return to disease oriented therapy if that is their desire. Euthanasia forecloses these options.

Beyond physical and psychological comfort, spiritual comfort is an important goal of hospice care. Patients who opt for euthanasia may miss the opportunity to transcend their suffering and find meaning in their lives for themselves and their survivors. Patient autonomy should not totally override the beneficence needs of the patient's family and community. Anticipatory grief work, which has value to both patient and family, would be truncated by the expedience of euthanasia. The request for euthanasia can aggravate the family's sense of failure to obtain adequate palliative care for their loved one.

There is a fine but important distinction between withholding or withdrawing treatments that sustain life and providing treatments that directly end it. The critical issue is the intent or goal of the therapy. Euthanasia is different in kind, not degree, from treatments that allow death to occur or even those which unintentionally hasten it. No patient need die in pain. Although the ideal goal of palliative care is to maximize comfort and function, effective symptom control in some patients causes forfeiture of cognitive function, discontinuation of eating and drinking, suppression of cough reflex, and depression of respiration. These unintended consequences may hasten the death caused by the underlying disease; they do not of themselves directly cause death.

Family members can often use this final period of peaceful, pharmacologically-induced sleep to begin to separate from their loved one in preparation for the time of actual physical death. This type of intensive symptom control is ethically acceptable and distinctly different from the administration of a drug whose primary intent is to end life. Achievement of comfort through intensive symptom control prior to death is less of a burden to the family and the caregivers than having to directly cause death as the only way to relieve the patient's suffering.

Hospice has done much to restore public trust in the health care delivery system. Even in families who fully accept euthanasia as beneficent, having to resort to an act that directly causes death leaves room for corrosive doubt regarding the completeness and expertise of care rendered prior to the request for euthanasia. The very presence of euthanasia as an option can erode trust that the health care delivery system will do everything possible to relieve suffering prior to terminating life. Euthanasia may be offered to patients disguised as the most compassionate care while, in fact, it represents an impersonal act of isolation. Distrust with the health care system already delays initial contact and decreases patient compliance with appropriate medical care leading to increased morbidity and mortality. The maleficence of euthanasia thus encompasses probable harm to the patient, the patient's family, and society at large.

Justice issues of equal access to care and allocation of limited resources apply more to the problem of abuse rather than the proposed use of legalized euthanasia. If euthanasia were to be legalized, policies and procedures would have to be enacted to assure ready access to euthanasia services by all interested patients. Such universal access is not yet available for general medial care, let alone hospice. Of greater concern is the potential of euthanasia being recommended to those patients whose disease, family system, financial status, or community resources denies them access to hospice care. Euthanasia could become a penalty for being too sick, too isolated, or too poor.

Legalization of euthanasia would also abort ongoing efforts to enhance the quantity and quality of palliative care. The administrative and financial requirements of developing and maintaining euthanasia as a component of the health care delivery system could competitively diminish the support needed to increase access to appropriate health care for the terminally ill. The scientific, ethical, and emotional energy that will be required to establish euthanasia as a safe and effective therapeutic option for the small number of terminally ill patients who might choose it is an unjustifiable drain on the use of that energy to advance the art and science of the more applicable and already proven option of hospice/palliative care.

The ethical dilemma created for health care professionals caused by legalizing euthanasia is its contradiction with their professional codes and standards. More importantly, even if these standards should change, clinicians have the right to have their own beliefs and values. Patients are not the only moral agents in this process. Ethical decisions are bilateral, not unilateral.

Health care professionals have traditionally had the option to transfer patients to another professional's care if the patient requests something with which only the latter professional can comply. If transfer is not possible and the clinical situation is imminently life-threatening, the initial health care professional's right and responsibility is to refuse to perform procedures which he or she deems will cause more harm than good to the patient, their family, or society.

Legalization of euthanasia would put undue pressure upon the vast majority of physicians who oppose euthanasia to perform an act which they feel is wrong. Merely diagnosing patients as terminal so that they might be eligible for euthanasia, would co-opt a physician's personal opposition to participating in euthanasia.

Beyond the immediate ethical pitfalls mentioned above, legalization of euthanasia has a high risk for over-expansion and corruption resulting in even more personal and social harm. The failure of policies, procedures, rules, and regulations to guarantee the safety and efficacy of the care currently being rendered to terminally ill patients in this country offers little security that proposed administrative "safeguards" will protect the public from such potential dangers.

Provision of euthanasia to competent, terminally ill adults can be expected to be extended to incompetent adults through advanced directives. Definitions of terminal illness and unbearable suffering may broaden and may stray from the patient's original intent. The immediacy and irreversibility of euthanasia allows no room for review and correction. Expansion of euthanasia to non-terminally ill patients with even vaguer definitions of quality of life engender the specter of totally bypassing upon the expansion of euthanasia as a cost effective alternative to rehabilitative or custodial care for the disabled, frail, elderly, and poor.

Laws are symbols of what society values. Legalization of euthanasia would devalue life and would add to the growing decay of social and moral values. Allowing unpreventable death to occur with dignity and comfort is quite different from accepting euthanasia as an expeditious way out of a difficult situation for individuals or society.

Hospice is an ethically sound model of compassionate, cost effective, quality assured, patient/family oriented, terminal care. Hospice must be expanded to reach more eligible patients. Public and professional education must be increased and appropriate reimbursement must be secured. Alternatives to traditional home settings must be created and inpatient care must be expanded to reach patients and families for whom home care will remain impossible. If there is any major drawback to hospice care it is that you have to be dying to get it. Hospice must share its expertise with professionals and programs that care for patients who cannot be diagnosed as terminal within the time frame of months that has proved to be relevant to the effective delivery and receipt of hospice care.

Through appropriate application to terminally ill patients and extrapolation of its principles to non-terminally ill patients, hospice can truly improve the quality of life for all patients and their families. Hospice must tell its story loudly and clearly, so that society will know that there are alternate ways of dealing with the fears that have led to the request for euthanasia. The call for euthanasia is a call for hospice to accelerate its evolution and expand its influence so that all terminally ill patients may live as fully and comfortably as possible.

CLIENT SELF-DETERMINATION IN END-OF-LIFE DECISIONS A STATEMENT OF THE NATIONAL ASSOCIATION OF SOCIAL WORKERS*

Background

End-of-life decisions are the choices made by a person with a terminal condition regarding his or her continuing care or treatment options. These options may include aggressive treatment of the medical condition, life-sustaining treatment, palliative care, passive euthanasia, voluntary active euthanasia, or physician-assisted suicide. For the purposes of this policy statement, these terms are defined as follows:

Terminal and irreversible condition means a continual profound comatose state with no reasonable chance of recovery or a condition caused by injury, disease, or illness, which, within reasonable medical judgment, would produce death within a short time and for which the application of life-sustaining procedures would serve only to postpone the moment of death. There is no universally accepted definition of "a short time," but in general it is considered to be less than one year (American Hospital Association, 1991).

Client self-determination means the right of the client to determine the appropriate level, if any, of medical intervention and the right for clients to change their wishes about their treatment as their condition changes over time or during the course of their illness. Self-determination assumes that the client is mentally competent.

Incompetent means lacking the ability, based on reasonable medical judgement, to understand and appreciate the nature and consequences of a treatment decision, including the significant benefits and harms of and reasonable alternatives to any proposed treatment decision.

Advance health care directive is a document in which a person either states choices for medical treatment or designates who should make treatment choices if the person should lose decision-making capacity. Although the term "advance directive" generally refers to formal, written documents, it may also include oral statements by the patient (American Hospital Association, 1991).

Life-sustaining treatment is medical intervention administered to a patient that prolongs life and delays death (American Hospital Association, 1991).

Medically inappropriate life-sustaining procedures means life-sustain-

---

*This statement was previously published in *Social Work Speaks: NASW Policy Statements, 3rd Edition*, NASW Press, 1994, pp. 58-61. Reprinted with permission.

ing procedures that are not in accord with the patient's wishes or that are medically futile.

Palliative care is medical intervention intended to alleviate suffering, discomfort, or dysfunction but not to cure (American Hospital Association, 1991).

Passive euthanasia is the withholding or withdrawing of life-sustaining treatment. It is the forgoing of treatment, sometimes called "letting die." The right-to-die rulings such as in the Karen Ann Quinlan case establish the right under certain circumstances to be disconnected from artificial life support.

Voluntary active euthanasia is a physician's administering a lethal dose after a clearly competent patient makes a fully voluntary and persistent request for aid in dying. This is the active termination of a patient's life by a physician at the request of the patient.

Physician-assisted suicide is a patient's ending his or her life with the means requested of and provided by a physician for that purpose. The physician and the patient are both involved. Nurses or significant others may also be involved, but the physician has the responsibility for providing the means. In all cases, the patient will have been determined competent to make such a decision.

Some argue that little distinction exists between euthanasia and physician-assisted suicide other than mechanical or technical difference as to who–the patient or the physician–triggers the event. Others (for example, Quill, 1991) maintain the difference is significant in that in assisted suicide the final act is the patient's; the risk of subtle coercion from doctors, family, or other social forces is reduced; the balance of power between patient and physician is more equal; and there is less risk of error, coercion, or abuse.

There has been a proliferation of state legislation related to assisted suicide, including Washington State's "Death with Dignity" initiative, which was narrowly defeated in a referendum in 1991, and bills that were in progress in 1993 in the California, Iowa, Maine, Michigan, and New Hampshire state legislatures. (The Michigan bill required social work counseling to qualified applicants for assisted suicide.) Currently, 37 states outlaw actively helping a patient to die (Brody, 1992).

The Patients' Self-Determination Act of 1990, included in the Omnibus Budget Reconciliation Act of 1990, requires all hospitals participating in Medicare or Medicaid to ask all adult inpatients if they have advance directives, to document their answers, and to provide information on state laws and hospital policies. Other health agencies such as home health and hospice have instituted similar requirements (American Hospital Association, 1991). In many of these facilities, social workers are called on to work with patients regarding advance health care directives and end-of-life decisions.

Issue Statement

Advances in medical capabilities and technology have made it possible to extend life through artificial means that were heretofore unimaginable. Although this level of care often provides enormous benefits for patients, it may also present difficult and increasingly complex ethical choices for patients, their families, and health care professionals. Inappropriate or unwanted utilization of medical technology may lead to lessened quality of life, loss of dignity, and loss of integrity of patients.

State and federal legislation related to advance health care directives has raised public awareness about the right of patients to participate in medical decision making, including end-of-life decisions. The individuals most immediately facing end-of-life decisions are those with a terminal and irreversible condition, a progressive chronic illness, or chronic intractable pain.

As advocates for the rights of individuals; as providers of mental health services; and as workers in hospitals, hospices, nursing homes, and crisis centers, social workers regularly deal with quality-of-life issues and choices related to life and death. Social workers have requested guidelines that are compatible with professional and personal ethics, legal parameters, and respect for client self-determination. Furthermore, other professionals look to social work for guidelines on these complex issues:

> Social work values, our traditional role as advocates and enablers, and our self-awareness and conscious use of self should serve as justification for engaging people in open and honest debate, recognizing the biases that society and the health care system have had with respect to the backgrounds, lifestyles, and illness of different groups of patients. . . . The social work community has the opportunity and the obligation to educate, organize, and advocate for a more widespread and extensive debate of these life and death matters. (Mizrahi, 1992)

In acknowledging and affirming social work's commitment to respecting diverse value systems in a pluralistic society, end-of-life issues are recognized as controversial because they reflect the varied value systems of different groups. Consequently, the National Association of Social Workers (NASW) does not take a position concerning the morality of end-of-life decisions, but affirms the right of the individual to determine the level of his or her care.

It is also recognized that de facto rationing of health care based on socioeconomic status, color, ability to pay, provider biases, and government policy differentially affects people's right to choose among viable service alternatives and their ability to give truly informed consent. The social worker should work to minimize the effect of these factors in determining the care options available to individuals.

In examining the social work role in working with clients around end-of-life decisions, the following issues must be addressed:

- the legal parameters that affect social work practice (for example, limits of confidentiality, state laws prohibiting assisted suicide, the potential for civil liability)
- the potential conflict of social work values with those of other health care professionals
- the emerging pressures for cost control and rationing of health care (for example, temptation of health care institutions and insurers to encourage use of end-of-life practices to control costs)
- the possibility of patients feeling obliged to choose death rather than becoming a burden (Brock, 1992)
- the societal limits on individual self-determination and autonomy
- the necessity to define safeguards to protect individuals and society in the implementation of end-of-life practices

Policy Statement

NASW's position concerning end-of-life decisions is based on the principle of client self-determination. Choice should be intrinsic to all aspects of life and death.

The social work profession strives to enhance the quality of life; to encourage the exploration of life options; and to advocate for access to options, including providing all information to make appropriate choices.

Social workers have an important role in helping individuals identify the end-of-life options available to them. This role must be performed with full knowledge of and compliance with the law and in accordance with the *NASW Code of Ethics* (NASW, 1993). Social workers should be well informed about living wills, durable power of attorney for health care, and legislation related to advance health care directives.

A key value for social workers is client self determination. Competent individuals should have the opportunity to make their own choices but only after being informed of all options and consequences. Choices should be made without coercion. Therefore, the appropriate role for social workers is to help patients express their thoughts and feelings, to facilitate exploration of alternatives, to provide information to make an informed choice, and to deal with grief and loss issues.

Social workers should not promote any particular means to end one's life but should be open to full discussion of the issues and care options. As a client is considering his or her choices, the social worker should explore and help ameliorate any factors such as pain, depression, need for medical treatment, and so forth. Further, the social worker should thoroughly review all available options including, but not limited to, pain management, counseling, hospice care, nursing home placement, and advance health care directives.

Social workers should act as liaisons with other health care professionals and help the patient and family communicate concerns and attitudes to the health care team to bring about the most responsible assistance possible.

Because end-of-life decisions have familial and social consequences, social workers should encourage the involvement of significant others, family, and friends in these decisions. Social workers should provide ongoing support and be liaisons to families and support persons (for example, caregivers, significant others) with care to maintain the patient's confidentiality. When death occurs, social workers have an obligation to provide emotional and tangible assistance to the significant others, family, and friends in the bereavement process.

Social workers should be free to participate or not participate in assisted-suicide matters or other end-of life choices, he or she has a professional obligation to refer patients and their families to competent professionals who are available to address end-of-life issues.

It is inappropriate for social workers to deliver, supply, or personally participate in the commission of an act of assisted suicide when acting in their professional role. Doing so may subject the social worker to criminal charges. If legally permissible, it is not inappropriate for a social worker to be present during an assisted suicide if the client requests the social worker's presence. The involvement of social workers in assisted suicide cases should not depend on race or ethnicity, religion, age, gender, economic factors, sexual orientation, or disability.

NASW chapters should facilitate their membership's participation in local, state, and national committees, activities, and task forces concerning client self-determination and end-of-life decisions. Education and research on these complex topics should be included in the social work role.

REFERENCES

American Hospital Association. (1991). *Put it in writing*. Chicago: Author.

Brock, D. W. (1992). Voluntary active euthanasia. *Hastings Center Report*, 22(2), 10-22.

Brody, J.E. (1992). Doctor-assisted suicide: Ever acceptable? *New York Times*.

Mizrahi, T. (1992). The direction of patients' rights in the 1990s: Proceed with caution. *Health & Social Work, 17*, 246-262.

National Association of Social Workers. (1993). *NASW code of ethics*. Washington, DC: Author.

Patients' Self-Determination Act of 1990, P.L. 101-508, 104 Stat. 1388 et seq.

Quill, T. (1991). Death and dignity: A case of individualized decision making. *New England Journal of Medicine, 324*, 691-694.

THE ONCOLOGY NURSING SOCIETY'S ENDORSEMENT OF THE AMERICAN NURSES ASSOCIATION POSITION STATEMENTS ON ACTIVE EUTHANASIA AND ASSISTED SUICIDE

The Oncology Nursing Society is a national organization of more than 25,000 cancer nurses dedicated to excellence in patient care, including end of life care. Despite advances in treatment, cancer is often a fatal illness, resulting in over 500,000 deaths annually in the United States. In accordance with our commitment to compassionate end of life care, we support the recent position statements by the American Nurses Association (ANA) on active euthanasia and assisted suicide.

The ANA believes that nurses should not participate in assisted suicide or active euthanasia and that such acts are in direct violation of the ANA *Code for Nurses with Interpretive Statements* and the ethical traditions of the profession. The ANA statements assert that, "Nurses individually and collectively have an obligation to provide comprehensive and compassionate end of life care which includes the promotion of comfort and the relief of pain, and at times, foregoing life-sustaining treatments."

In endorsing these positions statements, the Ethics Advisory Council acknowledges several important issues.

1. Issues of assisted suicide and active euthanasia are of particular significance to oncology nurses as cancer is often a life threatening illness. The current societal focus on issues of assisted suicide and euthanasia are a reflection of the failings of the health care system to respond to the needs of the dying by providing adequate end of life care.
2. The experience of cancer often involves loss of control, intense physical symptoms including pain, depression, hopelessness and fear of worsened suffering in the future.

3. Cancer is a family illness and decisions involving end of life care have consequences for family members as well as for patients.
4. Individual nurses may confront particular patient circumstances in which they believe that the most compassionate act is ending life to end suffering. While recognizing the inherent struggles that nurses face in cancer care, it is important to uphold the ethical mandates of the profession.
5. Terminal illness and requests for assisted suicide or euthanasia frequently involve existential suffering in addition to physical pain. Compassionate end of life care should include attention to these aspects of suffering as well as to the promotion of physical comfort.
6. Dedication to the well being of cancer patients continues through the continuum of cancer diagnosis until death. Aggressive attention to symptom control and spiritual distress are essential interventions in terminal care. Refusal to participate in assisted suicide or euthanasia does not constitute abandonment of patients.
7. Oncology nurses should continue to advocate for health care environments that provide humane and dignified care.

Oncology nurses are at the forefront of promoting quality of life as an essential component of cancer care. We support continued dialogue on the issues of assisted suicide and euthanasia. The Oncology Nursing Society recognizes the critical need for reform of end of life care. This position statement is an affirmation of the commitment of the Oncology Nursing Society to compassionate and competent care and as an expression of valuing life and the caring emphasis of cancer nursing.

June, 1995

PHYSICIAN-ASSISTED SUICIDE: TOWARD A COMPREHENSIVE UNDERSTANDING

Report of the Task Force on Physician-Assisted Suicide of the Society for Health and Human Values*

Before the issue of physician-assisted suicide seized the attention of the U.S. public in 1990, it had received less scholarly attention than many

---

*This slightly abridged version of the report of the SHHV Task Force on Physician-Assisted Suicide appeared in *Academic Medicine*, Vol. 70, no. 7 (July 1995), and is reprinted by permission of *Academic Medicine*. Copies of the full report (including a literary bibliography, tables, and an expanded list of questions for patients) may be obtained from the Society for Health and Human Values, 6728 Old McLean Village Drive, McLean, VA 22101.

other issues in medical ethics. Since then, academics have been trying to catch up with the popular media and with makers of public policy.

Origin and Preparation of the Report

In 1992, the Society for Health and Human Values (SHHV) (see note) established a task force on physician assisted suicide to develop a statement that would reflect the concerns and attitudes of its members. The SHHV's governing council selected active members for this task force, based on their previously published work on the topic and/or their contributions to the group's interdisciplinary mix and diversity of viewpoints. The task force soon discovered that no statement of a single position could adequately reflect the variety of views within the SHHV on this divisive topic. Moreover, the SHHV is an organization more committed to fostering the process of careful inquiry than to finding specific final answers. Hence, the statement of the task force that follows takes the form of a list of questions, designed to assure that discussions of physician-assisted suicide are thorough and searching, regardless of which side of the issue one eventually feels committed to defend. Before listing the questions, the task force found it necessary to examine some underlying assumptions, and also to reflect upon the perspectives of some of the scholarly disciplines within its membership.

Key Assumptions

First, as already suggested, the task force concluded that a set of final position statements, or even a majority report and a minority report, would ill suit the function of the SHHV as an organization committed to the thoughtful and careful inquiry into human-values issues in health care. It concluded that its product ought to be a guide and a prod to further careful inquiry, rather than an effort at closure.

Second, the task force found among its numbers informed, thoughtful, and decent people who disagreed as to whether physician-assisted suicide should be banned or should be permitted in unusual but compelling circumstances. Its deliberations seemed to show that the disagreement did not persist because one group was poorly advised about important facts, or because one group had simply not heard some of the arguments raised by its opponents. Instead, the disagreement ran deep and reflected importantly different views about what it means to be a health professional and what it means to live in a caring, compassionate society. These differences in turn reflect even deeper differences about the meaning and source of human life. Thus, premature efforts to arrive at consensus could well have misrepresented the nature of the debate.

Third, while most of the scholarly literature has addressed physician-assisted suicide as an ethical debate (drawing upon either secular-philosophical or religious-ethical frameworks), the SHHV is devoted to an interdisciplinary approach to values issues in health care. The range of humanities disciplines that ought to be incorporated into a comprehensive understanding of physician-assisted suicide is sketched under the next subsection.

Fourth, the members of the SHHV believe that the highest quality health care is an outgrowth of a partnership between the patient (and often the family) and the health professional or a professional team. Accordingly, a list of questions aimed solely at the health professional–in this case the physician, who by definition is most directly involved–would fall short of the model of dialogue and negotiation that the SHHV feels bound to promote. Our list of questions therefore includes a set of questions for patients to ask of themselves. We suggest that a careful review of the entire list of questions will promote a deeper understanding of physician-assisted suicide as a social and ethical issue, and that a dialogue between a physician and a patient about assisted suicide, after each party has reflected upon his or her own list of specific questions, will be the most therapeutically productive dialogue.

Approaches from Various Disciplines

The ethical, religious, and legal aspects of the debate are fairly obvious and are represented in the list of questions that begins the report. The contributions to the debate from history and from literature may be less easily discerned at first glance, and are less easily formulated as questions parallel in form to the others.

Historically, there is a rich body of material on changing conceptions of suicide in various cultures and historical periods, in some cases focusing upon the individual who chooses to commit suicide, and in at least some cases reflecting directly upon acts of assistance.[4] Relatively little of this material responds directly to the question of whether physicians ought to assist patients in committing suicide. To some opponents of physician-assisted suicide, appeal to the Hippocratic Oath suffices to end the debate. Others argue that the oath needs to be understood in its historical context, considering both who wrote it and why, and what medical practice consisted of in their culture.[5] Similarly, imaginative literature has proven to be a potent source of insight upon the entire range of ethical and values questions in health care, but there is only a very small body of literary work that speaks directly to physician-assisted suicide. We have prepared an annotated literary bibliography that is not included in the modified version of our report printed here but is available from the SHHV at the address given at the bottom of this article's title page.

PART 1: TOPICS AND QUESTIONS

A thorough discussion of physician-assisted suicide consists of efforts to answer certain questions and an analysis of why thoughtful individuals prefer different answers. Those questions, in turn, can be grouped under more general topic headings. We propose five: the moral status of suicide; the clinical and epidemiological aspects of suicide; the relevance of voluntary request; the nature of professional duty; and social implications.

1. The Moral Status of Suicide

Some argue that the moral question of suicide itself has been resolved within our society in favor of voluntary free choice; the only moral problems that remain have to do with seeking another's assistance. The law seems to reflect this view, as few if any state laws that regard suicide by itself as a crime now exist in the United States,[3,6] while assisting a suicide is illegal in 31 states (as of late 1993). But this view ignores a number of moral concerns, especially those arising from some religious traditions. According to those traditions, suicide raises profound questions that go to the core of the relationship between human beings and the transcendent realm: did the forces that granted us life also grant to us sole dominion over that life? Or do we better view ourselves as stewards caring for a valuable gift that was granted to us for our temporary use? Further, if we accept the role of stewards, do we have an absolute duty to protect the gift of life and to refrain from any premature act of closure? Or does the benevolent power whose steward we are recognize special circumstances in cases of terminal suffering, inability to function, and loss of dignity, such that an act of suicide would not violate the usual understanding of the responsibilities of stewardship?

An approach that to some extent bridges secular and religious concerns is to see a human life as a biographical narrative and to anticipate one's death as drafting the last chapter. What do we make of a biography in which the last chapter consists of a suicide? Is that narrative a coherent statement of the values that were embodied in, and served to guide, that individual's previous life? Or is that narrative radically incoherent, with the last chapter serving only as a renunciation of the positive value of what has gone before? Is it even sensible to think of ourselves as writing the final chapter in our autobiography; or is real "authorship" appropriately vested in a power outside of ourselves? If the "best" narrative of a life is one in which an individual discovers his or her own personal meaning in life events and patterns, what are we to make of individuals so beset with suffering and loss of function that they declare further life extension to be personally *meaningless?* Do we sympathize with them for the extremes to which disease and disability have brought them? Or do we exhort them to more strenuous efforts to find meaning in their present plight, citing instances of others who have successfully withstood terrible suffering, yet have affirmed life throughout?

One's answer to these questions to some extent guides one's reaction to a request for suicide assistance. If one views suicide itself as morally unproblematic, and morally defensible in a particular case, then assisting in that case would probably be viewed as morally praiseworthy. On the other hand, if one views suicide as a great moral wrong even under extenuating circumstances, then one will similarly denounce the act of assisting it, or even the act of telling the suffering individual where assistance might be available.

Of course, many would view suicide as more or less acceptable depending upon a variety of moral considerations peculiar to the case at hand, such as the likely length of life remaining, the perceived degree of suffering, and how thoughtful and enduring the patient's choice appears. These considerations may be relevant to the morality of other medical actions as well. How much weight these considerations deserve in decisions about whether to assist a suicide, as opposed to (for example) decisions to withdraw life-prolonging therapy or to administer high doses of narcotics or sedatives, may be informative.[7,8]

2. Clinical and Epidemiological Aspects of Suicide

An interesting feature of the current debate over physician-assisted suicide is the extent to which empirical assumptions are intermingled with value choices. These empirical assumptions often remain uninvestigated, partly because they may simply be confused with the value choices, and partly because no data are available to defend or challenge them. The data may be lacking, in turn, because no U.S. state has yet legalized physician-assisted suicide [except Oregon where voters approved legalization of assisted suicide by a 51 to 49% referendum vote; that measure was challenged in court and has not been implemented as this article goes to press] so the practical consequences of a permissive social policy are not known, and because the illegal, underground status of the assisted suicides and active euthanasia that presumably occur on a regular basis in the United States today render the gathering of reliable data difficult if not impossible. There are, of course, European precedents, in the open practices of active euthanasia in The Netherlands and assisted suicide in Germany; but the significance of these precedents for the United States is itself the subject of much heated debate.[9-11]

A great deal is known about suicide more generally; a major question is the extent to which that knowledge informs the debate over physician-assisted suicide. Opponents of physician-assisted suicide often extrapolate from the literature on suicide in cases of mental illness to the cases under discussion for possible physician assistance. They ask: since almost all suicides and attempted suicides can be traced to some sort of mental illness, isn't anyone requesting physician assistance for suicide probably irrational and mentally ill, and doesn't a failure to detect the psychopathology merely show that a thorough enough psychiatric examination was not performed?[12] Don't the data on the frequency of depression among those with serious medical illnesses support this assumption?[13,14] Since hospice and palliative care can relieve suffering in the vast majority of cases of terminal illness, isn't that further evidence that a request for suicide assistance cannot be rationally grounded?[13-17] Because many suicide attempts are disguised "cries for help," shouldn't a request to a physician for suicide assistance be viewed similarly? Since the surviving families of typical suicides *suffer* from prolonged grief, anger, and a variety of serious psychiatric consequences, isn't a patient who requests assistance with suicide being, at the very least, incredibly selfish in not considering the possibly devastating consequences for loved ones!

In reply, supporters of physician-assisted suicide ask whether the entire suicidology literature is not biased by the assumption that *all* cases of suicide reflect psychopathology, and simply fails to consider that in a small fraction of the cases, sufficient reasons for suicide may be present along with sufficient clarity of mind to weigh the options rationally. They ask whether applying the suicide-prevention model simply prejudges the case without considering the actual, individual facts. They also ask whether a suicide under a physician's care, chosen with calm reasonableness, would not in most cases be fully accepted by the family, who would in no way view this suicide as an angry rejection of their love and help. They emphasize the fact that no palliative techniques are effective 100% of the time; and moreover, while those techniques tend to address physical suffering, the suffering that leads one to request suicide assistance might be primarily emotional and spiritual. (Besides, hospice programs are set up to treat the terminally ill, and the worst cases of suffering might occur in not-yet-terminal conditions such as slowly degenerative neurological diseases.) Finally, the supporters might point to recent studies that have challenged the view that depression in the face of a major medical illness is a strong predictor of requests to discontinue life-prolonging medical therapy.[18] Might not requests for physician-assisted suicide be similarly free of psychopathology?

Despite these very different assumptions about empirical data, both opponents and supporters (except for the more strict libertarians) seem to agree that a desirable policy for screening any request for suicide assistance would involve a careful search for possible, treatable psychopathology before proceeding any further.[19,20] But even this point of agreement leads to some further thorny questions for supporters: how extensive a psychiatric evaluation, or a therapeutic trial of psychiatric intervention, is sufficient? How would one react to a patient who states that submitting to this very detailed psychiatric assessment is itself an insufferable indignity, given the very personal nature of suffering and of one's quality of life? Would the discovery of untreatable psychopathology, which by itself is causing the patient great suffering, justify assisting a suicide for that very reason?

The very few case studies of requests for physician-assisted suicide that have so far appeared in the medical literature suggest another set of questions.[21-23] How many apparently rational requests for suicide assistance in the face of irreversible illness are triggered by intolerable present suffering, and how many by a fear of intolerable suffering in the future? How often does a physician's agreement to assist a suicide later in the course of illness provide a patient with the assurance necessary to better enjoy the quality of his present existence for a longer period–in some cases never having to "cash in" on the promise of suicide assistance at all, as the later suffering turns out to be bearable? That is, can a promise to assist a suicide later on be, paradoxically, a form of suicide prevention, as well as a clinical assessment for the underlying causes of suffering that might be alleviated by other means?[24] Or would such discussions, under some circumstances, risk inducing suicide?

3. The Relevance of Voluntary Choice

The assisted-suicide debate highlights a larger question within medical ethics that has been much debated in recent years–the scope and limits of the principle of respect for patient autonomy. According to some, once one has established that the patient's request for suicide assistance is truly voluntary (and one has developed a clinical strategy to do so reliably), one has come to the end of the ethical discussion, and the choice must be respected. Others would argue that voluntariness of choice cannot overcome other negative features of assisting a suicide. In general, those arguing this way would cite as the opposing values either the wrongness of suicide itself (discussed in topic 1 in this report), the wrongness of physician involvement (topic 4), or negative social consequences for vulnerable populations (topic 5).

One possible restriction upon voluntary choice involves the appropriate role of the patient's family. Some proposals for safeguards in public policy envision mandatory notification of close family members, and good clinical care would seem to require facilitating family involvement in the decisions and the process to the extent that both patient and family are comfortable with this. But that raises the question of whether family members should have effective veto power over an individual's choice for assisted suicide.

One aspect of the "slippery slope" argument pertains directly to this topic. Some defenders of physician-assisted suicide advocate a policy in which now-autonomous patients might request and receive assistance, but in which physicians would never administer active euthanasia. Other defenders support both assisted suicide and active euthanasia for autonomous patients but refuse to consider administering euthanasia to patients who cannot currently issue an autonomous request. But critics question whether either of those supposed safeguards could be maintained in practice once a policy were established.[25,26]

Have not the U.S. courts refused to restrict the right to refuse life-prolonging medical treatment to the class of non-competent patients? And why would they not feel obligated similarly to extend the "right" of assisted death to non-competent patients (either by family consent or by advance directive) as soon as such a right were recognized in law? For example, if Patients A and B are both suffering terribly and both autonomously elect to die, but A is physically capable of ending his own life while B cannot physically end her own without the means that a physician could provide, should B's mere physical incapacity preclude her from physician assistance in dying while A's choice is respected? If Patients C and D are both suffering terribly and both have previously indicated their desires to die with physician assistance, but C is presently competent to choose while D has slipped beyond the stage of mental capacity to choose, then should D be denied assistance in death and made to suffer further simply because he has lost capacity? (Recent data from the Netherlands suggest that in cases like D's, some practitioners feel morally obligated to administer euthanasia even in the face of official guidelines that prohibit such an act.)[10,27]

4. The Nature of Professional Duty

Everything said up to this point can apply to assisted suicide regardless of who is doing the assisting. But important ethical issues arise from the specific designation for *physicians* as the appointed agents of assistance. Questions arise as to which of the strands that make up the entirety of a physician's professional duty to the patient should be seen to dominate in these cases. Should it be the duty to heal and to try to prolong life and to maintain a sense of awe for the proper functioning of the human being as a biological organism?[26,29] Or should it be the duty to serve the well-thought-out life plan of the patient through the judicious administration of technical skill; the duty not to abandon the patient during the course of terminal illness; and the duty to relieve suffering by available medical means?[30] (Another way to put this question is to note that the physician's basic duty is to "do no harm." Are there then circumstances in which causing the patient's death ceases to be a harm to the patient? What degree or type of suffering is necessary for this to be the case, and who should judge whether or not that suffering is present? Given these ambiguities, how is the physician to understand what *compassion* requires?)

Moreover, where does the physician turn for guidance in assigning relative weights to these various strands of professional duty? Does one read this in the Hippocratic Oath, in the historical record of medical practice through the ages, in the debates of today's "experts" in medical ethics, or in the social and cultural forces in contemporary society that shape medical practice whether we wish them to or not? If medicine is *both* a historically cohesive practice with its own tradition and also a service profession that must adapt to changing times and needs, then what balance between stability and change is appropriate?[31] And if thoughtful, committed physicians disagree among themselves on how to construe their professional duty in relation to requests for assistance in suicide, what does the inability to resolve that disagreement within medicine say about the moral nature of the enterprise?

One important set of questions relating to professional duty takes off from the current acceptance of withholding or withdrawing of life-sustaining medical treatment, where such actions may in at least some cases predictably result in an earlier death. We assume for purposes of this argument that such actions are fully consistent with a physician's professional duties. Can we then draw conclusions about whether the physician has a duty to take active measures to end the patient's life? Or are the two issues totally distinct, so that a willingness to withdraw implies nothing whatever about any willingness to assist a death? We may also assume that physicians have a duty to administer very high doses of pain medication in the face of terminal suffering, perhaps even to the point of coma; such a drug-induced coma may be predictably incompatible with survival beyond hours or days. Is it still important to maintain the distinction between intending the patient's death, as opposed to intending relief of pain alone? Or is such a distinction a semantic game with no real moral content?[32,33]

Other questions triggered by these reflections abound. If physicians cannot in good conscience as professionals assist a patient in suicide, but if the moral defense of suicide assistance in the face of serious illness and suffering is otherwise compelling, should a separate body of non-physicians be created for the purpose of offering this assistance? (Would other health professionals, such as nurses or pharmacists, volunteer?) Which will better cement the patient's trust in the physician; the knowledge that the physician will never directly act to end the patient's life? Or the knowledge that the physician will accede to the patient's voluntary request for assistance in certain specified circumstances?[34] What should we make of the clinical experience of the few physicians who have come forward with accounts of suicide assistance–especially the observation that once patients understand that the physician would assist them in the end, they will more openly discuss their true fears and needs, thereby leading in most cases to better alternatives for relief of suffering?[24]

We should note that raising this set of questions may have a salutary influence on medical education, quite apart from the discussion of assisted suicide. Some educators have been struck to observe that the notion of a *professional* duty, which one assumes simply by becoming a member of the medical profession and quite apart from one's personal or religious beliefs, is a novel concept for some medical students. The emphasis on individual autonomy and voluntary consent, for all of its value, seems to have spun off an unwillingness to accept any obligations for which one as an individual has not freely and explicitly contracted. One sees similar difficulties in getting medical students to perceive what is at stake in the debates over the duties of physicians to care for human immunodeficiency virus-positive patients and the duties of physicians to provide nonreimbursed care. These problems are very important for all who see membership in the medical profession as entailing a moral commitment, and who wish to view the profession as something more than an aggregate of private entrepreneurs.

5. Social Implications

Much of the debate over assisted suicide has focused upon the social implications, which may be subdivided into the more obvious and more subtle consequences of adopting a policy of legalized suicide assistance by physicians. Discussion of the subtle as well as the obvious consequences (in the face of almost total lack of empirical data by which to predict the likelihood of either) raises important methodological questions about the proper use of "slippery slope" arguments in medical ethics generally.[35] Does an argument from very subtle attitudinal changes that *could* result from legalizing suicide assistance simply betray the fact that the opponent has no really strong arguments to offer and must grasp at anything? Or are such subtleties precisely the bread and butter of ethical inquiry, and therefore the business of anyone trying to make responsible public policy in the face of great uncertainty?

Those who oppose physician-assisted suicide because of its likely social implications tend to make a number of assumptions about prevailing attitudes in the United States, and argue that these existing attitudes make it even more likely that the feared negative consequences will in fact occur. (Indeed, they may argue that the mere occurrence of a debate over physician-assisted suicide reinforces some undesirable social attitudes.[29]) The attitudes include:

1. Substantial prejudices against the elderly, the chronically ill, and people with disabilities, so that their quality of life is assumed to be poor and that a desire to die instead of persisting in that state is seen as *prima facie* rational;
2. Persistent difficulties in assuring access to care for the poor and members of minorities in the United States, raising the specter that someday assisted death could be seen as a form of medical cost control, or at least raising doubts about whether adequate alternatives to suicide, such as hospice care or intensive psychotherapy, will be available to those most in need;
3. Persistent imbalances within medical practice, with continued emphasis on curative, subspecialized medicine, and continued lack of support for hospice, mental health services, and primary care–thus raising questions about whether patients who might request suicide, especially the poor, will truly have a "personal physician" who can speak for them from a position of knowing intimately all of the better alternatives to suicide;
4. A persistent "death phobia" in our modern culture, with the loss of religious rituals and other ways of seeing meaning in death and dying, so that we have a tendency to seek mechanical or technical answers to what is at bottom a problem of meaning and of spirituality;[36]
5. Continued reliance in modern society upon violence and death as a way to resolve certain social problems (e.g., warfare, capital punishment, refusal to enact meaningful gun control), which might be exacerbated by projecting death as a medically assisted and hence sanitized event; and
6. Predictable fatigue among those who must care for the chronically and terminally ill, both family members and personal physicians, so that the ill person may receive a variety of subtle or not-so-subtle messages that he would be more valued by those around him if he elected a quicker end to his present state. (According to this assumption, having a personal physician who has accompanied one through the entire course of one's illness might actually be as much a liability as a safeguard.)[37]

Supporters of assisted suicide tend not to deny the validity of these assumptions, but instead rely upon various proposals for safeguards to assure that the negative consequences will be avoided–and tend to imply that our very knowledge of this list of attitudes is itself a form of assurance that we won't slide down the slippery slope unaware.[38,39] Opponents then proceed to question the adequacy of the proposed safeguards, sometimes pointing to evidence that at least some Dutch physicians have strayed from the official guidelines for approved active euthanasia in the country.[10,27] Safeguards may be challenged from either side: they may be too permissive and lead to a slippery-slope problem, or they may be too restrictive and may needlessly prolong the suffering of the patient while bureaucratic requirements are satisfied. The basic question is: assuming for the moment that some sort of legalized policy of suicide assistance is desirable, what types of safeguards and procedures would be sufficiently flexible to respond to the individual circumstances of the patient and the illness, and yet sufficiently stiff so as to assure that vulnerable populations are adequately protected? Assuming that no human system can be error-free, how great an error rate is acceptable in such a system of policing? (And how is one to monitor the system over time to assure that problems with the procedures are promptly brought to public scrutiny?)

Opponents of physician-assisted suicide may criticize the proposed safeguards without turning adequate attention to the dangers of leaving the present system in place. While data on the frequency of physician-assisted suicide and active euthanasia in the United States today are notoriously unreliable, a reasonable conclusion is that the rate is not zero, and that these actions may in fact be more common than is usually estimated. Is it prudent public policy to have this practice remain underground, concealed from public and professional scrutiny?[40] Could it even be that abuses of vulnerable patients are now fairly frequent, and that the total incidence of abuses would actually go down if we created an open system? How many patients who could be helped by thorough consultation with a physician, exploring all alternatives, are instead driven to a lonely suicide because they fear the legal implications of discussing their intention openly with either physician or family members?[23] The opponents, however, might reply that there are so many uncertainties involved in a policy of legally-permitted assisted suicide that there would have to be a great deal wrong with the present system to prompt us to plunge forward. Indeed, the very fact that assisted suicide is now carried out as an underground option for patients is viewed by some as an argument against changing the law or public policy in this regard.

A particularly important set of questions under this topic involves the impact on hospice care, which tends to be viewed with approval by both supporters and opponents of assisted suicide. Opponents fear that legalizing physician-assisted suicide would further undermine public support and funding (already marginal at best) for hospice programs, since society may be unwilling to spend money on hospice when suffering can quickly and easily be ended through suicide.[41] Supporters question whether a legal policy would not, instead, be a shot in the arm for hospice programs, since any appropriate set of safeguards would probably require that every candidate for assisted suicide must first receive what amounts to a "hospice work-up," and a substantial number of those patients will end up choosing hospice care as the preferable alternative.

PART II: CONSIDERATIONS FOR PATIENTS

The previous five topic sections have listed the questions that physicians should ask themselves before establishing a policy on assisted suicide. Turning now to the perspective of the patient, we must ask which questions would be advisable for patients to contemplate before they could assure themselves that their request for suicide assistance is as well thought through as humanly possible. Many of these questions parallel those listed earlier, yet they acquire a somewhat different slant when viewed from the patient's perspective. A short list of questions, which might simulate the appropriate dialogue between a patient, family, friends, and physician, includes:

- Why do I think that self-destruction is morally appropriate for me, given my present circumstances, suffering, values, and responsibilities?
- Why do I want to involve a physician? If I cannot kill myself, why should I ask someone else to help me do it?
- What persons may be harmed by my suicide? Are there ways in which I can minimize the harm brought to others by my suicide?
- If I am a religious believer, how can I reasonably conclude that killing myself is an acceptable act of stewardship over the life God has given me, and that it does not default on my obligations to God?
- What considerations should be taken into account to determine whether my request for suicide is a rational request?
- Might this request reflect an effort to exercise personal control over an illness that has seemingly robbed me of all choice? Might it be motivated by unexplored fears of the future consequences of a degenerative or terminal illness?

CONCLUSION

Some will find this document frustrating because the SHHV Task Force takes no substantive stand for or against physician-assisted suicide. Others will find it frustrating that we have taken an implicit stand simply by saying that there are two sides to the issue, instead of insisting that the issue is, by its very nature, not open to discussion. (For some, the admission that there is something reasonable to say in defense of assisting a patient's suicide is evidence that the feared slippery slope within medicine has already occurred.)

Therefore, to conclude this report, the SHHV task force members wish explicitly to review the substantive educational positions that they have adopted. We do, in fact, contend that discussion and debate on this issue are important and desirable, and that a simple "thou shalt not" is no longer an adequate guide for a program in education. We also strongly endorse the expansion of educational efforts to introduce medical students to the skills of palliative and hospice care and all methods of sharing control over medical decisions with the patient and family. In particular, a medical education establishment that would never think of allowing a student to graduate without having spent time in an intensive care unit, but routinely graduates students who have spent no time in a hospice setting, is in our opinion guilty of educational negligence.

Physician-assisted suicide poses profound questions about the degree of control over our deaths that we may optimally seek in modern society; about the relationship between individual moral choice and sound public policy; and about the role and duties of the medical profession. In some ways the debate is shaping itself to become as intractable as the debate over abortion. The policy maker's nightmare, however, is the educator's opportunity—so long as the educator is prepared to address the full range of questions, and not only those questions that suggest a particular position or that limit themselves to the approach of a single discipline.

NOTE

The Society for Health and Human Values (SHHV) is an association of dues-paying members who are health professionals concerned about the values dimensions of their work and scholars who teach human-values courses in health professional schools. Members of the SHHV Task Force that prepared this report were, in alphabetical order, Margaret P. Battin, PhD, James F. Bresnahan, SJ, PhD, JD, Baruch A. Brody, PhD, Howard Brody, MD, PhD (chair), Christine Cassel, MD, Robert Cassidy, PhD, Thomas Cole, PhD, H. Tristram Engelhardt, Jr., PhD, MD,

Edmund L. Erde, PhD, Eugene C. Grochowski, MD, PhD, Albert R. Jonson, PhD, Joanne Lynn, MD, William F. May, MDiv, PhD, Ronald B. Miller, MD, Stephen G. Post, PhD, Ann Folwell Stanford, PhD (literature consultant), S. Kay Toombs, PhD, Robert F. Weir, PhD, and William J. Winslade, PhD, JD.

REFERENCES

1. McCarrick, P.M. Scope Note 18: Active Euthanasia and Assisted Suicide. Kennedy Inst. Ethics J. 2 (1992): 79-100.

2. Campbell, C.S. Religious Ethics and Active Euthanasia in a Pluralistic Society. Kennedy Inst. Ethics J. 2 (1992): 253-277.

3. CeloCruz, M.T. Aid-in-dying: Should we Decriminalize Physician-assisted Suicide and Physician-committed Euthanasia. Am J. Law Med. 18 (1992): 369-394.

4. Brody, B.A., ed. Suicide and Euthanasia: Historical and Contemporary Themes. Boston, Massachusetts: Kluwer Academic Publishers, 1989.

5. Carrick, P. Medical Ethics in Antiquity: Philosophical Perspectives in Abortion and Euthanasia. Boston, Massachusetts: D. Radial, 1985.

6. Engelhardt, H.T., and Malloy, M. Suicide and Assisting Suicide: A Critique of Legal Sanctions. Southwestern Law J. 3, 36 (1982): 1003-1037.

7. Watts, D.T., and Howell, T. Assisted Suicide is not Voluntary Active Euthanasia. J. Am. Geriatr. Soc. 40 (1992):1043-1046.

8. Brody, H. Causing, Intending, and Assisting Death. J. Clin Ethics 4 (1993): 112-117.

9. van der Maas P.J., van Delden J.J.M., Pijnenborg, L., and Looman, C.W.N. Euthanasia and other Medical Decisions Concerning the End of Life. Lancet 338 (1991): 669-674.

10. Pijnenborg L., van der Maas P.J., van Delden, J.J.M., Looman, C.W. N. Life-terminating Acts without Explicit Request of Patient. Lancet 341 (1993): 1196-1199.

11. Battin, M.P. Assisted Suicide: Can We Learn from Germany? Hastings Cen. Rep. 22 (1992): 44-51.

12. Conwell, Y., and Caine, E.D. Rational Suicide and the Right to Die: Reality and Myth. N. Engl. J. Med. 325 (1991): 1100-1103.

13. Koening, H.G. Legalizing Physician-assisted Suicide: Some Thoughts and Concerns. J. Fam. Pract. 37 (1993): 171-179.

14. Brown, J.H., Henteleff, P., Baracat, S., and Rowe, C.J. Is it Normal for Terminally Ill Patients to Desire Death? Am J. Psychiatr. 143 (1986): 208-211.

15. Foley, K.M. The Relationship of Pain and Symptom Management to Patient Requests for Physician-assisted Suicide. J Pain Sympt Manag. 6(1991): 289-297.

16. Byock, I.R. The Euthanasia/Assisted Suicide Debate Matures. Am. J. Hospice Palliative Care 10 (March-April 1993): 8-11.

17. Cundiff, D. Euthanasia is Not the Answer: A Hospice Physician's View. Totowa, New Jersey: Humana, 1992.

18. Lee, M.A., and Ganzini, L. Depression in the Elderly: Effect on Patient Attitudes towards. Life-sustaining Therapy. J. Am Geriatr. Soc. 40 (1992): 983-988.

19. Benrubi, G.I. Euthanasia–The Need for Procedural Safeguards. N. Engl. J. Med. 326 (1992): 197-199.

20. Quill, T.E., Cassel, C.K., and Meier, D.E. Care of the Hopelessly Ill: Proposed Clinical Criteria for Physician-Assisted Suicide. N. Engl. J. Med. 327 (1992): 1380-1384.

21. Quill, T.E. Death and Dignity: A Case of Individualized Decision Making. N. Engl. J. Med. 324 (1991): 691-694.

22. Quill, T.E. The Ambiguity of clinical intentions N. Engl. J. Med. 329 (1993): 1039-1040.

23. Quill, T.E. Death and Dignity: Making Choices and Taking Charge. New York: W.W. Norton, 1993.

24. Quill, T.E. Doctor, I Want to Die. Will You Help Me? JAMA 270 (1993): 870-873.

25. Callahan, D. "Aid-in-Dying": The Social Dimensions. Commonweal, August 9,1991: Suppl: 12-16.

26. Kamisar, Y. Are Laws against Assisted Suicide Unconstitutional? Hastings Cen. Rep. 23 (1993): 32-43.

27. Dying Well? A Colloquy on Euthanasia and Assisted Suicide. Hastings Cen. Rep. 22 (1992): 6-55.

28. Kass, L.R. Neither for Love nor Money: Why Doctors Must Not Kill. Public Interest 94 (Winter 1989): 29-46.

29. Gaylin, W., Kass, L.R., Pellegrino, E.D., and Siegler, M. Doctors Must Not Kill. JAMA 259 (1988): 2139-2140.

30. Miller, F.G. and Fletcher, J.C. The Case for Legalized Euthanasia. Perspect. Biol. Med. 36 (1993): 159-176.

31. Vance, R. Medicine as Dependent Tradition: Historical and Ethical Reflections, Perspect. Biol. Med. 28 (1985): 282-302.

32. Truog, R.D., Berde, C.B., Mitcell, C., and Grier, H.E. Barbiturates in the Care of the Terminally Ill, N. Engl. J. Med. 327 (1992): 1678-1681.

33. Brody, H. Assisted Suicide: A Challenge for Family Physicians. J. Fam. Pract. 37 (1993): 123-125.

34. Cassel, C.K., and Meier, D.E. Morals and Moralism in the Debate over Euthanasia and Assisted Suicide. N. Engl. J. Med. 323 (1990): 750-752.

35. van der Burg, W. The Slippery Slope Argument. Ethics 102 (1991): 42-65.

36. Post, S.G. American Culture and Euthanasia; The Changing Definition of "Good Death." Health Progress 72 (December 1991): 32-38.

37. Miles, S.E. Physicians and Their Patients' Suicides. JAMA 271 (1994): 1786-1788.

38. Battin, M.P. Voluntary Euthanasia and the Risks of Abuse: Can We Learn Anything from the Netherlands? Law. Med. Health Care 20 (1992): 133-143.

39. Weir, R.F. The Morality of Physician-assisted Suicide. Law Med. Health Care 20 (1992): 116-126.

40. Winstade, W.J. Guarding the Exit Door: A Plea for Limited Toleration of Euthanasia. Houston Law Rev. 25 (1988): 517-524.

41. Teno, J., and Lynn, J. Voluntary Active Euthanasia: The Individual Case and Public Policy. J. Am. Geriatr. Soc. 39 (1991): 827-830.

Assisted Suicide and Euthanasia:
Cases and Commentaries

compiled and edited by

Sharon M. Valente
Judith M. Saunders

with case commentaries by

Charles Corr
Karen M. Corr
Peter J. Katsufrakis
Richard MacDonald
Fred S. Marcus

Barbara Jeanne McGuire
Jerome A. Motto
John Samuel Rozel
Judith M. Saunders

Bryan Tanney
Sharon M. Valente
James L. Werth, Jr.
Bruce D. White

INTRODUCTION

Enmeshed in their personal suffering and vulnerability, patients sometimes reach out to professional care givers to request help to end their own

---

Sharon M. Valente, RN, PhD, FAAN, is Assistant Professor, Department of Nursing, Center for Health Professions, University of Southern California, Los Angeles and Consultant, Department of Veterans Affairs, West Los Angeles. Judith M. Saunders, RN, DNSc, FAAN, is Assistant Research Scientist, City of Hope National Medical Center, Department of Nursing Education and Research, Duarte, CA and Assistant Professor, Department of Nursing, University of Southern California, Los Angeles.

Address correspondence to: Dr. Sharon M. Valente at 346 North Bowling Green Way, Los Angeles, CA 90033.

[Haworth co-indexing entry note]: "Assisted Suicide and Euthanasia: Cases and Commentaries." Valente, Sharon M., and Judith M. Saunders. Co-published simultaneously in *Journal of Pharmaceutical Care in Pain & Symptom Control* (Pharmaceutical Products Press, an imprint of The Haworth Press, Inc.) Vol. 4, No. 1/2, 1996, pp. 291-344; and: *Drug Use in Assisted Suicide and Euthanasia* (ed: Margaret P. Battin, and Arthur G. Lipman) Pharmaceutical Products Press, an imprint of The Haworth Press, Inc., 1996, pp. 291-344. Single or multiple copies of this article are available from The Haworth Document Delivery Service [1-800-342-9678, 9:00 a.m. - 5:00 p.m. (EST)].

© 1996 by The Haworth Press, Inc. All rights reserved.
291

lives, or the lives of their loved ones. Professional care givers often anguish over their responses to these requests for their participation in euthanasia and assisted suicide. In many fields of practice, this is a request that is rarely encountered, and clinicians have developed few guidelines to guide their practice. Values guiding clinical practice have been rooted in a tradition of preserving life, leaving clinicians with requests that touch the core of professional and personal intimate values. Rilke[1] pointed out that "we are unutterably alone, essentially, especially in the things most intimate and most important to us." Decisions about accepting and ending life matter, and we offer these seven cases and their twenty-two commentaries to illustrate not only different perspectives, but how different people deduced their positions.

We wanted to accomplish several goals in the discussion of these seven cases. First, we wanted to examine assisted suicide and euthanasia in the context of terminal illness and unrelieved symptoms and distress, a context involving the usual circumstances of discussion. While most of the cases involve people with terminal illness, it is not always clear if the individual is in the terminal phase of that illness. Second, we wanted to extend the discussion to circumstances outside of terminal illness, such as chronic depression and substance abuse. Third, we hoped that commentaries from individuals from many disciplines (pharmacists, nurses, psychologists, physicians, ethicists, etc.) might help dispel the distorted notion embedded in the common phrase, physician-assisted suicide, that only physicians deal with this situation. We also thought it might be helpful for readers to compare their own thinking with those in different fields of practice. Fourth, we hoped that the cases, along with their commentaries, might be useful as teaching cases for clinical and academic settings. Finally, we want to reinforce the viewpoint that "reasonable people disagree" and hope that the discussions and dialogue may increase respect and understanding of perspectives that differ from our own.

The commentaries are distributed unevenly across the seven cases. We invited people to respond to any or all of the adult cases as they chose. We sent the seventh case of an adolescent separately. All commentators have expertise in their clinical fields; most have expertise also in ethics or in suicide or euthanasia. As important as is their expertise, Tanney (personal correspondence) reminded us that more important is the perspective that each commentator brings to the case. Tanney states that . . . "Perspective is all important. I am a clinically active psychiatrist working in a psychiatric emergency environment. Decisions there are made quickly and pragmatically. After safety, compliance/adherence to a plan for using helping resources is our most important goal."

The cases provide a concrete context for discussing the clinical and ethical issues involved, rather than considering these issues outside of specific contexts, and in a more abstract manner. The cases also replicate the situation often found in clinical practice where professionals must make decisions with inadequate facts, and we encouraged each commentator to discuss the information needed and how it would be used. Each case is summarized as it was sent to each commentator, along with any specific perspective we asked the commentators to address. Following each case are all the commentaries related to that case. You are invited to identify areas of agreement and disagreement among the commentaries.

CASES AND COMMENTARIES

CASE #1. DAVE R.

Mr. Dave R. is a 40-year-old architect admitted to an open psychiatric unit. He reports depression, paranoia, violent impulses, guilt, low self esteem, insomnia, anxiety, unemployment, and hopelessness and more than 15 treatments for depression, alcohol and drug addiction. He has many years of sobriety. At present, he takes 16 mg of Xanax daily. He fears growing old alone and losing his good looks. He wants, but has little hope for, detoxification from his addiction to Xanax. He was admitted yesterday to the open psychiatric unit for detoxification and placed on an antidepressant (fluoxetine 20 mg qd), Librium (25 mg qid and 50 mg prn) to assist in detoxification and ibuprofen 400 mg for headache. He complains of increasing nausea, jitteriness, fatigue and headaches. He says, "I can't manage if these symptoms continue." He says he has wanted to die since age 14 and "this is my last try; if this treatment does not work, I'm going to kill myself."

You–a pharmacist–are asked to provide consultation regarding management of this case. Mr. R. asks you to keep this conversation confidential. He plans to leave the hospital without permission and to overdose on medications–he can't live with symptoms and without his Xanax. He asks how much medication he should take to kill himself? He says he cannot live with these chronic symptoms which interfere with his quality of life any more and he requests assistance in committing suicide.

COMMENTARY #1, CASE #1

Professionals in health care should bring to their work three principal competencies: (1) a caring presence and effective communication skills;

(2) technical proficiency in their knowledge of disease and their understanding of potential therapeutic interventions; and (3) an intelligent appreciation of their professional and ethical values. Caring involves empathy and the ability to enter into the world of the other so as to be able to grasp the problems and concerns which relate to that person's health. This needs to be supported by good interpersonal communication if professionals and ill persons are to work together successfully. Technical proficiency in this case relates to an understanding of the intersecting disorders experienced by Mr. R., the pharmacological resources which are currently available, and the implementation of those resources. Professional and ethical values are the foundation upon which professional conduct does and should rest, as well as the determinants of principles which guide action.

In this case, the pharmacist is challenged to enter into the world of, communicate effectively with, and take part in caring for a 40-year-old architect admitted to an open psychiatric unit who reports a history of depression and psychosocial disorders, along with extensive interventions for depression and addiction to alcohol and drugs. Mr. R. has multiple fears and concerns, along with apparent side effects from his treatment. His communications with the pharmacist request confidentiality, specifically include the possibility of suicide, and seek assistance in carrying out a suicidal plan.

In all of this, it will be apparent to the pharmacist that Mr. R. has great potential for a successful detoxification and treatment of his psychiatric disorders with appropriate drug therapy choices. For this reason, within a context of empathy for his concerns a pharmacist should direct discussion with Mr. R., not toward suicide, but toward a more positive outcome. Such discussions should not abruptly or brutally dismiss Mr. R.'s thoughts about dying and what he has said about suicide. Those thoughts and communications are a very important part of his diagnosis and final treatment.

Nevertheless, there is much to be discussed with Mr. R. about his problems and about the therapeutic modalities that are available to assist him. We recommend that effective communication should direct Mr. R.'s attention to these matters and that they should be presented to him as important subjects on which to begin to work together.

For example, the pharmacist will know that alprazolam (Xanax) is a particularly difficult drug to discontinue. Rebound anxiety can occur, as well as the other generalized signs and symptoms of withdrawal. This needs to be brought to Mr. R.'s attention as a framework for the positive program to follow. Furthermore, the pharmacist will be aware that a dose of 16mg/day of alprazolam is well above any recommended or documented doses for any of this drug's indications. Thus, a clinician must wonder if this medication has been misprescribed or (more likely) the patient has altered his drug regimen on his own–"increasing his medication to the desired effect," so to speak. Exploring such matters with Mr. R. will demonstrate to him the technical competencies of the pharmacist, may encourage him to be candid and forthcoming about the contributions that he may have made to his present difficulties, and may help to win his confidence and cooperation in a revised intervention plan. Clearly, the treatment plan for this patient could be modified to support Mr. R. through the physical detoxification and the psychological addiction. Death from an overdose of alprazolam alone is not likely. When implicated in suicides, it is in combination with alcohol and/or other drugs.

Because alprazolam, like many other benzodiazepines, is a difficult drug to discontinue and because its side effects are already quite disturbing to Mr. R., drug therapy to prevent the signs and symptoms of withdrawal should be aggressive. Doses of chlordiazepoxide (Librium) could be increased to 50mg four times a day for at least five days and then tapered slowly or combined with a slow discontinuation of the alprazolam as opposed to abrupt withdrawal.

In counseling the patient, the pharmacist can reassure Mr. R. that these physical manifestations do not last forever. With alprazolam, withdrawal usually peaks 2-3 days after discontinuation. The fluoxetine may be an adequate choice as an antidepressant. If panic disorder is a diagnosis, imipramine (Tofranil) is a more appropriate choice, combining antianxiety and antidepressant properties, and obviating the need for multiple medications. If the diagnosis is anxiety, then the patient can be treated with a drug such as buspirone (Buspar), which lacks psychological and physical addictive properties.

In communications with Mr. R. of the sort that have been described thus far, pharmacists who can draw upon professional and technical resources can present themselves as skillful and reliable allies in a difficult struggle. Without diminishing the problems and concerns that Mr. R. faces, pharmacists can ask him to invest briefly in a little patience and confidence. Every good result which follows from that investment can be identified and offered as the basis for further cooperative endeavors.

In addition, this patient has apparently had success in the past in overcoming his addiction to alcohol. This can definitely be used as an additional example of potential success to be achieved in overcoming his addiction to alprazolam. The pharmacist might hope that Mr. R. is an active participant in Alcoholics Anonymous and should inquire into this matter with him. If not, such involvement might be initiated. Similarly, directing Mr. R. to attend Narcotics Anonymous meetings may also prove to be beneficial. The pharmacist counseling Mr. R. can emphasize a number of issues that may dissuade him from his current thoughts of suicide:

1. The withdrawal symptoms that he is currently experiencing are likely to pass in a few days. An increase in the scheduled dose of chlordiazepoxide or a slow tapering of the alprazolam may facilitate this process.
2. The drug prescribed for Mr. R.'s depression may take a while to reach its full effect. Patience should be stressed.
3. Attendance at AA and NA support group meetings is essential to recovery from the disease of addiction.
4. Psychotherapy may prove beneficial in helping Mr. R. to focus on issues of low self-esteem, guilt, and hopelessness.

With respect to this last point, confidentiality is an important value in interactions between patients and health care professionals, but it is not an overriding value in all cases. The pharmacist will want to evaluate potential costs to the therapeutic relationship if confidentiality is breached in whole or in part in light of potential benefits to be achieved in assisting this patient to reevaluate his suicidal thoughts and to set aside his suicidal plan.

We do not regard it as professionally or ethically appropriate for a pharmacist or other health care professional to enter into a private and covert plan with this patient which would enable him to leave the hospital and overdose on medications. On the contrary, there is much to achieve for and with this patient in order to improve his present and future quality in living.

Karen M. Corr, PharmD
Clinical Pharmacy Coordinator
F.D.R. Veterans Hospital
Montrose, NY

Charles Corr, PhD
Professor, Department of Philosophical Studies
Southern Illinois University at Edwardsville
Edwardsville, IL

COMMENTARY #2, CASE #1

Clinical Issues

Contentious issues are often tentatively explored with a consultant before they become critical issues of treatment. Clarifying with Mr. R. that they are both part of the treatment team diminishes the possibilities for splitting and for "deadly secrets." More specifically, the consultant can indicate that there are no ethical or medicolegal grounds for confidentiality when suicide is the issue. Helping must address two issues: suicide risk and mental disorders. Do not assume that treatment of mental disorder issues will diminish suicide risks.

Suicide

Demographically (male, 40, unemployed), Mr. R. belongs to known at-risk groups. Affects of guilt and fearfulness, violent impulses suggesting an impaired capacity for affect regulation, and expressed hopelessness all indicate a person at risk for suicidal behavior. Comorbid affective disorder and substance abuse further confirm an elevated risk. He relates chronic suicidal tendencies and now proposes (albeit) contingent plans for ending his life. Finally, there are no indications of supportive interpersonal resources.

Mr. R. would definitely use suicide as a context for communicating. His "character" style presents issues in a dramatic and exaggerated fashion. He expresses no motivation or 'ownership' for either treatment or therapy. His active risk of suicidal behavior, valid over the next two weeks of hospitalization, is estimated at 2 on a 0-5 scale.

Mental Disorder

Axis I diagnoses are: Major Depressive Disorder, likely a double depression overlying chronic Dysthymia, and comorbid Substance Abuse. The roles of genetics, Post Traumatic Stress Disorder (PTSD), and other life history stressors in the development and chronicity of his mental disorders through more than 15 episodes are only speculation.

As an architect, we might assume he is an intelligent and creative man. His unemployment may stem from substance abuse issues, or from other interpersonal difficulties. There is a very strong suggestion of narcissism as a personality pathology.

Treatment

All elements of a biopsychosocial-spiritual approach deserve consideration. The present discussion focuses on biopharmaceutical and psychological aspects.

Addiction

Alprazolam detoxification is regarded as the most difficult among the benzodiazepine/anti-anxiety group of drugs and his use exceeds accepted daily maximums. Utilizing the pharmacokinetics of a long-acting benzodiazepine (chlordiazepoxide [Librium]), with multiple active metabolites and gradual self-tapering, is the historical approach to detoxification of this group of drugs. The dosing strategy chosen (baseline and then as needed [PRN]) is clinically appropriate if the PRN indications are specified. Many patients overusing alprazolam indicate that they experience significant withdrawal even in the presence of chlordiazepoxide. Fluoxetine is likely to significantly increase the chlordiazepoxide serum levels by inhibiting oxidation.

Detoxification is likely to be accomplished in 7-10 days with minimal physiological discomfort or danger. Rebound or return of original symptoms are a distinct possibility. Mr. R. can be given realistic hope that his ongoing efforts at eliminating substance abuse might be cumulatively successful. Emphasizing his many years of successful sobriety from alcohol is important.

Affective Disorders

Issues of dual diagnosis are involved. The fluoxetine (a serotonin selective reuptake inhibitor [SSRI]) is unlikely to relieve dysphoria linked to his dysthymia immediately, although it might reduce suicidality and relieve the severity of major depression. Is fluoxetine or any anti-depressant appropriate immediately at admission? I would be tempted to reserve the anti-depressant medication strategy for a later point in the treatment program. With respect to the dysthymia, it would be critical for Mr. R. to review all past therapies addressing recurrent themes, partial successes, and explanations for treatment failures. Negotiating a longer term helping contract, and ongoing process checking of his commitment and motivation will be essential.

Suicide

SSRIs, like fluoxetine, are indicated because they target suicidality. Mr. R. clearly indicates that his suicide solution is a response to intrapsychic pain. Has alprazolam been an effective pharmacological solution for this pain, despite its dependency-liability in the longer term? His chronic symptoms are not terminal or life-threatening physiologically. He is dissatisfied with his present quality of life, as interfered with by some or all of medication abuse, chronic interpersonal difficulties, and dysthymia. Mr. R. wishes to have his symptoms, and potentially his life difficulties, managed.

Though his request for assisted suicide could have a manipulative intent, any and all suicide ideation must be considered seriously and some intervention initiated. It is entirely inappropriate to provide instrumental assistance for his requests. It is appropriate to provide other support such as pharmacological advice concerning lethal dosages for his available medication, though I would not suggest the additive possibility of overdose using alcohol and benzodiazepines. Talking about suicide does not condone or support the act. Direct and open discussions of living and dying are an essential competency for mental health clinicians.

In these discussions, I would work towards a negotiation in which autonomy and decision making was respected on both sides. Never, *ever* would I ignore or "call his bluff" about acting on his suicide plan. Chronic suicide ideators may have a rigid and often dichotomous style of problem solving, and are especially unable to generate alternate problem solving solutions. It would be appropriate to offer various solutions related to specific issues to him. A straightforward discussion about alprazolam detoxification is a good starting point.

As to more restrictive security and containment, the consultant must be very aware of current state/provincial legislation. As a person at risk who has expressed a clear plan, there is a basis for formal commitment based on a "danger to self" criterion. With Mr. R., documenting serious and open discussions, and elaborating a dynamic estimation of suicide risk[2] would not require immediate containment, but might lead to cooperative work towards solutions other than suicide. Contracting, involving other team members for support, and scheduling regular meetings addressing the suicide issue are part of this strategy.

At present, an effective "first aid" intervention to prevent self-harm is the likely outcome. Working with Mr. R. beyond crisis would initially involve only issues for which successful action plans could be generated.

Moral Aspects

Assisted Death

Mr. R's condition is not terminal. It is chronically and intrapsychically painful. There are few acceptable measures of quality of life that would provide objective data about the impact and/or meaning of this pain to his life, but he is suffering. Unemployment, aloneness, needs met only by substance dependency, and low self-esteem can all, and each, be conditions contributing to his dysphoric mood.

Long term treatments operate from a rehabilitation, not cure, paradigm. Such a limited return to health should be acceptable to Mr. R. as "management" is his own stated goal. It is difficult to endorse assisted suicide as an option for him *at this time,* especially in light of the invitation to help which he initiated by sharing his plan for suicide.

Autonomy

Mr. R. invites intervention by his communication to the consultant. It signals his ambivalence and is not an assertion of personal autonomy with the hope that the consultant would endorse this solution. In an ongoing treatment situation, I would use the therapeutic alliance to test this hypothesis and to refine it by collecting further data. A respectful approach to Mr. R.'s autonomy requires that his discussion of suicide and his plan be taken seriously. Clinically, I believe that he is communicating a request not that he wishes to die, but that he hopes for some intervention on our part that will enable him to manage living. The emotional turmoil of detoxification, his affective impulsivity, and also the possible effect of alprazolam in disinhibiting both hostile and potentially suicidal impulses all suggest his suicide intention may be time-limited. Respectful of his decision making competency, it is still appropriate to question and challenge his thinking processes and their conclusions. While never ruling out suicide as an option for him, it is important to present other management scenarios and to move with him towards alternative helping strategies. Using this cooperative approach, it should be possible to discover which roles and themes are life-sustaining for him in the immediate present.

Containment/Committal

A societal belief that people are not expendable justifies intervention to prevent self-destruction. In most jurisdictions, legislation respects a clinician's "opinion" about the need for involuntary containment. This action is a temporary maneuver, undertaken in the hope that the person at risk is ambivalent and might be open to altered or other choices. The role of consultant is a significant advantage in the committal process. As a limited intervener, the consultant need not worry about the maintenance of an ongoing treatment alliance. The consultant role within a team may in fact be openly defined as that of making such difficult decisions. An effective helping team will find means to support the consultant's decision without jeopardizing their own provision of ongoing support for Mr. R.

For the competent helper, this issue of involuntary detention need never escalate to a conflict in working with Mr. R. It is more likely that the consultant will have to assure administrators and lawyers around their anxieties for Mr. R.'s safety or aid team members in processing their countertransference responses to this long-term patient.

Bryan Tanney, BSc, MD, FRCPC
Professor of Psychiatry
Calgary General Hospital
Calgary, Alberta, Canada

COMMENTARY #3, CASE #1

In this case analysis I focus on the potential rationality of the decision to suicide. Because, in my view, before a person should be assisted in a suicide the person's decision must be deemed rational, this assessment is a necessary precursor to any discussion of whether or not one ethically, morally, or legally should/could assist in the suicide of a particular individual. The criteria for such an assessment of rationality come from two national surveys of psychologists and are spelled out in more detail elsewhere.[3] Briefly, there are three criteria: (1) The person must have a hopeless condition; (2) the person must have made the decision to suicide without undue coercion from others; and (3) the person must have engaged in a sound decision-making process, which would involve (a) the presence of mental competence, (b) non-impulsive consideration of alternatives, (c) consideration of the congruence of the decision to suicide with personal values, (d) consideration of the impact on others, and (e) consultation with objective others and with significant others.

According to how the respondents in the surveys defined "hopeless," Dave R.'s condition would not necessarily be considered beyond hope yet since he is in detoxification treatment for his Xanax addiction. Although it is true that he has received multiple treatments before for various conditions, his condition is not necessarily hopeless because of the possibility of improvement following the breaking of his addiction. Regarding criterion two, there is no information provided about any potential coercion being placed on Dave to suicide. Thus, this is certainly an area to assess further—are there subtle pushes from people in the immediate environment or in the external world toward suicide?

There also is insufficient information to determine whether or not Dave has followed a sound decision-making process. Is someone who is in a detoxification program competent to decide to suicide? Perhaps; perhaps not. This would require an assessment of the several components of competence, such as being able to understand and remember relevant information, appreciate the consequences of the decision, and be able to use the information to make a decision[3] for a more complete description of competence relevant to life-and-death decision-making. We also do not have enough data regarding the alternatives that have been tried and considered and the thoroughness with which the options have been explored. However, it may be an acceptable assumption that Dave is currently not able to make a non-impulsive examination of options while in the midst of his detoxification program.

Further, we do not have anything more than a hint about Dave's value system. What is important to him? What is his spiritual belief system?

How would his values relate to the decision to suicide (the use of one's values are also a part of making a competent decision). What would he be sacrificing by suiciding (note that because I do not consider suicide a crime that is "committed" I am using "suicide" as a verb without the modifier "commit")? We also do not know if Dave has considered the impact of his suicide on others in his life or, if there are no significant others, is this isolation and loneliness something that, if ameliorated, would reduce or eliminate the desire to die? Finally, from the information provided, it is not clear whether or not any external resources, such as people who have successfully made it through detoxification, have been consulted.

Therefore, without much more information I would not be able to declare that Dave had made a rational decision to suicide. In fact, at present a case may be made that he cannot make a rational decision while he is being detoxified from Xanax. Yet, if he successfully completes the detoxification process and maintains a drug-free life and his depression still cannot be alleviated, then he may qualify as having a hopeless psychological condition–provided all appropriate treatments for depression have been tried once he is clean and sober. He may also then be clearly competent and we may have enough information about his values, alternatives which have been considered, and the availability of a support system to determine that he meets the criteria for rational suicide.

James L. Werth, Jr., BS
Psychology Intern
Counseling and Consultation
Arizona State University
Tempe, AZ

COMMENTARY #4, CASE #1

Dave R. is a young man with depression, hopelessness, and Xanax addiction who has just been hospitalized and placed on an antidepressant and Librium. His distressing symptoms require attention. Although it is difficult for him to imagine he will feel better, he needs to know that his psychiatrist and nurse care about him and will be active in managing his care. Establishing an alliance that helps Dave in the next few days and weeks is critically important because his risk of suicide is high. He seems ambivalent because he wants help and yet is planning his death. I would engage the part of him that wants to live. I would strongly encourage him to take time for the treatment he wanted and subsequently to consider his options carefully when he is thinking more clearly. If Dave were to leave prematurely, he would not give the treatment enough time to work. I would encourage Dave to defer leaving the hospital because he needs better symptom control immediately and his depression creates a negative and perhaps unrealistic view of the future.

A pressing concern is his hopelessness regarding withdrawal from Xanax and his fear of continued and intolerable symptoms. Withdrawal from Xanax is stressful and difficult and will increase anxiety. Because Dave worries that he will not manage detoxification if his symptoms continue, he will benefit from symptom control, supportive counselling and education. I would encourage him to recognize his past strengths–he has been sober and he has come for help. We can help him build on those strengths and get better.

The first and very important task is to assure Dave that the treatment team will control his poorly controlled symptoms. His withdrawal symptoms need better control. The dose of Librium is too low to substitute for the amount of Xanax he was taking, so his nausea and jitteriness are expected withdrawal symptoms. First, a clinical pharmacist should be consulted and the dose of Librium should be increased to control withdrawal. I would suggest that we need to work together to control his withdrawal–we will increase his medication, and his symptoms should diminish. He needs to report his ongoing symptoms promptly so we can assess medication effectiveness and calculate new dosages. Once the withdrawal symptoms are controlled, we can work together so Dave can learn constructive ways to manage his anxiety and attain a better understanding of the factors involved in his addiction.

The next important focus is on the depressive symptoms. Although the new antidepressants work more promptly than the traditional tricyclic antidepressants, effects will still take about 3-7 days. Dave needs to understand that these medications will not be effective until therapeutic blood levels are achieved. If Dave unrealistically expects his depressive symptoms to be controlled immediately and they are not, he may feel more discouraged and hopeless. Dave needs to be engaged in psychotherapy where his anxieties and feelings can be discussed and where he can be invited to learn cognitive strategies to manage his depression. I would encourage Dave to move to the locked psychiatric unit which provides more supervision and support during the stressful time of detoxification.

I would not agree to keep Dave's requests confidential because his depression and his anxiety cloud his judgment, but I would suggest that he has many choices. His current and anticipated symptoms have prompted his wish for death, and his depression clouds his thinking and has left him blind to other options and solutions to his problems. I would engage Dave in a partnership so we could reduce these symptoms and approach available options together. In forging the partnership with Dave, I would propose that we assess his medication regimen's effectiveness in relieving his distressing symptoms, rather than addressing medication dosage necessary to kill himself.

In therapy, I would encourage Dave to work on learning cognitive strategies and ways to manage his anxiety, hopelessness, and depression. I would also invite him to engage in activities to build his self esteem. I would want Dave to be closely supervised. I would invite him to talk about his suicidal ideas and feelings so we could understand them. I would also talk about Dave's fears of aging and being alone, and we would explore options to reduce some of these fears. Dave's concerns suggest that he needs to be in control, and I would design his treatment to include his active involvement in choices and planning solutions. When the acute symptoms were controlled, I would direct psychotherapeutic discussions around the chronic nature of his past depressions and examine ways to prevent or reduce these episodes. Dave has many concerns and effective therapy needs to consider his concerns seriously and strengthen his coping strategies and self esteem.

Sharon M. Valente, RN, PhD, FAAN
Assistant Professor, University of Southern California
Department of Nursing, Center for Health Professions
Los Angeles, California
Consultant, Department of Veterans Affairs,
West Los Angeles, CA

Judith M. Saunders, RN, DNSc, FAAN
Assistant Research Scientist, Department of Nursing Research
City of Hope National Medical Center
Assistant Professor, Department of Nursing
University of Southern California
Duarte, CA

COMMENTARY #5, CASE #1

The Clinical/Ethical Right Action

The first step would be to determine if the patient is making a rational decision, which in this context means that his desire to end his life is based on a thorough and realistic assessment of all the available and pertinent facts. A clear state of mind is not sufficient. After assuring that the suicidal impulse is not the result of a thought or mood disorder, this determination requires reviewing with the patient all important aspects of his life, especially those elements that are seen as unbearable and generate a sense of hopelessness. It would include such issues as the compatibility of suicide with the patient's personal philosophy and prior approaches to problems that seemed insoluble; the possible effects of suicide on others in his life; the attitudes of significant individuals, such as parents (even if they are deceased); the degree of ambivalence about the suicide plan; the resolution of unfulfilled obligations, projects, or goals; and conflict with spiritual values.

If the patient seems to see all the facts clearly and still opts for suicide, the second step would be to assure that all alternatives to suicide have been thoroughly explored, including simply temporizing. One's outlook can be altered by time alone, and delaying the act does not require relinquishing the option. This inquiry is dictated by a profound respect for the utter finality of suicide, so if another alternative might be even temporarily bearable, it deserves serious consideration.

The third step would be a detailed scrutiny of the patient's "more than fifteen treatments" for depression and substance abuse, to clarify whether the disorder is undertreated, treatment resistant, or untreatable due to its characterological origins. Did the alcohol and drugs represent self treatment for depression? Was the depression brought on by losses generated by substance abuse (e.g., jobs, friends, family, health, professional standing)?

If the patient has wanted to die since age 14, the dysphoria would seem to be primary. How aggressive were the "treatments"? Were there trials of adequate duration and dosage with the known types of antidepressants? These would include tricyclics, selective serotonin reuptake inhibitors, bupropion, venlafaxine, nefazodone, and electroconvulsive therapy. At least one of each of these categories in combination with psychotherapy should have been tried before accepting that the unbearable symptoms cannot be relieved. If these measures are ineffective, the patient should be offered the possibility of a neurosurgical procedure (cingulotomy) that has helped about 40% of persons with chronic, complex mood disorders unresponsive to traditional treatment.

The fourth step is to shift the focus from "detoxification" to relief of dysphoria. Though admitted for detoxification, the patient "has little hope for detoxification from his addiction to Xanax," and states he "can't live with symptoms and without his Xanax." I find no evidence of toxicity in the data provided, nor of addiction. Physical dependence on Xanax is certainly present, but this poses relatively little risk of serious harm, either by chronic use or overdose. It would be desirable to substitute a longer-acting agent (e.g., chlordiazepoxide, clinaxepan, phenobarbital), which has already been done with Librium. If his continued use of Xanax or an equivalent provides life-sustaining hope, it should be continued.

The increasing nausea, fatigue, jitteriness and headache are common side-effects of fluxetine, which may be relieved by reducing the dose to 5 mg/day and gradually increasing it to a therapeutic level. Starting at 30 mg/day probably accounts for the symptoms increasing after admission. If we find by trial or by history that the patient is unresponsive to pharmacological agents, electroconvulsive therapy deserves consideration. A series of twelve treatments should be recommended in the absence of a prior history of lack of response to this medium.

Throughout the period of medication trials or electroconvulsive therapy, an ongoing program of psychotherapy, both supportive and dynamic, should be recommended. This can have considerable impact on feelings of hopelessness and despair, even if other symptoms persist. Both the duration of symptoms, suggesting a dysthymic disorder, and the hint of narcissistic personality traits limit treatment optimism, but it is important that the therapist maintain a firm conviction that relief will be found if the therapeutic effort is sustained.

If all traditional measures fail to provide relief, recommending a cingulotomy might be regarded as a "final resort." This procedure provides a realistic alternative to giving up on attempts to find relief of symptoms. It should be emphasized to the patient that none of the therapeutic measures requires that he relinquish his thoughts regarding suicide, only that he give himself every feasible chance of recovery before resorting to such a solution.

It remains to assure ourselves that the patient is not subject to any external coercive influence, that pertinent family members are consulted and their input seriously considered, and that another consultation be obtained from a mental health professional for a second opinion as to the outcome of the considerations enumerated above.

The patient's request, that his plan to elope from the hospital and take an overdose remain confidential, cannot be honored. It should be made explicit that at this stage, his well-being has priority over all other considerations.

Rationale

It seems clear that much remains to be done in this case before any consideration can be given to physician-assisted suicide. The record reflects only one request for such assistance, and this at a point of discouragement and despair, heightened by the threat of "detoxification" from an agent that has helped the patient survive in the past. Verbal reiteration of an ongoing desire to end his life would be needed.

It is not yet evident that he suffers an untreatable or a progressive disorder, though it has apparently been chronic. Further, his degree of disability is not such that he is unable to care for his everyday needs and cooperate with a treatment program. A number of alternatives apparently remain to be explored.

The second consultation with another mental health professional would need to confirm that he is not significantly influenced by a cognitive deficit or a mood or thought disorder, and that he has come to a decision in a rational way.

In the absence of these criteria for consideration of his request for assistance with his suicide plans, it would not be appropriate to go further at this time than to respond to his question about how much medicine would be lethal. The most accurate answer would be that it would depend on the unique characteristics of his metabolic system, and that the amount needed would therefore be unpredictable.

If the patient refuses voluntary ongoing treatment, involuntary measures would be indicated to the extent that the law permits, after which caregivers can take some satisfaction from the fact that they have done as much as could be done. The likelihood that this patient would become a candidate for assisted suicide appears quite low, as at this point he does not fit either the "terminal illness" or the "unbearable and untreatable" model.

Jerome A. Motto, MD
Department of Psychiatry
Langley Porter Psychiatric Institute
University of California, San Francisco
San Francisco, CA

CASE #2. LAURA

Laura was in her late 50s when she was diagnosed with Stage IV colo-rectal adenocarcinoma. Her palliative surgery included both a colostomy and removal of her rectum. Since her diagnosis Laura has persistently told friends she would commit suicide rather than endure unnecessary pain and suffering. Although she has an expert pain consultant, her pain and suffering have never been relieved adequately. Gradually, as her disease progressed, Laura's energy evaporated when she attempted small projects, and she required increasing amounts of both sustained release morphine sulfate and immediate release morphine sulphate for break-through pain. She lives at home. She complained that managing her complex drug arsenal was becoming both a full-time job and a bulky dietary intake, as she balanced antacids, stool softeners, sleeping pills, vitamins, and various analgesics to supplement the morphine. Always a socially active person, she was surprised that she dreaded friends' visits more than welcoming them, as they robbed her precious energy. She thought more and more about suicide, but was uncertain about what lethal drugs to take and the necessary dosages. She methodically read Derek Humphry's publications (e.g., Final Exit, Let Me Die Before I Wake) *but remained unclear about the combination of drugs and dosages.*

You have been her local pharmacist or clinician for the last decade so you have a close relationship. When Laura calls to schedule an appointment with you to discuss her medications, you are not surprised but wonder how to answer her questions about safe/unsafe/fatal doses of medications.

Assume next that Laura asks you to sit with her after she has taken a presumably lethal dose of barbiturates, morphine, antiemetic, and alcohol. The most excruciating ethical dilemma then occurs as she continues to breathe and wakes up in a groggy state and wonders why she is not dead. Discuss whether you should take additional measures to end Laura's life because she is too weak to do this herself and begs for assistance. Should a physician or care provider actively intervene?

COMMENTARY #1, CASE #2

There are several troubling aspects to this scenario. Laura has "an expert pain consultant" but still inadequately relieved symptoms. In this particular malignancy it is often the indignities and loss of normal control which the patient finds even more distressing than the pain, and attention to amelioration of such compromised conditions must be of prime importance to the care givers. If it is indeed the degree of pain that is the major complaint of Laura, this suggests that there is some problem in communication with the pain consultant, and that full discussion about relief of her pain should be part of my intervention with her, as her long time clinician. Morphine would be increased with the hope of giving her enough relief that she would wish to continue living if such relief permitted her to enjoy some social interaction with family and friends. If it proved that adequate pain control could not be accomplished then, the next concern I have relates to the possibility that Laura is depressed as well as suffering the indignities and pain attendant to this form of cancer. Therefore, in the appointment to discuss medication with Laura, it would be incumbent upon me to assess the possibility that a trial of an adequate antidepressant would be indicated, to improve her mood as well as help in her pain control. No such medication is mentioned in the armamentarium listed in the scenario.

If, after a trial of an adequate antidepressant, there is still no relief obtained, I would wish to explore her confusion regarding lethal dosage of barbiturates, and I would advise her on those medications which have been accepted to be extremely effective and adequate in the experience of physicians and patients in the Netherlands, as well as those who have followed the directions given in such publications as *Final Exit* by Derek Humphry. In other words, her questions should be answered honestly and completely, with attention to possible complications or problems with taking the medication. This should obviate the quandary which is related in the case, that Laura had less than sufficient quantity of medication and awoke. However, with the scenario described, since she roused enough to ask why she is not dead, this suggests that she may follow one of two possible courses. A further mixture of barbiturates could be offered at that time, if she is able to consume a further oral dosage. An alternative might be to wait until she is fully awake and have Laura accomplish her deliverance with a level of medication which is increased over that used in her failed attempt.

Because of the legal prohibition to assisting by active intervention, at the time I would not feel comfortable in proceeding in the manner that would be possible in the Netherlands. In that country, a physician could help a patient actively, with injectable medication, if the patient were unable to successfully do so without assistance. However, if she "begs for assistance" it would be very difficult not to work with her. If she had asked her physician to stand by while she took her life with medication, and with use of a plastic bag, as is recommended by Humphry, and if she had no close family or friend who would be available to sit with her, then I would accommodate that request. My consideration would be to ensure that Laura did not find herself in a situation of permanent vegetative state by compromising the brain cortex, but not the brain stem.

In this case, if no family or close friend is available, I would feel obligated to give Laura the best information possible to assist her in being successful with ending her life in the "least worst way."

Richard MacDonald, MD
Medical Director, The Hemlock Society
Megalia, CA

COMMENTARY #2, CASE #2

As the long time care provider for this patient, you are in an excellent position to counsel and advise; she will trust your advice, whereas her new consultants are not familiar to her. She has undergone radical cancer surgery (resection) and even after that sacrifice has non-curable metastatic cancer. Her emotional state is fragile and her future is uncertain (except for the fact that she is going to die from her disease) and the role of the primary provider must be to assure an understanding of the situation and then to provide assurance against her worst nightmare–symptom control. She must be assured that suicide is not needed for symptom control and you will be there for her.

Although seeing a pain specialist, Laura's symptoms are not controlled adequately and this must be done for her. Symptom control for a person with advancing and incurable cancer is just as important as aggressive therapy for the person with potentially curative cancer. Laura is overwhelmed by her medical regimen and cannot cope by herself. She has become socially withdrawn. This is an extremely important time for intervention by her primary care provider–active intervention with office visits to assess and reassure her and home care and hospice referral for help with symptom control and coping. Laura should not have had to resort to *Final Exit* on her own, there should have been dialogue with her provider regarding these issues. She is contemplating active euthanasia because her symptoms are not controlled and because she has no emotional support. I believe that issues to be discussed should include: dealing with fear and despair, providing an assurance of maximal symptom control, ensuring her ability to remain at home if desired, and supporting her ability to go to the hospital at any time if desired. She needs to know that I will always be there for her, no matter what–so there is no feeling of abandonment. And lastly she needs to know that aid may be available under the right circumstances.

Some clarification of terms and definitions is appropriate here so that confusion and misunderstanding are not perpetuated. Active euthanasia is defined as an intentional act that causes death. Passive euthanasia is defined as an intentional act to avoid prolonging the dying process ("pulling the plug"). It is critically important to distinguish between clinical suicide and the desire to hasten death when death is inevitable, as in terminal illness. In clinical suicide, the patient is depressed or despondent, the act is planned in secret and carried out in a violent manor and the survivors are left with feelings of shock, confusion and sometimes, guilt. In situations of hastened death in the setting of terminal illness, the patient is exhausted by the dying process, and often has consulted family or loved ones. Moreover, the process is nonviolent and occurs at rest. Hence, the survivors feel gratitude that the ordeal of dying is finally over and that the person is at peace.

The ethical dilemma presented after you agree to sit with Laura and the suicide is botched is a very difficult one. As her adviser and care giver, you have given her permission to proceed, presumably because you agree with her wishes. My position regarding the moral actions of the care giver is that the relief of pain and suffering are paramount. This concept reflects one of the four basic principles of biomedical ethics: nonmalficence–provide comfort and relieve suffering. In our current legal environment, assisting in suicide is not permissible. I would participate through a family member or friend and provide the expertise that is needed to allow Laura to complete her wishes. I strongly believe in the right of self determination and that providing the means and guidance is part of the continuum of complete medical care, up to and including the dying process. Based on the same moral principles, I believe it is only right to further assist when the attempt at self deliverance fails. The suffering has not ceased, and the goal must remain the same–not to abandon the patient and to relieve suffering. I believe there should be no emotional turmoil thereafter on the part of the care giver–you have adhered to moral and ethical principles you believe in and you have provided the best of care to your patient.

The situation here points out clearly why there needs to be legislation passed that would protect the care giver in this setting and allow active administration of a lethal injection to hasten death by a qualified care provider, if the adult, terminally ill patient has consented. Such legislation needs to carefully define who is a suitable candidate for such a procedure. Such qualifying candidates would include only adults who are terminally ill, with no evidence of active depression and should also include written and repeated requests as well as a defined waiting period.

If the concepts and principles discussed here could have been applied to Laura, she would have been able to have had a dignified dying process and not have been in the position to beg for final relief when the living process had no more life to give.

Fred S. Marcus, MD
Medical Oncologist, Redwood Medical Group
Attending Physician
Sequoia Hospital, Redwood City and
Stanford University Hospital, Stanford, CA

COMMENTARY #3, CASE #2

In this case, there is additional information that I would want before I could agree that Laura's decision to suicide is rational. Although I am not a medical professional, I would venture to guess that her physical condition may be hopeless, if not in terms of the progressive nature of her condition then at least regarding the amount of pain she is experiencing. The criteria for rational suicide include as a hopeless condition terminal illness, both physical and psychological pain that cannot be adequately alleviated, physically and mentally deteriorating and/or debilitating conditions and, finally, quality of life unacceptable to the individual. If consultation with one or more medical professionals confirmed that her condition was hopeless then I would see this criterion as satisfied.

The second item of my criteria for rational suicide (see my discussion of the first case), not experiencing undue coercion to suicide, is more complex. We do not have information about how others have responded to her condition, do not know if she has succumbed to the ageist prejudices of society, and cannot tell if she has any potential inheritors who are pressuring her not to use up all her financial resources on her own treatments. Thus, this area would need much more assessment.

I also have questions about the soundness of her decision-making process. There is no indication that an assessment of her competence to make such a profound decision has been conducted. The case presentation indicates that she *may* be experiencing a reactive depression but, even if such a depression is present, this may not be sufficient to lead to a determination of incompetence. I do not want to give the impression that I am trying to find a way for her to be declared unable to make such a decision, rather I merely would want an assessment performed before I would be willing to view her decision as rational. I also would want to know more about the alternatives to suicide she has considered. It sounds as if she has done quite a bit to alleviate her pain but there may be other options which have been successful for other people which have not been tried yet, such as self-hypnosis. Again, I would want more information before I could consider this sub-criterion satisfied. And, likewise, I would want to know more about Laura's value system and how suicide would fit within her views.

The vignette mentions that Laura is a social person and has had to cut back drastically on her engagements and, further, that she has mentioned suicide to some friends. But it does not state how her friends have reacted to her declining sociability and her statements about death. Nor is there indication that she has considered the potential impact on her friends and/or any family members. There is no mention of living parents or siblings, or the presence of children or grandchildren, but I would not want to assume that she is therefore without family. She may well decide that the potential impact on her friends (and family?) does not offset the actual impact of the suffering she is presently experiencing; this certainly could be a valid decision. It is just another factor that needs to be assessed and worked into the equation.

Overall, therefore, I would want more information before I could feel confident that Laura's decision to suicide was indeed rational. However, there is the distinct possibility that she could adequately address each of the criteria and I would then agree that her decision is rational.

James L. Werth, Jr., BS
Psychology Intern
Counseling and Consultation
Arizona State University
Tempe, AZ

CASE #3. JON D.

Mr. Jon D. is a 50 year old married man with two pre-teen children. He receives antidepressants and family therapy for his major depression and has low self-esteem. He reports he is not going to die "the terrible death as his mother did from Huntington's Chorea" and that he will kill himself first. His diagnosis of Huntington's Chorea is confirmed but he is asymptomatic. After his antidepressant (imipramine 250mg daily) was changed to amitriptyline 300 mg daily, and he developed his first tremors and jittery movements–he interpreted these jitters as symptoms of progression of the Huntington's Chorea. He receives Sinequan 50 mg at bedtime for sleep. He fears his Huntington's Chorea symptoms will rapidly become full-blown and tells his sons and wife that "if he attempts suicide" they are not to intervene. They are clearly uncomfortable with this mandate, but they do not argue.

He expects his Huntington's Chorea will progress rapidly and leave him incapacitated very quickly. He asks for help to commit suicide.

COMMENTARY #1, CASE #3

Given the information provided, Jon D., the main figure in this case, presents a tricky situation for the first criterion for rational suicide (see my commentary on the first case), because there is a hint that his condition (which in its later stages may be considered hopeless) is not progressing as fast as he thinks it is. I would definitely want a consultation with at least one and perhaps two physicians regarding his prognosis at this point. Is his disease actually progressing or are his "symptoms" actually side effects of medication? Is his experience with his mother coloring his expectations so that he is hypervigilant about any hint of overt illness which leads to an inability to enjoy life while he is asymptomatic or experiencing only mild symptoms? In terms of the presence of a hopeless condition, if his physicians concur that he is facing the immediate onset of symptoms then he may be considered to have a hopeless condition, but if they declare that he has lots of time left then steps need to be taken to try to alleviate his concerns so that he can live life to the fullest.

The second criterion, not being coerced into suiciding, appears to be met since Jon's wife and sons are "clearly uncomfortable" with his decision to suicide. However, there may be an implicit message (or Jon may infer a message) in their not arguing with him about his wanting to die. Therefore, an assessment of family dynamics would be necessary to determine the messages associated with this lack of opposition.

The first two criteria may be met, depending on information gleaned from further consultation with physicians and family; however, Jon clearly does not meet the sub-criteria associated with a sound decision-making process. We would definitely want an assessment of Jon's competence to make this decision for at least two reasons. First, because the disease may have affected his decision-making abilities; second, his fear of dying like his mother may be interfering with his ability to follow the other four sub-criteria. One of the biggest obstacles to finding Jon's decision rational is his apparent inability to consider alternatives to suicide. He seems to be determined to suicide regardless of others' beliefs. This would be especially problematic if his physicians can provide him with options based on their diagnosis of his current condition.

Regarding the third sub-criterion, examination of values, we do have a sense that Jon (perhaps quite rationally) fears suffering the way his mother did and from this we can infer some of his values but I would want a more thorough examination. Another major reason to question the rationality of Jon's decision is the apparent lack of consideration of the impact of his suicide on his family. Not that he would have to acquiesce to their wishes but, rather, he should at least consider them in his process and converse with them so as to attempt to help them understand why he has decided to die instead of face the progression of the disease. Finally, there is no indication that Jon has consulted with others (such as other physicians) regarding his condition and ways to cope with it. Again, they may not change his mind but it is difficult to view his decision as rational if he has not consulted with people who may provide him with a way to continue living.

Overall, then, at this point I would not consider Jon's decision to suicide rational. I would see his decision to suicide instead of face the ravages of the disease as a potentially rational choice provided he meets the decision-making sub-criteria (especially those related to exploring alternatives and considering the impact on significant others and consulting with them). Once again I want to reiterate that Jon is not obligated to give in to the wishes of others nor to try every alternative presented by other people; it is his apparently premature foreclosure of these issues that leads to my view of his decision as being irrational, not the decision itself.

James L. Werth, Jr., BS
Psychology Intern
Counseling and Consultation
Arizona State University
Tempe, AZ

COMMENTARY #2, CASE #3

It is helpful to be as clear as possible about the facts of this or any other case before undertaking professional or ethical comment. We are told that Mr. Jon D. is a 50-year-old married man with two children who has a confirmed diagnosis of Huntington's Chorea. We know that Huntington's Chorea is a disease which advances slowly, generally spanning 15 to 20 years before death occurs. The disease is relentless in its progression, combining both motor disorder and dementia.

We have not been told when Mr. D. was diagnosed with this disease or the present state of its progression. Because of his age and current asymptomatic condition, we might assume for purposes of this discussion that Mr. D. is in the early stages of his disease. If that were not true, a somewhat different analysis might apply.

In recent years, Huntington's Chorea has been found to have a special feature which adds to its frightening prospects: sophisticated genetic testing can determine whether or not a family member carries the gene for the disease. If genetic testing were to determine that an individual did not carry the relevant gene, that could provide great relief. In Mr. D.'s case, however, genetic testing has confirmed that he does have the gene for Huntington's Chorea. This has significant implications both for him and for his children.

In addition, Mr. D. has experienced his mother's struggles with this disease over a period of what can be assumed to be a number of years. Thus, he knows how devastating this disease can be for a loved one and he is aware that in the present circumstances he has little hope for escape from the ravages of this incurable disease. Not surprisingly, he declares that he does not intend to suffer "the terrible death" that his mother experienced from Huntington's Chorea.

In the case of a disease such as Huntington's Chorea, one with a relentless and extended course, it can be assumed that Mr. D. would receive palliative treatment and supportive care for the rest of his life–unless, of course, a cure is found. We are hesitant to hold out unwarranted hope as a standard tactic in health care, but the possibility of a cure should not be too lightly excluded in this case. Overnight cures are perhaps too often mentioned in discussions of this sort and too rarely realized. But if we couple the extended course which we project for Mr. D.'s disease with advances being made in medical research on a daily basis, the possibility of a cure or other intervention emerging for Huntington's Chorea is not a totally unrealistic view.

In the meantime, the present situation calls for the health care professional to undertake a complex set of actions with Mr. D. The challenge for any health professional is threefold: to improve the patient's quality of life; to attempt to obey the basic rule in health care to "do no harm"; and to respect the patient's right to make decisions about his care. Certainly, the ideal situation for the pharmacist would be somehow to accommodate or respond effectively to all three of these challenges. With Mr. D. that may prove difficult.

Improving this patient's quality of life, especially at the latter stages of the disease, will be difficult. In addition, helping to extend a patient's life does not necessarily mean that it will be improved–from a clinical standpoint or from the patient's perspective.

In terms of the mandate to "do no harm," it may be helpful to note that in most areas of the United States, pharmacists do not themselves have prescriptive authority. In most cases, pharmacists work as consultants or advisers to those who do have such authority. Moreover, the mandate is not to "allow no harm to occur." Quite often, whether or not harm comes about or might arise is beyond the control of the pharmacist. It may even be beyond all human control. The responsibility of the professional pharmacist may not extend to the prevention of all harm, but it surely encompasses the governance of his or her own actions, both as an individual professional and as a member of a health care team.

The third set of challenges in this case concerns the patient's right to make decisions about his own care. In order for the patient to exercise that right in an informed way, it will be necessary to engage with him in a thorough discussion of his disease, its prognosis, his present situation, the therapeutic modalities that are currently or potentially available, and their likely effects. In addition, health care providers should conduct a frank discussion with Mr. D. as to his wishes in the case of extreme life-saving measures and as to the implications of his projected suicide. One would want to explore with Mr. D. the probable implications of his wishes and possible actions for him, his family members, and all concerned. Only then can a treatment plan be mapped out for Mr. D. which is likely to include supportive drug therapy and intensive professional counseling for both the patient and his family. The counseling should address Mr. D.'s disease, its genetic implications for his children, and issues associated with the possibility of his suicide.

At the moment, Mr. D. is clearly depressed. He is currently being prescribed two different tricyclic antidepressants, amitriptyline (Elavil) and doxepin (Sinequan). In treating the depression associated with Huntington's Chorea, response has been seen with the use of tricyclic antidepressants. The combination of amitriptyline and doxepin which Mr. D. is currently receiving, however, could be modified to derive more benefit for the patient. Before doing so, it will be useful first to comment on the current regimen.

We are not told why Mr. D. was switched from imipramine (Tofranil) to amitriptyline or how long he had been on the imipramine. If the imipramine had been given an ample trial, then the switch would seem appropriate. The fact, however, that Mr. D. is experiencing what appears to be a side effect of the new drug (the tremor) should cause some concern, since he is misinterpreting this as a sign of progression of his disease. Imipramine is a suitable choice for a patient such as Mr. D., provided that the drug is given an appropriate trial (at least 6-8 weeks), at appropriate doses, and administered at bedtime to avoid the sedative side effects during the day. If his imipramine had not been administered properly, daytime sedation could also be contributing to his depressive symptoms. The additional use of doxepin offers no real benefit in this patient.

Dosed at bedtime, the imipramine should provide adequate sedation at least for a short period of time. A sedative/hypnotic could also be prescribed. In an overtly suicidal patient, this may present the prescriber with a dilemma, since sedatives are often implicated in deaths due to overdose. Providing only small quantities per prescription is one alternative to avert this potential problem.

Aside from the antidepressant, Huntington's patients have at times benefitted from a neuroleptic to help suppress the choreic movements and agitation. Phenothiazines, haloperidol, or reserpine may be used until side effects supervene.

With the number of resources currently available to the public related to assisted suicide and the types of drugs he is likely to be prescribed for his condition, Mr. D. would have little trouble committing suicide. Pharmacists in good conscience provide these medications to patients believing that they will relieve the patients' suffering. Huntington's Chorea is a devastating disease, one that is life-altering for those family members who have witnessed its ruinous effects. The long progression of the disease, the dementia, and the chorea give family members time to dwell on the specifics and potential implications of every jittery movement and every deranged outburst that the patient makes. Mr. D. was privy to all of this as he watched his own mother die of the disease. It is no surprise that someone like him who in a sense "knows his destiny" would find it almost unbearable.

Medications can provide relief from suffering and pain. In so doing, such medications may help patients to achieve a sense of control and a quality of life that will permit them to live the life they desire in the present moment. Any pharmacist working with Mr. D. and with other health care providers in this situation should focus on improving his present quality of life and on achieving a skillful balance between one's professional obligation to "do no harm" and the patient's right to make decisions about his care. For this, health care providers should not precipitously inject into the present their expectations of the eventual outcome of a disease with a very long course. That anticipated outcome might never be realized; Mr. D. is just as likely as the rest of us to die in a motor vehicle accident before his disease progresses much further. Long-term prospects should not be excluded in a case like this, but they need to be viewed in proper perspective. Pharmacists involved in this case should be sensitive to the potential therapeutic value of skilled professional counseling both for Mr. D. and for his family. Finally, no pharmacist or other health care professional can rightly be asked to violate his or her own ethical values and principles in order to accommodate the wishes of a patient or another professional.

Karen M. Corr, PharmD
Clinical Pharmacy Coordinator
F.D.R. Veterans Hospital
Montrose, NY

Charles A. Corr, PhD
Professor, Department of Philosophical Studies
Southern Illinois University at Edwardsville
Edwardsville, IL

CASE #4. KEN S.

Dr. Ken S. is a divorced, 39-year-old physician who is diagnosed with advanced AIDS with Kaposi's sarcoma and many past opportunistic infections. He lives with his lover and receives home care nursing. When he was alert and free of mental status changes, he completed his written requests for a no-code. He complains of increasing distress from diarrhea, pain, shortness of breath, fatigue, chest pain, headaches, oral pain, and painful peripheral neuropathy. Most problems are now well managed except for shortness of breath and pain. He consistently uses oxygen but remains short of breath. Previously he refused AZT and DDI because of side effects. A regimen of 120 mg oral sustained release morphine every 12 hours with either carbamazepine or sodium valproate failed to control pain. He received limited relief from a four week trial of epidural opioids administered through a lumbar epidural catheter. He takes Dalmane for insomnia and Xanax for anxiety. He barely survived a recent episode of status epilepticus. His grand mal seizures are now controlled with phenytoin 200 mg three times daily. He has experienced episodes of delirium and currently has dementia with memory loss and confusion. During bouts of illness, he talks about wishing to die and not burden his lover and children. He argues that he deserves the right to die with dignity. He asks that his seizure medications be discontinued so he may die quickly of natural causes. Alternatively, he asks for a continuous morphine drip that he can control by turning up the rate, volume and dosage.

COMMENTARY #1, CASE #4

The first word in this case tells us that the patient we are dealing with is a physician. Often, when we treat physicians, nurses and other health professionals, we make the error of treating them as colleagues, assuming that they are completely informed and thus not in need of a careful discussion of their care, all treatment options, their feelings, and the other actions that we take in attending to our patients. While in another situation Dr. Ken may have been a colleague, he is presently a patient and his professional training should not taint our current relationship with him. Ironically, we sometimes provide less than optimal care to our colleagues, and need to consider this patient's actions and wishes as carefully as we would those of any other, lest we fall into the trap of taking his words at face value because of his training as a physician.

In reviewing his case, we find that this is a man who has had multiple manifestations of the opportunistic complications of HIV disease and is currently symptomatic with pain and shortness of breath. Additionally, he has dementia with memory loss and episodes of delirium, which may materially affect his judgement and other cognitive processes. His other symptoms and seizure disorder are reported to be controlled at present.

Although he is reported to be demented, the degree of dementia is not quantified. People with HIV often have subtle changes in cognitive function very early in the course of their illness which don't materially affect their livelihood or activities of daily living; many patients retain sufficient cognitive function to participate in treatment decisions in an informed and conscious manner right up until the time of their death. Thus, the *degree* of dementia in this patient may be important in assessing his expressed wishes to die, as his current comments and judgement must be interpreted in light of his cognitive abilities.

Even if Ken is markedly demented, his current wish to die may be consistent with his previous wish for no code status that was expressed when he was alert and fully functional. This prior wish suggests that when he was fully capable, he felt that there were certain measures he would not want instituted to prolong his life. From this we *may* also infer that he would not want to continue living if the quality of his life deteriorated beyond a certain point. However he did not explicitly state this, and it requires somewhat of a leap of logic to infer that a person would desire assisted death simply from the fact that they had previously expressed a wish not to be resuscitated. "No code" is not equal to "no care," so we may not infer from Ken's previous request for no code that he does not desire any care at this time. In sum, although he is presently demented, his current wishes to die are *consistent with* his previous thoughts and actions though not an inevitable conclusion from his previous comments.

There are suggestions that perhaps Ken's current wish to die is more a cry for help than a reasoned evaluation of his desire to end his life. The case presentation states that *"during bouts of illness,* he talks about wishing to die and not burden. . . . " It may be that his request to die is a response to the frustration of transient changes in his health status and not representative of a consistent wish on his part. His statement of being a "burden" may more accurately reflect his own guilt over his illness and the demands it forces him to make on others than his desire to end his life, and reassurances from his lover and children might diminish this stated wish to die. Additionally, although he receives treatment for both insomnia and anxiety, these may be manifestations of an underlying depression that is causing him to express suicidal ideation. Medical illness and depression must always be thoroughly evaluated and treated before judging the validity of a patient's request to die even in a patient in the final stages of a terminal illness, as requests for suicide may represent a cry for another form of help.

Finally, if we fully analyze this situation and agree that Ken is making a conscious, reasoned decision based upon an accurate assessment of his life circumstances and not a distorted perception of transient difficulties, we must realize that it is within his right as a patient to refuse treatment such as seizure medications, even if to do so would result in his death. However, the withdrawal of seizure medication in no way guarantees that his death would be forthcoming, prompt, painless or humane, nor can we be certain that his eventual death would not be preceded by a series of distressing, non-lethal seizures. The alternative requested by the patient, intravenous morphine that is completely patient-controlled, is also problematic. Although physicians are legally allowed to prescribe medication for pain even with the knowledge that appropriate treatment of pain may otherwise shorten the natural life span, physicians are prohibited by law from prescribing any medication to induce death. Additionally, the choice of morphine as a sole agent in this patient would be a poor one, as the patient is already receiving 240 mg of morphine every 24 hours; we can expect that he would be fairly tolerant of high doses of morphine that would otherwise be lethal. He may be more susceptible to other drugs, or morphine used in combination with other drugs, but these are simply finer points that address the mechanism of inducing death, and skirt the greater issue of an individual's right to die in the manner and at the time of his or her choice versus the right and responsibility of society to intervene.

Peter J. Katsufrakis, MD
Associate Dean for Student Affairs
Clinical Assistant Professor of Family Medicine
and Director of Clinical Training,
Pacific AIDS Education and Training Center
University of Southern California School of Medicine
Los Angeles, CA

COMMENTARY #2, CASE #4

For Dr. Ken S., with his written advance directive for "No Code" in place, it is clear that, in the event of a cardiopulmonary arrest, his request should be honored. What is not so clear in the scenario is whether Ken also had a power of attorney naming his lover or other person as his surrogate. He has asked that his seizure medication be discontinued, but there is no guarantee that such a step would afford the death with dignity which he has hoped for. Indeed, the possibility of a PVS may be more likely. His request for morphine intravenously via a patient controlled analgesia (PCA) pump appears reasonable to me, since he has been in continuous pain for some time, and this may well permit him some period of time which is more acceptable to him, in which to enjoy social interaction with his partner, his children and friends, in order to make his farewells. If he decides that further comfort care is no longer acceptable due to the multiplicity of his symptoms which are not controlled, he should be permitted the option of increasingly larger dosage of morphine in order to shorten his dying time, accepting the principle of "double effect." During a time when he is free of impaired thinking, a discussion of his options should include his partner and his children, assuming they are of an age to make this meaningful.

Richard MacDonald, MD
Medical Director
The Hemlock Society
Megalia, CA

CASE #5. LOU A.

Mr. Lou A. is a 44-year-old man with chronic renal disease. For three years, his treatment has included dialysis three times a week. He lives in a group residence adjacent to his dialysis treatment center. One event that made his life better was an activity program conducted by one person at the residence. Recently, that program was stopped. Mr. A.'s complaints about the loss of this program provoked no response to his distress so he stopped complaining. Mr. A. decided to stop dialysis because his quality of life had become unacceptable since the end of the program. The renal dialysis staff arranged for their affiliated psychiatric hospital to admit Mr. A. on a 72-hour involuntary hold for evaluation of suicide risk. Mr. A. seemed fully aware of the consequences of his decision and explained to the psychiatric staff, "If I am careful with my diet, exercise, etc., I would probably live about a month to six weeks after ending dialysis. I would have decreased energy and increased difficulty breathing. I would expect to die within 4-6 weeks." Mr. A. wants to be discharged from the psychiatric unit and allowed to end his dialysis.

In discussing your reactions to this case, please explain your view of whether Mr. A. demonstrates the capacity to make the decision to halt dialysis? Clarify whether you think the 72-hour involuntary hold was appropriate or the right thing to do. How should Mr. A.'s requests and his situation be handled?

COMMENTARY #1, CASE #5

This case features two important bioethics topics: *decision making capacity* and *quality of life*. Both are quite controversial and both are very difficult to analyze and discuss without reference to one person's values. Numerous pieces about these subjects have been published, many quite recently. (In fact, some articles carry titles that reek of sensationalism.) Moreover, the ethics dilemmas that have played out as court cases during the last two decades–and which have helped define society's responses have stirred public emotions.[7] The Karen Ann Quinlan, Elizabeth Bouvia, and Baby M cases were discussed. Also known were the Cruzan case[8,9] and the Baby K. case.[10] Dr. Jack Kevorkian's first case, that of Janet Adkins, also received media attention.[11]

The facts of this hypothetical situation–involving Mr. A., a 44-year-old group home resident with chronic renal failure who is dialyzed three times a week at a clinic next door–offer unique twists to these common themes:

> One event that made his life better was an activity program conducted by one person at the residence. Recently that program was stopped. . . . Mr. A. decided to stop dialysis because his quality of life had become unacceptable since the end of the program.
>
> The renal dialysis staff arranged for their affiliated psychiatric hospital to admit Mr. A. on a 72-hour involuntary hold for evaluation of suicide risk. Mr. A. seemed fully aware of the consequences of his decision and explained to the psychiatric staff, "If I am careful with my diet, exercise, etc., I would probably live about a month to six weeks after ending dialysis. I would have decreased energy and increased difficulty breathing. I would expect to die within four to six weeks." Mr. A. wants to be discharged from the psychiatric unit and allowed to end his dialysis.

It might be well to discuss these issues out of the order in which they appear in the given scenario and look at the decision making capacity question first. This is important chronologically to practitioners as well because, if a given patient lacks decision making capacity, providers must turn to a surrogate for permission to provide or to continue treatment unless there is need for emergency intervention.

Decision Making Capacity

The term *decision making capacity*–rather than *competency*–is preferred by most healthcare practitioners.[12] American law presumes that every adult person is competent unless declared incompetent by a judicial authority with proper jurisdiction. Whether or not a person is legally competent is usually less important in a patient care setting than determining if the patient has sufficient mental judgment to make rational, informed decisions about medical treatment options.[13] This notion flows from the accepted doctrine that all individuals should be respected because they are autonomous persons and requires that even legally incompetent patients be afforded a courteous and complete explanation of proposed procedures and treatments if at all possible.[14]

In the *Cruzan* case, the United States Supreme Court held that competent adults have a legal right to refuse life-sustaining medical treatment, limited only by constitutionally-valid, state-by-state procedural safeguards.[15] The Court skirted the capacity issue by dealing almost exclusively with *competent* patient issues. Therefore, physicians and other health care providers must continue to interpret interactions with patients and to assess decision making capacity much as they always have to give the "patient's right to refuse medical care" vitality. Is this something of a Catch-22? Some authors have suggested that practitioners rarely raise the question of decision making capacity except when the patient disagrees with a proposed treatment plan.[16]

Experienced practitioners will readily admit that establishing decision making capacity is not an easy task in some cases.[17] Temporary incapacity (as from trauma or from metabolic or neurological disease) does not render patients *incompetent* automatically in the legal sense; but on the other hand, and most particularly in non-emergent cases, healthcare providers cannot deliver care as if these patients fully possess decision making capacity either (if they could they would not seek out patients' representatives to discuss diagnoses, prognoses and treatment options or ask representatives to sign consent forms). Of course, much of the difficulty in establishing a clear algorithm for answering decision making capacity concerns arises from the facts of the cases which present the issues. Some scholars have suggested universal, "three-step" methodologies for establishing decision making capacity but with little practical impact on care.[18] In the end, practitioners must make an initial appraisal about decision making capacity at the bedside based on reasonable medical judgment; if they feel uncomfortable with an independent assessment, they seek assistance from others. This procedural framework reinforces the legal standard of medical care required in such circumstances: physicians should act circumspectly in determining decision making capacity and then respond as would a reasonably prudent practitioner with similar qualifications in that locale.[9]

Unfortunately, the hypothetical facts here leave the impression that Mr. A.'s healthcare providers thought he was "suicidal" because he wanted to stop dialysis after the activity program ended. One might ask if they thought he was trying to intentionally kill himself–the dictionary definition of *suicide*[19]–by refusing to continue treatment *or* if he was stopping dialysis for what they presumed to be an irrational reason. In these circumstances, it might be helpful to know whether Mr. A.'s decision making capacity had ever been questioned earlier, that is, before he "decided to stop dialysis because his quality of life had become unacceptable. . . ." Regardless, the team moved quickly to have him involuntarily placed in a psychiatric facility for evaluation and observation after he expressed his preferences regarding treatment.

The facts also seem to indicate that Mr. A. was upset–or concerned (?) or depressed (?) or despondent (?)–over the activity program ending. The degree of distress is not clear, but appears material. The exact reason for the distress is not given either. One might ask: Was the activity program his one enjoyable escape or outlet? Was his distress related in any way to the fact that the "one person at the residence" who conducted the program was not there any more? Was the program discontinued because of funding reasons? Or, was he distressed because no one responded to his complaints? All these questions are important; the answers might shed some light on Mr. A.'s mental capabilities and condition.

More troubling though was the almost reflexive-like action of the facility staff in moving to place him *involuntarily*–against his will–into a psychiatric facility. It leaves one with the feeling that they did so simply because he expressed his desire to stop dialysis. This may indicate that the staff was uncomfortable about Mr. A.'s exercising his right to refuse this medical treatment–for whatever reason. The medical team cannot force (or coerce) patients into accepting unwanted medical care without risking a malpractice claim for "overtreatment."[20] Was the involuntary commitment really necessary here? Probably not, unless Mr. A. was a danger to himself or others. Psychiatrists are not absolutely necessary to the process of determining decision making capacity. Mr. A. may need psychiatric care, but this is not readily apparent from the facts given, particularly in light of his seemingly rational response (he understood the physiological progression of worsening symptoms–including death as an endpoint–from withholding dialysis).

Quality of Life

Walter and Shannon,[21] in the preface to their anthology *Quality of Life: The New Medical Dilemma,* state the reasons for reflecting on quality of life in healthcare contexts.

The critical issue here is that certain lives [are] considered unworthy of being lived. Today quality of life is often used in a neonatal context, and its application initiates a process of decision making when there is, for example, a genetic abnormality or a major physiological defect. In this situation the child's life is not considered unworthy, but perhaps it is so burdened or compromised that continued existence itself may be too onerous.

Quality of life has also been used in reference to the conditions under which one lives. In many ways this term refers to the traditional concepts of "burdensomeness" or "extraordinary means" that are found in traditional moral analysis. The insight here is that the conditions under which one lives or is forced to live may be so burdensome that there is no obligation to pursue medical treatment in order to preserve life. Yet this concept, too, has been extended in ways that are quite controversial, e.g., abortion for sex selection. While this practice does not appear to be common, it is nevertheless a reality.

Finally, one can also think of quality of life as referring to how a person chooses to live under the constraints imposed by biological and social conditions and the limits (technical or ethical) of modern medicine. In other words, the term can refer to personal choices about one's own life, how it is to be lived and the extent to which medicine will or will not be used in achieving one's own goals. This individualist perspective (grounded in the principle of autonomy), which is also open to the problems of the consumerist model, can effectively blunt any social evaluation of the conditions under which people should live or of the personal qualities that they should possess.

Thus, the real dilemmas for the healthcare team in Mr. A.'s case are: (1) If Mr. A. has decision making capacity, does he have to give them a morally valid reason for his decision to stop dialysis? And (2), if he is required to give a reason, what reason is sufficient? Are reasons such as "I'm tired of living period," "I'm really tired of dialysis treatments," "I just don't want to be stuck with another needle," or "If I can't participate in that activity program anymore, I just don't want to live" good enough? This problem vividly illustrates the tension between the classic bioethics principles (and control mechanisms) which guide the shared decision making model: *patient autonomy* v. *practitioner beneficence and nonmaleficence*. Just as the paternalistic physician cannot impose one treatment plan on the patient, the patient cannot elect a treatment choice without physician agreement.[22]

In the final analysis though, it remains for the parties involved (practitioner and patient) to resolve these questions between themselves to their own satisfaction. Each are morally responsible for their own actions and bear the consequences of continued association and interaction. If the attending physician feels that discontinuing medical care is not in the patient's best interests, the physician is ethically obligated to explain to the patient why such a choice may be ill-advised. But if the patient insists on what the physician feels is an unwise course, the physician does not have to continue participation in the case—the physician may, and should, withdraw after appropriate transfer is effected. Similarly, the competent patient is at liberty to seek another physician's counsel.

Conclusion

It is difficult to talk about *decision making capacity* and *quality of life* without at least thinking about the continuum extremes of both issues and the rights and responsibilities of autonomous patients and practitioners who act beneficently and nonmaleficently. It is these extremes of actions after all that cause the most anxiety about dealing with the problems in the first place. Uncertainty, though, is part of healthcare. Patients and practitioners must not fear the dangers of the "slippery slope" just because it exists.[23] Cases like this allow another opportunity to expand the horizons of the patient-healthcare team relationship.

Bruce D. White, DO, JD
Clinical Director
Clinical Ethics Center
Saint Thomas Hospital
Nashville, TN

COMMENTARY #2, CASE #5

This patient proposes to end his life by discontinuing a life-preserving medical procedure. His action is clearly intentional, knowledgeable and likely to end in his death through his own behavior. This is suicide. His autonomy in making this choice must be respected. However, his discussion of suicide must also be recognized as a means of communication about the state of his living. Using life as a bargaining chip is a characteristic wager in the chronically physically ill when issues of control are involved. It attracts immediate attention from committed health caregivers. It may also represent an indirect means to exert personal control over a physical body which has disappointed and failed them.

For Mr. A., suicide represents his adjustment to the program cancellation and to the lack of response on the part of his supports to his complaints and distress about this event. The lack of response crystallizes his feelings of helplessness. It is unclear whether the communication of suicide intent reflects a low level adaptive coping capacity or the only response left available to him which can effectively communicate his level of distress. Directing the message to the dialysis team and not to the group residence where the stressor was initiated suggests the former explanation.

His decision for suicide must be accepted with sadness, but there should be no efforts to assist his death. As much as possible it is important to ensure that his autonomy and wish in this regard is respected. Most importantly, the useful helper must re-open the possibility of alternate solutions to his present distress. Truly listening to this patient is critical and may be life-saving.

Competency

His capacity and competency to make a decision for "Selbstmordt" must be assessed. He shows every evidence of having rational intellectual capacities. He communicates a choice, understands relevant information, appreciates the current situation and its consequences, and is able to manipulate information rationally in his discussions with dialysis treatment staff. The process behind his decision-making is clearly understandable.

However, stress impairs coping and problem-solving capabilities, and Mr. A. has experienced important "exit" stressors. His decision-making apparatus is intact, but its operation may be seriously distorted because feelings of powerlessness and impaired self-worth impair his insight. His capacity to appreciate his decision is now much more difficult to discern. We are in the dark as to whether his present solution represents a new integration of his life circumstances, or is a further example of low level coping capability. Living in a group residence suggests that there are other issues impacting his social and societal functioning. For unspecified reasons, there is a clear suggestion that he does have a limited adaptive coping ability. Some would argue that the *"parens patriae"* stance is applicable, but most clinicians now accept that this well meaning approach is morally invalid.

Distorted or limited abilities to problem-solve are not sufficient to argue that the process of making competent decisions is functioning improperly. Accepting this argument is a "slippery slope" which could be used to suppress autonomous choices whenever patients disagreed with their caregiver(s).

Autonomy

The decision by the dialysis staff to arrange a 72-hour involuntary hold for evaluation of suicide risk was entirely appropriate. Mr. A.'s age, gender and his chronic illness condition are all risk indicators.[26] There is controversy for dialysis patients, but the weight of literature still tends to see them as experiencing an elevated risk of suicide, because of their chronic illness and because of the availability of means. Mr. A. openly expresses a suicide plan which he has the means to carry out. The presence of a specified "loss" stressor, his suicidal response and his (assumed) feeling of helplessness, warrant a *provisional* diagnosis of "Adjustment Disorder with Depressed Mood." Together the mental disorders and the identified risk of self-destructive behaviour meet the criteria for involuntary hold in most jurisdictions. Although not every person who chooses self-death is mentally disordered, it is entirely appropriate that treatable mental disorders be explored and evaluated before acceding to such requests.[27] A full socio-environmental assessment is also needed to examine the possibility of modifiable external stressors. Finally, the security/containment decision is appropriate as it 'buys some time' and, potentially, some emotional distance from the stressor events. In a different and supportive environment, it is common for the distortion or coloration of problem-solving capacities to diminish markedly.

Without more history, I am unsure if such discussions and ruling out demand an involuntary hold. I hope that major efforts at resolving the situation in the group residence have already been made. Such optimism is probably unrealistic. Psychiatric facilities in North America have become a "dumping ground" for difficult patients, difficult problems and difficult decisions. (Informed readers will appreciate this moment of ventilation.) It is not unusual for other medical caretakers to expect that a suicide risk will immediately be translated into mental disorder, and from there to a finding of incompetency to make treatment decisions. Buchanan and Brock[24] counter this issue: "Treatment refusal does reasonably serve to trigger a competency evaluation. On the other hand, a disagreement with the physician's recommendation or a refusal of a treatment recommendation is *no basis or evidence whatsoever* for a finding of incompetence."

Management

In approaching Mr. A., I would utilize the Person in Environment System. This re-working of the biopsychosocial-spiritual model is a multi-axial classification of social functioning problems. Mr. A. is a person in an outpatient role who has a power problem due to conflicts with the mental health system. The severity of his problem is moderate, one to six months in duration, and he brings to the problem a somewhat inadequate coping style. The description confirms that psychopharmacology is not required. Finding a solution to the environmental/personal situation should resolve the issue of suicidality because his at risk status is likely contingent on external circumstances. Get more information. Establish with the group residence staff whether and why Mr. A.'s communications verbally were (according to him) not heard. Meet with the renal dialysis staff to clarify and to support their decision-making strategy.

Whatever their origins, Mr. A.'s response is based on real and painful feelings. This pain makes suicide real. Death may represent the only means left which will effectively express and relieve his level of distress. Alternatively, the solution of suicide for Mr. A. is a means to escape a living situation which has become unacceptable for him. In either situation, a management approach is indicated for there is no clear expression of an intent that Mr. A. is embracing death. He wishes to live differently and will choose death if his living environment cannot be adjusted.[25]

Offering to cancel the 72-hour involuntary hold as an initial evidence of good-faith negotiation enhances possibilities for further discussion. Inpatient care should continue because of availability and intensity of resources. A community rich in integrated community health resources would never have used an involuntary hold. Whatever the venue, it is vital that Mr. A. have a personal experience that his concerns and his distress are listened to and appreciated. There are *two* loss issues. The first is the real time event of losing an important support in his social world. Establishing whether the person or the program was more important as a loss event for him will direct further environmental advocacy efforts. The second and probably more important is the loss of worth and esteem which he experienced when there was no response to his feelings of distress. Ventilation, validation and support may build a therapeutic alliance that will lead to cooperative problem solving. There may even be opportunities to improve Mr. A.'s coping repertoire, as this is the optimal result afforded by any crisis.

Affectively, it is important to be a "yea-sayer" for life. This means accepting and respecting Mr. A.'s decision, but reserving the right to disagree with it, to argue against it, and to express realistically felt sadness at losing him as a human being if he insists on refusing dialysis.

There is one final issue. When Mr. A. clinically deteriorates, it would not be unusual for well meaning medical or social resources to attempt further interventions to coerce him into dialysis. Usually, this involves requesting another competency evaluation. This distressing likelihood must be recognized as meeting the needs of his caregivers and not those of Mr. A. In such situations, although disagreeing with his life-ending decision, I would advocate for and respect his autonomy and competency to end his own life. Such active advocacy could only be undertaken if Mr. A. were engaged with a caregiver who could address his competency based upon a current assessment. Difficult although it might be, maintaining this relationship even until death might afford important and respectful protection for Mr. A.

Bryan Tanney, BSc, MD, FRCPC
Professor of Psychiatry
Calgary General Hospital
Calgary, Alberta, Canada

COMMENTARY #3, CASE #5

This case recalls one experienced some years ago, before the availability of peritoneal dialysis, when a patient who lived at home with his wife and three children discontinued his treatments because of loss of any further joy in his life, due to the illness and the increasing frequency required in his treatments to maintain any vitality. He died within a short time. In this case, Lou has been undergoing dialysis for three years, but his reason for wishing to suspend treatment is more related to social issues, and to the loss of the entertaining programs which had given him some reason to live. In my opinion, intervention should have included a multidisciplinary conference, including an advocate for the patient, a social worker, a psychologist or psychiatrist, a representative of the home in which he resides, family members if available and interested, his physician(s), a renal dialysis nurse, and his surrogate, if he has named one in an advance directive. The peremptory admission for an involuntary hold of 72 hours infringes on his rights, and was improper.

The decision of the patient in this case appears premature, and may have been a cry for help or attention. Lou may be an example of an inadequate personality, considering the stated fact that his desire to stop treatment was based only on the loss of his favorite activity program. With a conference of all concerned, it would seem that many avenues are open to explore as to improving the situation. This would include seeking placement in another facility if the present residence failed to respond to a request to include activities which Lou found enjoyable. Psychological consultation is certainly indicated, and counseling and assessment of possible treatable depression must be undertaken. He should be discharged from the psychiatric unit with a "contract" to include a conference looking into his complaint regarding the program at this residence, while he agrees to delay his cessation of dialysis. This is a situation which should never have occurred in the first place, if adequate communication had been part of his relationship with his various care givers.

Richard MacDonald, MD
Medical Director
The Hemlock Society
Megalia, CA

CASE #6. DONALD

Since his diagnosis of HIV disease ten years ago, Donald and his lover Bret, talked often about how this disease would shorten Donald's life. Donald's CD_4 count had been below 20 for about eighteen months now. Donald made out his will and his durable power of attorney. His family of origin understood that Bret would be manager of the estate and major beneficiary.

What they had not talked about, however, was Donald's attitude toward an unacceptable quality of life. Donald was very much an "in charge" patient and actively managed his own therapeutic regimen. He complained of severe, recurrent headaches, and despite vigorous diagnostic tests, the physicians could not determine precise etiology; they also could not provide effective relief. Donald read avidly about new treatments in clinical trials and occasionally persuaded his physician to prescribe one of these new drugs.

He worked to stay as healthy as he could by eating a carefully balanced diet and taking prescribed medications. Donald's vision grew steadily worse ending in blindness; his Cytomegalovirus (CMV) retinitis did not respond to ganciclovir or foscarnet prescribed individually or concurrently. While Donald was reconciled to losing his vision, he had not anticipated the onset of acute confusion, ataxia and forgetfulness. Donald's ability to talk or communicate became severely impaired, but he often held his head as though in severe pain. Bret was clearly distressed at seeing Donald in this condition of suffering and incompetence. The home hospice team taught Bret to use the PCA (patient controlled analgesia) pump and started IV morphine to reduce Donald's restlessness and non-verbal indications of headache. Bret asked many questions during this session, and many questions related to morphine dose levels. Bret wondered if it were his responsibility, as Donald's lover, to do what Donald could not–facilitate a dignified death. He asked the hospice team to help him facilitate a prompt and dignified death for Donald.

COMMENTARY #1, CASE #6

As usual, when given a written case history to respond to, I feel the need for more data. When dealing with such extreme issues as assisted suicide and euthanasia that need seems to double! On the face of it, given the data I have to work with, I would recommend against either Bret or the hospice team *intentionally* causing Donald's death. For the remainder of my commentary, I will attempt to explain my recommendation.

Any thought of "facilitating" a dignified death for Donald seems very premature to me. As I read this case, I think that it is a relatively safe bet that Donald is in pain—possibly severe pain—but we, as yet, do not know Donald's response to the IV morphine. I see no reason to assume, *prima facie,* that the morphine will not control his pain. Donald's pain control will need continued evaluation, and therefore, we are in a bit of a mess. It seems that we have no reliable way to communicate with Donald. This might have been avoided. The onset of "acute confusion . . . and forgetfulness" and severe impairment of "Donald's ability to talk or communicate" could probably have been anticipated by his hospice team and some provision could have been made for, at least, rudimentary communication. For me, this seems like a relatively common intervention, and I am disturbed that it was overlooked in this instance. Our evaluation of pain relief will now be limited to Donald's decreased "head-holding" and a more relaxed body posture. This is not entirely unreasonable as these are the indicators we used to determined that Donald was in pain in the first place. It would have been better, however, if we had more indicators to rely on.

I am struck by Bret's question—whether it is his responsibility to facilitate Donald's death. I can't imagine any situation where someone has the *duty* to hasten someone else's death. One might have the desire to hasten death, but that is different from a duty one is morally obligated to perform. But, clearly, at this juncture, Bret is unsure of exactly what is expected of him. This is understandable since apparently neither Bret nor Donald were able to discuss "Donald's attitude toward an unacceptable quality of life." Given that Donald was such a "take charge" kind of person—at least as far as his disease process was concerned—I am surprised by this omission. As we know, what is *not* said is often as important as what is said; when I don't hear something I would expect to hear, I wonder why.

I am also prepared to wonder about the "many questions related to morphine dose levels" that Bret asked. We could assume that these questions related specifically to a determination of lethal dose, but we might be in error. I would suggest that it is just as reasonable to assume Bret's many questions might indicate anxiety on his part–perhaps anxiety about how to operate the PCA pump or even anxiety that he might unwittingly cause Donald's death through unintentional overdose. The profile we have of Bret seems to suggest to me that he is in crisis and deserves some further evaluation by the hospice team.

I would like to say a word here about "double effect."[13] Most people would agree that to adequately control Donald's pain, the possibility exists that the morphine might hasten or cause his death. For me, this result does not fall into the category of euthanasia. First of all our intent is to control Donald's pain–a morally good action. Secondly, we foresee, and even permit this administration of morphine to cause or hasten death, but death is not our intent. Thirdly, it is the morphine that we anticipate will control the pain–not Donald's death. And finally, adequate control of Donald's pain is important enough to outweigh the possibility, or even probability, of hastening or causing his death. Therefore, all four conditions specified by the principle of double effect have been met to my satisfaction.

I believe that we need more of a feel for the family of origin. I would be concerned about how they would view Bret's facilitating Donald's death, especially considering Bret's beneficiary status. This is the stuff that lawsuits are made of and, unless I miss my guess, Bret wouldn't benefit by putting himself in this position. I also wonder how ready Bret and Donald's family of origin are to "let go" of Donald. Although this would never be my *primary* consideration in this situation, I tend to think it is an important consideration, and requires further assessment by the hospice team. If we can make Donald and Bret comfortable, along with the rest of Donald's family, I see nothing "undignified" about how he is dying.

Finally, if I need to justify my recommendation on a "principle based approach" to ethical decision making (also known as the "Georgetown mantra") I would rely on the principle of nonmaleficence, that is "Do no harm." However, our reliance on principles should never substitute for an adequate assessment of the patient and family. If I should err in my assessment of this case study, let me err on the side of life.

Barbara Jeanne McGuire, RN, MN, PhC
The Fielding Institute
Santa Barbara, CA

COMMENTARY #2, CASE #6

In this case, the impetus for action arises from Bret, the patient's lover, when he questions whether it is his responsibility to facilitate a dignified death for Donald. From a legal standpoint, it is clearly *not* Bret's responsibility, as facilitating the death of another is against the law. It is a more complex matter to consider this question from an ethical and moral standpoint. I will first consider the matter of assisting Donald's death, and then address the question raised by Bret.

As a result of his progressive HIV disease, Donald currently is blind, confused, ataxic and forgetful, and has limited ability to communicate. Although he has not or cannot express pain verbally, he demonstrates behaviors which suggest that he has ongoing headaches and pain. This set of circumstances distresses his lover, causing him to question whether it is his responsibility to facilitate Donald's death. While many would certainly agree that this set of circumstances would characterize a poor quality of life and be justification for suicide, it is less apparent that this would be Donald's wish were he able to express himself. Lacking direct evidence of Donald's criteria for an unacceptable quality of life, we must infer his attitude from his previous actions.

As described in the case presentation, Donald aggressively pursued various therapies throughout the course of his illness, and underwent aggressive evaluation of his headaches. He actively participated in the management of his treatment, complying with medication and diet orders and reading avidly about new treatment options. He also tolerated significant losses in the quality of his life produced by blindness and severe recurrent headaches that were not amenable to treatment, without expressing a wish to end his life. Thus, Donald had expressed through repeated actions a desire to aggressively battle his HIV infection and pursue life-prolonging therapies.

As stated in the case, Donald had not previously expressed any wishes regarding acceptable quality of life or a point at which he would not want his life to continue; while not unprecedented, this set of circumstances in someone who has lived for years with a terminal illness is somewhat unusual, and close friends and family should be carefully questioned to ascertain as best possible the patient's wishes. In the absence of a previously expressed wish to terminate his life if he were to deteriorate beyond a particular point, and in the presence of actions which suggest that Donald desired aggressive treatment for his illness, we must assume that his desire would be for continued care until the point of his natural death. Appropriate treatment *would* include effective pain management, and if Donald is demonstrating signs of pain he should be treated aggressively for this, but pain management should not be used to mask an assisted death by loved ones or caregivers.

An interesting issue that this case highlights is the suffering of the patient's family and loved ones as they grapple with the events surrounding

Donald's demise, particularly that of his lover who wonders whether to end the patient's life. Bret's distress is real, justified, and in need of treatment. Appropriate care for Donald would include helping Bret understand and cope with Donald's impending death, educating him about the expected sequence of events, and exploring ways to make this easier for both Donald and Bret. However, Bret's distress is *not* justification for premature termination of Donald's life, and Donald's wishes should take precedence over those of his loved ones. The pattern of action pursued by Donald throughout the course of his illness suggests that he would want aggressive treatment to sustain his life until such time that this was no longer possible.

Finally, we look again to Bret's original question, which is whether or not it is his "responsibility" to facilitate Donald's death. If we accept the premise that in certain instances it is right for an individual to wish to terminate his life prematurely, then where should the responsibility for this action rest if the patient is unable to act? Is this the responsibility of a lover, family, friend or health care provider? Should health care workers be permitted, or required, to take such action? These practical considerations contribute to the multi-faceted question of euthanasia and assisted suicide, and must be addressed in any attempt to resolve this issue.

Peter J. Katsufrakis, MD
Associate Dean for Student Affairs,
Clinical Assistant Professor of Family Medicine
and Director of Clinical Training
Pacific AIDS Education and Training Center
University of Southern California, School of Medicine
Los Angeles, CA

COMMENTARY #3, CASE #6

This appears to be a situation in which the patient has reached that stage in his disease when no improvement can be anticipated, at least to any satisfactory quality of life in the apparently short time remaining. As part of the hospice team attempting to give Donald comfort care, I would have little difficulty in working with Bret to ensure that Donald was released from this condition which is clearly without possibility of mitigation.

Since his advance directive is in place, with Bret as his designated surrogate, a full discussion with Bret should explain the options available, and I would act as advocate to Bret, recommending increasing the dosage of the PCA (patient controlled analgesia pump used to administered medications intravenously at preset rate and dosage) in incremental fashion, so that Donald may slip into unconsciousness. Respirations would be compromised to the point that death will ensue, with as little discomfort for Donald as is possible. It is my firm opinion that the responsibility of the care givers in this case is to support Bret in his decision to follow the advance directive of Donald, thus relieving Bret of the anxiety which he might experience with any possible conflict with the medical team regarding that decision. Donald's family should be included in any discussion which would help them understand why it was time to discontinue any further futile efforts to maintain life.

This case would be considered differently depending on the legal situation in the state of residence. If in Oregon, and, after legal challenges are exhausted in the effort to rescind Measure 16, the care giver could act within the law to provide oral barbiturates to satisfy the request to end the suffering, if the patient were able to ingest the medication. In all states, on the other hand, in the legal climate of today, increasing the morphine dosage to control discomfort and suffering is accepted by many under the "double effect" principle. Clearly, the intent is to shorten the time of dying, and the effect is the same as in providing a lethal dosage of barbiturates, in my opinion. Following Donald's death, I would feel comfortable in recording the cause of death as related to his disease.

Richard MacDonald, MD
Medical Director
The Hemlock Society
Megalia, CA

COMMENTARY #4, CASE #6

This vignette is another one which involves HIV disease; however, in this case the person's mental condition has moved past the point of intermittent competence (therefore differentiating this situation from case 4) to apparent incompetence. Therefore, since the criteria for rational suicide require competence on the part of the suicidal person they are not applicable in this case. For decision-making related to individuals who are incompetent the reader is referred to *Deciding for Others: The Ethics of Surrogate Decision Making*, among other sources.[24]

James L. Werth, Jr., BS
Psychology Intern
Counseling and Consultation
Arizona State University
Tempe, AZ

CASE #7. NIRINA JOY

Nirina Joy S. is a 14-year-old identical twin and the youngest of four children. Their family immigrated from Jamaica six decades ago to New York. Nirina is a talented dancer who is popular and successful in school and an active participant in the church choir, youth group and other activities. She wants to become a lawyer but may also decide to teach dance to children. During her recent illness, her classmates at school sent notes, balloons, and cards wishing her a speedy recovery. Several months ago, Nirina completed a successful bone marrow transplant for leukemia. She responded well to treatment and her family was very supportive. Her prognosis is excellent. Nirina has now returned to school but seems to have lost interest in everything. She does not attend dance class or the activities she previously enjoyed. She says she is too tired and too ugly. She often fails to join the family at meals because she is not hungry. Although she previously loved these activities she does not go out with her twin sister and avoids going skating or bike riding with her friends. In school she has had trouble concentrating but is working efficiently on a paper on current issues. She has decided to write a paper on self deliverance and has done extended research on this topic. She writes in her diary, "I have no reason to live–my hair fell out, I feel like a freak." "Even though my hair has grown back–I've lost my beautiful body, skin and beautiful hair. Nobody will ever love me." She includes a note about the many, expensive cancer medications left over from treatment for her pain, insomnia, nausea and other symptoms. She says that the cancer treatment has ruined her life forever, and she wishes she never had the treatment. The family believes that with proper rest, prayer, and good food, Nirina will return to her previous levels of energy and well being.

The cancer treatment team believes she probably will not have any recurrence of cancer. When she sees her cancer treatment team, Nirina comes to the appointment with a copy of Final Exit *and asks if patients can use the medical library to look up medications. If asked, Nirina would say that she needs to know about the medications for this paper she is writing on self deliverance. The treatment team assures her that her tests are normal and everything looks great. How would you respond?*

COMMENTARY, CASE #7

Nirina Joy S. is a 14-year-old woman in remission from leukemia. She has asked her physicians for access to a medical library to do research on "self deliverance." She may or may not be suicidal and her research may or may not be related to her suicidal ideation. What are the ethical questions her physicians must now resolve? First, note that ethics is not about the standard of care or liability or what is "good" medicine in a scientific sense. Ethics is about making decisions for and because of the effect on other peoples' rights and autonomy. That much said, any questions about the Nirina Joy case regarding legal liability, clinical management of suicidality, or even Constitutional questions about the restriction of information can be discarded.

There are three questions left derived from two interpretations of the Nirina Joy case. If one interprets the case at a basic, trusting level, Nirina Joy is not suicidal. The only purpose of her reading *Final Exit* and her only motivation in seeking access to the medical library is academic interest. The primary ethical question her physicians face relates to their role as gatekeepers of medical information: How should Nirina Joy's physicians handle the distribution of sensitive information? Perhaps a more realistic interpretation acknowledges that Nirina Joy is suicidal and she intends to use *Final Exit* and the medical library to develop her suicide plan. Thus, the first question from this interpretation is about preventing suicide.

Should suicide be prevented and should different types of suicidality warrant different responses?[28] The final question relates specifically to Nirina Joy. Should any significance be attached to Nirina Joy's age in determining the answers to the second question? I will respond briefly to the first two questions and at some length to the third.

If one assumes that Nirina Joy is telling the truth about her intended use of the information in *Final Exit*, then her physicians must come up with some compelling reason not to allow her access to the library. I would imagine that the most valid reason for barring access to the library is to limit access to potentially dangerous information (i.e., lethal combinations and dosages of information). This argument seems weak. Nirina Joy already has substantial information; *Final Exit* provides readers with lists of medicines lethal by dosage or combination and details of which symptoms to fake to procure prescriptions for such medications. There is little information Nirina Joy could gain from the library that would be more dangerous than to what she already has access. (One could argue that *Final Exit* does not discuss chemotherapy drugs and that Nirina Joy wishes to learn more about their toxic effects. However, if her physicians have not already disclosed such information to her then they have egregiously breached their role in informed consent.) All Nirina Joy would gain from research in the medical library would be the biochemical and metabolic processes causing the toxic and lethal effects about which she already knows. In short, she would only learn the details and basis of the broader concepts she already knows. Even if one could justify limiting the dissemination of potentially dangerous information–and I doubt one could–then even here it would serve no purpose.

The second question essentially describes the problem of determining how much one should assist or resist a patient's suicidal ideation. So much has been written on this subject that there is little to be added. I will make some basic observations first, however. If Nirina Joy is suicidal then she is making a decision to die and attempting, to some small degree, to enlist the assistance of her physicians in the process. (She is not asking for the physicians to actively assist, but she is asking for them to help her understand what will happen to her body at a metabolic level if she takes a lethal dosage or combination of medicines.) Nirina Joy is, then, making a decision. Further, if she is considered autonomous, then her decisions must be judged on process–not outcome. Suicide is a choice as living is a choice. If a person is allowed to choose life but not death, then the person is not truly allowed to act autonomously. Dogmatic arguments against the right to suicide and assisted suicide are often internally inconsistent or inconsistent with the concepts of autonomy and informed consent. Thus, physicians should not actively prevent or interfere with any decision that is appropriately made by an autonomous person. For Nirina Joy's physicians to justify interfering with her suicide plan they would have to prove, somehow, that either Nirina Joy is not autonomous or her decision-making system is flawed. Those are the only grounds for usurping another person's autonomy.

Thus, the two criteria for decision-making are autonomy and the ability to form and use decision-making systems.[29] Is Nirina Joy automatically incapable of making decisions simply because of her age? Many would argue this to be so; the misperception that young people are categorically less capable than adults is pervasive in our culture. Informed consent is the gold standard for evaluating medical decisions for adults. Surely, if a child or young woman like Nirina Joy can fulfill the requirements of informed consent then there is little reason to abrogate her rights. If one assumes that suicide can be a medical decision then one can use the informed consent model to evaluate Nirina Joy's decision to die. Consider several commonly recognized elements of informed consent decisions: voluntariness, disclosure, recommendation, understanding, and capacity.

A valid informed consent decision must be voluntary. Nirina Joy is as capable of acting voluntarily as a person of any age in her situation. The decision must be made independently; the ideas of other people may be incorporated into the decision making process but without allowing those opinions more weight than would normally be allowed. Admittedly, Nirina Joy's sensitivity towards her family will play a major role in her decision. I doubt that the presence of siblings or parents would have any more influence than would a spouse and children have upon an adult. One could also argue that Nirina Joy cannot act voluntarily because her parents or physicians will not let her do so; whose fault is this? Certainly not hers. Nirina Joy can and will act voluntarily if allowed to do so.

Disclosure and recommendation are the duties of the physician to educate the patient about his or her condition and about the treatment options. These are intended to lead to understanding. For informed consent to be impeached based on any of these three criteria, then the decision would have to be grounded in misinformation or misunderstanding. Nirina Joy understands her condition: she knows that she is in remission, that there is a small chance of complications in the future, that she is not happy with her current quality of life, and that, for her, death would be preferable to her current life. (It is true that physical therapy and counseling may change her perceptions and her quality of life, however, that inadequacy of information is the obligation of the physicians to fulfill.) In short, Nirina Joy can understand her situation well enough to render informed consent. Her physicians seem to have failed to meet their obligations in disclosing Nirina Joy's condition to her.

The most important element of informed consent may be the capacity to make decisions. What does decision making entail? In essence, making a decision entails selecting and using an appropriate value system for evaluating a situation and devising a plan of action. There are, then, three orders of decision making. The first order decision is the decision itself (e.g., I want chocolate ice cream). The second order decision is the use of a value system to make a decision (e.g., I want chocolate ice cream because I want something that tastes good and I like the taste of chocolate). The third order decision is determining the appropriate value system for evaluating the decision (e.g., I am using taste as a criterion instead of calories in picking out ice cream because sensual pleasure is more important to me than nutrition).

How does this apply to informed consent? If a person can make medical decisions at the second and third order level, then they meet a reasonable standard of capacity. Note that this is not true, broad-based competency. Instead, it is the task-oriented competency for medical decision making. For informed consent to be fulfilled, a decision must be derived from an internally consistent value system and that value system must be appropriate for medical decision making. Nirina Joy's reasoning may be that she wants to die (first order decision) because she finds death preferable to her current quality of life (second order) and that quality of life is a valid criterion for deciding whether to continue to live (third order). If this is true and she can express as much, then she has successfully demonstrated her capacity for self-evaluation and decision-making. Suppose that Nirina Joy is not thinking this. Instead, perhaps her reasoning is more like "I normally like to consider my options slowly and carefully, but my gut instinct is telling me to kill myself so I will." In this case, Nirina Joy is demonstrating first and second order decision making but has also shown explicitly flawed third order decision making. If she is unable to identify and correct this inconsistency then she is incapable of making the informed consent decision to die.

The validity of the informed consent decision to die is derived in its entirety from the process that creates the decision. A person of any age or capacity who can demonstrate three-order decision making and an informed consent process is morally entitled to act on their decisions. Age is not a criterion: it is morally invalid and clinically inappropriate. Decision making capacity and the other elements of informed consent are the only criteria I am applying to Nirina Joy. They are also the only criteria I would apply to her if she were four years or forty years old instead of fourteen. If Nirina Joy can demonstrate that her decision to die is an informed consent decision then there is no moral justification for interference by her physicians.

John Samuel Rozel, BA (Medical Ethics)
Medical student
Brown University School of Medicine
and Consultant on the ethical and clinical management
of suicidal and violent behavior
Providence, RI

SUMMARY

The commentaries for these seven cases provide differing perspectives on the issues involved for the health care giver in relation to euthanasia and assisted suicide. No extreme views were voiced, i.e., suicide and euthanasia are never acceptable or suicide and euthanasia are acceptable upon demand. The commentaries reflect a multitude of clinical and ethical concerns embedded in each case scenario for the reflective clinician, but may have not addressed all the relevant issues for everyone.

REFERENCES

1. Rilke RM. Letters to a young poet. (J.M. Burnham, Trans.) San Rafael, CA: The Classic Wisdom Collection New World Library, 1992.

2. Maltsberger JT, Buie DH. The Practical Formulation of Suicide Risks. Cambridge, Firefly Press, 1983.

3. Werth Jr. JL. Rational suicide? Implications for mental health professionals. Washington, DC: Taylor & Francis (in press).

4. Werth Jr. JL. Rational suicide and AIDS: considerations for the psychotherapist. The Counseling Psychologist 1992;20:645-659.

5. Werth Jr. JL. Rational suicide reconsidered: AIDS as an impetus for change. Death Studies 1995;19:65-80.

6. Rogers JR, Britton PJ. AIDS and rational suicide: a counseling psychology perspective or a slide on the slippery slope. The Counseling Psychologist, 1994; 22:171-178.

7. Pence GE. Classic cases in medical ethics. New York: McGraw-Hill, 1990.

8. White BD, Siegler M, Singer PA, Iserson KV. What does Cruzan mean to the practicing physician? Arch Intern Med 1991;151:925-928.

9. Annas GJ. The rights of patients. 2nd rev. ed. Carbondale, IL: Southern Illinois University Press, 1989.

10. Annas GJ. Asking the courts to set the standard of emergency care: the case of Baby K. N Engl J Med 1994;330:1542-1545.

11. Oregon woman who chose death is remembered at upbeat service. The New York Times, p. A14, June 11, 1990.

12. White BD. Current ethical and legal issues in gastroenterological endoscopy. Gastrointestinal Endoscopy Clinics of North America 1995;5:421-432.

13. Joint Commission for the Accreditation of Healthcare Organizations (JCAHO). Accreditation Manual for Hospitals, 1995. Chicago, Joint Commission for the Accreditation of Healthcare Organizations, 1995.

14. Beauchamp TL, Childress JF. Principles of biomedical ethics. 3rd ed. New York, Oxford University Press, 1989.

15. Annas GJ, Arnold B, Aroskar M et al. Bioethicists' statement on the US Supreme Court's Cruzan decision. N Engl J Med 1989;323:686-687.

16. Abernethy V. Compassion, control, and decisions about competency. Amer J Psychiatr 1984;141:53-58.

17. Drane JF. The many faces of competency. Hastings Center Report. 14 (Apr), 17-21, 1985.

18. Appelbaum PS, Grisso T. Assessing patients' capacities to consent to treatment. N Engl J Med 1988;319:1635-1638.

19. de Mello VF. (ed.-in-chief). The American Heritage Desk Dictionary. Boston: Houghton Mifflin, p. 927, 1981.

20. White BD, Singer PA, Siegler M. Continuing problems with patient self-determination. Amer J Med Qual 1993;8:187-193.

21. Walter JJ, Shannon TA. Quality of life: The new medical dilemma. New York: Paulist Press, 1990.

22. Siegler M. The progression of medicine: from paternalism to patient autonomy to bureaucratic parsimony. Arch Intern Med 1985;145:713-715.

23. Keown J. Dutch slide down euthanasia's slippery slope. The Wall Street Journal, p. A18, November 5, 1991.

24. Buchanan AE, Brock DW. Deciding for others: The ethics of surrogate decision making. Cambridge, Cambridge University Press, 1989.

25. Pulakos J. Two models of suicide treatment: evaluation and recommendations. Am J Physcotherapy 1993;47:603-612.

26. McKegney FP, Lange P. The decision to no longer live on chronic hemodialysis. Amer J Psychiatr 1971;128:267-273.

27. Neu S, Kjellstrand CM. Stopping long-term dialysis: An empirical study of withdrawal of life-supporting treatment. N Engl J Med 1986;314:14-20.

28. Schowalter JE, Ferholt JB, Mann NM. The adolescent patient's decision to die. Pediatr 1973;51:97-103.

29. Powell CJ. Ethical principles and issues of competence in counseling adolescents. The Counseling Psychologist 1984;12:57-68.

Index

Abortion analogy, 129-130,170-173
Absorption, 220
Abuse. *See* Slippery slope argument
Academy of Hospice Physicians
 position statement, 246
Accumulating drugs. *See* Stockpiling
Acquired immune deficiency
 syndrome. *See* AIDS/HIV
Adkins case, 323. *See also*
 Kevorkian, Dr. Jack
Administration routes, 199-202,204
Admiraal's manual, 197-198,204-205.
 See also Netherlands
Adolescent suicidal ideation and body
 (case/commentary), 338-342
Advance directives, 258,267,
 319-322,332-337
Ageism, 17-18,266
Aging as motivation for suicide,
 232-236
AIDS/HIV, 6,169,179,
 228-229,231-232
 case/commentaries
  incompetency, 319-322
  intermittent competency,
   332-337
 empowerment and multiple
  bereavement, 106-107
 end-of-life issues in, 91-107
 licensure issues in, 162
 pain and suffering in, 103-104
 prevalence of psychiatric
  disorders, 94-96
 psychiatric considerations in, 94
  anxiety, 98-101
  depression, 96-97
  organic mental disorders,
   101-103,319-322

 suicidal ideation, 97-98
 social factors in, 105
 Wink case, 144
Alcohol
 abuse/recovery, 293-307
 as potentiator,
  181,202,217-218,258
Alcoholics Anonymous, 295-296
Alprazolam (Xanax), 293-307. *See*
 also Benzodiazepines
Alzheimer's disease, 162,169,235
American Association of Poison
 Control Centers, 212
American Cancer Society position
 statement, 246-248
American Hospital Association,
 267-268
American Medical Association
 (AMA) Code of Ethics, 34
American Nurses Association
 ANA Code of Ethics, 34,37,
  56-57,248-256
 position statements
  on active euthanasia, 254-256
  on assisted suicide, 248-253
American Pharmaceutical
 Association (APA) Code of
 Ethics, 37,47-48
Americans with Disabilities Act, 140
Amitriptyline, 313-318. *See also*
 Antidepressants
Amobarbital. *See* Barbiturates
Analgesia. *See* Pain control; Pain;
 Suffering
Analgesics. *See* Opioid analgesics
Angarola, Robert T., 6,113-123
Animal studies of lethality, 213
Antacids, 220

© 1996 by The Haworth Press, Inc. All rights reserved.

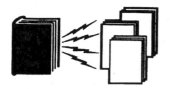 Haworth

DOCUMENT DELIVERY
SERVICE

This valuable service provides a single-article order form for any article from a Haworth journal.

- *Time Saving:* No running around from library to library to find a specific article.
- *Cost Effective:* All costs are kept down to a minimum.
- *Fast Delivery:* Choose from several options, including same-day FAX.
- *No Copyright Hassles:* You will be supplied by the original publisher.
- *Easy Payment:* Choose from several easy payment methods.

Open Accounts Welcome for ...
- Library Interlibrary Loan Departments
- Library Network/Consortia Wishing to Provide Single-Article Services
- Indexing/Abstracting Services with Single Article Provision Services
- Document Provision Brokers and Freelance Information Service Providers

---

MAIL or *FAX* THIS ENTIRE ORDER FORM TO:

Haworth Document Delivery Service
The Haworth Press, Inc.
10 Alice Street
Binghamton, NY 13904-1580

or FAX: 1-800-895-0582
or CALL: 1-800-342-9678
9am-5pm EST

PLEASE SEND ME PHOTOCOPIES OF THE FOLLOWING SINGLE ARTICLES:

1) Journal Title: _____
   Vol/Issue/Year: _____ Starting & Ending Pages: _____
Article Title: _____

2) Journal Title: _____
   Vol/Issue/Year: _____ Starting & Ending Pages: _____
Article Title: _____

3) Journal Title: _____
   Vol/Issue/Year: _____ Starting & Ending Pages: _____
Article Title: _____

4) Journal Title: _____
   Vol/Issue/Year: _____ Starting & Ending Pages: _____
Article Title: _____

(See other side for Costs and Payment Information)

COSTS: Please figure your cost to order quality copies of an article.

1. Set-up charge per article: $8.00
   ($8.00 × number of separate articles)   _____

2. Photocopying charge for each article:

                       1-10 pages: $1.00   _____

                       11-19 pages: $3.00   _____

                       20-29 pages: $5.00   _____

                       30+ pages: $2.00/10 pages   _____

3. Flexicover (optional): $2.00/article   _____

4. Postage & Handling: US: $1.00 for the first article/
                       $.50 each additional article   _____

                  Federal Express: $25.00   _____

                  Outside US: $2.00 for first article/
                       $.50 each additional article_____

5. Same-day FAX service: $.35 per page   _____

                                  GRAND TOTAL: _____

METHOD OF PAYMENT: (please check one)

❏ Check enclosed   ❏ Please ship and bill. PO # _____

               (sorry we can ship and bill to bookstores only! All others must pre-pay)

❏ Charge to my credit card: ❏ Visa; ❏ MasterCard; ❏ Discover;
                    ❏ American Express;

Account Number:_____ Expiration date:_____

Signature: ✗_____

Name: _____ Institution: _____

Address: _____

_____

City: _____ State:_____ Zip:_____

Phone Number: _____ FAX Number: _____

MAIL or *FAX* THIS ENTIRE ORDER FORM TO:

Haworth Document Delivery Service	or **FAX**: 1-800-895-0582
The Haworth Press, Inc.	or **CALL**: 1-800-342-9678
10 Alice Street	9am-5pm EST)
Binghamton, NY 13904-1580	